Map 1. *General reference map.*

Map I

GENERAL REFERENCE MAP

100   50   0   100
MILES

° Vologda

Volga R

° Rostov

° Gorki

trov

OSCOW

U. S. S. R.

a

k

° Voronezh

Oskol R.

Don R.

° Kupyansk

° Stalingrad

Donets R.

Volga R

° Stalino

Mius R.

Taganrog

Rostov

Astrakhan

of

CASPIAN

SEA

Novorossysk

° Maikop

° Grozny

Batumi

Baku

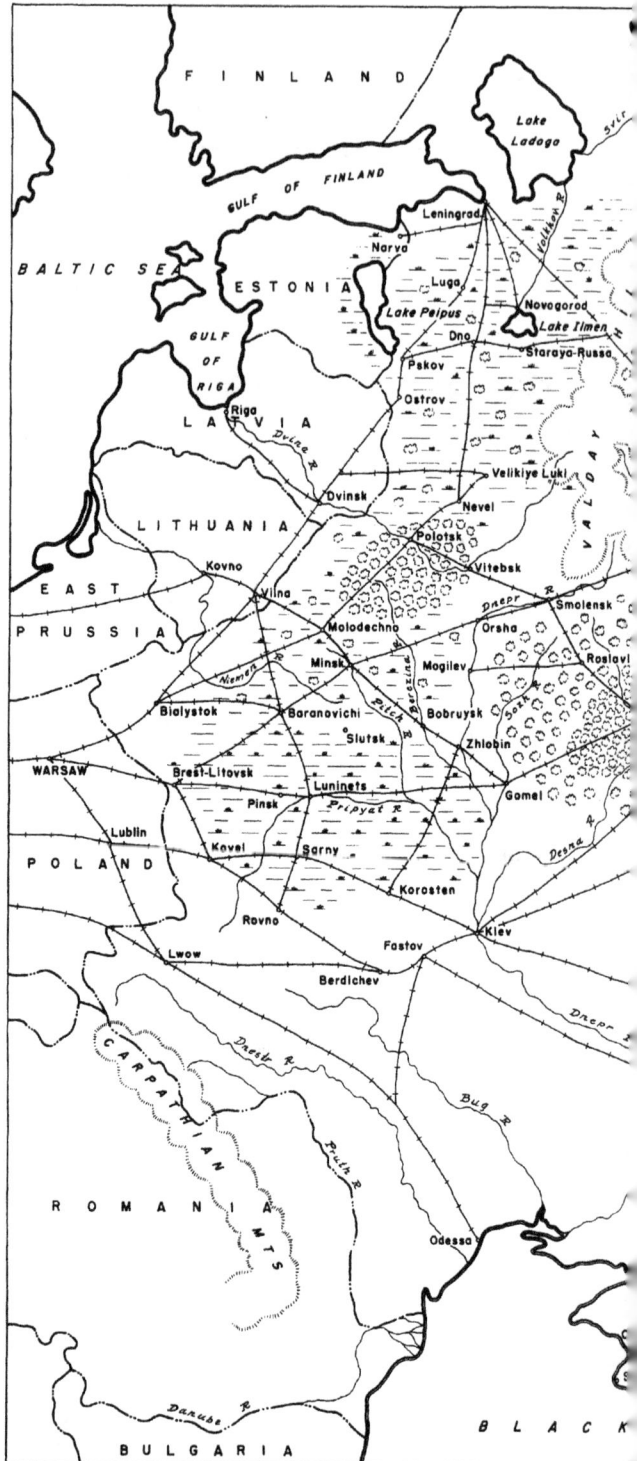

Map 2. *Principal rail lines in European Russia, 1941–1944.*

PRINCIPAL RAIL LINES IN
EUROPEAN RUSSIA 1941-1944

Map 2

100   50   0   100

MILES

- Scattered Swamp Areas
- Dense Swamp Areas
- Swamp and Forest Areas
- Heavy Forested Areas
- Light or Scattered Forested Areas

MOSCOW

Tula

U. S. S. R.

Voronezh

Volga R

Don R

Donets R

Stalingrad

Volga R

Don R

Rostov

ovsk

CASPIAN

SEA

A O F

O V

E A

THE
SOVIET PARTISAN
MOVEMENT
1941-1944

By
EDGAR M. HOWELL

FOREWORD

Unconventional warfare has gained in importance along with the increase in range and destructiveness of weapons. It was a particularly potent factor in several theaters of operations during World War II, but in none did it play a more significant role than on the Eastern front during that conflict. There the guerrilla movement behind the Axis forces gained in importance as the Soviet Army withdrew deeper and deeper into its homeland, trading space for time until mobilization could be completed and winter act as an ally.

If *The Soviet Partisan Movement, 1941–1944* is studied in connection with operational studies of the war on the east European front during World War II, it should prove to be of great value to students of that conflict. It should also prove of particular value to the Army staff and schools and colleges as a reference work in partisan warfare.

iii

PREFACE

The purpose of this text is to provide the Army with a factual account of the organization and operations of the Soviet resistance movement behind the German forces on the Eastern Front during World War II. This movement offers a particularly valuable case study, for it can be viewed both in relation to the German occupation in the Soviet Union and to the offensive and defensive operations of the Wehrmacht and the Red Army.

The scope of the study includes an over-all picture of a quasi-military organization in relation to a larger conflict between two regular armies. It is not a study in partisan tactics, nor is it intended to be. German measures taken to combat the partisan movement are sketched in, but the story in large part remains that of an organization and how it operated. The German planning for the invasion of Russia is treated at some length because many of the circumstances which favored the rise and development of the movement had their bases in errors the Germans made in their initial planning. The operations of the Wehrmacht and the Red Army are likewise described in considerable detail as the backdrop against which the operations of the partisan units are projected.

Because of the lack of reliable Soviet sources, the story has been told much as the Germans recorded it. German documents written during the course of World War II constitute the principal sources, but many survivors who had experience in Russia have made important contributions based upon their personal experience.

The study was prepared in the Special Studies Division, Office of the Chief of Military History, under the supervision and direction of the chief of that Division. Maj. Edgar M. Howell, AUS-Ret., initiated the project and carried it through to completion. He was assisted in his research in the German records by Lt. Larry Wolff, Lt. William Klepper, Jr., and Miss Leopoldina Novak.

CONTENTS

PART ONE

GERMAN PLANNING FOR THE INVASION AND OCCUPATION OF RUSSIA

CHAPTER 1

BACKGROUND

In the military history of few countries of the world have topography, climate, and population played such decisive roles as in Russia. The sheer size of the land, its formidable array of natural obstacles, the violent seasonal variations of climate, and the single-mindedness of the Russian populace in the face of alien pressure are unmatched. Time and again great powers have invaded Russia with powerful military machines, winning striking victory after victory, only to be ultimately defeated and driven out.

The USSR, which comprises the eastern half of Europe and the northern and central part of Asia, is the largest continuous political unit in the world. Occupying some 8,400,000 square miles, roughly one-sixth of the habitable land surface of the earth, it is nearly three times the size of the United States, and larger than all of North America. It extends from Romania, Poland, the Baltic Sea, and Finland in the west to China, Manchuria, and the Pacific Ocean in the east, a distance of some 6,000 miles. From north to south it stretches from the Arctic Circle to Turkey, Persia, Afghanistan, and Mongolia, a maximum distance of some 3,000 miles.

In this huge area are something over 200 million people, about one-tenth of the world's population, including 174 races, nationalities, and tribes, speaking 125 different languages or dialects, and professing faith to some 40 different religions. Of the 174 ethnic groups, however, only 93 are composed of more than 10,000 people. Of the total population, over 153,000,000 are of Slavic origin, divided roughly as follows: Great Russians, 105 millions; Ukrainians, 37 millions; and White Russians, 8½ millions, with a scattering of Poles, Bulgars, and Czechs. The Slavs are chiefly of the Greek Orthodox faith. In addition, there are some 21 million Turko-Tartars, predominantly Mohammedan.

European Russia

European Russia—with which this study is primarily concerned—may be considered that portion of the USSR lying between Central

1

Europe and the Ural Mountains. Although it represents but a fraction of the entire country, by European standards it encompasses a tremendous expanse of territory. The distance from the 1941 Polish border to Moscow is some 600 miles, to Leningrad, nearly 500; to Stalingrad far to the east on the Volga River, 900; to the foothills of the Caucasus Mountains, 950. Laterally, the distance from Leningrad to the north to Odessa on the Black Sea is 900 miles.

Topography

Almost all European Russia is taken up by the East European Plain. This plain, which is actually a series of low plateaus, has an average elevation of some 500 feet, reaching a maximum of 800–900 feet in the Valday Hills. In a broad, general sense, the land is of very low relief with no abrupt geographical changes. Despite this topographic monotony, however, the land offers a series of natural obstacles as protection for the heart of the country that is matched by no other area of comparable size.

The greatest single natural barrier in the country is the Pripyat Marshes which lie between White Russia and the western Ukraine and comprise more than 150,000 square miles of densely forested swamps. Other than for a few man-made routes they are impassable except when frozen. Adjoining them on the north is a wide belt of forests and swamps which covers western White Russia. This belt together with the deep woodlands in the Gomel and Bryansk areas and between Vyazma and Moscow forms a succession of natural defenses against any thrust toward Moscow. The topography of the Baltic States and northwest Russia is similar, with forests, swamps, and numerous small lakes predominating. In the south are the broad, treeless steppes of the Ukraine.

Completing this natural defensive network are the rivers. The principal ones, the Dnestr, the Bug, the Niemen, the Dvina, the Dnepr, and the Don, do not provide ready routes of access into the interior but cut across the paths of invasion and, together with their tributaries and swampy watersheds, form in themselves an excellent defense system. Not only do they require innumerable crossings, but due to the low relief of the country and resultant periodic floodings both banks tend toward marshiness and make the construction of approach roads a more difficult engineering feat than the actual bridging. Only between the headwaters of the Dnepr and Dvina in the "dry" Vitebsk-Orsha-Smolensk triangle, or Orsha Corridor, is the defensive value of the river net minimized. But this corridor with its paramount strategic importance is protected by the belt of forests and swamps running north from the Pripyat Marsh. However, in a normal winter all the rivers freeze and, for a period at least, are virtually eliminated as natural barriers.

Climate

The climate is as much an obstacle to extensive military operations as the physical barriers, and at certain seasons is even more effective. The bulk of the land lies in the same latitudes as Canada; the southern Caucasus is on the same parallel as Philadelphia, central Crimea as Bangor, Maine, and Moscow as Hudson Bay, with Leningrad nearly 300 miles farther north. In winter the entire country, with the exception of the southern Crimea, suffers from extremely low temperatures, often far below zero. The climate of the northwest, influenced by the warm Atlantic drift coming across Scandinavia is rather humid and somewhat less rigorous in the winter, but the northeast and central regions and the steppes of the south, being unprotected in the east since the Urals are too low to form an effective climatic barrier, are swept by the prevailing frigid northeast winds from Siberia. Stalingrad, lying along the 48th parallel, has an average January temperature of 15°, while Leningrad, some 950 miles to the north, has a January mean of 18°. Cold weather sets in suddenly and lasts five to six months. Snows are extremely heavy. The spring thaws and the fall rainy season bring heavy flooding and deep mud. The majority of the roads become bottomless and travel across country impossible, throwing excessive weight on the rail lines.

Population

Of the roughly 200 million peoples in the USSR, better than 80 percent are concentrated in European Russia in three well-defined regions, Great Russia, White Russia, and the Ukraine. Although the inhabitants of all three areas are predominantly of Slavic origin, they have kept their separate identities despite invasions and migrations. The division is still reflected today in the three basic dialects generally confined to the three geographical regions. Great Russia is that area generally centering around Moscow lying east of the line Smolensk-Lake Peipus and north of the line Gomel-Orel, as opposed to White Russia bounded by the Pripyat Marshes, Great Russia, Lithuania, and Poland, and the great steppe area of the Ukraine to the south.

The Great Russians

The Great Russians, concentrated as they are in the old Muscovite kingdom, are perhaps more truly Russian in the general acceptance of the term than those to the west and south. Certainly they are more communistic, concentrated as they have been about the center of Bolshevism since the fall of the Imperial government. They have been dominant over the rest of the Russian peoples since the second partition of Poland in 1793 which ceded them the western Ukraine and White Russia.

The White Russians

The White Russians have lived alternately under Polish, Lithuanian, and Russian rule for centuries, plagued throughout history with perpetual invasions. This combined with unproductve soil has kept the standard of living low and the level of illiteracy high. They possess no semblance of a natonal homogeneity or feeling, and only the language has kept their name alive.

The Ukrainians

The Ukrainians are perhaps the least Russian of all the Russian peoples. Historically they have had little sympathy with the Great Russians. The whole of their area which is the richest agricultural land in the Eurasian land mass, was part of the Polish-Lithuanian Empire until 1667 when the portion east of the Dnepr River fell to the Tsar. The remainder was ceded to the Imperial government in 1793. Those inhabiting the western and northern regions are descended from the Kievan Russians, while the eastern and southern portions were populated by Ruthenes who came down from the north to escape the Polish and Lithuanian invasions and from whom evolved the Cossacks. Individually they have always exhibited a marked degree of independence; as a mass, however, beyond a certain consciousness of their history as Ukrainians due to their language and way of life, they have shown only a desultory sort of national consciousness. Despite efforts of the middle-class intelligentsia in the middle of the 19th century to unite all Ruthenes into a Ukrainian nation and the actual creation of a Ukrainian state for a short time during the Revolution, there is little evidence that except in very limited circles there was any real desire for political separation. A restoration of local autonomy and a settlement of the land tenure question would have satisfied any and all demands of the people. At the time of the German invasion in 1941, despite the claims of the separatists as to the national aspirations of the populace, the people sought only a release from the collectivist system and demonstrated only vague and apathetic ideas about the future political configuration of the Ukraine.

The Balts

The inhabitants of the Baltic States, Lithuania, Latvia, and Estonia, are not historically or ethnically Russians. Predominantly Indo-European rather than Slavic, they came under Russian rule only with the disintegration of the Lithuanian and Polish kingdoms and the defeat of Charles XII of Sweden by Peter the Great. All three states gained their independence in 1918, but were occupied by the USSR in 1940.

Taken together they comprise some 6,000,000 people of whom better than 80 percent are pure Balts. The Lithuanians, once a powerful people in their own right, never seem to have lost their sense of nationality. But the Letts and Estonians for centuries were subject peoples, serfs and small holders, under the heavy hand of the great German land-owning class descended from the Teutonic Knights.

The Transportation Net

The tremendous territorial extent of Russia and its low industrial capacity, capping the natural difficulties of its terrain and climate, have been a great handicap to the development of an adequate transportation system. As a result, compared to central and especially western Europe, Russian rail and highway nets are extremely deficient both quantity and qualitywise. European Russia is a land of rivers, and while these streams provide a ready means of transportation at least part of the year, at the same time they sharply limit the expansion of the railroad and highway systems because of the necessity for innumerable bridges. Since most of the country lies in the northern latitudes, both construction and maintenance are hampered by extremes of weather with alternate freezing and thawing, frozen subsoil and consequent lack of drainage, and deep mud during the spring thaw and the autumn rainy period. In addition, because of a lack of hard, granite-like rock for foundation work, the subgrade has to be limited generally to river gravels, with a consequent deterioration under heavy use and extremes of weather. This is especially true of the road net.

The most extensive portions of the transportation net were north of the Pripyat Marshes, running from Poland and Lithuania through White Russia to Moscow. In the Ukraine the net was much more sparse, although, militarily speaking, this was compensated for to some degree by the open, flat terrain which was highly suitable for mobile warfare. In the northwest and the Baltic States the net was equally limited, but unlike the Ukraine the terrain was unsuitable for cross-country maneuver and the few roads and rail lines had to carry the bulk of all movement.

Railroads

In 1941 the USSR had for its 8,400,000 square miles of territory only 52,000 miles of railroads, the greatest portion of which lay in European Russia. Of this trackage, less than 15 percent could be classed as heavy capacity, as opposed to medium and light. As a means of comparison, the density of the rail lines was 17.6 miles per 1,000 square miles for European Russia as against 155 miles per 1,000 square miles for Germany.[1]   The gauge differed from the standard European gauge,[2] necessitating transshipment at the western border.

The three major geographical areas—the Ukraine, White and Great Russia, and the Baltic States—were each served by one heavy-capacity double track rail line.   In the Ukraine this was the line Krakow-Lwow-Kiev-Kursk or Dnepropetrovsk.   Only to a small extent could it be supplemented by the tortuous and winding medium-, and often low-, capacity line Przemysl-Stanislaw-Cernauti-Odessa on the southern slopes of the Carpathian Mountains.   Through White Russia to the east the primary trunk was the Warsaw-Brest-Litovsk-Minsk-Smolensk-Moscow. This was paralleled on the south by the low- and medium-capacity line through the Pripyat, Brest-Litovsk, Pinsk-Gomel-Bryansk-Moscow. Several lateral lines of medium capacity, however, and one diagonal route from Kovno in Lithuania southeast through Minsk and Bobruysk to Gomel offered possibilities for alternate routes.   To the north the one trunk was the Warsaw-Bialystok-Vilna-Dvinsk-Pskov-Leningrad line.   With the exception of the stretch Dvinsk-Ostrov, it was double track.   The few alternate lines, for the most part to the north of Pskov, were all of low capacity.

Roads

The road net was generally poor, comprising some 60,500 miles of all types of surfacing, from plain unimproved dirt track to asphalt and concrete highways, for the whole of the USSR.[3]   The majority of this net was in European Russia.   Generally the paved arteries paralleled the rail lines.   Of the entire net, only the stretch westward from Moscow through Smolensk to Minsk, where it terminated could be classed as a superhighway in the American sense of the term.   All but the few hundred miles of concrete and asphalt deteriorated rapidly under heavy use and became bottomless during the spring and fall muddy seasons, thus throwing an added burden on the rail system.

---

[1] *Militaergeographische Angaben ueber das europaeische Russland, Allgemeiner Ueberblick, 1.IX.41., Gen. St.d.H. Abt. fuer Kriegskarten und Vermessungswesen (IV. Mil.-Geo.)*, pp. 38–40. 29/IDZ.11.   Postwar estimates of the 1940 trackage total have raised this estimate to just over 60,000 miles, of which 16,000 were double-track. See: P. E. Garbutt, *The Russian Railroads* (London, 1949), p. 12; Nikolae A. Voznesensky, *The Economy of the USSR During World War II* (Washington, 1948), p. 59.
[2] Standard European gauge: 4 feet 8½ inches; Russian gauge: 5 feet.
[3] *Militaergeographische Angaben ueber das europaeische Russland, Allgemeiner Ueberblick, 1.IX.41., GenStdH. Abt. fuer Kriegskarten und Vermessungswesen (IV. Mil.-Geo.)*, pp. 38–40. 29/IDZ.11.   A 1938 American estimate placed the total at 64,200 miles, of which some 2,400 miles were believed to be asphalted.   See: E. J. Simmons, *USSR, A Concise Handbook* (Ithaca, 1947), ch. XIV.

Rivers

Despite the fact that rapids were few in the Russian rivers and that canals connected several of the major streams, their extensive use as an aid to invasion was limited by their general north-south courses and by their freezing in the cold months and heavy flooding in the spring. Prior to World War II, less than 8 percent of Russian freight traffic moved over these inland waterways.[4]

The Transportation Net and Irregular Resistance

The difficulties of Russian terrain and climate pose an added problem to an invader should any determined guerrilla resistance develop, that is, the protection of the lines of communication against organized armed attack. Whereas in the Ukraine the general absence of cover virtually precludes the chance of irregular raiding, in the central and northern sectors the danger is a very real one. From the southern edges of the Pripyat to the Gulf of Finland all orderly movement is channeled by the terrain into a few narrow corridors where for long stretches it is exposed to easy interdiction. This also is true of the heavy forests about Gomel and Bryansk and before Moscow. Not only does the terrain offer the attackers protection in the execution of their raids, but secures their movements and hides and protects their bases. The many rivers add to this problem, for the bridges and culverts are very ready targets for sabotage. The climate too exercises a very real effect in this respect. The heavy snows during the winter and the mud in the spring and fall sharply limit the value of the road net which in turn places an added load on the rail system and a few good highways and makes any interruption of them doubly effective.

---

[4] Garbutt, *op. cit.*, p. 12.

CHAPTER 2

PREINVASION PLANNING

The Decision To Attack Russia

After the swift and successful conclusion of the French campaign in June 1940, Hitler thought he was invincible. France was completely in his grasp and it seemed impossible that Britain, with its army shattered, would attempt to hold out in the face of the German threat. But when Britain showed it had no idea of admitting defeat and intended to fight to the finish, Hitler started preparations for an invasion of the island kingdom in the event he could not bomb it into submission.

Actually he did not favor such an operation. Not only was he well aware of the risks involved in such an amphibious attack in view of Germany's undeniable inferiority at sea—and he was seconded in this by his naval leaders [1]—but also he disliked the political implications which he believed an actual military defeat of Britain would entail. He wanted surrender not destruction, for in destruction he saw a collapse of the Empire which in the long run would benefit Japan and the United States rather than the Reich. He and his advisors concluded that Britain's intransigency stemmed from the hope of Soviet Russia's entering the picture, since the latter obviously had every reason not to want a powerful Germany on its western border.[2] As he cast about for alternatives, Hitler saw the possibilities inherent in confronting his enemies with a solid political front from the North Cape to Morocco. An international bloc including Spain, Italy, and Russia, he thought, would demonstrate to the British the futility of continued resistance.[3]

On 21 July 1940 at a conference between Hitler, Grossadmiral Erich Raeder, Commander in Chief of the Navy, and Generalfeldmarschall Walther von Brauchitsch, Commander in Chief of the Army, all the skepticism relative to the invasion, Operation *SEELOEWE,* was aired.[4]

---

[1] See: Memo, Raeder to OKW, 11 Jul 40. Cited in *Brassey's Naval Annual, 1948* (New York, 1948), pp. 113–15, 117–18.

[2] *Ibid.,* "The Private War Journal of Generaloberst Franz Halder" (hereafter cited as "Halder's Journal"), IV, pp. 115–17. Copy in Foreign Studies Br., OCMH. Halder was chief of the German General Staff from 1938 to Sep 1942.

[3] "Halder's Journal," *op. cit.,* IV, pp. 115–16. Negotiations for some sort of an alliance with Spain continued fitfully throughout the fall of 1940.

[4] There are two accounts of this conference extant, one by Raeder and the other, much more detailed, by Halder who had been briefed on the meeting by Von Brauchitsch. See "Halder's Journal," *op. cit.* IV, pp. 126–28; *Brassey's Naval Annual 1948, op. cit.,* p. 119.

Still doubting the feasibility of the attack, Hitler believed that it should be made only if all other means of bringing Britain to terms failed. Britain was sustained, he insisted, by the hope of assistance from Soviet Russia and a change of attitude on the part of the United States. For this reason Germany's attention had to be turned to the Russian aspect of the picture. The Army should study the problem in the light of a possible operation against the Soviet Union and should begin planning.

Although this conference was mainly concerned with Operation *SEELOEWE* Hitler had previously been briefed on the broad operational and political aspects of a campaign in the East. Among these was the idea that the political objectives of such an operation should include the creation of a Ukranian state and a confederation of Baltic States under German domination.[5]

On 31 July, at another conference of his leaders, Hitler, reiterating that the British were hanging on only because they hoped the Russians would enter the war on the side of the Allies, declared that Germany would have to attack and destroy the Soviet Union the following spring. The Communist state had to be eliminated from the European scene. He would shatter it in one rapid, driving campaign and then break it up along ethnic and geographic lines, absorbing some parts bodily into the Reich and making puppet states of others. The Army (*Oberkommando des Heeres—OKH*) was to immediately initiate preparations for such an attack, later named Operation *BARBAROSSA*.[6]

This was no random speculation on the part of the Fuehrer. Rather, it was a clear-cut military and political decision to wage war on two fronts simultaneously. As such it might well be taken as the turning point of World War II.

German Occupation Policy and Practice

In planning a campaign of the scope of *BARBAROSSA* and with its sweeping military and political objectives, the preparations had to go far beyond purely operational aspects, for during the interim between the launching of the initial attack and the actual end of hostilities, as well as during the transition period between the attainment of military victory and the final political goal, the land would have to be occupied by military or political agencies, or both.

To the Germans, theoretically, all territory in their possession in which military operations might take place was a theater of war (*Kriegsgebiet*). This theater of war consisted of a zone of operations (*Operationsgebiet*),

---

[5] "Halder's Journal," *op. cit.*, IV, p. 128.

[6] *Ibid.*, pp. 144–45: The directive for Operation *BARBAROSSA* is contained in OKW/WFSt/Abt. L (1), Nr. 33408/40g.K.Chefs., 18.XII.40. in "Fuehrer Directives and Other Top-Level Directives of the German Armed Forces, . . . 1939–1945" (hereafter cited as "Fuehrer Directives"), tr. by Office of Naval Intelligence. I, pp. 127–30.

that portion of the theater of war where the armed forces operated against the enemy, and a zone of the interior (*Heimat-Kriegsgebiet*). The zone of operations was always under a German military administration (*Deutsche Militaer-Verwaltung*).[7] Upon the cessation of operations the newly seized territory was placed under either a military or a civilian political administration according to the particular ethnic, geographic, and strategic considerations of the area occupied. The early occupation administrations had followed no specific pattern and were the products of no particular pre-formed plans. In each case it had been Hitler who determined the method.[8] The Soviet Union was another case presenting new problems.

Military Occupation

Organization

According to German standing operating procedure, the executive power in the zone of operations was vested in the military. This zone of operations was divided into a combat zone (*Gefechtsgebiet*) and a number of army rear area commands (*Rueckwaertige Armeegebiete*) or *Koruecke* one behind each army operating at the front.[9] [See *chart 1.*]

The *Koruecke* were in charge of supply and administration and were responsible for military security in their particular zones.[10] To carry out these duties they were given special security units. For purposes of administration and local control, they had several gradations of subordinate headquarters: *Feldkommandanturen,* regional military government offices, *Kreiskommandanturen,* district offices in rural areas, and *Ortskommandanturen* in the smaller urban areas and towns. For normal police work and security of lines of communication they were assigned units of military police (*Feldgendarmerie*).[11]

These *Koruecke* corresponded in effect to the communictions zone of the American Army, and, although nominally agencies of their respective armies, were under the direct control of the Army Chief of Supply and Administration (*Generalquartiermeister-GenQu*). *GenQu* had as his province all the functions of the supply and administration of the

---

[7] *"Handbuch fuer den Generalstab im Krieg, 1.VIII.39."* pts. 1, 4. Copy in CRS, TAG.

[8] See: Directive No. 5, *30.IX.39., OKW, Nr. 171/39 g.K.Chefs., WFA/L I,* in "Fuehrer Directives," *op. cit.,* I, p. 55; *Berlin den 20. Oktober 1939, Besprechung des Fuehrers Mit Chef OKW ueber die kuenftige Gestaltung der polnischen Verhaeltnisse zu Deutschland* (*Vom 17.X.39. abds.*) in *Trial of the Major War Criminals Before the International Military Tribunal,* (hereafter cited is *I.M.T.*). (Nuremberg, 1947), XXVI, pp. 378–83.

[9] *"Handbuch fuer den Generalstab im Krieg, 1.VIII.39.",* op. cit. I, p. 4.

[10] *Ob.d.H., 6. Abt.* (*IV*), *Gen.St.d.H., "Versorgung des Feldheeres* (*V.d.F.*)",* (Berlin, 1940), pp. 21–25. Copy in H.Dv.90/40.

[11] *Ibid.,* pp. 29–30, 33–34; WD MID, "Order of Battle of the German Army" (Feb 44), pp. 49–50.

Chart 1—Organization of the German Theater of War (Kriegsgebiet) as of 1 August 1939, showing a Typical Army Sector*

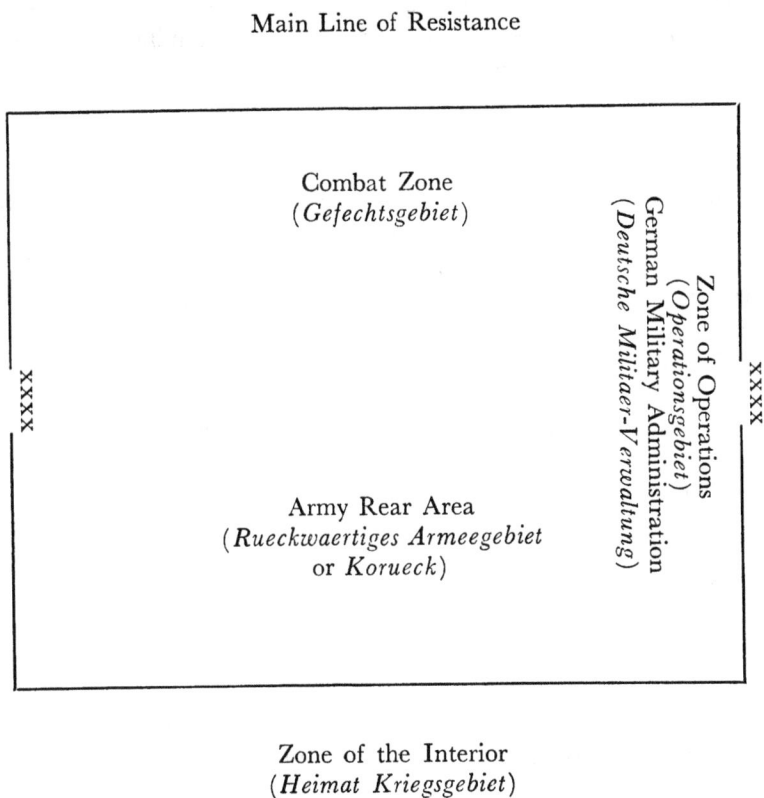

Main Line of Resistance

Combat Zone
(*Gefechtsgebiet*)

xxxx

Army Rear Area
(*Rueckwaertiges Armeegebiet*
or *Korueck*)

Zone of Operations
(*Operationsgebiet*)
German Military Administration
(*Deutsche Militaer-Verwaltung*)

xxxx

Zone of the Interior
(*Heimat Kriegsgebiet*)

*Source: CRS, TAG. Grundlegende Befehle, Gliederung des rueckw. Gebiets, H17/6.

field army. Besides the planning and organization of supply in the field, he was responsible for the establishment and security of all lines of communication and supply installations and for military government control of the areas behind the operating armies.[12]

By the time detailed planning for *BARBAROSSA* was well under way following the December publication of the actual directive for the attack, the Armed Forces High Command (*Oberkommando der Wehrmacht—OKW*) had made it clear that the occupation of the Soviet Union was to be civilian and political, not military, and had placed definite limitations on the extent to which a strictly military jurisdiction was to be exercised. The area under the control of the Army was to be kept as shallow as possible, and as the campaign moved farther and farther to the east the forward boundary of the political administration zone, which was to be established behind the Army's zone of operations, was to be progressively advanced. With the termination of hostilities the entire area was to go under a political occupation.[13] In other words, a planned administration was to be put into effect in the occupied portions of the USSR only after they had left the jurisdiction of the military.

With the policy thus set, *GenQu* made his preparations accordingly, planning only those security measures necessary to guarantee the unimpeded progress of the armies and the exploitation of the land for their immediate use.[14]

The Security Commands

In March *GenQu* received his allotment of staffs and troop units. These comprised three army group rear headquarters (*Rueckwaertige Heeresgebiete*) and nine security divisions (*Sicherungs Divisionen*) activated from three regular infantry divisions. These security divisions were units "specially created," as OKH described them, to handle the "security, exploitation, and military administration" behind the front lines. One army group rear area headquarters and three security di-

---

[12] TM E 30–351, "Handbook on German Military Forces" (1945); *"Versorgung des Feldheeres,"* op. cit., pp. 12–15. The information in these sources was corrected and brought up to date by Gen Maj Alfred Toppe, *GenQu* during 1944–45, in interview in Aug 52.

[13] See: Helmuth Greiner, "Draft Entries in the War Diary of Def Br [Definite Branch] of Wehrmacht Operations (Dec 40–Mar 21)" (MS 065k, Hist Div, EUCOM), pp. 102–04. Copy in Foreign Studies Br, OCMH. Supplement to Directive 21, "Directive for Special Areas (Operation *BARBAROSSA*)," *OKW/ WFSt/Abt. L (IV/Qu), Nr. 44125/41 g.K.Chefs., 13.III.41.,* in "Fuehrer Directives," op. cit., I, pp. 158–60.

[14] "Special Directives for the Supply," 3 Apr 41, in *Trials of War Criminals Before the Nuernberg Military Tribunals* (hereafter cited as *N.M.T.*), V, *U.S.* vs *Wilhelm von Leeb, et al* (Case 12), von Roques 2. Copy in CRS, TAG.

visions were assigned to each of the three army groups set up for the operation.[15] In the initial phases of the campaign, the *Koruecke* were to be responsible for security, with the security divisions assigned to them. As soon as the tactical situation permitted, however, the army group rear area commands would take over, committing the security units laterally according to the army sectors. As in the case of the *Koruecke*, these commands, although subordinated to their respective army groups, were to receive their operational directives from and report directly to *GenQu*.[16]

Each security division received one infantry regiment and an artillery battalion from the cannibalized formations. At least six of these infantry regiments, which were to constitute the "alert units" (*Eingreifgruppen*) of the security divisions, had had front line experience in the Polish or French campaigns. The remainder was made up of *Landesschuetzen* battalions, formed into regiments, and field and local administrative headquarters, with small complements of signal, engineer, and similar troops. In addition to the strictly army units, each division was assigned one motorized police battalion from the *Ordnungspolizei*.[17]

The staffing and equipping of the security divisions reflected the quality of the troop units they comprised. In general they were staffed with retired or overaged officers and inexperienced reservists. The G–4's were inadequately trained and the G–2's were admittedly inept in intelligence matters and generally had no knowledge of counterintelligence methodology.[18] The alert regiments for the most part were well armed and equipped, as were the motorized police battalions, but in the *Landesschuetzen* battalions and the field and local administrative headquarters much organic equipment was lacking and many weapons were

---

[15] *OKH, Chef der Heeresruestung und BdE, AHA: Ia (II) Nr. 591/41 g. Kdos., 3.III.41., in Befh. rueckw. H. Geb. 103, Ia, Taetigkeitsbericht, 13.III.41.–21.VI.41.* 16407/1.

[16] *N.M.T., op. cit.,* V, *U.S.* vs. *Wilhelm von Leeb, et al* (Case 12), pp. 5012–13; "Special Directives for the Supply," Von Roques 2 in *ibid.*

[17] There is no adequate English equivalent for *Landesschuetzen* or *Ordnungspolizei.* The *Landesschuetzen* were troops of poor quality generally drawn from the *Landwehr* classifications, the 35- to 45-year-old classes. The *Ordnungspolizei* were German regular or uniformed police formed into troop units. They included the municipal, rural, river, and building inspection police, the firefighting police, and the air raid protection services. They should not be confused with the *Sicherheitspolizei,* or security police. See: TM 30–451, "Handbook on German Military Forces" (1945), II–8, II–31; "Order of Battle of the German Army," *op. cit.,* pp. 102–06; *Anl. z OKH 1600, Kriegsgliederung des Feldheeres, 15.V.41. H1/93b; Befehl RFSS, 21.V.41.* NOKW 2079.

[18] Notes of CG of Rear Area at Stargard on G–2 conf at Hq, 9 May 41 (indexed under No. 22, H 3/482) ; *KTB, Ib, 281 Sich. Div., 1.V.41.* 15954/6.

14   THE SOVIET PARTISAN MOVEMENT

substandard.   In the *281st Security Division,* for instance, all rifles,
carbines, and pistols were from stocks captured from the French, Belgian,
Dutch, and Czechoslovakian Armies.   All vehicles were of foreign make
with no spare parts.   Some had no tires.   Division headquarters had no
vehicles of any sort.[19]   Of the units of the 9 security divisions, 3 infantry
regiments and 9 *Landesschuetzen* battalions were equipped with bicycles,
while 15 police battalions and 1 *Wachbataillon* (guard battalion) were
motorized.   The bicycle troops were considered suitable for local commitment only.[20]

Training: The specific operational missions given the rear area commands and the training of the security and police units allotted them
closely mirrored the Army's occupation role as outlined by OKW.   The
Koruecke and army group rear areas had as their primary tasks the security of supply installations, supply routes and lateral routes, supply
transports (by convoy if necessary), airfields, and depots of captured
materiel; the guarding and evacuation of prisoners of war; and traffic
regulation.   The heaviest emphasis was placed on the security of supply
points.[21]

The field and local administrative headquarters, which were to be
permanently set up at key points along supply routes and lateral roads,
were to work with the security and police units in establishing a series of
strong points to protect the supply lines and insure control of the populace.   They were to immediately suppress any active or passive resistance on the part of the Russian civilians by severe punitive measures.
In addition they were to watch the population carefully in order to determine which elements were anti-Soviet and thus possibly useful to
German interests.[22]

The training of the troop units reflected these tasks, and at the same
time took into consideration the military capabilities of each.   The
Landesschuetzen units and the *Wachbataillone* were specifically trained
in the security and defense of supply installations, troop billets, and airfields; in reconnaissance and patrol duty along communication axes; for
attacks on objectives of limited scope such as clearing villages and small
wooded areas of stragglers; in convoy duty; and in working in close cooperation with the *Feldgendarmerie* and *Ordnungspolizei.*   The police
units were schooled in traffic regulation on the supply routes and in the
general maintenance of order.   In addition they were given enough small
unit infantry training to enable them to assist other units in attacks on

---

[19] *Bericht, Ib, 281 Sich. Div. 1.V.41., KTB 281 Sich. Div.* 15954/6.
[20] *Anl 2 z. KTB 1, H Geb Mitte, 1.IX.41.* 14684/3; *KTB, H Geb Nord, 22.IV.-7.VIII.41.* 14768/2; *Anl z. OKH 160.00 Kriegsgliederung des Feldheeres, 15.V.41.* H 1/93b.
[21] *OKH/Gen.St.d.H/Ausb. Abt. (Ia), Nr. 700/41 g., 21.III.41., Anl. Bd. 2, z. KTB 1, Hefter 1, 286 Sich. Div., Ia, 31.III.–7.VIII.41.* 16182/2.
[22] *Ibid.*

limited objectives and in the guarding and evacuation of prisoners of war and captured materiel. The alert regiments were trained as normal infantry units with emphasis on offensive work in keeping with their role as mobile reserve forces.[23]

Summary

This was the extent of the preparation for the military occupation. Beyond planning for the period between the launching of the initial attack and the actual end of hostilities there was nothing. The deficiency was the same one that underlay the *BARBAROSSA* plan as a whole; all planning for the attack was predicated on a winning campaign of no more than four months' duration.[24] The Army expected to win and win quickly. There was no preparation for unforeseen contingencies, such as especially adverse weather, which might prolong the campaign beyond expectations, or for the possibility of failure to achieve complete victory. Such eventualities, following German army practice, were not considered the province of the planners, but of "command responsibility."[25] Despite the fact that as early as December 1940 Hitler had indicated to Von Brauchitsch and Halder that he intended leaving some 60 divisions in Russia as occupation troops, the General Staff had no definite plans for utilizing these units, only a "vague concept."[26]

Political Occupation

The occupation and partition of Russia were to be political. In order to bring the war to a successful conclusion according to Third Reich standards, which meant the satiation of all its war aims, Germany would have to do more than merely defeat the Red Army. It would have to split up the entire area into socialist, political entities, dependent on Germany, with which peace might be concluded. According to Hitler's directive, this was not a task for the Army.[27]

The territory overrun in the course of the campaign was to be divided into states with separate governments as soon as the progress of the war permitted. The rear boundary of the Army's zone of operations was to

---

[23] *Ibid.*

[24] *Besprechung mit den stellvertretenden Kommandierenden Generalen am 5.I.42., KTB, Chef des Stabs, Chef Heeresruestung und Befehlshaber des Ersatzheeres, 19.XII.41.–20.III.42.;* Directive No. 32, "Preparations for the Period After *BARBAROSSA*," *OKW/WFSt/Abt. L (I Op.), Nr. 44886/41 g. K. Chefs., 11.IV.41.,* in "Fuehrer Directives," *op. cit.;* Heinz Guderian, *Panzer Leader* (New York, 1952), p. 143.

[25] Interview with Gen Maj Alfred Toppe, 13 Aug 52.

[26] Helmuth Greiner, "Operation *BARBAROSSA*," (MS C–065i, Hist Div, EUCOM), p. 47. Copy in Foreign Studies Br, OCMH. See also: Interview with Gen Maj Alfred Toppe, 13 Aug 52. The phrase "vague concept" is Toppe's.

[27] Greiner, "Draft Entries in the War Dairy of Def Br of Wehrmacht Operations (Dec 40–Mar 41)," *op. cit.,* pp. 202–04.

be moved progressively eastward with the fighting and the area so formed given a civilian political administration. At first it was to be divided into three administrative divisions or *Reichskommissariate* corresponding roughly to the Baltic States, White Russia, and the Ukraine on the basis of ethnic differences and the boundaries between army groups. Here the administration was to be in the hands of Reich commissioners or *Reichskommissare* who were to take their orders from the Fuehrer. Military tasks in the *Reichskommissariate* were to be handled by armed forces commanders (*Wehrmachtbefehlshaber*) subordinate to OKW. They were to provide military protection for the area and maintain close liaison with the *Reichskommissare* in order to support them in their political tasks.

Since this war was to be far more than a mere passage of arms, or as Hitler said, a fight to a finish between "two opposite political systems," the invaded territory was to be "prepared" for the political occupation to follow. This task of "preparation" was given to Heinrich Himmler, leader of the SS troops (*Reichsfuehrer SS*) and chief of the German Police, to carry out independently of all other agencies and on his own responsibility.[28]

For the mission Himmler formed special task groups called *Einsatzgruppen* from the personnel of the SS, SD, and Gestapo [29] which he made generally responsible for all political security tasks within the operational area of the Army and the rear areas so far as the latter did not fall under the civil administration. Specifically they were to clear the operations zone of both Jews and Communist officials and agents by liquidating all racially and politically undesirable elements seized. The armies were to supply the *Einsatzgruppen* with quarters, food, gasoline, and the like, but were to have no control over them whatever. A Himmler representative was assigned to each army group with an *Einsatzgruppe* at his disposal. When the attack was launched, these groups followed directly behind the troops as they moved into Russia.[30]

The detailed planning for the political administration took form under the direction of Alfred Rosenberg, Hitler's deputy for ideological matters

---

[28] "Directive For Special Areas (Operation *BARBAROSSA*)" in *OKW/WFSt/Abt. L (1), Nr. 33408/40 g. K. Chefs., 18.XII.40* in "Fuehrer Directives," I, pp. 127–30.

[29] SS—*Schutzstaffeln,* the elite guard of the Nazi Party (combat units of the SS were known as the Waffen SS); SD—*Sicherheitsdienst,* SS security and intelligence service; Gestapo—*Geheime Staatspolizei,* secret state or political police.

[30] *N.M.T. op. cit.,* IV, *U.S.* vs *Otto Ohlendorf, et al* (Case 9), I, pp. 75–77; Ohlendorf affidavit, doc. 2890 in *ibid;* "Regulation for Assignment of Security Police and SD in the Army Organization," *OKH, 26.III.41.* (doc. 256), prosecution document book in *ibid.; I.M.T., op. cit.,* IV, pp. 312–18.

and philosopher of the Nazi Party.[31] Early in April he was first oriented
on *BARBAROSSA* and its aims and was successively appointed political
advisor to Hitler for the operation,[32] Commissioner for the Central
Control of Questions Connected with the East-European Region,[33] and
finally on 17 July Reich Minister for the Occupied Eastern Territories.[34]
In starting his preparation, Rosenberg gave top priority to safeguarding
the war effort in its operational stages and assuring a supply of raw
materials and food for the armies and the occupation force.[35] To him
the long-range goal was the end of Pan-Russian (*Grossrussisch*) pressure
and the elimination of any military or political threat from the east.[36]

His plans to achieve this goal followed closely the political premises
laid down in the 21 and 31 July conferences the previous year: occupied
Russia was to be broken up into separate political entities according
to historical and racial conditions, each with a different political aim.
Some were to be absorbed into the Reich, others set up as puppets.
During the interim period between the actual end of hostilities and the
achievement of the final political goal, the *Reichskommissare* operating
under his direction were to carry forward the administration toward
the final form.[37]

He believed that in an undertaking of such size the ultimate political
goal could be more quickly and efficiently reached if the plans of all
Reich agencies in the East, including police, economic, and propaganda,
be made to conform with those laid down by his office and their activities
subordinated to him as Hitler's representative.[38] This was a practical
approach, and had it been adopted would have eliminated a duplication

---

[31] Rosenberg was an old line National Socialist, having joined the Nazi Party in
1919 and worked steadily in it through the years Early recognized as the party
ideologist, he developed and spread Nazi doctrines both in the newspaper *Voelkischer
Beobachter,* which he edited, and in numerous books he wrote. He was never a
member of Hitler's inner circle, and beyond the scope of his editorial work was never
influential in party affairs.

[32] *I.M.T., op. cit.,* XI, pp. 476–77; *Anhang zur Denkschrift Nr. 2, Personelle
Vorschlaege fuer die Reichskommissariate im Osten und die politische Zentralstelle
in Berlin, 7.IV.41. Ibid.,* pp. 555–60.

[33] See: Hitler's decree of 20 April 41 concerning the appointment of Rosenberg
as his agent for matters relating to eastern Europe. *I.M.T., op. cit.,* XXVI, pp.
383–84.

[34] *Abschrift zu Rk. 10714 B, Erlass des Fuehrers ueber die Verwaltung der neu
besetzten Ostgebiete, Vom 17, VII.41.* in *I.M.T., op. cit.,* XXIX, pp. 235–37.

[35] *Allgemeiner Aufbau und Aufgaben einer Dienststelle fuer die zentrale Bearbeitung
der Fragen des osteuropaeischen Raumes, 29.IV.41* in *I.M.T., op. cit.,* pp. 550–66.

[36] *Allgemeine Instruktion fuer alle Reichskommissare in den besetzten Ostgebieten,
8.V.41.* in *I.M.T., op. cit.,* XXVI, pp. 576–80.

[37] See: "Halder's Journal," *op. cit.,* IV, pp. 126–28, 144–45.

[38] *Anhang zur Denkschrift Nr. 2, Personelle Vorschlaege fuer die Reichskommis-
sariate im Osten und die politische Zentralstelle in Berlin 7.IV.41* in *I.M.T., op. cit.,*
XXVI, pp. 555–60; *Denkschrift Nr. 3, Betrifft: UdSSR, Berlin, den 25.IV.41.*
Doc. 1020–PS. Files of Office of the Chief of Counsel for War Crimes. DRB, TAG.

of functions and a constant conflict of jurisdictions, which was to do much harm to the occupation, and would have given the whole venture a singleness of purpose that it was to need so badly later. But both Goering [39] and Himmler, however, insisted on complete independence.[40]

The form the final political structure was to take is not completely clear. As Rosenberg saw it, White Russia was to be developed into a German protectorate with progressively closer ties to Germany; the Baltic States were also to become a protectorate, transformed into a part of the greater German Reich by Germanization of the racially acceptable elements, the settling of Germans there, and the deportation of all those racially undesirable; the Ukraine was to be set up as an independent state in alliance with Germany; and the Caucasus with its contiguous northern territories was to become a federation of Caucasian States with a German plenipotentiary, German military and naval bases, and extraterritorial military rights for the protection of the oil fields which would be exploited by the Reich.[41]

Hitler's views were much the same: generally, the Crimea was to become Reich territory, evacuated by all foreigners and settled by Germans only; the Baltic States and the Don-Volga area were to be absorbed into a greater Germany; while the Caucasus was to become a military colony. The future status of the Ukraine and White Russia remained vague, however, and the forms of the structures were never drawn out in detail.[42]

Except for the operations of the economic administration and Himmler's police functions (Himmler was given as much authority in Russia as he exercised in Germany proper), Rosenberg was to have jurisdiction of all territory west of the operations zone and was to be responsible for the entire administration there.[43] From his Ministry for the Occupied Eastern Territories at the top, control was to descend through the *Reichskommissare* in their political-ethnic areas, to general, main, and

---

[39] At the same time Himmler had been given his task of preparing for the political occupation, Goering had been placed in charge of the economic exploitation of the USSR. See: "Directive For Special Areas (Operation *BARBAROSSA*)," *op. cit.*

[40] *Aktenvermerk, Fuehrerhauptquartier 16.VII.41.*, memo for the record, notes on the Fuehrer conf, 16 Jul 41, in *I.M.T. op. cit.*, XXXVIII, pp. 86–94.

[41] *Instruktion fuer einen Reichskommissar im Kaukasien, 7.V.41.* Doc. 1027–PS. Files of Office of Chief of Counsel for War Crimes. DRB, TAG: *Instruktion fuer einen Reichskommissar im der Ukraine, 7.V.41* in *I.M.T., op. cit.*, XXVI, pp. 567–73; *Instruktion fuer einen Reichskommissar im Ostland, 8.V.41* in *ibid.*, pp. 573–76; *Allgemeine Instruktion fuer alle Reichskommissare in den besetzten Ostgebieten, 8.V.41* in *ibid.*, pp. 576–80.

[42] See: *Aktenvermerk, Fuehrerhauptquartier, 16.VII.41.* in *I.M.T., op. cit.*, XXVIII, pp. 86–94.

[43] *Abschrift zu Rk. 10714 B. Erlass des Fuehrers ueber die Verwaltung der neu besetzten Ostgebiete, Vom 17.VII.41.* in *I.M.T. op. cit.*, XXIX, pp. 235–37.

district *Kommissare.* A higher SS and police leader was to be assigned to each *Reichskommissariat.*[44]

Taken together with Himmler's "preparation," there was to be nothing benevolent about this administration. What the Russian people thought or felt did not matter, and there was to be no real attempt to draw them over into the German camp. The occupation was to be permanent. That was the final goal as Hitler set it, and nothing or no one was to be allowed to interfere with the attainment of it.[45] This was a struggle of ideologies, not nations.[46] The "Jewish-Bolshevik" intelligentsia was to be exterminated. In Great Russia force was to be used "in its most brutal form." [47] Moscow and Leningrad were to be leveled and made uninhabitable so as to obviate the necessity for feeding the populations through the winter.[48] The land was first to be dominated, then administered and exploited.[49]

Martial law was to be established and all legal procedures for offenses committed by enemy civilians were to be eliminated. Guerrillas were to be ruthlessly killed at any time. Civilians who attacked members of the Wehrmacht were to be treated in like manner and on the spot. In circumstances where individuals attacking the armed forces could not readily be identified collective punitive measures were to be carried out immediately upon orders of an officer with the rank of battalion commander or higher. Suspects were not to be retained in custody for trial at a later date. For offenses committed by members of the Wehrmacht against the indigenous population, prosecution was not to be compulsory even when such acts constituted crimes or offenses under German military law. Such acts were to be prosecuted only when the maintenance of discipline required it.[50] All Communist Party functionaries and Red Army commissars, including those at the small unit level, were to be

---

[44] *Erster Abschnitt: Die Organization der Verwaltung in den besetzten Ostgebieten,* an undated, unsigned paper found in the Rosenberg files outlining the organization and administration of the occupied eastern territories, in *I.M.T., op. cit.,* XXVI, pp. 592–609. According to Rosenberg, "[This paper] is not a direct instruction of the Ministry for the Occupied Eastern Territories but it was the result of discussions with the various agencies of the Reich government officially interested in the east. In this document there are contained instructions for the Eastern Ministry itself." (See: *I.M.T., op. cit.,* XXXVIII, pp. 86–94.

[45] *Aktenvermerk, Fuehrerhauptquartier, 16.VII.41. I.M.T., op. cit.,* XXXVIII, pp. 86–94.

[46] Greiner, "Draft Entries in the War Diary of Def Br of Wehrmacht Operations (Dec 40–Mar 41)," *op. cit.,* p. 202.

[47] "Halder's Journal," *op. cit.,* VI, p. 29.

[48] *Ibid.,* p. 212.

[49] *Aktenvermerk, Fuehrerhauptquartier, 16.VII.41.,* in *I.M.T., op. cit.* XXXVIII, pp. 86–94.

[50] "Order concerning martial law in the area of Operation *BARBAROSSA* and special measures for the troops," *Fuehrer HQ, 13.V.41.,* in "Fuehrer Directives," *op. cit.,* I, pp. 173–74.

eliminated as guerrillas not later than at the transit prisoner of war
camps. This was the well-known "Commissar Order." [51]

Preparation for the Economic Exploitation

Germany's ultimate objectives in the attack on the Soviet Union were
primarily of an economic nature. The campaign was intended to in-
troduce the vast food resources of Russia into the European economy and
make Russian raw materials available for the Four-Year Plan.[52] With
the USSR's "boundless riches under her control," as Hitler put it,
Germany would be "unassailable" and would control the necessary potential for waging "future wars against continents." [53]

The systematic economic exploitation, such as the Germans planned,
had three basically different aspects: exploitation with the aim of supporting the troops in the field; exploitation in terms of obtaining raw
materials and food stuffs for Germany proper; and lastly the permanent
control and exploitation of all economic production in Russia within
the framework of a European market under German hegemony.

Goering, as plenipotentiary of the Four-Year Plan, was given jurisdiction over the whole program and empowered to issue all orders concerning it, even to the Wehrmacht.[54]   He in turn delegated this authority
to the Policy Directorate of the Economic Staff East (*Wirtschaftsfueh-
rungsstab Ost*) headed by the chief of the Armed Forces Economic Office,
General der Infantrie Georg Thomas.[55]

In Russia itself, control was to be vested in Economic Staff Oldenburg
for Special Duties (*Wirtschaftsstab z. b. V. Oldenburg*) under the command of Generalmajor Schubert.   Staff Oldenburg was to exercise its
command and administrative functions through five economic inspec-

---

[51] See: *Abt. Landesverteidigung (IV/Uq) F. H. Qu., den 12.V.41., Betr.; Behand-
lung gefangener politischer und milit. russischer Funktionaere* in *I.M.T., op. cit.,*
XXVI, pp. 406–08; *OKH/Az. Gen zbV ObdH (Gr R Wes), Nr. 91/41g. Kdos.
Chefs., 8.VI.41.* in *Fr Heere Ost, Chefsachen Band I.* H 3/1.

[52] *Wirtschaftspolitische Richtlinien fuer Wirtschaftsorganisation Ost, Gruppe Landwirtschaft, Wirtschaftsstab Ost, Gruppe La, 23.V.41.* in *I.M.T., op. cit.,* XXXVI,
pp. 135–57; see also: *Vortragsnotiz uber Vierjahresplan und Vorbereitung der
Kriegswirtschaft, Abt. Landesverteidigung 3.XII.36.* in *ibid.,* pp. 478–80. The
Four-Year Plan was set up in 1936 with Hermann Goering as plenipotentiary to
"Within four years . . . put the entire economy in a state of readiness for war," and
in peacetime to safeguard ". . . the independent basis of the life and economy of
the German people," i. e., to make Germany self-sufficient in such strategic war
materials as gasoline, rubber, and steel.

[53] Greiner, "Operation *BARBAROSSA*," *op. cit.,* p. 70.

[54] Hitler Decree "concerning the Economy in the Newly Occupied Eastern Territories," 20 May 41, in *Nazi Conspiracy and Aggression* (Washington, 1948), III,
p. 832.

[55] *Unterabschnitt Ostpreussen I, IV Wi, "Der IV Wi des AOK,"* 12.VI.41., in
KTB.2, Korueck 584. 35615/2; *Besprechung mit den Wehrmachtteilen am Dienstag,
den 29.IV.41.* in *I.M.T., op. cit.,* XXVII, pp. 32–38.

torates, one of which was assigned to each army group rear area, one for the Caucasus, and the fifth held in reserve. In the army rear areas, a liaison officer of the industrial armament office was to be attached to each of the army commands. For his work in the combat zone this liaison officer was to have technical battalions and reconnaissance and recovery units for raw materials, agricultural machinery, and production facilities. In the army rear areas he was to work through economic specialists in the subordinate commands, supplying the troop units from the country and preparing for the general exploitation to follow.[56]

Such an exploitation was nothing new. Following the defeat of the Polish armed forces in the fall of 1939, Goering had ordered that all raw materials, machinery, scrap metals, and the like, which might be of use for the German war economy, be removed from those areas of Poland which were not to be politically incorporated into the Reich. He directed that all industries that were not absolutely necessary for "the meager maintenance of the bare existence of the population" were to be dismantled and transferred to Germany.[57]

Th policy in Russia was to be similar but more drastic. German needs were to be satisfied without any consideration for the native population. The minimum aim was the provisioning of the Wehrmacht from enemy territory in the third year of the war, and, if necessary, in later years. This was to be attained at any price. Since the grain surplus of Russia was determined not by the size of the crop but by the level of domestic consumption, isolating the grain-producing black soil areas from the less productive regions would place sizeable surpluses at German disposal. Such an isolation would cut off supplies to the entire forest zone, including the industrial centers of Moscow and Leningrad. The people of these areas would naturally face serious distress from famine. If any attempt was made to save them from death by starvation by importing surpluses from the black soil zone it would be at the expense of supplies to Europe, and was unthinkable as it would reduce Germany's staying power in the war and undermine her ability to resist the blockade. This isolation of the forest regions thus was in accord with the political policy, that is, the preservation of the Baltic States, White Russia, the Ukraine, and the Caucasus and the destruction of Great Russia.[58] Throughout the planning period it was taken for granted that the Wehrmacht would destroy the Red Army. But in connection with

---

[56] *Besprechung mit den Wehrmachtteilen am Dienstag, den 29.IV.41.* in *I.M.T.*, *op. cit.*, XXVII, pp. 32–38.

[57] *Ministerpraesident Generalfeldmarschall Goering, Beauftragter fuer den Vierjahresplan, Vorsitzender des Ministerrats fuer die Reichsverteidigung, St. M.Dev. 9547, 19.X.39.* in *I.M.T.*, *op. cit.*, XXXVI, pp. 482–83.

[58] *Wirtschaftspolitische Richtlinien fuer Wirtschaftsorganisation Ost*, in *I.M.T.* *op. cit.*, XXXVI, pp. 135–57.

the proposed economic program many of the German leaders expressed concern over the possible negative reaction of the Russian natives to so obvious an exploitation and the effect it might have on the whole war effort.

Ernst von Weizsaecker, State Secretary in the Foreign Office, admitted the inevitability of the military victory, but doubted that it could be turned to account in the face of Slavic passive resistance.[59] Thomas believed that if the campaign lasted longer than a few months the success of his program would depend among other things on the collaboration of the people with the economic authorities,[60] while Staff Oldenburg, in much the same vein, estimated that unless the people were won over, a permanent distribution of 250,000 security troops over the occupied territory would be necessary to ensure the accomplishment of the economic mission.[61] Even Rosenberg had his misgivings about the exploitation, fearing the political reaction in Russia when the extent of German economic intentions became known.[62] But all these forebodings went unheeded.

Propaganda for Russia

Despite the intensive preparation in other fields that had been under way for several months, it was not until June that OKW issued a directive for handling propaganda in Operation *BARBAROSSA*.[63] Apparently no great amount of thought had been given the matter, for even this directive was considered neither final nor complete and the choice of permissible propaganda themes was greatly restricted. Many subjects which had been used in previous campaigns, as statements of German intentions, appeals to nationalistic sentiments or ambitions of ethnic minorities, and references to new pro-German national governments, were outlawed. Such themes as were allowed were to be used against both the Red Army and the civilian population.[64]

The greatest emphasis was to be placed on the thesis that the enemies of Germany were not the people of the Soviet Union, but the Jewish-Bolshevist Soviet government and the communist party working for

[59] Memo, State Sec in German Foreign Office to Reich Foreign Minister, 28 Apr 41, *Nazi-Soviet Relations, 1939–1941* (Washington, 1948), pp. 333–34.

[60] Georg Thomas, *Grundlagen fuer eine Geschichte der deutschen Wehr- und Ruestungswirtschaft* in *I.M.T., op. cit.,* XXX, pp. 259–80.

[61] Notes on conf between economic office and Rosenberg Ministry, in *OKW/Abt. Landesverteidigung, Gruppenleiter II, 28.V.41.* OKW/1759.

[62] Decree of the Fuehrer Concerning the Economy in the Newly Occupied Eastern Territories, 20 May 41, and attached remarks of Rosenberg, in *Nazi Conspiracy and Aggression, op. cit.,* III, pp. 832–33.

[63] "Directive for Handling Propaganda for Operation *BARBAROSSA*," *OKW/ WFSt/WPr, Nr. 144/41 g.Kdos.Chefs., Juni 41,* in "Fuehrer Directives," *op. cit.,* I, pp. 180–83.

[64] For a definitive treatment of propaganda used against Russia, see: John Buchsbaum "German Psychological Warfare on the Russian Front." MS in OCMH.

world revolution. An especial point was to be made that the Wehrmacht was not entering Russia as an enemy of the people, but to free them from Soviet tyranny. Nevertheless, the natives were to have impressed on them that should any part of the non-Bolshevist populace offer resistance of any kind, the German armed forces would be obliged to break it whenever and wherever it appeared.

The people were to be constantly warned not to participate in the fighting and to remain calm and orderly. They were to have impressed on them the importance of "work as usual" and be made to understand that looting, waste, and destruction of machinery and industrial installations would lead to poverty and famine. For the same reason it was to be announced that the collective farms were not to be broken up and the land distributed immediately, but at some later date. Propaganda was not to lead prematurely to the conclusion that the Soviet Union was to be dissolved.

The expressions "Russia," "Russians," and "Russian armed forces" were to be avoided, and the terms "Soviet Union," "people of the Soviet Union," and "Red Army" used instead.

Wherever it should be found possible to control the press, several large newspapers were to continue to appear under German censorship, especially in the Baltic States and the Ukraine. Similar use was to be made of such radio networks as were captured undamaged. In the use of these media, special emphasis was to be given to policies which would exercise a calmning influence on the inhabitants and dissuade them from committing any acts of sabotage. In places where it might be found impossible to control the press, the activities of information bureaus were to be suppressed entirely.[65]

Just where this negative approach originated is unknown. The evidence points to Hitler himself as the author, or at least the inner Nazi Party circle.[66] In publishing the directive the Wehrmacht Propaganda Division, which was strictly an operating and not a policy-making body, was merely passing on to subordinate propaganda commands instructions it had received from above. For the execution of this directive, one propaganda company of five platoons was assigned to each field army. Of the platoons, only one was actually to engage in propaganda operations, three being allotted respectively to newspaper, film, and radio reporting for German consumption, and the fifth being a service unit.[67]

---

[65] "Directive for Handling Propaganda for Operation *BARBAROSSA*," *op. cit.*

[66] See *Aktenvermerk, Fuehrerhauptquartier 16.VII.41.* in *I.M.T.*, *op. cit.*, XXXVIII, pp. 86–94; ltr, Lammers (on behalf of Hitler) to Keitel, 20 May 41, in Buchsbaum, *op. cit.*; memo on Briefing of the Chiefs of Staff of Rear Area Commands, 11 June 41, in Buchsbaum, *op. cit.*

[67] Buchsbaum, *op. cit.*, ch. IV, pp. 17–18.

388413—56——3

Invasion Planning

The German Lineup

Under the German plan of operations, the immediate task of the Army was the destruction of the Red Army in the western border zones of the USSR by means of deep penetrations and encirclements by armored spearheads. Special emphasis was to be placed on the prevention of a strategic retreat into the void of the Russian land mass where space might be traded for time and German communications stretched to the breaking point. The final aim of the entire operation was the erection of a barrier against the infinity of Asiatic Russia along the Archangel-Astrakhan line.

The attack was to be launched by three army groups simultaneously, two to the north and one to the south of the Pripyat Marshes, with the main effort in the north. *Army Group Center,* under the command of Generalfeldmarschall Fedor von Bock was to move directly eastward and encircle and destroy the enemy forces in White Russia. This would cover the right flank of *Army Group North* and enable it to advance swiftly to the north to capture Leningrad and free the Baltic States coast to the German navy. Once the Baltics were secure, and his left flank thus anchored, he was to throw the entire weight of his armies at Moscow. His force for this task consisted of the *Second Panzer Group* (General-oberist Heinz Guderian), the *Third Panzer Group* (Generaloberst Hans Hoth), the *Fourth Army* (Generaloberst Guenther von Kluge), and the *Ninth Army* (Generaloberst Adolf Strauss), the whole totaling 48 divisions of which 9 were armored and 7 motorized.[68]

The assault was to be spearheaded by the two panzer groups attacking from points some 120 miles apart in a series of gigantic double envelopments, the *Third Panzer Group* on the extreme left and the *Second Panzer Group* to the south in the vicinity of Brest-Litovsk. The infantry was to push forward all along the line and reduce the tank-encircled pockets.

Opposing *Army Group Center* was Timoshenko's West Front,[69] comprised of the Second, Third, Tenth, and Twelfth Armies, made up of some 45 rifle and 2 armored divisions.

Poised in East Prussia for the thrust through the Baltics to Leningrad was Generalfeldmarschall Wilhelm Ritter von Leeb's *Army Group North,* made up of the *Fourth Panzer Group* (Generaloberst Erich Hoeppner), the *Sixteenth Army* (Generaloberst Ernst Busch), and the *Eighteenth Army* (Generaloberst Georg von Kuechler), totaling 27 divi-

---

[68] All figures for the German order of battle at the beginning of the campaign are taken from DA Pam 20–261a, *The German Campaign in Russia, Planning and Operations (1940–1942).*

[69] In the Red Army a "front" corresponded roughly to a German army group.

sions, of which 3 were armored and 3 motorized. Despite the obvious fact that the Baltic topography would channelize Von Leeb's movement and throw his armor along but a few avenues of advance, the attack was expected to roll rapidly.

Von Leeb planned to attack with his *Fourth Panzer Group* in the center generally along the line Vilna-Dvinsk-Pskov-Luga-Leningrad with the *Sixteenth Army* covering his right flank and the *Eighteenth Army* on the left where it was to clear the coastal regions and occupy the Baltic ports.

Facing him were the Eighth and Eleventh Armies of Marshal Voroshilov's Northwest Front consisting of an estimated 32 divisions, of which at least 2 were armored.

To the south of the Pripyat barrier was *Army Group South*, commanded by the dean of the German officer corps, Generalfeldmarschall Gerd von Rundstedt. Von Rundstedt's task, a secondary one, was to roll up and destroy the southern Russian armies along the course of the Dnepr River with a force consisting of the *First Panzer Group* (Generaloberst Ewald von Kleist), the *Sixth Army* (Generaloberst Walther von Reichenau), the *Seventeenth Army* (General der Infanterie Henrich von Stuelpnagel), and the *Eleventh Army* (Generaloberst Eugen Ritter von Schobert), the latter including the *Third Romanian Army* under General Ion Antonescu. The force totaled 40 German divisions, of which 5 were armored and 3 motorized, and 14 Romanian divisions.

Von Rundstedt planned to make his main effort on the left of the line with the *Sixth* and *Seventeenth Armies,* holding back the panzers until the infantry had breached the immediate border defenses. Assembling on the Romanian border, the *Eleventh Army,* separated from the remainder of the army group by a 150 mile stretch of the Carpathian Mountains, was not expected to be ready to move before the beginning of July.

Facing Von Rundstedt were the four armies of Marshal Budenny's Southwest Front, the Fifth, Sixth, Twelfth, and Second, from north to south, estimated at a strength of 64 rifle divisions and the equivalent of 5 armored divisions.

In OKH reserve was the *Second Army* (Generaloberst Maximilian Freiherr von Weichs) consisting of seven infantry divisions, later to be added to von Bock's forces. The attack was to be supported by the tactical aircraft of three air forces, one for each army group.

Minor operations were to be undertaken in Finland by *Army, Norway* under the command of Generaloberst Nikolaus von Falkenhorst, and the *Finnish Army* commanded by Field Marshal Carl Gustaf Emil von Mannerheim. These two forces comprised a total of 16 divisions, 13 Finnish, and 3 German, plus one German brigade.

PART TWO

1941–1942: THE PERIOD OF GERMAN ADVANCES

CHAPTER 3

GERMAN OPERATIONS TO THE STALINGRAD DEBACLE [1]

The Attack Through White Russia

The general assault was mounted on 22 June 1941. In the pre-dawn hours Von Bock launched his attack from two points near the center of the front, the *Fourth Army* attacking on the right and the *Ninth Army* on the left. Tactical surprise was almost complete. Bridges in the Brest-Litovsk area were seized intact and crossings further north were quickly established in the face of slight opposition. The infantry, moving through the only partially manned border defenses, rapidly opened holes through which the armored and motorized units of the *Second* and *Third Panzer Groups* could start their operations. Their immediate task was to close a gigantic pair of pincers on Minsk in order to trap both the Russian forces along the frontier and the reserve units hastily committed to stem the assault, while the infantry at the same time enveloped a large Russian concentration about Bialystok. Hoth moved rapidly and by the 24th was less than 30 miles from his goal, while Guderian drove more slowly eastward along the Warsaw-Minsk highway, repeatedly checked by local counterattacks. On the 29th the two linked up beyond Minsk, but, constantly harassed by attacks in their rear and on their inner flanks and lacking the mass of the more slowly moving infantry, they were unable to completely close the gap before large numbers of Russians managed to escape to the east.

In the first 10 days the tank units of *Army Group Center* moved some 190 miles into Russian territory but still were unable to achieve complete operational freedom. Strong opposition was encountered on all sides: the enemy units caught in the pincer movement were wildly attempting to break out in all directions. Minsk fell on 30 June, but the inner pocket was not completely reduced until 10 July. During the three-week period, 323,000 prisoners were reported captured and 3,000 tanks and 1,800 guns taken or destroyed.

---

[1] For a detailed account of German operations in Russia in 1941–42, see DA Pam 20–261a, *The German Campaign in Russia, Planning and Operations (1940–1942)*.

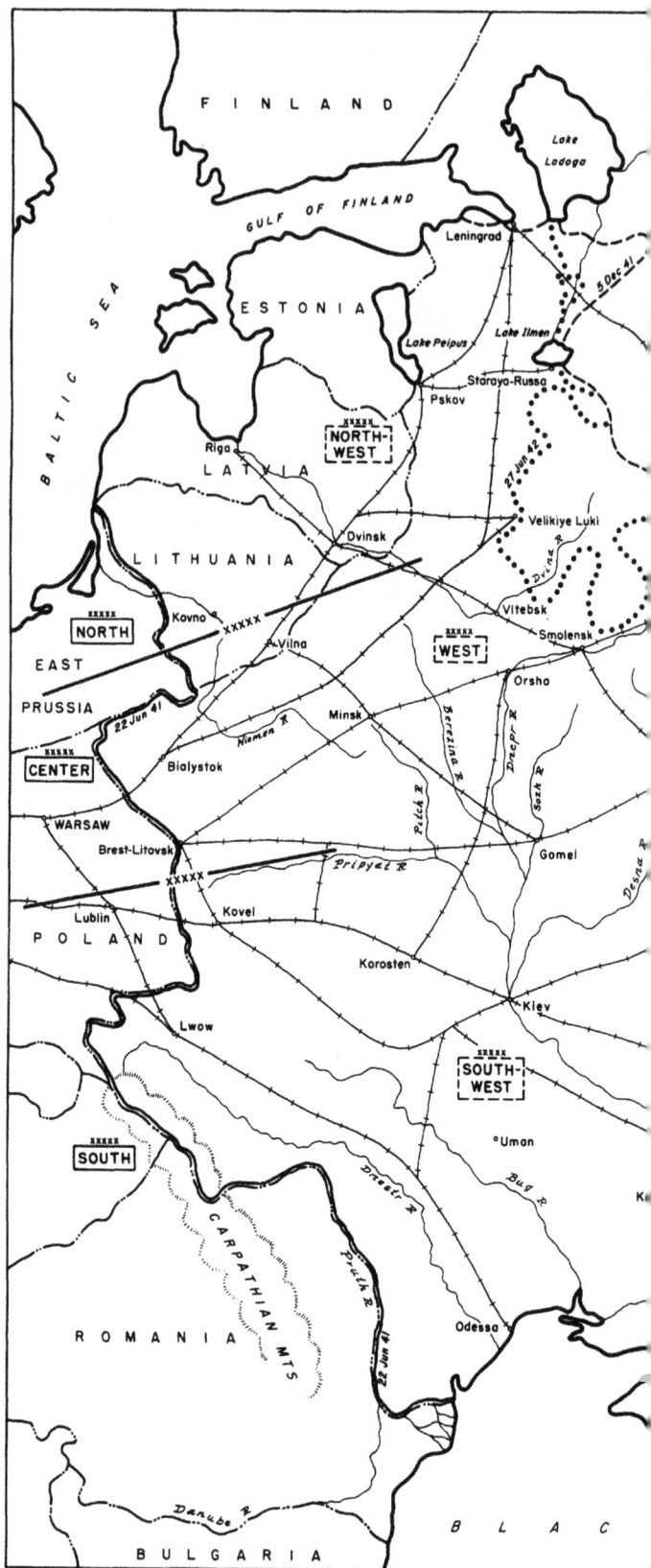

Map 3. *Period of German Offensives, 1941–1942.*

Map 3

)D OF GERMAN OFFENSIVES,1941-1942

WITH FRONT INDICATED AS OF

———— 22 June 1941
— — — 5 December 1941
•••••• 27 June 1942
—•— 18 November 1942

+—+ Railways
▭ German
⊏‡⊐ Russian

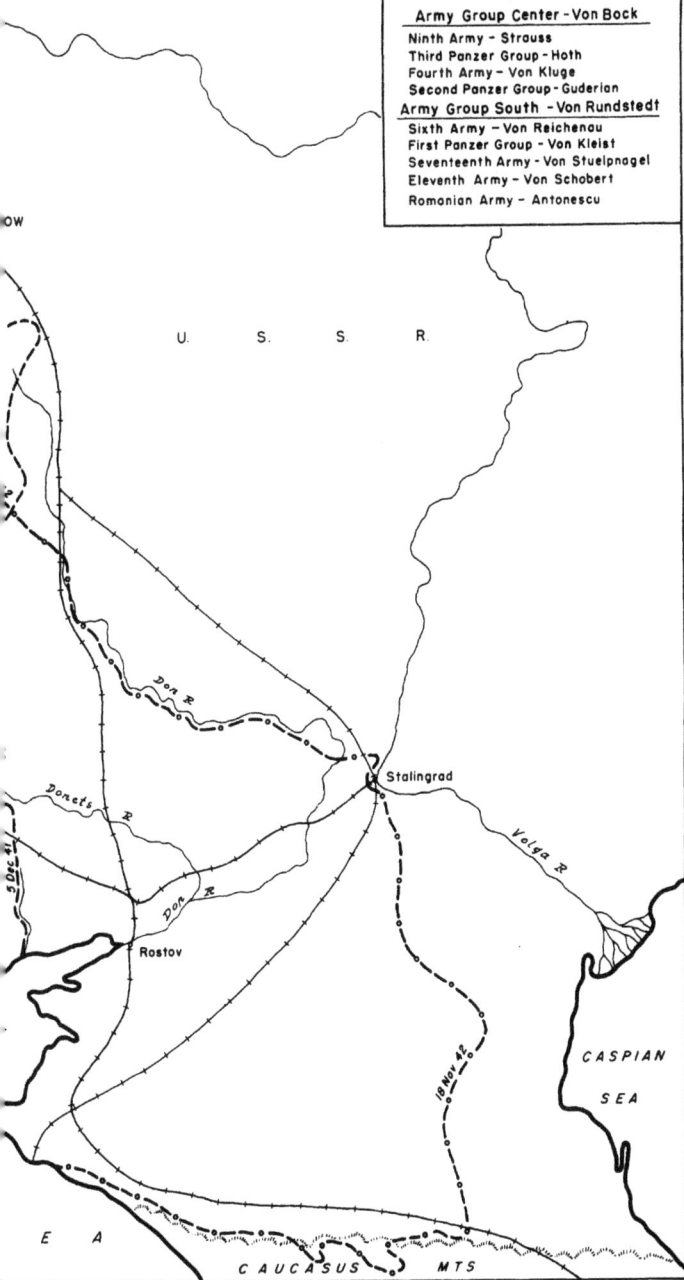

50 0 100
MILES

ORDER OF BATTLE

RUSSIAN
Northwest Front-Voroshilov

West Front-Timoshenko

Southwest Front-Budenny

GERMAN
Army Group North-Von Leeb
Eighteenth Army – Von Kuechler
Fourth Panzer Group – Hoeppner
Sixteenth Army – Busch

Army Group Center-Von Bock
Ninth Army – Strauss
Third Panzer Group – Hoth
Fourth Army – Von Kluge
Second Panzer Group – Guderian

Army Group South – Von Rundstedt
Sixth Army – Von Reichenau
First Panzer Group – Von Kleist
Seventeenth Army – Von Stuelpnagel
Eleventh Army – Von Schobert
Romanian Army – Antonescu

OW

U. S. S. R.

Don R.

Donets R.

Stalingrad

Volga R.

5 Dec 41

Don R.

Rostov

18 Nov 42

CASPIAN

SEA

E A

18 Nov 42

C A U C A S U S MTS

Following the fall of Minsk units were quickly regrouped for the drive to the next important objective, the "dry route" to Moscow between the headwaters of the Dvina and Dnepr Rivers through the triangle Vitebsk-Orsha-Smolensk. On 3 July Von Kluge with his *Fourth Army* headquarters, redesignated the *Fourth Panzer Army,* took over command of both panzer groups, his infantry divisions going to *Second Army,* which had moved up from OKH reserve to carry on the mopping up west of Minsk in conjunction with the *Ninth Army.* On the same day Hoth and Guderian resumed the attack, making good progress against stiff opposition. By 16 July the latter reached Smolensk. Hoth meanwhile reached out east of Vitebsk and cut to the north to pinch off the enemy forces still in the west against the swamps south of Lake Ilmen. Heavily counterattacked day after day along their extended communication lines and on their exposed flanks, both groups soon found that the supply lag and the need for rest and rehabilitation of troops and materiel precluded a continued eastward movement. Any further thrust toward Moscow had to be postponed until the infantry could move up to stabilize the rear and liquidate the huge pocket formed west of Smolensk. Again enemy attempts to break out were aggressively executed, and it was not until 10 August that the trap was completely sprung with the capture of 310,000 prisoners and 3,200 tanks. Even with such a bag the Germans were unable to prevent an almost wholesale escape of thousands of others. By the middle of August the Smolensk operation was complete.

The Drive to Leningrad

Meanwhile *Army Group North* moved north through the Baltic States at the same fast pace. Kovno fell to the *Fourth Panzer Group* on 23 June with little opposition and Dvinsk on the Dvina River was occupied by noon on the 26th. The infantry elements of the *Sixteenth* and *Eighteenth Armies,* on the right and left respectively, maintained the swift pace, Liepaja falling to the *291st Division* on the 27th and advance elements of the *61st Division* entering Riga on the 30th.

On 2 July Hoeppner renewed his attack out of the Dvina bridgeheads, and on the first day advanced elements of his command halfway to Pskov. Ostrov, thirty miles below Pskov, was reached two days later with armored units fanning out to the right to occupy the exposed flank between Velikiye Luki and Lake Ilmen. Von Kuechler's *Eighteenth Army* moved north to clear Estonia, and Busch drove hard on the right flank to relieve the panzers there and free them for further offensive action in the center.

The drive was continued, but by the middle of the month the panzers had been perceptibly slowed down by a combination of bad roads, difficult terrain, and increasing pressure from the right and direct front. During the next six weeks their gains were modest: they were canalized by Lakes Ilmen and Peipus to routes through swamps and deep forests heavily defended by the enemy. The *Eighteenth Army,* moving more surely against lighter opposition, reached the Gulf of Finland on 9 August and swung eastward toward Leningrad, leaving one corps to mop up the coastal areas. The progress in the center continued to be slow, both terrain and strong enemy resistance preventing any clean breakaway. This drive was considerably strengthened when one armored and two motorized divisions were shifted to it from *Army Group Center,* and by 1 September the spearhead stood within 20 miles of Lake Ladoga. Continued attacks on the ring of defenses around Leningrad counted for little gain, even with the *Eighteenth Army* moving over from Estonia and joining in the assault. Finally, with the capture of Shlisselburg, a fortress on Lake Ladoga, the isolation of the old Tsarist capital was complete, and a stalemate set in. By 21 September most of the armor was out of the area and the *Eighteenth Army* took over the siege zone.

Clearing the Dnepr Bend

Concurrently with the twin attacks of Von Leeb and Von Bock further to the north, Von Rundstedt struck across the border with the panzer group and two of the three armies which comprised his *Army Group South.*

As elsewhere along the line, almost complete tactical surprise was achieved, and by noon the border areas had been sufficiently cleared for Von Kleist to move out his *First Panzer Group* to the attack. Given an opening and protected on both flanks by Von Reichenau's *Sixth Army,* the panzers thrust rapidly forward, reaching the Styr River on 24 June and taking Dubno the following day. But on the 26th strong armored counterattacks developed on their right flank and progress was slowed. Such gains as were made, however, threatened the Soviet forces holding up Von Stuelpnagel's *Seventeenth Army* and made untenable their salient in the vicinity of Przemysl, forcing them to withdraw. Thus freed of opposition the *Seventeenth Army* drove to Lwow by the 27th and occupied the city three days later.

To the south of the Carpathian barrier, Von Schobert attacked across the Pruth River with his *Eleventh Army* on 2 July. The attack made slow progress, the Russians fighting stubborn rear guard actions as they fell back, and the Dnestr River was reached only on the 15th. On the right of Von Schobert the Romanian Army began to move forward as the Soviets evacuated Bessarabia.

The main effort continued with Von Kleist's armor still in the van, the *Seventeenth Army* to the south moving more slowly on a broad front.

By 11 July one panzer unit had reached the outer defenses of Kiev, but violent tank-led counterattacks from both north and south in the vicinity of Zhitomir and Berdichev, the twin cities that controlled the western approaches to the Ukrainian capital, brought forward movement to a halt and inflicted heavy casualties on several of the armored divisions. Meanwhile, the *Seventeenth Army*, moving deliberately, was pulling up on the right.

During the first three weeks of the campaign Von Rundstedt pushed steadily to the east, but had scored no gains comparable to those of Von Bock in the center. Kept off balance by Budenny's counterblows, he had been unable to encircle any large groups of the enemy or prevent large-scale withdrawals to the Dnepr. From a strategic point of view, Budenny's fighting retreat was a success, for it provided the time necessary for withdrawing much of the Ukrainian industry to the east.

By 16 July Von Kleist had eliminated the opposition about Zhitomir and Berdichev and began a series of moves designed to place his armor behind the Reds being slowly forced back by the *Seventeenth* and *Eleventh Armies*. Despite heavy pressure from the north which virtually tied down the *Sixth Army* in the Kiev-Korosten area and the appearance of fresh enemy units on his immediate left flank which at times occupied the attention of an entire armored corps, Von Kleist swung all of his available units to the south and drove hard on Pervomaysk and Uman to trap the Russians against the eastward-moving infantry. By 3 August the trap was sprung on a number of Red divisions, although others were able to make good their escape to the east.

The Pervomaysk-Uman pocket was reduced and by 7 August the line of the Bug River secured. The tank units then drove on toward Kirovo and Krivoi Rog—the iron ore center of European Russia—and occupied the latter on the 14th. Meanwhile the Romanians had reached Odessa and were preparing an assault. Two days later the Soviet forces were in retreat along the whole southern front, and on the 17th Von Rundstedt moved to clear the entire western bank of the Dnepr. The Russian salient around Kiev held fast, but the Soviet Fifth Army, which had battered so hard against the northern flank of the army group at Korosten, withdrew across the river followed by Von Reichenau who forced a crossing above Kiev on the 25th. The same day Von Kleist secured a bridgehead at Dnepropetrovsk, and on the 30th the *Eleventh Army* was over the river at Kherson. Two days later the *Seventeenth Army* established another bridgehead east of Kremenchug. Thus by 1 September *Army Group South* had cleared the right bank of the Dnepr with the exception of the Ukrainian capital and had established bridgeheads for each of its armies out of which to resume the offensive. In the far south the Romanians had launched their assault on Odessa, but with little immediate success.

In two months time the Germans had advanced some 400 miles into the Soviet Union and had reached the line generally Leningrad-Smolensk-Dnepr River. The first phase of operations was ended, and Moscow lay only 180 miles further on. Although the Germans had exacted a terrific toll of their enemies, they had not destroyed the Red Army and their own casualties had been high. By 11 August OKH had committed the last of the German reserves, and had identified 360 Red divisions as against an expected 200; by 13 August German casualties totaled 389,984 in killed, wounded, and missing; and by 24 August German infantry divisions had declined in strength an average of 40 percent, and armored units 50 percent.[2]

The Diversion to the South

During July Hitler had begun to vacillate as to the ultimate direction of his major effort. Because of the development of strong pressure on both flanks of *Army Group Center*, the adverse supply conditions, and the need of the armored formations for rehabilitation, on 30 July he ordered Von Bock to halt all forward movement and shift to the defensive.[3] This order was reiterated on 12 August. Finally on the 21st, and against the advice of both the troop leaders and the army high command, he shifted the emphasis of the campaign from Moscow and redirected it toward the Donets Basin and the Caucasus with the focus on *Army Group South*. Von Bock was ordered to assign Von Rundstedt such of his forces as were necessary to enable the latter to trap the Russians in the Kiev sector and gain a secure foothold east of the middle section of the Dnepr River. Moscow was to wait.[4]

In accordance with these orders, Von Weichs and Guderian pivoted their commands to the southeast and pushed toward Kiev. Despite violent counterattacks on his exposed left flank, Guderian made good progress and by 11 September was through Konotop to Romny, with the *Second Army* moving steadily on his inner flank and closing on Nezhin in conjunction with the *Sixth Army*. The German plan called for Von Kleist to strike northward out of the Seventeenth Army's Kremenchug bridgehead for a junction with Guderian on the Sula River, and the two to make a joint attack on the Kiev salient with an inverted front. The *Seventeenth Army*, after enlarging its bridgehead, was to strike to the northeast to secure the flank and rear of the enveloping forces. Although heavy enemy counterattacks and poor weather slowed the *First Panzer Group*, by 10 September German pressure on the Reds pinned against the Dnepr had begun to tell and resistance became in-

---

[2] "Halder's Journal," *op. cit.*, pp. 36, 63, 74.
[3] Directive No. 34, *OKW/WFSt/Abt. L. (I Op.), Nr. 441298/41, g. K. Chefs., 30.VIII.41.*, in "Fuehrer Directives," *op. cit.*
[4] Dir, Hitler to Von Brauchitsch, 21 Aug 41, in *ibid.*

creasingly disorganized. On the 14th the two armored units linked up near Lubny. By the 16th the ring was tightly sealed and at 1200 on the 19th the Swastika was raised over the citadel of Kiev. The Germans claimed 665,000 prisoners, 3,718 guns, and 886 tanks captured or destroyed. The armies of Budenny's Southwest Front were destroyed for all intents and purposes, and for the time being the Soviet marshal was left without an effective fighting force.

Von Rundstedt's Fall Offensive

With the springing of the trap on the Kiev salient, Von Kleist reversed his field and moved southward, while Guderian quickly regrouped his units and turned back to join *Army Group Center* in its renewed offensive toward Moscow. Moving rapidly, Von Kleist took the still tenaciously contested Dnepropetrovsk bridgehead in reverse and then pushed on to the south and southeast toward the Sea of Azov and the city of Rostov at the mouth of the Don River, the gateway to the Caucasus.

As a result of the Kiev disaster, Budenny had been relieved of his command and replaced by Timoshenko, Zhukov taking over the West Front defending before Moscow. Under the new commander the remaining units of the shattered Southwest Front conducted a general withdrawal toward the Don River north of Kharkov, though remaining in the city itself.

The Sixth Army in the meantime, having completed the liquidation of the Kiev pocket during the last days of September, began to move eastward as left flank cover for the *Seventeenth Army* which had made slow progress in its push to the east from the Kremenchug crossing. As early as 19 September the infantry units had taken Poltava, where Charles XII of Sweden had been defeated by Peter the Great in 1709, but the fall rains and resultant bottomless roads held them to insignificant gains beyond. With the advent of better weather and with Von Reichenau's pulling up on the left, Von Stuelpnagel bypassed Kharkov to the south, leaving his colleague to invest the city, and joined Von Kleist's panzers in the advance into the Don Basin. Kharkov fell to the *Sixth Army* on 24 October; the *First Panzer Group* crossed the Mius River and reached the outskirts of Rostov by the beginning of November; and the *Seventeenth Army* meanwhile had pushed slowly into the Don bend.

The *Eleventh Army* in the meantime moved out of its Dnepr crossing at Kherson, drove toward the Crimea, and on 14 September reached Perekop at the head of the isthmus that joined the peninsula to the mainland. Resistance on the narrow neck of land was bitter, and it was not until 29 October that Von Manstein [5] was able to storm the last of the defenses and break free, capturing Simferopol, the capital, two days

---

[5] Generalleutnant Fritz-Erich von Manstein had replaced Von Schobert who was killed in a plane crash on 12 Sep.

later.   Odessa, having withstood the Romanian assault, was finally evacuated by the Russians on 16 October.

The Crimea had a special strategic importance in that the possessor of its air fields could effectively dominate the maritime trade routes of the Black Sea as well as easily reach the vital Ploesti oil fields in Romania. With the capture of Simferopol, the Soviets withdrew within the fortress of Sevastopol and into the Kerch Peninsula, but returned in two large sea-borne raids, on 26 and 29 December 1941 respectively, which so occupied Von Manstein that he was unable to mount an assault on the great Russian fortress until the following May.

Advance elements of the *First Panzer Group* entered Rostov on 23 November, but it was an exhausted army that stood at the mouth of the Don.   Men and machines alike were worn with fighting both a stubborn enemy and the autumn mud and rain.   A week later the Soviets viciously counterattacked on the exposed left flank, and the sagging columns were forced back to the line of the Mius River, some 60 miles to the west, despite Hitler's orders not to retreat one step.   (This was the order which caused Von Rundstedt to ask to be relieved.)   Thus the year ended in the south, and although operations closed on a note of defeat, the Ukraine with its grain fields and the Don Basin with its industry lay within the German perimeter.

The Battle for Moscow

On 6 September Hitler, apparently emboldened by the prospect of Budenny's destruction in the "biggest battle in world history" and believing that as a result *Army Group South* would be able to proceed with its drive to the Caucasus unaided, reversed his decision of 21 August and revived the original OKH blueprint for the main effort toward Moscow, at the same time ordering Von Weichs and Guderian back to *Army Group Center* control as soon as the situation behind Kiev would permit.[6]   The plan was to trap and crush Zhukov's West Front before the Soviet capital by means of another double envelopment converging on Vyazma with strong supporting task forces on the flanks.   The *Third Panzer Group* and the *Ninth Army* were to form the northern pincer arm, with the *Fourth Panzer Group* (to be released from *Army Group North*) and the *Fourth Army* comprising the southern half of the ring. After the completion of this "operation of annihilation" the army group was to attack Moscow along a front bounded by the Oka River on the right and the upper Volga on the left.   It was further provided that Guderian's *Second Panzer Group,* when released from the Kiev encirclement, would swing northward along the Orel-Tula axis and join

---

[6] Notes on Fuehrer conf, 5 Sep 41, in "Halder's Journal," *op. cit.,* VII, p. 84; Directive No. 35, *OKW/WFSt/Abt. L.* (*I Op.*), *Nr. 441492/41, g. kdos, Chefs., 6.IX.41.,* in "Fuehrer Directives," *op. cit.*

the attack, forming an outer arc of the Vyazma trap.[7]   For this final drive Von Bock had at his disposal 69 divisions, of which 14 were armored and 7 motorized.   In general the supply situation was satisfactory.   Time was the important element, for the early Russian winter was approaching and the attack had to be launched regardless of other considerations.

This final drive opened on 2 October, and by the end of the second day had broken the resistance along almost the entire front.   Meanwhile Guderian had disengaged his units from the Kiev front and before the end of September was pushing hard to the northeast to join the lower jaw of the trap.   By the day of the opening of the attack he had gained considerable operational freedom and his advance elements were nearing Orel.   On 4 October he was past Orel and driving hard for Tula, his left flank units at the same time aiding the *Second Army* in an envelopment of Bryansk.   On the 7th tanks of Hoth and Hoeppner linked up at Vyazma closing the circle, with the *Fourth Army* pushing in sharply to release the armor for operations further to the east.   During the next week the ring was tightened and the Germans announced the capture of 600,000 more Russians.   Actually the resistance of some of the cut-off Red Army groups was not completely broken until later in the month.   Meanwhile the heavy autumn rains and logistical difficulties slowed the advance perceptibly.

Progress from the middle of October until 15 November was slow. Swamps and heavy forests channeled the advance along a few passable roads and a desperate defense along successive lines and behind antitank obstacles and mine fields held the attack to but a few miles a day.   By 15 November the *Fourth Army* had passed through Mozhaysk and come to within 40 miles of Moscow where it was halted by the line of the Nara and Oka Rivers.   Guderian meanwhile reached the vicinity of Tula.

The final drive on Moscow was to consist of another double envelopment coordinated with a frontal assault by the *Fourth Army*.   The *Fourth Panzer Group* supported by elements of the *Third Panzer Group* on its left flank was to form the northern jaw of the trap; Guderian was to comprise the southern arm, attacking from Tula toward Kolomna to come at Moscow from the rear.

The attack was launched on 16 November.   Moving slowly because of the intense cold and a stubborn defense, the northern force reached the Moscow-Volga Canal on 25 November where the fighting grew even heavier.   On the southern arm Guderian, unable to take Tula, bypassed it to the east and pressed on, though with both flanks exposed.   German casualties were very heavy, and deep snows and temperatures as low

---

[7] Directive No. 35, *OKW/WFSt/Abt. L. (I Op.), Nr. 441492/41, g. Kdos. Chefs.,* in "Fuehrer Directives," *op. cit.*

as $-40°$ F. punished the troops. The turning point came on 5 December. One element of Hoeppner's *2d Panzer Division* fought to within sight of the Kremlin while an infantry unit drove into the Moscow suburbs. But that same day Von Bock reported his troops at the end of their strength. Three days later the army group was ordered to go over to the defensive, and for the first time in World War II the Wehrmacht was stopped.[8]

The Winter of 1941–42

Despite the German successes of the summer and fall and the staggering losses suffered by the Red Army, this halt definitely shifted the advantage to the Russians. It was a thinned German army which stood on the outskirts of the Soviet capital, at the end of a long and overworked supply line, hundreds of miles from its bases, and with the last of its reserves long since committed. The Red divisions facing it were operating in familiar terrain close to their bases on interior lines and still had the manpower to give strength to their moves. The Germans were unprepared for the severe weather, while the Russians were acclimated and equipped for winter operations. The morale of the Germans was low; they were exhausted by long months of fighting and haunted by the spectre of Napoleon's retreat.[9]

On 6 December the Soviets struck back. With two armies [10] they launched an attack on the German left flank along the border between *Army Group North* and *Army Group Center* in the vicinity of Kalinin, and with a third drove into the right wing north of Tula. The German line, thin and with no depth, wavered and then slowly gave way. The Soviet pressure was maintained, and then increased, and before the first of the year *Army Group Center* was forced back generally to the line from which it had launched its final offensive late in November.

The Russian counterstroke, for the first time since the start of the war, was supported by an impressive propaganda campaign. The German troops were constantly reminded by leaflet and public address systems of the French campaign of 1812, the deep snow and bitter cold to which they were unaccustomed, the immediate danger of death by freezing far away from the German homeland, the resurrection of Soviet strength, and the turn of the tide of battle, all of which made a strong emotional impression on the German command and, to an even higher degree, on the troops.[11]

---

[8] Directive No. 39, *OKW/WFSt/Abt. L. (I Op.), Nr. 442090/41, g. kdos. Chefs., 8.XII.41,* in *ibid.*

[9] See: Liddell Hart, *The German Generals Talk* (New York, 1948), p. 185.

[10] A Russian army approximated a German corps in size.

[11] General der Infanterie Guenther Blumentritt, "Strategy and Psychological Warfare," pp. 11–12. Foreign Studies Br, OCMH.

Faced with a virtually impossible situation and influenced "to some extent" by the Russian winter propaganda,[12] Von Bock and Von Kluge requested permission to withdraw behind the Ugra River. At this juncture, Hitler made the pivotal decision of the entire campaign. Against the advice of many of his military leaders who had continually argued in favor of a general withdrawal to a winter line in the rear, he ordered the armies to stand "regardless of enemy breakthroughs at the flanks or in the rear."[13] Although the move could hardly be called sound militarily, there seems little doubt that it saved this particular situation. "It was his one great achievement," General der Infanterie Kurt von Tippelskirch has stated. "At that critical moment . . . if [the troops] had once begun a retreat, it might have turned into a panic flight,"[14] for there were no prepared positions to withdraw to.

By the middle of January the earlier Russian tactical successes threatened to develop into a strategic disaster for the Germans. Reinforcing their initial assault units, the Soviets continued to press the attack. With two armies they forced a sizeable wedge between the *Second Panzer Army* and the *Fourth Army* in the vicinity of Kaluga, thus menacing army group headquarters at Smolensk; with four others they struck heavily between Rzhev and Kholm along the army group boundary, threatening to cut off *Army Groups Center* and *North* from one another and at the same time wholly envelop Von Kluge's northern flank.[15] The *Fourth Panzer, Ninth,* and *Fourth Armies* stood in grave danger of complete encirclement should this drive succeed in reaching to Smolensk.

Too weak to maintain a continuous line, the Germans pulled their units into a series of hedgehog defenses around key communication centers. Despite the deep enemy penetrations and the dropping of a number of Soviet airborne detachments in and behind the German defense sectors, the fiercely held German strong points denied important areas to the Soviets and forced them to spread their offensive strength thin. This had the effect of taking the edge off any enemy gain of strategic value. Several of the hedgehogs were cut off for weeks at a time and could be supplied only by air, but all were held. Thus a

---

[12] *Ibid.*
[13] Hitler Dir, *Nr. 442182/41 g.K.Chefs WFSt/Abt. L. (I Op.), 16.XII.41.* in "Fuehrer Directives," *op. cit.*
[14] Quoted in Hart, *op. cit.,* p. 189.
[15] Following the defeat at Moscow, Hitler radically shuffled the German command. He dismissed Von Brauchitsch and assumed direct command of the Army itself. Halder was retained as Chief of the General Staff, but his authority was heavily curtailed. In *Army Group North,* Von Kuechler replaced Von Leeb and Von Rundstedt was relieved in command of *Army Group South* by Von Reichenau. The latter died in January and was replaced by Von Bock who had given way to Von Kluge in *Army Group Center.* The commands of the individual armies were likewise radically reshuffled.

diseaster was averted, but this "one great achievement" of Hitler's had the ironic effect of exalting his faith in himself and his inelastic defense, and, in so doing, foreshadowed the final denouement.

During the same period heavy attacks were launched against *Army Group North*. The *Eighteenth Army* was forced back of the Volkhov River just south of Lake Ladoga and the line of the *Sixteenth Army* below Lake Ilmen was shattered; the entire *II Corps* was cut off and had to be supplied by air for several months, while the principal lateral communications line between *Army Groups Center* and *North* was completely overrun with the exception of the hedgehog at Kholm.

In the southern sector, the Russians late in January scored a signal success when they broke through between the *Sixth* and *Seventeenth Armies* at Izyum and drove halfway to the Dnepr bridgeheads, threatening to cut off and pin the *First Panzer* and *Seventeenth Armies* against the Black Sea coast. They lacked the reserves to follow up and exploit their gains, however, and were forced to a halt by strong German pressure on the shoulders of the penetration.

By the beginning of March the Soviet offensives had spent themselves, and the coming of the spring thaws brought all activity along the entire front to an end. Both sides began to regroup and prepare for the summer campaign. There was no further change in the line until May.

The German Summer Offensive, 1942

In making the strategic decision on the objectives of his next offensive moves, Hitler veered past intermediate goals. Still convinced that the Soviet nation was tottering, he focused his immediate planning on the basic objectives of the whole Russian venture: the destruction of Soviet manpower and the seizure of a source of food supply and raw materials for the German people and German economy.

Generally the plan called for a stabilized front in the center; a limited offensive in the north to isolate Leningrad; and an all-out drive in the south to destroy the Red Army units in the Don River region, block off the Soviets from the south by cutting the Volga River at Stalingrad, and capture the Caucasian oil fields.[16]

Since the manpower shortage precluded a general attack all along the southern front simultaneously, the offensive was to be launched to the east and southeast in a series of strikes unrolling from north to south in such a manner as to make maximum use of all arms at decisive points. It was to open with an assault east of Kursk by the *Second, Fourth Panzer*, and *Second Hungarian Armies* to take Voronezh on the Don

---

[16] Hitler Dir 41, *OKW/WFSt Nr. 55616/42 g.K.Chefs., 5.IV.42*, in "Fuehrer Directives," *op. cit.*

River. Immediately on achieving this objective, the infantry divisions of the northern arm of the pincer were to set up strong defensive positions on the line Livny-Voronezh to anchor the northern flank of the whole army group. With this wing secure, the armor was to move southward along the right bank of the river in support of the second attack. In this second phase, the *Sixth Army,* now commanded by Generaloberst Friedrich Paulus, was to strike northeast from Kharkov to link up with the *Fourth Panzer Army* along the Don and then swing downriver with it in support of the third phase, which was to be launched eastward from the Mius River line by the *First Panzer* and *Seventeenth Armies.* These latter were to join the units sweeping into the Don bend, with one element swinging to the south to retake Rostov and secure bridgeheads over the lower Don in preparation for the final drive to the Caucasus. The payoff phase was to be the final securing of the long left flank of the army group as a defensive front with the capture of Stalingrad and the rapid overrunning of the whole Caucasus region by the *First Panzer* and *Seventeenth Armies.*[17]

On 28 June the *Fourth Panzer* and *Second Armies* opened the offensive, sweeping eastward against light opposition. By 4 July the armor reached the Don at Voronezh and on the 7th established firm contact with the *Sixth Army* which had launched its phase of the attack on the last day of June. Despite this progress, all had not gone according to plan; a stubborn defense at Voronezh delayed the armored units' swinging downriver just long enough for several large Russian forces to evade the trap and escape to the east.

The third phase of the offensive was opened on 9 July with the combined *Fourth Panzer* and *Sixth Armies* pushing down the Don as planned and the *First Panzer* and *Seventeenth Armies* moving out from their Mius River line. Fear of the armor being delayed by a strong defense at Rostov caused a last minute change of plan and the main effort of the *First Panzer Army* was made much further to the north and across the Donets River instead of in the bend closer to Rostov. The *First* and *Fourth Panzer Armies* linked up on the 15th with the former forcing the Donets and closing on Rostov, and the latter driving steadily to the south. As the armor moved into the lower reaches of the river, the Russians withdrew before it, while the *Sixth Army* forged slowly into the Don bend opposite Stalingrad. By the 22nd the *First Panzer Army* reached Rostov, holding four bridgeheads over the Don, and the *Fourth Panzer Army* secured a crossing further to the east.

Meanwhile, on 8 May, Von Manstein opened operations with his *Eleventh Army* to sweep the Crimea as a prerequisite to the drive to the Caucasus. He first turned his attention to the Russians in the eastern end of the peninsula and by 2 June was able to focus his efforts on the

---

[17] *Ibid.*

enemy garrisons in the ancient fortress of Sevastopol. Despite fanatical
Soviet resistance from a stronghold that contained 19 modern forts and
more than 3,600 pillboxes, he snuffed out all resistance and secured the
entire peninsula by 2 July.

Preliminary to a continuation of the offensive into its final phase,
Army Group South was radically reorganized. Von Bock was relieved
and his command split into two new army groups. The force in the
northern zone, consisting of the *Second, Hungarian Second, Fourth
Panzer,* and *Sixth Armies,* was designated *Army Group B* and placed
under the command of Von Weichs. The units in the southern sector,
the *First Panzer, Seventeenth,* and *Eleventh Armies,* were grouped into
Army Group A under Generalfeldmarschall Wilhelm List. Hitler's op-
timism was at its peak. He was convinced that the campaign was all
but over despite the fact that the Russian forces had largely been able
to avoid encirclement and that the northern flank along the upper Don
was but thinly held, since the satellite divisions that were to man the
greater portion of it had not yet had time to move into position. He
therefore ordered the attack continued according to plan.

The Drive to the Caucasus

In the drive to the Caucasus, List's mission was threefold. *Army
Group A* was first to encircle and destroy the last major enemy forces,
which Hitler believed to be south and southeast of Rostov, by a strong
armored attack across the Don. For this operation elements of the
Fourth Panzer Army were attached to his command. Then, with the
Eleventh Army crossing the Kerch Straits from the Crimea, he was to
push to the south, capturing the entire east coast of the Black Sea and
the last bases of the Russian Black Sea fleet. The *Seventeenth Army*
was to strike across the Kuban River, occupy the Maikop area, and then
push across and join the drive down the coast toward Batum. A third
force, to be formed mainly of units of the *First Panzer Army,* was to
push to the southeast, capture the Grozny oil fields, and then press to
the Caspian Sea and down its coast to the Russian oil center at Baku.[18]

Army Group B was given the task of establishing the flank defenses
along the Don and blocking the Volga by taking Stalingrad and destroying the enemy forces there. Subsequently, fast armored units were to
drive down the Volga to Astrakhan.[19]

List opened his attack as planned, but the blow that was to destroy
the last enemy forces fell on thin air; no coordinated defense of the whole
Don area developed, and Rostov was quickly occupied. By 30 July the
Soviets were falling back along the line and by 3 August the German

[18] Hitler Dir 45, *OKW/WFSt/Op. Nr. 551288/42 g.K. Chefs.,* 23, VII.42., in
ibid.
[19] *Ibid.*

armor was over and beyond the Kuban River. The *Seventeenth Army,* moving behind the panzers, captured the Russian naval base at Novorossiysk on 6 August, while two armored corps rapidly overran the Maikop area and turned southeast behind a third that was driving deep into the Caucasus toward Grozny. Following these successes, however, attempts to force the passes east of Tuapse bogged down in the face of stiff resistance, and the armored units, after a dash all the way to the Terek River, were halted by fuel shortage.

Stalingrad and the Soviet Counterblow

Army Group B was meanwhile making slow progress toward Stalingrad. The *Sixth Army* had moved well into the Don bend, but due to logistical difficulties and the fact that the *Fourth Panzer Army,* which had reverted to Von Weichs, had been forced over to the defensive by a shortage of fuel, no all-out assault had been mounted on the city. By 11 August, however, Paulus had eliminated all of the enemy west of the river with the exception of two small bridgeheads. Then on 23 August he made a surprise crossing and drove a mechanized unit clear to the Volga.

As black as the situation looked for the Soviets, with all of the Don Basin industry, the rich wheat lands of the Kuban area, and the Maikop oil fields in enemy hands, the German position from a tactical standpoint, was far from favorable. *Army Groups A* and *B* together held a front some 1500 miles long and were separated by over 400 miles of territory undefended except for occasional patrols. Their left flank, more than 360 miles in length, was for the most part held by satellite divisions of questionable quality. Each army group was supplied by but one medium capacity rail line. And the autumn rains were fast approaching. To make matters worse, List had asked to be relieved as a result of violent disagreements with OKW over what he considered to be impossible demands made of his command. (Halder was dismissed at this time as the result of a difference of opinion with Hitler as to the feasibility of continuing the offensive.)[20]

With a restoration of *Army Group B's* supply situation the attack moved on again. The *Sixth Army* exploited its penetration to the Volga and closed directly on Stalingrad, while the *Fourth Panzer Army* attacked from the south. When the Russians were forced to retreat before the German push, they dropped back and joined the defenders of the city, where a new Soviet command, the Stalingrad Front, had been formed to hold the city at all costs. The nearer the German divisions came to the city, the more it seemed to grow in importance in Hitler's

---

[20] Halder was replaced on 22 Sep by Gen Kurt Zeitzler. Von Kleist took command *Army Group A* on 10 Sep.

eyes, and as the defense rose to fanatical heights he became obsessed with its capture. The mere name of the place—"the city of Stalin"— became a challenge as it were. He seemed to believe the fate of the whole war would be decided there,[21] and all other considerations of the campaign seemed to wane in comparison. The assault devolved into a dull process of battering at block after block of houses and factories. It was an exhausting struggle for both attacker and defender, and as early as 20 September the German troops were beginning to show signs of the strain.[22] Casualties grew increasingly heavy on both sides. As the battle progressed, more and more German divisions were drawn from the defensive flanks and thrown into the fight, replaced by new satellite units. By mid-October the Germans were near the heart of the city, barely a half mile from the Volga. But troop morale had degenerated in the face of heavy losses and a growing sense of frustration, and discouragement grew even among the commanders. Still Hitler drove them on.

During October and November Paulus reported growing Soviet concentrations on his northern flank and suggested withdrawal to a winter line in the rear. Hitler saw these reports and seemed to expect some sort of a Russian counter.[23] Still he insisted on continuing the offensive, and persisted in weakening the flanks by withdrawal of German units for commitment in the Stalingrad cauldron. On 19 November the storm broke.

All during the fall the Soviets had been preparing their counterstroke. Under security measures, which proved highly successful in deceiving the Germans as to his true strength, General Zhukov had built up and placed two strong army groups northwest and south of Stalingrad opposite the satellite units. Three armored and three cavalry corps of Rokossovski's Don Front on 19 November broke out of the Serafimovich bridgehead—one of those which the Germans curiously enough had never tried to reduce. The next day, two armored and one cavalry corps of Yeremenko's Stalingrad Front penetrated the defensive positions south of Stalingrad. Both breakthroughs were quickly exploited and on the 23d the two forces linked up west of Stalingrad at Kalach on the Don. The headquarters of the *Fourth Panzer Army* and several of the Romanian divisions escaped, but the *Sixth Army* was firmly entrapped with the enemy in position to attack from all sides.

The German position was desperate. Von Manstein was hurriedly brought in from *Army Group North,* where he had been sent to direct

---

[21] See "Halder's Journal," *op. cit.,* VII, p. 363.

[22] *Ibid.,* p. 396.

[23] See: Helmuth Greiner, "Notes on the Situation Reports and Discussions at Hitler's Headquarters from 12 August 1942 to 17 March 1943" (MS C–0652, Hist Div. EUCOM), entries 16 Oct–18 Nov 42. Foreign Studies Br, OCMH.

a projected assault on Leningrad, and given a newly formed task force designated *Army Group Don* with the specific mission of breaking through and relieving Paulus.   With the Romanian divisions that had escaped the trap and five armored and motorized divisions hastily brought from as far away as France he attacked toward Stalingrad along the Kotelnikov-Stalingrad axis.   But the Soviet armies were too well in command of the situation and the attempt fell short.   The *Sixth Army* with its 250,000 men was doomed.

Although Hitler had ordered Paulus to hold at all costs, he saw the folly of attempting to remain in the Caucasus   Accordingly he ordered Von Kleist to withdraw the *Seventeenth Army* to the Crimea and the *First Panzer Army* to the Ukraine through Rostov.   With Von Manstein fighting desperately to hold open an escape gap for Von Kleist at the mouth of the Don and with Paulus hanging on to a steadily diminishing perimeter in the face of tremendous pressure, the withdrawal was successfully completed.   Only on 2 February when the evacuation through Rostov had been completed did Paulus capitulate.

CHAPTER 4

EARLY RUSSIAN RESISTANCE AND GERMAN COUNTERMEASURES

The initial German attack in June 1941 was hardly under way before the first signs of guerrilla-like opposition appeared. There was no question of a popular rising: the mass of the people had no part in it. It consisted in the main of the continued resistance of groups of bypassed Red Army personnel, some scattered demolitions by small groups of saboteurs parachuted or infiltrated into the Gearman rear, and the activity of hastily formed units of Communist Party members and officials of the Peoples' Commissariat of Internal Affairs (NKVD) directed toward maintaining some sort of political control over the natives or completing the destruction initiated by the Red Army in its "scorched earth" policy.

The First Resistance

Bypassed Red Army Units

Of the groups offering the earliest opposition, the bypassed Red Army units posed the most immediate problem because for the most part they were still armed and in many cases retained some semblance of military organization. Tens of thousands of such personnel were scattered over the rear in troop units of all sizes,[1] and while huge numbers were taken prisoner the nature of the terrain was such, especially in the central and northern sectors and to some extent on the left flank of *Army Group South* that the final elimination of all of their many small centers of resistance proved well nigh impossible. The task, which would have been difficult for even the first-line infantry units in the face of difficult and relatively unmapped terrain and inadequate intelligence, became almost insurmountable for the security divisions and police battalions that took over the job as the fighting moved further to the east. The expanse of territory to be covered was too great an obstacle, and many enemy units remained—a sizeable reservoir of manpower to harass communications. Even as early as the first days of July their stubborn resistance to mopping up operations created many critical situations, and pockets continued to appear far to the rear as late

---

[1] *Teil 2, KTB 1, H. Geb. Sued, 21.VI.–31.VIII.41. 16407/17.*

as the middle of the month.² The nuclei of these die-hard groups were Red Army officers and political commissars, who were often part or the entire staff of units that had been ordered to set up partisan organizations when cut off.³

As early as the third day of the campaign *Army Group Center* reported that Red Army "stragglers and guerrillas" were attacking supply routes and field hospitals and striking at elements of the security divisions.⁴ And before the first of July infantry units of *Army Group North* were harassed from all sides by bypassed Red elements. Numbers of Soviet troops were still roaming the swamps and forests, von Leeb reported to OKH, many in peasant clothes, and effective countermeasures were frustrated by the expanse and difficulty of the country and by manpower limitations.⁵ Even though this activity was sporadic and unorganized OKH became seriously concerned⁶ and OKW worried to the extent of ordering captured French tanks transferred to the security divisions in the east for use against the "bandits."⁷

Parachutists

Adding to the diversion caused by the Red Army groups were small units of parachutists dropped behind *Army Group South* on sabotage, espionage, and terrorist missions. (There were no reports of similar groups being parachuted in behind *Army Groups Center* or *North.*) Interrogation of prisoners indicated that they had been assigned tasks ranging from the collection of information on German and Romanian troop units and the reconnaissance of airfields and destruction of rail lines, bridges, highways, cable lines, and pipelines at strategic spots to terrorization designed to create panic in the rear and the marking of targets for bombing raids. The groups normally comprised six to eight men, almost all of whom were former natives of the districts into which they were dropped. They had been given short periods of training in schools at Odessa, Cuipaiov, Nikolayev, or Moscow, and had received rudimentary parachute schooling consisting of one jump from a training tower.⁸ On several occasions they succeeded in blasting sections of trackage, but the manner in which they executed the demolitions indi-

² "Halder's Journal," *op. cit.*, VI, pp. 204, 208, 239, 246; *KTB, 221 Sich. Div. 24.VI.41.* 16748/9.
³ "Halder's Journal," *op. cit.*, VI, p. 208; *Pugatslov Interrogation Meldung 23, Einsatzgruppe B, 12.VII.41.* 62/4.
⁴ *Anl. z. KTB 403 Sich. Div., 24.VI.41.* 15701/3; *KTB 221 Sich. Div., 24.VI.41.* 16728/9.
⁵ "Halder's Journal," *op. cit.,* VI, pp. 181, 183.
⁶ *Ibid.,* p. 190.
⁷ *Auszugsweise Abschrift, 5.VII.41.* (signed by Keitel). OKW/1938.
⁸ "Paratroopers and Sabotage Agents, Terrorists, and Soviet Partisans and Their Activities." *Anl. z. KTB, LIV Corps, 24.VII.41.* (Canadian trans.). 15420/5.

cated little technical knowledge of such work.[9]   Most of them were scattered widely in their drops, and few were jumped anywhere near their objectives.[10]

Because of the short period of training, the carelessness of drops, the small numbers involved, and the variety of objectives, the entire action was regarded by the Germans as an experiment or wild idea conceived in the heat and confusion of the early days of the fighting and not as an attempt to foment unrest among the people and instigate a resistance movement.[11]

Communist-Led Units

Other agents were infiltrated through the lines, especially in the northern sector.   For the most part these were Communist Party functionaries of the middle and older age groups who had been given the task of organizing and directing partisan activity and political work in the overrun areas.   Operating through local Communist Party cells and informal groups of pro-Soviet natives, they formed a number of loose-knit guerrilla organizations and set up a communications net of sorts.   These partisan units comprised some 50 to 80 men, subdivided into 10-man groups.   They were headed by local party leaders, members of the NKVD border guard, and managers of collective enterprises.   Twenty-two such organizations were identified behind *Army Group North* prior to 13 July.[12]   Their general mission was to foment rebellion in the German communications zone, but they also offered some direct resistance in form of sabotage and launched a minor reign of terror among the natives, thereby creating considerable unrest and a decided reluctance on the part of many to collaborate with the invader in any way.[13]

Annihilation Battalions

During this same period, armed units of another type began to appear, causing some disruption along the supply lines and considerable unrest among the natives.   These were "Annihilation" or "Destruction" battalions, organized by the NKVD of Communist Party members, factory workers, overage members of the Red Army reserve, and volunteers. They averaged some 100 men and women to a unit, at least 90 percent

---

[9] "Final Report on Combating Partisans and Parachutists Along the Slucz River, 213th Security Division," 31 Aug 41. (Trans.).   14424/2.

[10] *Anl. z. KTB, LIV Corps, 24.VII.41.*   15420/5.

[11] *Ibid.*

[12] "Political Report of the Administration of the Political Propaganda of the Northwest Front" (German translation from the Russian dated 15 July 41), in *Anl. z. KTB. 1, H. Geb. Nord, 21. III.–19.X.41.* 14768/5.

[13] *KTB, 281 Sich. Div., 31.VII.41.* 15954/1; *Meldung 26, Einsatzgruppe A, 18.VII.41.*   Footlocker 62, folder 4.

of whom had to be party members or former members of the Komsomolsk,[14] and the remainder reliable in a political sense. Their primary mission was the maintenance of internal security in the Soviet rear, defense against German parachute attack, and the destruction of all installations not demolished by the Red Army in its retreat. In the event of the continued advance of the enemy, they were to allow themselves to be bypassed and then operate as partisan units in the German rear, carrying out sabotage missions and waging a campaign of terror among the natives to prevent political deviation.[15] They were normally formed into regiments of 10 battalions, each having its own commissar and surgeon. In addition to the commissar, or perhaps to supplement him, in each battalion there was one group entrusted with the political security of the unit with police power over the remainder. The battalions were further subdivided into five groups of 20 to 25 men each, including at least one man considered especially safe politically. A majority of the personnel wore civilian clothes, none a complete uniform. Although they were armed with Red Army ordnance, they were not trained for formal combat and were not expected to be used in the line. Under normal circumstances they lived off the land. At the end of July the *285th Security Division* reported it had identified 10 of these regiments in its area of responsibility alone.[16]

The Soviets Organize the Movement

By the first days of August a definite pattern of insurgent activity was beginning to take form. The appearance of the annihilation battalions, the parachute agent groups, and the local bands formed around Communist Party cells and led by party functionaries and NKVD personnel was the first evidence of any attempt on the part of the Soviet government to set up and sustain a centrally directed irregular movement.

On 3 July Stalin had made his first public statement to the Soviet people since the German attack. In this radio broadcast he stated:

In case of the forced retreat of Red Army units, all rolling stock must be evacuated; the enemy must not be left a single engine, a single railroad car, not a single pound of grain or a gallon of fuel. Collective farmers

---

[14] The Communist youth organization.
[15] *KTB, 213 Sich, Div.,* 14424/4; radio announcement found 3 Jul 41 in Lwow radio station, in *Meldung 23, Einsatzgruppe C, 15.VII.41.* 62/4; "Political Report of the Administration of the Political Propaganda of the Northwest Front," in *Anl. z. KTB. 1, H. Geb. Nord, 21. III–19.X.41.* 14768/5; *Meldung 51, Einsatzgruppe A, 13.VIII.41.* 62/6; *Meldung 31, Einsatzgruppe B, 23.VI.41.* 62/5; rpt 2, 14 Aug 41 (doc. 2652), prosecution document book in *N.M.T., op. cit.* (Case 9); *Meldung 95, Einsatzgruppe A, 26.IX.41.* Footlocker 62, folder 5.
[16] "Final Report on Combating Partisans and Parachutists Along the Slucz River, 213th Security Division," 31 Aug 41. 14424/2; *KTB, 285 Sich. Div., 31.VII.41.* 14878/3; *Meldung 51, Einsatzgruppe A, 13.VIII.41.* 62/6.

must drive off their cattle, and turn over their grain to the safekeeping of the state authorities for transportation to the rear. All valuable property, including nonferrous metals, grain and fuel that cannot be withdrawn, must be destroyed without fail.

In areas occupied by the enemy, partisan units, mounted and on foot, must be formed; sabotage groups must be organized to combat the enemy units, to forment partisan warfare everywhere, blow up bridges and roads, damage telephone and telegraph lines, set fires to forests, stores, and transport. In occupied regions conditions must be made unbearable for the enemy and all his accomplices. They must be hounded and annihilated at every step, and all their measures frustrated.[17]

He also announced that "in order to ensure the rapid mobilization of all the strength of the peoples of the USSR" a State Committee of Defense had been set up.[18] The concentration of defense powers in this new agency was necessitated by the obvious need to stiffen the resistance of the entire nation at all levels. At the top of the list was the immediate improvement of the morale and combat initiative of the Red Army. But hardly second in importance was the necessity for reasserting control over the natives of territory overrun by the Germans—and thus no longer under control of the party—where the chances of deviation from Soviet principles under German propaganda were great. And finally the need to tighten direction of the Communist Party and NKVD units in the enemy-occupied areas which had been caught as unprepared as the Red Army and had their liaison with Moscow destroyed was recognized. Such a reassertion of party domination behind the enemy lines with the clandestine reconstruction of an underground Soviet administrative and party organization there went hand in hand with the possibilities for developing an effective irregular movement under centralized control.

The effects of this tightening of control were felt almost immediately through the entire political structure of the Red Army. Reading into the continued defeats of the Army a lack of initiative on the part of the Army political commissar in matters of morale and leadership, General Mechlis, the head of the armed forces political system, on 15 July issued stringent orders that political agitation and propaganda be immediately intensified, that commissars and party members among the troops be placed in the front lines for morale and leadership purposes, and that units be made to understand that they were never to cease resisting and they had a definite mission of sabotage and terrorism behind the enemy lines should they be cut off.[19] He further ordered all Army political officers to maintain an especially close relationship with local Communist

---

[17] *Soviet Foreign Policy During the Patriotic War*, trans. Arthur Rothstein (London), I, pp. 21–24.

[18] *Ibid.*

[19] Order 81, 15 Jul 41 (signed by Mechlis) in *Anl. 11a, 29.VII.41., KTB, AOK 18.* 13787/20.

Party organizations in order to be able to expand the partisan movement in the occupied territories and incite the people there to greater heights in undermining the enemy effort.[20]

Establishment of Partisan Combat Battalions and Diversionary Units

On 10 July the Partisan Movement was officially organized and placed under the control of the Tenth Department of the Political Administration of the Army, a portion of Mechlis' command as chief of the Main Administration of the Political Propaganda of the Red Army,[21] which in turn was under the direct control of the Central Committee of the Communist Party. Great emphasis was continually placed on the need to bring all the irregular units under the central control of Moscow at the earliest possible date.

Almost immediately the effect of this centralized control was perceptible. On 11 July [22] Mechlis issued to the ranking political officers of all the army fronts and, apparently, to the Central Committee of the Communist Party in all the Soviet Republics endangered by the Germans detailed orders to form partisan units.[23] These political leaders were directed to organize irregular groups in "the main zone of operations . . . where the principal units of the enemy troops [were] located." Depending on their commitment these groups were to be divided into partisan combat battalions [24] and diversionary units. The combat battalions were to be well armed and of sufficient strength for offensive action. Comprising from 75 to 150 men, they were to be

---

[20] Directive of the People's Commisar for Army Matters, 20 Jul 41 (signed by Stalin and Mechlis), in Wehrmacht propaganda files. *Ausland Abwehr, Nr. 03443/41 geh. 23.IX.41.* OKW 688.

[21] Shigunov Interrogation, 14 Apr 42. EAP 3-a-11/2(C), p. 175842. Shigunov was an NKVD agent captured by the Germans. "Political Report of the Administration of the Political Propaganda of the Northwest Front," in *Anl. z. KTB. 1, H. Geb. Nord, 21. III–19.X.41.* 14768/5.

[22] This date is rather arbitrarily taken. On 10 Jul the partisan movement came under Mechlis' control; on 15 Jul the chief of the Administration of the Political Propaganda of the Northwest Front, Brigade-Commissar Rjabtsch, reported to Moscow that he had put such an order into effect on 13 Jul. See: "Political Report of the Administration of the Political Propaganda of the Northwest Front," in *Anl. z. KTB. 1, H. Geb. Nord, 21. III–19.X.41.* 14768/5. Rjabtschi passed this order on to his command on 20 Jul. See: "Instructions for the Organization and Activity of the Partisan Units and Diversionary Groups," 20 Jul 41 (signed by Rjabtschi) in *OKH GenStdH, O.Q. IV–Abt. Fde.H. (II) Nr. 1600.41, 31.VIII.41,* to H. Gr. *Sued,* and annex *Merkblatt ueber Organisation und Taetigkeit der Partisanen-Abteilungen und Diversiongruppen, Uebersetzung aus dem Russischen,* in *Heeres Gruppe Sued, Ic, Russland 20. VIII.–9.XI.41.* 15417/6.

[23] See leaflet distributed to partisans by the People's Commissars, White Russia, and the Central Committee X of the Communist Party in White Russia in *Anl. z. KTB 2, 1.IX.–7.XI.41., Korueck 553.* 20383/8. This leaflet is undated, but its content indicates that it was distributed soon after Stalin's radio proclamation.

[24] The German translation of the Russian phrase is *Kampfabteilung,* literally "combat battalion."

divided into 2 to 3 companies and the companies into 2 to 3 platoons. The normal combat unit was to be the company or the platoon. Generally they were to operate only at night and from ambush. Their mission was to attack troop columns and assemblies, motorized infantry, camps, transports of fuel and ammunition, headquarters, air bases, and railroad trains previously halted by rail demolitions. They were to operate in regions where the terrain was broken enough or the cover was heavy enough to afford concealment for their movements and bases. They were to act only along the principal communication axes of the enemy. It was considered desirable that there be at least one combat unit per *rayon*.[25]

In addition to the combat battalions, diversionary units of from 30 to 50 men each were to be organized in each *rayon*. These units were to consist of from 5 to 8 groups of 3 to 10 men each. They were to be so organized that the individuals comprising one group would not be acquainted with those of another. The small units were to be concentrated into a larger organization only to control their activity and to facilitate the formation of new groups in the *rayon*. Their fundamental mission was sabotage, cutting telephone lines, firing fuel and ammunition dumps, raiload demolition, and attacks on individual or small groups of enemy vehicles.[26]

In all areas still occupied by the Red Army, the local headquarters of the NKVD and NKGB (People's Commissariat for State Security) were directed to organize annihilation battalions to combat enemy air landings. In the case of a withdrawal by the Red Army, these annihilation battalions were to allow the German attack to pass over them and then operate as partisan units in the enemy rear.[27]

Local Partisan Units

A similar order was passed down through the People's Commissars and the Central Committees of the Communist Party in the Soviet Republics that lay in the path of the German attack to all local administrative headquarters, both urban and rural. Partisan units were ordered formed in all industrial plants, in the transportation system, and in the state and collective farms. These were to be volunteer units, formed of men, women, and youths physically capable of serving. Organizationalwise, they were to be set up along the same lines as the Soviet local

---

[25] *Rayon*—a Soviet political and administrative subdivision similar to the American county.

[26] "Instructions for the Organization and Activity of the Partisan Units and Diversionary Groups," 20 Jul 41 (signed by Rjabtschi) in *OKH Gen.St.d.H., O.Q. IV— Abt. Fde.H. (II) Nr. 1600.41, 31.VIII.41*, to *H. Gr. Sued, and annex Merkblatt ueber Organisation und Taetigkeit der Partisanen-Abteilungen und Diversiongruppen, Uebersetzung aus dem Russischen*, in *Heeres Gruppe Sued, Ic, Russland 20.VIII.– 9.XI.41. 15417/6.*

[27] *Ibid.*

government. The basic unit was to be the battalion, with the battalion commanders chosen by the local party councils from among the officer reserve of the Red Army, local leaders with previous military service, and commissars of proven political reliability. Staffs for the battalion commanders were to be formed in the Jurisdictional Committees and the local Labor Councils. These battalions, further broken down into companies and platoons, were given the various missions of securing industrial plants and state and collective farms, resisting river crossings by the enemy, destroying bridges and rail lines, and maintaining liaison between partisan groups and between the partisans and the Red Army. They were to live off the country and supply themselves with arms, clothing, and signal equipment.[28]

Early Partisan Operations

Thus as the German advance continued, the partisan groups fell into four more or less distinct categories, each at least originally independent of the others: the annihilation battalions, the groups formed by the local Soviet administrations which approximated a loosely thrown together "home guard," the battalions formed by the commissars under Mechlis' order, and a miscellany of groups of bypassed Red Army personnel. After the first weeks of the war, no effective groups of parachutists appeared for some months. By 26 August the Germans were aware that some of the partisans were in more than casual communication with the Russian rear and had established a radio net of sorts.[29]

At best these early organizational efforts of the Soviets, made in the midst of the wild confusion following the German attack, produced only meager results. There had been no prewar planning for guerrilla warfare on a national scale and only some scattered preparation locally.[30]

In the annihilation battalions morale was not of the best, for recruitment was often forced, even within the ranks of the politically reliable, and training was carried on after the long Soviet work day. The farther the Germans penetrated the country the greater the signs of panic and the larger the number of desertions. When leaders fled or were killed, the battalions fell apart.[31] And the "home guard" units, which were poorly armed and trained, were never a factor. The largest unit identified as such was soon dispersed when its leaders fled.[32]

---

[28] Leaflet distributed to partisans by the People's Commissars, White Russia, and the Central Committee X of the Communist Party in White Russia in *Anl. z. KTB 2, 1.IX.–7.XI.41., Korueck 553.* 20383/8. This leaflet is undated, but its content indicates that it was distributed soon after Stalin's radio proclamation.

[29] *KTB, 281 Sich. Div., 26.VIII.41.* 15954/6.

[30] See: Interrogation of Capt M. Pugatslov in *Meldung 23, Chef der Sicherheits Polizei und SD, 15.VII.41.* Footlocker 62, folder 4; supplement to Eugenev Koslov interrogation in *KTB H. Geb. Nord.* 14768/5; Shigunov interrogation, 14 Apr 42. EAP 3–a–11/2(C).

[31] *Meldung 80, Einsatzgruppe C, 11.IX.41.* Footlocker 62, folder 10.

[32] *Ibid.*

Thus the first irregular units actually were few in number; they were not overly aggressive and seldom appeared in the more populous areas or near German troop concentrations, confining their activities to forest and swamp areas where heavy natural cover provided maximum protection and where opposition was lightest. Their attacks were scattered and appeared to conform to no set pattern, the majority being aimed at the more lightly guarded secondary supply links. They made a few raids on individual German vehicles and small convoys,[33] and in several regions in the central sector were reported sabotaging installations left intact by the Red Army and terrorizing the natives.[34] The Soviet high command early realized that the few serviceable supply routes through the vast Russian land mass were of paramount importance to any invader and that in view of the great distances involved and the poor general state of Russian highways the greatest burden of German supply and troop movements would necessarily fall on the rail lines. Stalin, in his 3 July broadcast speech to the Russian people, could only have been echoing a basic strategic concept when he said: "In case of a forced retreat of Red Army units, all rolling stock must be evacuated, the enemy must not be left a single engine, a single railway truck. . . ."[35]

Certainly the Soviets' reactions in this sphere indicate that they clearly saw this weakest link in the Wehrmacht chain—the utter German dependence on long and therefore vulnerable communication lines over an inadequate rail and road system—and they struck at it even in the first confused months. Between 22 June and 16 September, 447 rail culverts and bridges were damaged or destroyed by the Russians either in front of or behind the German armies and rails were broken at some 250 places. The aggregate length of blasted bridges alone was more than several thousand yards.[36]

Just what percentage of this sabotage was due to partisan action and what to systematic devastation by the Red Army is impossible to determine. Destruction of communication facilities is normal practice for any well-trained army in retreat, and considering the generally poor state of organization and discipline within the partisan units during the first months of the war and the lack of reliable communications with the Soviet rear, it is highly probable that a large percentage of these demolitions were carried out by the Red Army in execution of a "scorched earth" policy.

In the sector of *Army Group North* more than 70 percent of all bridges destroyed were in the area before Leningrad between Lake Ilmen and

---

[33] *Meldung 71, Einsatzgruppe B, 2.IX.41.* Footlocker 62, folder 6.

[34] *Meldung 34, Einsatzgruppe B, 26.VII.41; Meldung 43, Einsatzgruppe B, 5.VIII. 41.* Both in footlocker 62, folder 5.

[35] *Soviet Foreign Policy During the Patriotic War, op. cit.,* I, pp. 21–24.

[36] *Streckenzustandskarte, Stand vom 22.VI.–16.IX.41.* H 14/570.

Lake Peipus where the Red defenders had resisted stiffly and virtually immobilized Hoeppner's panzers for some weeks. Here probably few of the demolitions can be credited to the irregulars. Still the fact that the annihilation battalions were sent out from Leningrad in such numbers—and apparently with considerable effectiveness since as early as 3 August they controlled almost the entire area behind the *Fourth Panzer Group*—with the primary mission of destroying all important installations which the Red Army had been forced to bypass indicates that at least a portion of the demolition work fell to them.[37] After the middle of September, when the Russian operational units had been driven within the Leningrad perimeter, all sabotage in the northern sector must be considered to have been carried out by the partisans.

In *Army Group Center,* however, where Von Bock struck with great speed and overpowering weight of armor, the Red Army was apparently far too disorganized to carry out any planned destruction of rail facilities. Of a total of 117 bridges and culverts destroyed or heavily damaged, only 22 lay in the strategically vital entrance to the "dry route" to Moscow, the triangle Vitebsk-Orsha-Smolensk, and none were so badly damaged as not to be in use again before 15 September. Along the main supply route, the double-track rail line Brest-Litovsk-Minsk-Orsha-Smolensk, there were no bridges blown or tracks broken west of the entrance to the "dry route" triangle. The bulk of the demolitions occurred in areas exposed to partisan pressure, in the Pripyat Marshes and in the marshy forests to the south of Lake Ilmen and the Valdai Hills.[38]

In Von Rundstedt's sector, where the German advance was relatively slow, it is evident from the area in which the demolitions were concentrated that Budenny was able to carry out considerable sabotage on the rail net. Of the 141 rail bridges destroyed, a number of them were on major connections directly to the west of the Kiev bastion and in the Dnepr bend industrial area west and northwest of Dnepropetrovsk. These must be attributed directly to Red Army action. But in the lower edges of the Pripyat along the Korosten-Mozyr line and in the Sarny-Rovno-Kovel area, where the irregulars exerted considerable pressure on the security units, there were a large number of bridges blown and long sections of trackage destroyed. The same was true in the eastern foothills of the Carpathian range and in the marshes along the upper courses of the Bug River. It is probable that these latter were due directly to irregular action. As inconclusive as these figures and the surmises made upon them appear, especially in light of the low level of efficiency of the partisans during the first months of the campaign and

[37] *Ibid; Lage Ost,* 3 Aug. 41.
[38] *Streckenzustandskarte, Stand vom 22.VI.–16.IX.41.,* H 14/570.

the fact that often the demolitions were very crudely executed,[39] it is evident that Moscow had ordered the bands to pay major attention to enemy communications and that a continuation of such attention was to be expected.

German Counteractions

The Security Commands

The rear area commands had been specifically charged with maintaining the supply of the field armies and guaranteeing the exploitation of the land for the immediate use of the military. Thus the task of crushing the embryonic partisan bands in so far as they threatened the lines of communication and the supply points and depots or the rear in general fell to them. Nine security divisions were available for this mission, each one comprising an infantry "alert" regiment of three battalions and a *Landesschuetzen* regiment of from three to four *Landesschuetzen* battalions and a guard battalion. Seven of the nine had an integral motorized police battalion. *Army Group North Rear Area* and *Army Group Center Rear Area* each had a security regiment of bicycle troops in general reserve while the former had an additional police regiment. *Army Group South Rear Area* also had several satellite security brigades for commitment in the deep rear and the Carpathian Mountains.[40]

Basically the employment of the security divisions was the same in the three army group sectors. Generally one division closely followed the main effort of the army group, keeping the major communication axis clear of interference, occupying the key population centers along the line of advance, and furnishing local protection for the operational headquarters. The others fanned out on either side, occupying the larger towns and cities and covering the roads and railroads feeding the flank armies and the more important lateral links betweens units. The majority of this work fell to the *Landesschuetzen* units, patrolling the roads and rail lines and guarding important bridges, supply dumps, and the like, while the "alert regiments" either aided in clearing up the encircled pockets of Red Army personnel or were held as a mobile reserve for any serious insurgent outbreak. The police units concerned themselves with the general maintenance of order and handled traffic on the highways.

As the armies pushed farther and farther into the Russian interior and the rear grew larger and larger, and as the "alert" regiments were pulled out of the rear for front-line duty, two newly activated infantry

---

[39] *Meldung 95, Einsatzgruppe A, 26.IX.41.*, Footlocker 62, folder 5.
[40] *Anlagen z. OKH 1600, Kriegsgliederung des Feldheeres.* H 1/93b; *Anl. z. KTB, H.Geb. Mitte.* 14684/3; *Anl. z. KTB, H.Geb. Nord. 22.VI.–7.VIII.41.* 14768/2; *KTB, H. Geb. Sued.* 16407/11.

divisions [41] and several SS brigades were assigned to the security commands. To furnish special protection in critical areas or to curb especially troublesome resistance, security and police units were sometimes formed into group (*Gruppe*) commands.[42]

To further supplement these security troops, especially in difficult and unmapped terrain, units of native volunteers were recruited. The first of these were Ukrainian security units formed by the *Army Group South Rear Area* when several partisan groups early in August began disrupting communications in the southern edge of the Pripyat Marshes. Because of their knowledge of the almost trackless terrain, these local Ukrainians gave considerable assistance in rooting out the sources of trouble.[43] During the same period the rear area command in the northern sector organized a number of Estonian police units (*Schutzmannschaft Abteilung*) for security and antipartisan work in Estonia. They were formed into battalions of 330 men each with one German officer and several German NCO's per unit.[44]

On 25 July, Lithuania, Latvia, Estonia, and the extreme western portion of White Russia were detached from army jurisdiction and incorporated into the *Reichskommissariat Ostland,* and the *Army Group North Rear Area* and *Army Group Center Rear Area* were ordered to assign one security division each to the *Reichskommissar.*[45] Similarly, on 1 September the *Reichskommissar Ukraine* assumed jurisdiction of that portion of the Ukraine west of the line Slucz River, with the Romanian, Hungarian, and Slovak security units there being transferred to the command of the *Wehrmachtbefehlshaber.* On 20 October the *Reichskommissariat Ukraine* was further extended eastward to the course of the middle and lower Dnepr.[46]

As to the security divisions themselves, the first two months of operations indicated a number of organizational deficiencies within them which foreshadowed a decline in their effectiveness just at the time the partisans were growing in numbers and experience. Operations indicated they were not equipped for the mobile, hard-hitting type of action

---

[41] These were the *707th* and *339th Infantry Divisions.* Both had been activated only in 1941 and had but two infantry regiments each. See: "Order of Battle of the German Army," *op. cit.*

[42] For dispositions and movements of the security units, see the *Lagen Ost* for the period.

[43] "Final Report on Combating Partisans and Parachutists Along the Slucz River, 213th Security Division," 31 Aug 41. 14424/2.

[44] *KTB, Ia, 281st Sich. Div., 8.IX.41.* 15954/2.

[45] *Bhf. H.Geb. Nord, Nr. 749/41 geh., 21.VII.41.* in *KTB, 281 Sich. Div.* 15954/2. Actually Estonia continued under the jurisdiction of the Army for purposes of local requisitioning of food supplies and the security of supply lines, while the political authorities administered the country in a purely civil sense. See overprint on *Lage Ost* for 6 Dec 41.

[46] *OKW/WFSt/Abt. L. (IV), Nr. 684/41. 11.X.41., Anl. 5 z. KTB 1, H. Geb. Sued, Ia, 5.X.–26.X.41.* 16407/7.

required for success against an irregular foe. They were woefully short of motor vehicles, and those available to them were in a poor state of repair;[47] they rarely had enough gasoline or other types of supplies;[48] the personnel, being for the most part from the *Landwehr* classifications (35 to 45 years old), were proving poorly equipped physically for anti-partisan work.[49]

From an operational standpoint the level of efficiency of the security divisions left a great deal to be desired. Due to the failure of OKH to prepare for an irregular rising, they were badly handicapped from the start by a lack of understanding of partisan resistance and training in methods of combating it. The operational directives issued them prior to the campaign had been drawn up without any clear conception of the type of warfare they were to face and were too generalized for poorly staffed, relatively untrained units. General missions and responsibilities had been outlined in these directives, but methodology was left completely to the discretion and initiative of the individual commanders. Initially, this lack of direction resulted at times in a "wild state of anarchy" in antipartisan operations and the unnecessary killing of numbers of innocent civilians. Coordination of effort was lacking and there was little or no interchange or pooling of information even among units of the same parent organization. Operations varied sharply according to the character of the commanders of the individual units and the qualities of the troops.[50]

At best their tactical employment was desultory. Because of the expanse of country which had to be covered, they took positive measures against the partisans only when the supply lines and installations were openly threatened. Even then they stuck closely to the roads and rail lines and the urban areas, and avoided the more difficult terrain and back-country regions. Seeing little of the growing opposition, unaware of or indifferent to the possibility of a developing pattern of hostility in the rear, and victorious in a few insignificant incidents over small insurgent groups, the security units gained in confidence and foresaw an early advent of complete peace and quiet there. They felt they were winning their war and that their areas of responsibility would be completely under control in a matter of weeks or days.[51]

---

[47] *KTB, 213 Sich. Div., 31.VIII.41.* 14424/2.

[48] *KTB, 281 Sich. Div., 14.VII.41.* 15954/6; *Anl. 77 z. KTB 221 Sich. Div., 15.VIII.41.* 16748/24.

[49] "Final Report on Combating Partisans and Parachutists Along the Slucz River, 213th Security Division," 31 Aug 41. 14424/2.

[50] *Bericht, Korueck 582, 27.IX.41.* 17262/11; *I.M.T., op. cit.,* IV, pp. 479–80.

[51] *Anl. z. KTB, AOK 16, 19.VII.41.* 35615/2; rpt, Economic Office at Smolensk, 3–16 Sep 41. Wi/ID 2.319.

Laxity in the Rear

The lack of general security consciousness in all the German units heavily accentuated the shortcomings of the security units and made their work increasingly more difficult. The *XXXIII Panzer Corps* admitted that its troops were "too softhearted and trusting" toward the indigenous population and that as far as 13–14 miles behind the front lines suspicious individuals continually roamed the highways without check.[52] Officers often demonstrated extreme carelessness regarding the protection of troop installations.[53]

Passes and identification papers were continually counterfeited and successfully used.[54] A number of captured partisans obtained safe conduct passes from local administrative commanders merely by stating that they were liberated Soviet political prisoners.[55] The political commissar of the 1st Partisan Regiment reported to Moscow: "Several of our partisans, when captured by the Germans, identified themselves as escapees from the Russian regime or prisons. After obtaining identification papers from the German headquarters in Yemilchino in this manner, they reconnoitered the area and returned to the Russian lines."[56] Legal identification papers were issued civilians without termination dates which made it easy for irregulars to use them in carrying on their activities for long periods of time without hindrance; partisan reconnaissance missions became more uniformly successful and messenger service improved when it was discovered that Nazi troops would not stop or harm elderly, well-dressed people.[57] Even after considerable casualties, single vehicles continued on the road and German soldiers still roamed the countryside alone or in groups of only two or three, a condition not ordered corrected until late in September. Even then, convoys continued to travel at night when they were more vulnerable to partisan action.[58] Considerable trust was placed in village elders and mayors who were often informed of impending antipartisan operations and as often passed the information along to irregular groups. The elders were entrusted with the task of collecting all firearms from the people under their jurisdiction and only after some time was it discovered that while

---

[52] *Bericht, XXXIII Pz Corps, Ic, 29.IX.41., Anl. z. KTB, 112 Inf. Div.* 19643/24.

[53] *Gen.St.d.H./Ausb. Abt., Nr. 2200/41 geh., 22.IX.41., Anl. z. KTB, H. Geb. Nord.* 14768/3.

[54] *H. Geb. Nord. Nr. 153/41, 8.VIII.41.* 14768/5; *AOK 18, OQu KTB, 3.VI.– 8.X.41., Anl. 11a*, quoting *AOK 18, Ic, Nr. 1047/41, 31.VIII.41.* 13787/20; *H. Geb. Mitte Nr. 51/41, 11.IX.41.*, in *Tgb., Ic, H. Geb. Sued, KTB 1, 1.IX.–31.XII.41., Teil 3.* 16407/18.

[55] *Anl. z. KTB, Wi Stab Ost, 16.IX–30.IX.41.* Wi/ID 2.345.

[56] *Tgb., Ic, XXX Corps, 7.X.41.* Himmler collection, footlocker 57, folder 15.

[57] *KTB, 281 Sich. Div., 24.XI.41.* 15954/2; *Tgb., Ic, H. Geb. Sued, Okt 41, Teil 3 z. KTB 1, H. Geb. Sued, 1.IX.–31.XII.41.* 16407/18.

[58] *KTB, 281 Sich. Div., 19.IX.41.* 15954/2.

the weapons were being collected in many cases they were being handed over to the partisans rather than to the German authorities.[59]

Security units were too often committed on the basis of old or unchecked information and mere rumors which led to fruitless dispersion of strength. It was found that the natives often reported the presence of partisans in order to obtain arms.[60] Too often the security troops when occupying a town failed to take a census of the civilian population which made it possible for nonresidents to move freely and enabled Red Army personnel to commit sabotage in civilian clothes. In one instance the failure to check civilians enabled a Russian officer in mufti to penetrate near a high German command post and gain valuable information. The Soviets found that the security units occupied only villages and towns located along the main highways, leaving untouched the more remote villages, and ordered these used as partisan strongpoints.[61]

It was only after captured Soviet documents indicated that the Russians had perceived and were exploiting this laxity that measures were taken at high level to correct these deficiencies. Late in September OKH issued a directive calling for stringent measures to be taken by all officers to improve security discipline.[62]

Passive Measures by the Army

In addition to the uncoordinated and none too aggressive active measures taken by the Germans in the first few weeks of the campaign, a number of more passive attempts were made to check the growth of the partisan movement. In the latter part of July rewards as high as 3,000 rubles ($1,500) were offered to the native population for information leading to the arrest of Soviet insurgents.[63] Apparently the offers brought only meager results, for within two weeks the proffered bribes were changed to threats. On 9 August it was proclaimed in one sector that any person belonging to a partisan formation, any person furnishing aid or comfort, directly or indirectly, to such partisans, or any person withholding information of partisans would be shot. As an afterthought was added the note that anyone furnishing useful intelligence on irregulars would be rewarded with cash and rations.[64] All weapons were ordered turned in and local Russian officials were made responsible for the compliance of the people. After a given deadline, all persons found

[59] *Bericht, 4/260 Ls. Bn., 30.IX.41., Anl. z. KTB 281 Sich. Div.* 15954/2; *KTB, 286, Sich. Div., 13.X.41.* 16182/3; *Anl. 79 z. KTB, 286 Sich. Div., 12.IX.41.* 16182/3.
[60] *KTB 1, H. Geb. Sued, 24.VIII.41.* 16407/17.
[61] *Tgb., Ic, H. Geb. Sued, Okt 41, Teil 3 z. KTB 1, H. Geb. Sued, 1.IX–31.XII.41.* 16407/18.
[62] *Gen.St.d.H./Ausb, Abt., Nr. 2200/41 geh., 22.IX.41., Anl. z. KTB, H. Geb. Nord.* 14768/3.
[63] *KTB, H. Geb. Nord. 25.VII.41.* 14768/2.
[64] *Heeresfilmstelle, 9.VIII.41., Struge-Krasnyje.* (No file number.)

in possession of firearms were to be shot as partisans. If a conspiracy was proven, entire villages were to be burned down.[65] In the Ukraine all radios, both receivers and transmitters, were confiscated, despite the absence of partisan opposition there and without regard for the loss of a valuable propaganda medium.[66] Late in August a further step was taken: in the northern sector the native male population of several critical areas was evacuated and placed in detention camps in an effort to curb unrest.[67]

Prisoner of War Status of the Partisans

OKH Directives

Even OKH, weighed down as it was with directing the campaign, found itself pulled into the partisan picture by the problem of control of the huge number of prisoners taken in the successive encirclements. Due to the speed of the advance and the shortage of manpower, thousands of surrendered Red Army soldiers roamed unrestricted through the rear areas in search of food, pillaging and marauding, and often allied themselves with the partisans. The problem grew to such an extent that the rear area commands found it increasingly difficult to differentiate between prisoners and partisans, and to control the one and combat the other.

In an attempt to clarify the situation and establish a basis for separating the legal from the illegal, OKH on the advice of the Chief of the Army Legal System (*Der Chef des Heeres Justizwesens*), issued a series of directives defining the prisoner of war status of combatants and noncombatants under varying situations of belligerency. On 3 July it directed that: "Soldiers in uniform, with or without arms, are considered lawful belligerents. Those in civilian clothes, with or without arms, according to age and looks considered draftable, are to be accorded rights as prisoners of war. Civilians in mufti or half uniform found with arms are to be considered guerrillas." [68] On 18 July this was supplemented to the extent that members of partisan units, in front of or behind the German lines, when not wearing a uniform or insignia recognizable by the opposing forces, were to be considered as guerrillas and treated as such. Inhabitants of cities and villages who aided such persons were to be treated accordng to the same rules.[69] And further, on 25 July, individual soldiers roaming the rear areas in uniform or

[65] *KTB, H. Geb. Sued, 23.VIII.41.* 16407/17.
[66] *KTB, H. Geb. Sued, 25.VII.41.* 16407/17.
[67] *KTB, WiKdo., z. b. V., "Goerlitz," 21.VIII.41.* WI/ID 2.357.
[68] *AOK 9, Ic, Nr. 2058/41, 3.VII.41., Anl. z. KTB, Ic, Korueck 582.* 17326/15.
[69] *OKH/Gen. z. b. V./Jag., Nr. 1260/41, g.Kdos. Chefs., 18.VII.41.*, appears as *AOK 2, Ic, Nr. 1560/41, 30.VII.41., Anl. z. KTB, 112 Inf. Div.* 19643/24.

civilian clothes were to be advised by means of public address systems, radio, or posters that they should give themselves up to the nearest German organization. Should they fail to do this by a certain date, to be determined by the rear area commander, they were to be considered as guerrillas and treated as such.[70] These directives were all legally well within the provisions of the Geneva Convention of 1929 relative to the treatment of prisoners of war (PW's) [71] and stood in sharp contrast to Rosenberg's flat declaration that the Hague Rules of Land Warfare were not applicable to BARBAROSSA since the Reich considered the USSR dissolved as a sovereign power.[72]

Following the leads at OKH, *Army Group Center Rear Area* ordered its units to issue a proclamation stating that all Russian soldiers found west of the Berezina River after 15 August would be considered as guerrillas (*Freischaerler*) and treated as such.[73] When large numbers of stragglers surrendered as a result of this policy, the time limit was extended to 31 August.[74] The *Ninth Army* issued declarations to the effect that former Red Army personnel who had been forced to join partisan groups would be accorded PW status if they surrendered prior to 5 September.[75] Even parachutists, who in the first weeks of the war were all considered saboteurs and treated as such, were ordered accorded rights as PW's when captured in uniform. Civilians found with weapons or captured in or after skirmishes were still to be considered partisans and shot or hanged.[76]

The same general attitude existed in the southern sector where notices were posted stating that all Red Army stragglers were to give themselves up by 18 August or be treated as partisans.[77]

In September the armies received from Hitler what apparently was intended as the last word relative to the prisoner of war status of combatants in the rear areas. Russian combat troops under the command of an officer who got behind the German lines on a definite mission were when captured to be treated as prisoners of war so long as they were not a part of units which had previously surrendered. Any soldiers

---

[70] *OKH/Gen.z.b.V./Jag., Nr. 1332/41 g.Kdos. Chefs., 25.VII.41., Anl. z. KTB, Ic, Korueck 582.* 17326/15.

[71] See: FM 27–10, "Rules of Land Warfare," pars. 9, 12, 350, 353–54.

[72] *Erster Abschnitt: Die Organisation der Verwaltung in den besetzten Ostgebieten.* Undated unsigned paper found in the Rosenberg files outlining the organization and administration of the occupied eastern territories. *I.M.T., op. cit.,* XXVI, pp. 592–609.

[73] *Anl. 492 z. KTB 2, 221 Sich. Div., 12.VIII.41.* 16748/10.

[74] *Bfh. H. Geb. Mitte, Nr. 40/41., Anl. 521 z. KTB 2, 221 Div.* 16748/10.

[75] *AOK 9, Ia, Ic/AO, Nr. 3600/41 geh., 18.VIII.41., Anl. z. KTB, Ic Korueck 582.* 17326/15.

[76] *AOK 9, Ia, Ic, Nr. 254/41 geh., 10.IX.41, Anl. z. KTB, Ic, Korueck 582.* 17326/15.

[77] *Tgb., Ic, H. Geb. Sued, 1.VIII.–31.VIII.41., Teil 2 z. KTB 1, 21.VI.–H. Geb. Sued, 31.VIII.41.* 16407/17.

who came out of hiding after actual combat was over and renewed the fight in the rear were to be treated as guerrillas. All soldiers who were involved in actions with a "people's war" tinge—sabotage, attacks on single vehicles, and the like—were to be considered guerrillas. Troop commanders were to draw the distinction on their own initiative.[78]

The OKW Approach

The reaction of OKW to these beginnings of resistance was but an elaboration of the policies regarding the treatment to be accorded the Russian people laid down in the political and economic planning. The whole of the occupied territories had to be pacified as quickly as possible. The resistance there had to be crushed. The best method was a strict reign of terror.[79]

When the security commands encountered increasing difficulty in keeping the lines of communication clear and began to request more units for security duties, the OKW reply was typical:

> The troops available for securing the conquered eastern areas will, considering the vast expanse of these stretches, suffice only if the occupying power meets all resistance, not by legally punishing the guilty, but rather by spreading that type of terror which is the only means of taking from the population every desire for opposition.
>
> The respective commanders are to be held responsible, together with the troops at their disposal, for quiet in their areas. The commanders must find the means to keep their districts in order by employing suitable draconian measures, not by requesting more security forces.[80]

The approach to pacification was to be heavyhanded. There was to be no other. Resistance was to be crushed in a ruthless manner, not turned into more harmless channels.

As the weeks passed the evidences of revolt did not lessen, and in mid-September OKW took an even more repressive approach:

* * *

> The measures taken up to now to deal with this general insurrection movement have proved inadequate. The Fuehrer has now given orders that we take action everywhere with the most drastic means in order to crush the movement in the shortest possible time.

* * *

> Action taken in this matter should be in accordance with the following general directions:

---

[78] *AOK 9, Ic, Nr. 271/41 geh., 20.IX.41., Anl. z. KTB, Ic, Korueck 582.* 17326/15. This is not the Hitler directive, but a digest of it by the *Ninth Army* for distribution to lower echelons.

[79] *Aktenvermerk, Fuehrerhauptquartier, 16.VII.41.,* in *I.M.T., op. cit.,* XXXVIII, pp. 86–94.

[80] Supplement to Dir 33, 23 Jul 41, *OKW/WFSt/Abt. L (I Op). Nr. 442254/41 g. K. Chefs.* in "Fuehrer Directives," *op. cit.*

a. It should be inferred, in every case of resistance to the German occupying forces, no matter what the individual circumstances, that it is of Communist origin.

b. In order to nip these machinations in the bud, the most drastic measures should be taken immediately on the first indication, so that the authority of the occupying forces may be maintained, and further spreading prevented. In this connection it should be remembered that a human life in unsettled countries frequently counts for nothing and a deterrent effect can be attained only by unusual severity. The death penalty for 50–100 Communists should generally be regarded in these cases as suitable atonement for one German soldier's life. The way in which sentence is carried out should still further increase the deterrent effect. The reverse course of action, that of imposing relatively lenient penalties, and of being content, for purposes of deterrence, with the threat of more severe measures, does not accord with these principles and should therefore not be followed.[81]

                 *   *   *

There is little evidence that these directives were carried out by the line armies. The indications are that, with but few exceptions,[82] they were ignored and the OKH policy was generally followed in the zone of operations.

There was no attempt to soften the effect of such tactics by a change in the psychological approach. Propaganda remained negative, and even verged on the hypocritical. It was designed primarily to keep the population from joining or supporting the partisans. They were to be promised nothing. Beyond threats, warnings, and prohibitions, the emphasis was to remain on the role of the Germans as "liberators" come to create "a new system of social justice." The people in the individual Soviet republics were to be given no expectation of the restoration of their national sovereignty and no encouragement toward the development of a national consciousness. There were to be told merely that their political future would be worked out after the war. The peasantry was to be cautiously told that for the time being the collective farms were not to be broken up, that such would lead to too much economic dislocation. The one concession granted was in the matter of religion. The religious question was to be viewed as the business of the individual, to be tolerated but not encouraged.[83]

---

[81] *Kommunistische Aufstandsbewegung in den besetzten Gebieten, Der Chef des Oberkommandos der Wehrmacht, WFSt/Abt. 1 (IV/Qu), Nr. 002060/41. g. Kdos., 16.IX.41.* in *I.M.T.*, *op. cit.*, XXXIV, pp. 501–04; *Nazi Conspiracy and Aggression, op. cit.*, VI, pp. 961–63.

[82] See: *Verhalten der Truppe im Ostraum, Armeeoberkommando 6, Abt. Ia-Az., 7, A. H. Qu., den 10.X.41.* in *I.M.T.*, *op. cit.*, XXXV, pp. 84–86.

[83] *OKW/WFSt/WPr (1a) Nr. 486/41 g. K., 21.VIII.41.* OKW/1939.

CHAPTER 5

GERMAN OCCUPATION POLICIES IN OPERATION

Russian Reaction

General Conditions

In the central and northern sectors as the front passed further to the east it left the Polish and Lithuanian border areas, where anti-Soviet feelings ran high, and entered the western fringes of old Russia. As had been the case with Napoleon's army in 1812, the farther the Germans pressed their advance the more rapidly the first heat of excitement over the "liberation" cooled and the less friendly the people became.

Their mood took on a progressively negative tinge as the full import of the war began to come home to them. Those who had openly welcomed the invasion appeared to be watchfully waiting for signs of improvement in the general standard of living under their new rulers. The shortage of food and uncertainty as to future developments cast a pall on the effects of their release from the Soviet system. Many villages and cities had been almost completely destroyed, and some areas showed a "deplorable state of chaos." In the war-devastated urban areas many natives were "half-starved." Looting and stealing were rife, and few people evidenced interest in anything beyond securing enough to eat. In some regions food stocks were nearing exhaustion.[1] Beyond the Russo-Baltic States border and east of Minsk, where the people for the most part were Great Russians, a definite change was visible, and in places there were signs of genuine hostility.[2]

In the rural areas of the Ukraine, on the other hand, the attitude of the natives remained at least neutral as late as December even in the face of a deteriorating economic situation and despite the fact that the Germans had openly snubbed the Ukrainian Nationalist groups.[3] Outside the cities there was food enough for local consumption, but in the

---

[1] *Meldung 40, Chef der Sicherheitspolizei und SD, 1.VIII.41.* Footlocker 62, folder 5; rpt, CO, 284th Inf Regt, 96th Inf Div, 29 Oct 41. Wi/ID 2.1355. Files of the Economic Office; *Meldung 34, 26.VII.41., Meldung 43, 5.VIII.41., Meldung 71, 2.IX.41., Einsatzgruppe B.* Footlocker 62, folders 5, 6.

[2] *Meldung 34, 26.VII.41., Meldung 43, 5.VIII.41., Meldung 71, 2.IX.41., Einsatzgruppe B.* Footlocker 62, folders 5, 6; rpt 34, 26 Jul 41 (doc. 2924), prosecution document book in *N.M.T., op. cit.* (Case 9).

[3] *Rue In Ukraine, Inspekteur an den Chef der Wi Rue Amtes, 2.XII.41*, in *I.M.T., op. cit.,* XXXII, pp. 71–75.

industrial areas there was some suffering and morale was low. Although the crops were generally good and sufficient manpower was available for the harvest, the farm machinery so necessary for harvesting on other than a small scale had either been removed or demolished by the Reds and the draft animals driven off. Cattle were not to be found.[4] This situation was accentuated by a complete lack of initiative on the part of the peasants. Unless closely supervised they would do no work beyond that necessary to fill personal needs and once they had harvested enough to carry their families through the winter they had to be driven to work further.[5] Only rarely had they complied with Stalin's order to destroy all crops rather than allow them to fall into German hands, but groups of the younger generation in several areas instituted a minor reign of terror on their own, burning a number of farm installations and openly declaring that all barns and silos in the occupied areas would be destroyed after the crops had been gathered.[6] Such action did nothing to improve the morale and will-to-work of the peasants, and the Germans found it difficult to combat.

In White Russia in many cases the collective farms had resumed operation but since the Germans had requisitioned all available trucks there was never enough transport to carry food supplies to the cities where the people were in need.[7]

In the northern sector matters were even more critical. Many crops were not or could not be harvested, and farmers began to fear they would be unable to feed what stock they had left during the winter. As late as November, 35 percent of the potatoes and other bulbar roots were still in the ground, destroyed by the frost.[8] The general food situation was considerably worsened by the plundering of German troops.[9] Despair and suffering appeared even in the undevastated urban areas, and the spectre of unemployment hung over the land. Large numbers of people in Pskov and the Leningrad region were without work.[10] The "white collar" groups, which had been relatively privileged under the Soviet regime, walked the streets in most places.[11] The people complained that they had been misled by German propaganda. The occupation authorities countered, rather ineffectively, that the cause of short rations was to be found among the Russians themselves, in the

---

[4] *Meldung 40, Chef der Sicherheitspolizei und SD.* Footlocker 62, folder 5.
[5] Rpt of agricultural staff with *Army Group South*, 16 Oct 41, in *Wi Stab Ost.* Wi/ID 2.1355; *Bericht, Wi Stab Ost, 26.I.42.* Wi/ID 2.317b.
[6] *KTB, H. Geb. Sued, 27.VIII.41.* 16407/17.
[7] *Meldung 43, Einsatzgruppe B, 5.VIII.41.* Footlocker 62, folder 5.
[8] *Meldung 131, Einsatzgruppe A, 10.XI.41.* Footlocker 62, folder 11.
[9] *Anl 12 z. Bericht Wi Stab, Krasnowardeisk, Okt 41.* Wi/ID 2.189; *Meldung 43, 5.VIII.41., Einsatzgruppe B.* Footlocker 62, folder 5.
[10] *Bericht, Wi Stab Ost. 16.IX.–30.IX.41.* Wi/ID 2.345.
[11] *Meldung 106, Chef der Sicherheitspolizei und SD, 7.X.41.* Footlocker 62, folder 7.

looting and destruction of food stocks by the Communists.[12] The change of popular temper became so obvious and food so short that *Army Group North*, realizing that such conditions created fertile ground for the spread of the partisan movement, early in November ordered large-scale evacuations from the worst affected areas in order to avoid possible riots and epidemics.[13]

The Communists and partisan bands did much to lower public morale even further and add to the general feeling of insecurity. With party functionaries and NKVD personnel concentrating on the cities, the partisans launched a number of deliberately designed terror attacks on small rural communities. Appearing in sizeable groups, they struck at state and collective farms, machine tractor stations, and villages, forcibly requisitioning livestock and food supplies or wantonly destroying agricultural stockpiles, demolishing machinery, and butchering cattle.[14] These attacks were designed both to remove a possible source of provender for the Germans and supply the needs of the bands, and at the same time pose a constant reminder on the people that the Soviet arm was long and the hand of the party ever present. The pressure readily showed and in several districts all agricultural pursuits came to a complete standstill, so greatly did the peasants fear these raids.[15]

Under such compulsion the reluctance of the people to work closely with or even to approach the occupation authorities spread, and a number of partisan reprisal murders of German-appointed mayors and elders made it difficult to find individuals willing to serve in such capacities. Thus the establishment of a workable administration was definitely hampered.[16] In some areas the native volunteer units were similarly affected.[17] The fear of an eventual Soviet return was especially prevalent among the urban population, which had seen the NKVD at work at closer hand than had the peasants; and in areas where the German advance slowed down or the front became stabilized there were instances of passive resistance.[18]

Russian Propaganda

In conjunction with the terror attacks, the Soviets launched a virulent propaganda campaign. Although some of this propaganda was put

[12] *Befehl 44, Wi Stab Ost. anl. z. OKH/GenStdH/GenQu, Nr. 7732/41 geh., 4.XI.41., KTB H. Gp. Nord.* 75133/32.

[13] *KTB, Ia, 281 Sich. Div., 3.XI.41.* 15954/2.

[14] *KTB, 281 Sich. Div., 22.IX.41.* 15954/2; *KTB, Wi. Kdo. z.b.V. 'Goerlitz' 9.VI.–30.IX.41.* Wi/ID 2.357; *Anl. 58 z. Bericht Wi Stab Ost, 16.IX.–30.IX.41.* Wi/ID 2.345.

[15] *Bericht, Wi Stab Sued. 3.IX.–16.X.41.* Wi/ID 2.1355; rpt, econ officer with *Fourth Army*, 16 Oct 41, in *Wi Stab Ost.* Wi/ID 2.319.

[16] *KTB, 285 Sich. Div., 23.IX.41.* 14878/10.

[17] *Meldung 106, Chef der Sicherheitspolizei und SD, 7.X.41.* Footlocker 62, folder 5; *Bericht Wi Stab Ost, 16.IX.–30.IX.41.* Wi/ID 2.345.

[18] *Meldung 38, Chef der Sicherheitspolizei und SD, 30.VII.41.* Footlocker 62, folder 5; *Bericht Wi Stab Ost, 16.IX.–30.IX.41.* Wi/ID 2.345.

out by the partisan groups, the majority of it, in the form of printed
material dropped from aircraft, originated with the Soviet high command. There was a leaflet "News of the Soviet Fatherland," and a
newspaper published in Moscow.[19] The partisans turned out smaller
sheets on hand presses in the field.[20] During September when the offensive in the central sector came to a temporary halt, the Soviets gave
heavy play to the news that the German advance was stalemated and
that the tide would soon turn with the resultant return of the NKVD.
All who collaborated with the invaders were threatened with assassina-
tion or trial and death after the war. No one could remain neutral;
every citizen was to support the Soviet defense effort in every possible
way or face the consequences. That the Red Army and the party would
return was iterated and reiterated. This was not lost on the people.[21]
Wide play was given the criminal acts of the German SS and police
units, and the satellite troops.[22]

The people were continually urged to strike at the enemy: ". . . if
the Germans wish a war of annihilation, they shall get it . . . Destroy
to the last man all Germans . . . No quarter to the German Occupation
Forces!"[23] And again: "Love of the Soviet fatherland and hatred
of the foe are your strongest weapons. Scorn of death, your duty . . .
Forge all powers of the people together for the war of annihilation
against the German intruders!"[24]

Propaganda aimed particularly at the partisans stressed the need for
aggressiveness: ". . . Think of one thing; the fundamental law of
partisans is attack, attack, and attack again. If you act half-heartedly
and stick to your place, you will waste your strength to no purpose and
deliver yourself to the enemy. Resolve on offensive activity. These are
the pledges of success in the partisan war."[25] And such general exhorta-
tions as: "The enemy who has trodden on our soil shall perish on it! . . .
May [he] find out how our soil can burn under his feet."[26]

The people grew progressively uneasy under such psychological
attacks and began to wonder at the true nature of these self-styled
"liberators" with their inept policies and conflicting jurisdictions. The

[19] *Meldung 90, Chef der Sicherheitspolizei und SD, 21.IX.41.* Footlocker 62, folder 6; *Bericht, Korueck 559, 19.IX.–29.XI.41.* 13512/3.
[20] *KTB, Wi. Kdo, Pskov, 27.IX.41.* Wi/ID 2.357.
[21] *Meldung 90, Chef der Sicherheitspolizei und SD, 21.IX.41.* Footlocker 62, folder 6; *Bericht, Korueck, 559, 19.IX.–29.XI.41.* 13512/3.
[22] *Meldung 80, Einsatzgruppe C, 11.IX.41.* Footlocker 62, folder 11.
[23] From Stalin's speech of 6 Nov 41 in *Banden Bekaempfung, RFSS und Chef d. deutschen Polizei, IX.42.* EAP 170–a–10/7.
[24] From Stalin's speech of 7 Nov 41 in *ibid.*
[25] Excerpt from the brochure *Soviet Partisans* ("Young Guard" Publishing House; Moscow, 1941) in *Banden Bekaempfung, RFSS and Chef d. deutschen Polizei, IX.42.* EAP 170–a–10/7.
[26] Russian propaganda leaflet, "Directive for Partisans in the German Zone of Communications," found 19 Jul 41 by *293 Div.* OKW 1263.

German soldier, under good discipline and acting in a reasonably circumspect manner, had left a favorable impression. In his wake, however, had come the field administrative units with no well-integrated plan who were unable to either control the indiscriminate killing and looting of the police forces and the *Einsatzgruppen* or provide an adequate food supply. They wondered further at the rude treatment accorded Red Army prisoners, numbers of whom they had seen drop dead from starvation.[27] They were used to having every detail of their lives regulated and to being told what they might do and when they might do it. Without this close control they became restless and wondered further.[28] Since the radios in many areas had been confiscated, the official Wehrmacht broadcasts often went unheard and the people were uninformed of German plans for their welfare, of the German orders they were expected to obey, and of German desires and occupational intentions. There were few public-address systems in use outside the large population centers.[29]

Such a dearth of information provided a fertile breeding ground for rumors of all kinds and played directly into the hands of the Soviet propagandists. News that the Poles in eastern Galicia and the Volhynian border areas were treated with more consideration than the Ukrainians farther to the east did little to improve matters.[30] Still, despite all these indications of lowering morale, the people did not go over to the partisans in any numbers and, other than Communist Party members, few showed any open antagonism.

The Partisan Movement Becomes Independent

In the early fall, apparently some time in September, the control and direction of the partisans was taken from Mechlis' command and placed under the Central Staff of the Partisan Movement. This was a new department which was to operate independently of both the Red Army and the NKVD under the direct control of the Central Committee of the Communist Party. Red Army Marshal Voroshilov was its first head.[31]

---

[27] *Bericht, Wi. Stab Ost, 16.IX.41.* Wi/ID 2.345.

[28] *Bericht, Wi. Stab Sued, 16.X.41.* Wi/ID 2.1355.

[29] *Meldung 38, Chef der Sicherheitspolizei und SD, 30.VII.41. KTB, H. Geb. Sued, 25.VII.41.* 16407/17. Footlocker 62, folder 5.

[30] *KTB, H. Geb. Sued, 25.VII.41.* 16407/17; *Meldung 100, Chef der Sicherheitspolizei und SD, 1.X.41.* Footlocker 62, folder 5; *Bericht, Wi Stab Ost, 16.X.41.* Wi/ID 2.1355.

[31] Little factual material on the first set-up is available. See: ID, "Survey of Soviet Intelligence and Counter-Intelligence," (S) ARM-A G–2 1 SIC. OCMH, Gen Ref Br; "Organization and Mission of the Soviet Secret Service," (TS) (hereafter cited as NKVD Document). SD–9129, ID Library. This is a translation of a German appreciation of the Soviet Secret Service, made in 1944 on the basis of three years of war with the Soviet Union. The translation was made by the 258th Interrogation team and is undocumented.

Possibly as a result of this move, or at least coincident with it, the bands began to increase their activity. Although they were still far from being tight-knit military units and their liaison with Moscow and with each other was exceedingly tenuous when it existed at all, their operations started showing some semblance of order and purpose. In some cases their discipline was much improved and in portions of the central sector they followed Moscow-issued directives in both training and operations.[32] Some with radios had some limited success in establishing liaison with the Red Army units opposite the German divisions in whose rear they were working.[33]   A few received leaders who had been trained at special partisan schools in the Soviet rear.[34]

Change in German Tactics

Having found that they could not operate successfully except in terrain which protected their movements and bases and made German counteraction difficult, and not being particularly aggressive in any case, the partisan bands that were not broken up by the Germans or did not melt away from their own lack of organization and discipline began concentrating in the heavy forests and swamp areas, the Pripyat Marshes, the wooded regions of White Russia, and the almost trackless area south of Lake Ilmen behind the *Sixteenth Army*. This made the organization tasks of the Central Staff much easier and at the same time presaged grouping into larger units and future operations on more than a hit-and-run scale. Even during October the demolitions in these areas were increasing, and behind the right wing of *Army Group North* the number of bands visibly multiplied to such an extent that the army commander there was forced to assign areas for partisan control to his combat divisions.[35]

The tactics of the bands appeared to keep pace with these forward steps in organization and discipline. They seldom launched a raid without previous reconnaissance, often carried out by civilians pressured into the job, and generally struck or failed to strike in relation to the number of German troops in the area. They never remained in a district in the face of strong opposition and made every effort to avoid a standup fight. Forced from a particular sector by aggressive German action, they subsequently began raiding in another less well protected. In general

---

[32] *Meldung 71, Einsatzgruppe A, 2.IX.41.* 62/6.
[33] *Ibid.; Meldung 97, Einsatzgruppe B, 28.IX.41.* 62/5.
[34] *Wi. Inspektion AOK 6, 2.XI.41.* Wi/ID 2.294; *Bericht, Bfh. H. Geb. Sued. 29.IX.–30.IX.41.; 5.XI.41.* 16407/18.
[35] Bericht, Ia, H. Geb. Nord. Nr. 1424/41, 2.XI.41. 14768/4; "Protection of Troops Against Partisans and Sabotage," *12 Inf. Div.*, Nr. 604/41, 17 Nov 41 in *Nazi Conspiracy and Aggression, op. cit.* VII, pp. 49–51; Gen. d. Inf. Walther von Unruh, CG, Fourth Army Rear Area, "War Experiences in Russia." MS D–056. OCMH, Foreign Studies Br.

they operated in areas with which they were well acquainted and set up their bases on swamp islands and in deep forests difficult of access. They made their marches only by night and over prearranged routes. They were armed with Russian or captured German ordnance, their ammunition coming from bypassed Soviet depots or raids on German convoys and installations. Occasionally they received arms, generally automatic, and ammunition by air drop. They lived off the country, forcibly requisitioning what they needed from the natives. They deliberately attempted to demoralize the local civilians with sudden raids, rumor-mongering, and general heavy-handed terror tactics.[36] There is some evidence that they attempted to gather and transmit information on German troop dispositions and the locations of German supply installations, and in several instances the Germans were given reason to believe that Red Army countermoves were made on the basis of partisan-supplied information.[37]

This improvement in the organization and operational capabilities of the bands did not go unobserved by the Germans. As early as the middle of September the security commands were aware that the resistance they faced was not of a passing nature but the opposition of irregular groups under some sort of a centralized control. They saw the fallacy in their earlier overconfidence and realized that the antipartisan tactics they were then using were faulty and that a change of method was called for.[38] Through observation, PW interrogation, and collation of captured documents they had been able to pinpoint the types of groups they had to contend with: the annihilation battalions, units of Red Army soldiers led by Army commissars, local groups comprising predominantly young Communists who worked on the collective farms during the day and gathered into previously established units at night to operate against German communications, and Communist Party members and NKVD personnel infiltrated or parachuted into the occupied areas on special sabotage missions or with the task of fomenting rebellion among the natives.[39] Of these the annihilation units appeared to be the backbone of the movement, furnishing most of the opposition. As the Red Army per-

---

[36] *Bhf, H. Geb. Mitte, Nr. 1001/41 geh., 12.X.41., Anl, Bd. II. KTB 1, H. Geb. Mitte, 1.IX.–31.XII.41.* 14684/3; *H. Geb. Nord, Ia, Ic/AO, Nr. 1198/41 geh., 14.IX.41., Nr. 1236/41 geh., 20.IX.41., Nr. 1328/41 geh., 7.X.41., KTB, H. Geb, Nord. 14768/4; Lagebericht, Wi Stab Ost, 16.IX.–30.IX.41., Anl. 58 z. KTB, Wi Stab Ost.* Wi/ID 2.345.

[37] *Meldung 71, Einsatzgruppe A, 2.IX.41.* 62/6; *Meldung 97, Einsatzgruppe B. 28.IX.41.* 62/5.

[38] *Korpsbefehl Nr. 52, H. Geb. Mitte, Ia, 14.IX.41., Anl. 125, Anlagenband II. KTB 1. H. Geb. Mitte, 1.IX.–31.XII.41.* 14684/3.

[39] *Anl. 1 z. AOK 16, Ic/AO, Nr. 52/41. 13.VIII.41., KTB, Korueck 584.* 35615/2; *H. Geb. Nord. Ia, Ic, Nr. 1198/41 geh., 14.IX.41., KTB, 281 Sich. Div.* 15954/2; ltr, *Bfh. Sicherheitspolizei und SD to Bfh. H. Geb. Nord.,* 14 Aug 41, in *KTB, H. Geb. Nord.* 14768/5.

sonnel took active command, leaving the party members only political functions, these units took on something of a military tinge, becoming more active and their operations more uniformly successful.[40] To combat the partisans the security commands evolved an antipartisan blueprint founded on the basic assumption that to be successful in a rear area war they had to be as mobile and as tricky as the partisans themselves, so much so that it would be the Germans who were feared, not the partisans. Highest priority was given to obtaining accurate and up-to-date information of the bands as to location, strength, composition, armament, mission, etc., in order to obviate faulty or scattered commitment of security forces. The establishment of a reliable net of informers from the civil population—*Vertrauensleute* or V men—in each area was considered an absolute must. All information brought in by these V men was to be immediately evaluated and checked for accuracy, and all false or overexaggerated reports punished severely. High emphasis was placed on aggressiveness and general alertness.

Frontal assaults in difficult county had proved abortive, too often splitting the enemy units into groups small enough to slip through the lines of the attacking force. Mobility and surprise rather than superiority of force were believed to be the best guarantee of success, since the majority of the bands were still small. The alert regiments and SS brigades therefore were to be re-formed into highly mobile task forces of several companies each and held in constant readiness at strategic points. Roads and rail line right of ways were to be patrolled continuously in order to maintain pressure on the bands and keep them off balance. Surprise offensive operations of ample strength were to be executed in such a way that they would be unable to escape annihilation. Where a composite force of German military and paramilitary units was to be committed, a clear chain of command and responsibility was to be established prior to the action. The troops of the *Landesschuetzen* battalions and any spare police forces were to be dispersed down to platoon size over as many villages as possible so as to give support to the inhabitants against the terror raids, deny the partisans bases and food, and prevent the natives from aiding them. Once an area was considered pacified, it was still to be patrolled and important localities and installations guarded. Native volunteer units, wherever recruited, were to be used for reconnaissance and static guard duty only, and never committed in an offensive operation except as a last resort, and then under close and immediate German command. The areas surrounding important depots and rail junctions were to be evacuated of all natives, although it was realized that such a move would not necessarily allow for a reduction of the security garrison there; admittedly rail lines and highways, even when guarded and patrolled, would still be vulnerable to attack.

---

[40] *Meldung 97, Einsatzgruppe B, 28.IX.41.* 62/5.

A better clearing house for the assembly and collation of information on the partisans was to be set up; complete reports of all partisan actions and countermeasures taken were to be submitted and detailed interrogations of all prisoners forwarded to higher headquarters in order that experience gained might be used in future operations.[41]

The New Tactics in Operation

The application of these new approaches to the partisan question was fairly universal throughout the three army group sectors. Additional measures were taken by individual units. The *Army Group Center Rear Area* revamped its procedure for guarding rail lines: a battalion of security troops was assigned to every 60 miles of track, two men to each half-mile. The remainder of the battalion was to be used on patrol duty or held as a reserve. All bridges were to have a sentry at both ends with an additional guard underneath at night. Patrols were to constantly check rail connections and the inside of tracks for mines. A similar procedure was ordered for the express highways.[42]

The armies themselves experienced no opposition from the partisans in the immediate combat zone other than scattered attacks on single vehicles,[43] yet they seemed fully aware of the possible effect of such action on their supply and took steps accordingly. The *Ninth Army* was particularly specific. In the combat area each corps was made responsible for security and control of the population in its sector. Patrols were ordered out to round up all village leaders and males not originally from the area. Mayors appointed by the corps were to be made responsible for registering all strangers. Passes and identification cards issued by any agency outside the jurisdiction of the army were declared invalid, and in the army area no pass was to have any value nor were any to be issued. Any partisans captured before 15 September were to be accorded prisoner of war status. Interrogation of partisan prisoners was to be comprehensive, covering data on irregular organization, intelligence system, and missions. Those persuaded to talk were to be forwarded to corps headquarters for further interrogation.[44] The commandant of the army rear area was considered responsible for all matters pertaining to partisan resistance and German countermeasures. If he became unable to control the situation, the army would take over.[45]

[41] Dir, *Bfh, H. Geb. Nord, Ia/Ic, Nr. 1198/41 geh., 14.IX.41., KTB, 281 Sich. Div. 15954/2; H. Geb. Sued. Ia/Ic, Nr. 1337/41 geh., 24.VIII.41., KTB, H. Geb. Sued, Aug 41–Dez 42, 75905; Korpsbefehl Nr. 52, Bfh, H. Geb. Mitte, 14.IX.41., Anl. 121, Anlagenband II, KTB 1. H. Geb. Mitte, 1.IX.–31.XII.41.* 14684/3.
[42] *Anl. 144 z. KTB 1, H. Geb. Mitte, 12.X.41.* 14684/3.
[43] On this, see: *Bericht N. 264/41 geh., 3.IX.41., Geheime Feldpolizei Gruppe 580, KTB, AOK 9.* 14162/7.
[44] *AOK 9, Ic/Abw/OQu, Nr. 238/41 geh., Anl. z. KTB, AOK 9, Ic, 2.III.–26.XI.41.* 14162/7.
[45] *Befehl, AOK 9, Ia/Ic/Ao. Nr. 254/41 geh., 10.IX.41.* 14162/7.

In an attempt to penetrate any radio net the partisans might have established, an order was passed that all signal data and signal equipment captured from the partisans was to be forwarded to the chief signal officer of the army and any signal personnel captured was not to be be shot but sent to army headquarters with the equipment.[46]

Convoy regulations were revamped in many units. The *XXXXIV Panzer Corps* ordered that vehicles and personnel be kept close together on the road with more guards and no advance reconnaissance riders. One empty truck was to be included in each convoy to pick up all persons found wandering through the countryside.[47] Many line units had antipartisan duty added to their combat roles.[48]

In both the northern and central sectors local officials were made responsible for the good order of their districts, and reprisals were ordered in retaliation for partisan-inflicted casualties in an attempt to curb popular support of the bands. The mayors or elders of towns and villages, after a security check by the SD, were armed and given responsibility for the security of their areas, but their offices were moved to the nearest German headquarters in order that they might be closely watched. They also were made accountable for quiet not only in their community itself but for the area halfway to the next settlement. For added support, local civilians were drafted for static guard duty. As reprisal for positive partisan activity, in the *Fourth Army Area* two inhabitants were ordered shot for every German killed. In the case of an attack on an important installation three persons were to be executed. Any native who harbored strangers was to suffer a like penalty.[49] Persons found wandering in the streets after dark or found near rail or highway bridges at any time were to be shot on sight.[50]

The German units in the operations zone, seeing that much of the last-ditch resistance of some of the Red Army divisions as well as the determined opposition of a number of the partisan bands centered around the fanatical leadership of the political commissars, repeatedly requested the "Commissar Order" be rescinded. As long as the commissars saw themselves faced with certain death, the *XXXIX Corps* wrote the *Sixteenth Army*, they would fight to the last because of the threats against them. Yet if the individual commissar knew that he could save his life by deserting, the inner unity of the political leadership would dissolve.[51]

---

[46] *Befehl, AOK 9, Ia, Ic/AO, Nr. 284/41 geh., 25.IX.41.* 14162/7.

[47] *Befehl, XXXXIV Pz. Corps, 29.IX.41. in KTB, 112 Inf Div.* 19643/24.

[48] See: *Bericht, Nr. 264/41 geh., 3/IX.41., Geheime Feldpolizei Gruppe 580, KTB, AOK 9.* 14162/7.

[49] *Befehl Nr. 52, 21.IX.41., 286 Sich. Div., Anl. 102 z. KTB 1, 286 Sich. Div.* 16182/3; *Anl. 2 z. Befehl Nr. 25, 403d Sich. Div., 10.X.41.* 15701/3.

[50] Order of commandant of the *Fourth Army Rear Area* to *137 Inf Div* in *Lagebericht, 18.X.41., Korueck 559.* 13512/2.

[51] Memo, *XXXIX Corps* to *Sixteenth Army*, 17 Sep 41, "Possibilities of Disrupting Bolshevik Resistance from Within." *Anl. z. KTB, XXXIX Corps.* 23584/8.

The request was passed along through OKH to OKW, but was turned down. In answer Jodl noted only: "The Fuehrer has declined any modification of previously published orders on the treatment of commissars." [52]

In a less violent and perhaps more practical vein, OKH, to whom it had become obvious that the partisan threat would be greatly minimized and would eventually die if it were denied popular support, recommended that the armies make every effort to wean the people away from the partisan cause and as far as possible provide work for them so that there would be no idleness to breed discontent. [53]

Antipartisan Directives

On 25 October OKH issued its first "Directive for Anti-Partisan Warfare" for distribution to all units in the east. Based on the experience and recommendations of the security commands, this directive actually offered little new information on the partisan movement and ordered only remedial measures which had been in use for several weeks in various portions of the occupied territories. It did, however, establish a uniform course of action based on experience and set up at least the beginning of a German antipartisan doctrine. Emphasis was placed on general aggressiveness, careful planning founded on extensive reconnaissance and reliable information, and swift execution in all operations against the bands, with encirclement and annihilation always the ultimate objectives. [54]

This was not to be a static doctrine. The security commands were directed to supplement their activity reports with all information of value on the partisans, both general and in answer to specific queries, in order that the principles as laid down might be kept abreast of new developments. [55]

Following the publication of the directive, the armies visibly tightened up their security procedures. For example, individual units of the *12th Infantry Division* of the *Sixteenth Army* were assigned areas for permanent partisan control. All villages, roads, and paths in those areas were ordered patrolled 24 hours a day and on an irregular schedule to keep any partisans there off balance. Pro-German village elders were to be installed in all communities and directed to compile

---

[52] Note penciled on the margin of ltr, OKH to OKW, 23 Sep 41, in planning file *BARBAROSSA.* OKW/1938.

[53] *Anl. z. OKH/GenStdH/GenQu., Nr. 23766/41 geh., 18.X.41. in KTB, H. Geb. Nord.* 14768/4; *OKH/Gen. z.b.V/JAG., Nr. 453–1332/41 geh., in KTB, Ic, H. Geb. Nord. 21.III–19.X.41.* 14768/5.

[54] *Richtlinien Fuer Partisanenbekaempfung, Gen.St.d.H/Ausb. Abt. Ia, Nr. 1900/41, 25.X.41.* H 26/6.

[55] *OKH/Gen.St.d.H./Gen.Qu.Nr. 7562/41 Geh. 29.X.41., Anl. 154, Anlagenband II z. KTB 1, H. Geb. Mitte, 1.IX.–31.XII.41.* 14684/3.

a census of the population in which all individuals not native to the place were to be shown with the date of their arrival. These lists were to be constantly checked by means of snap roll calls. Collective punitive measures were to be carried out for noncompliance of orders. Natives were forbidden to travel from one village to another and no one was to be allowed to leave his community except in exceptional cases and then only with the permission of the garrison commander. Permits for such travel were to be dated and bear the route and the place to be visited, and were to be valid for but one day. All permits were to be turned in on the date of expiration and any person found on the roads without a pass was to be arrested and, if not belonging to the nearest village, executed as a partisan.[56]

Effect of the Manpower Shortage in the Rear

Even with this increased awareness on the part of the Army High Command of the turn events in the occupied areas and the improved procedures for dealing with it, the efforts to establish secure control of the rear left much to be desired and did little to retard the growth of the movement. This was due primarily to the attitude of the people. Even the victory at Vyazma in October only momentarily stayed a steady deterioration of public morale and a growing hostility toward the Germans. The reasons were always the same—fear of a Soviet return, the German failure to improve the food situation, and, as ever, the land tenure question. In the central and northern sectors the individual Russian more and more was coming to look on the German as an enemy, not as a "liberator." As a result he became obstinate and disrespectful, and began to support the partisans, tacitly if not openly. The unchecked "clearing" actions of the *Einsatzgruppen* and police units, during which many people were executed without proof of Communist Party affiliation or Jewish blood, hurt the German cause immensely, and the continued pilfering and illegal requisitioning by the troops, especially that of the security units, did nothing to improve the situation.[57]

In these matters there was little the security commands could do. As far as feeding the people in the devastated areas, they faced the hard and fast policies of the economic administration, and when some limited food stocks were available there was insufficient transportation for equitable distribution. There was no chance for a practical psychological approach with OKW refusing to allow the *Wehrmacht Propaganda Division* to make any open commitments on any subject; as a result many

---

[56] *12 Inf. Div., Ic/Ia, Nr. 607/41. 17.XI.41.* in *Nazi Conspiracy and Aggression, op. cit.,* VII, pp. 49–51.

[57] *Bericht, Wi Stab Sued, 16.X.41.* Wi/ID 2.1355; *Lagebericht, Ortskdtr "Rshev", 8.XI.41.,* in *KTB, Korueck 582.* 17326/11; *Anl. 12 z. Lagebericht, Wi Stab "Krasnowardeisk," Okt 41.* Wi/ID 2.189.

points of difference between the occupiers and the occupied, often simple in themselves but with explosive possibilities when taken in aggregate, went unresolved. And the land tenure question was out of the Army orbit. Although the forces in the field made repeated recommendations that the state and collective farms be broken up and the acreage distributed to the peasants as a gesture of German good will, their recommendations were ignored.[58]

The army and army group rear areas had been specifically charged with guaranteening the unimpeded supply of the armies and the exploitation of the country for the use of the military. Had the natives accepted matters quietly as in Poland and France, the units originally allotted for this task would have sufficed. But with the campaign as yet unended and the partisan movement and general civilian disaffection on the rise, there were simply not enough troops available to protect the supply lines and still bring the huge territories under adequate police control.

It was strictly a problem of men and materiel. On 1 October the *Army Group Center Rear Area*, where the greatest amount of resistance existed, was responsible for the security of some 137,000 square miles of country, an area slightly smaller than the state of Texas and more than five times Pennsylvania. For this task it had available on paper three security divisions, two second-rate infantry divisions,[59] and an SS brigade. Several of the better elements of these units had been drawn into the front lines. The *707th Infantry Division*, with but two infantry regiments and only one motorized supply company, had an area of responsibility of 35,000 square miles.[60] *Korueck 582* in the rear of the *Ninth Army* covered 6,900 square miles including more than 1,500 villages plus collective farms. To secure this area it had available, in addition to headquarters personnel, 16 companies of 80 to 90 men each, a total of less than 1,400, for railroad, supply installation, headquarters, and PW camp guards. Of these, once the static details were mounted, less than 300 men remained for patrols and antipartisan action.[61] On 5 October the commandant of the army group rear area reported that the security divisions and the *339th Infantry Division* were so far understrength that after static rail line guards were posted there were too few troops remaining to mount any offensive action against the partisans or exercise effective control.[62]

---

[58] Op. Sit. Rpt 86, 17 Sep 41 (doc. 3151), prosecution document book in *N.M.T. op. cit.* (Case 9); rpt, *Army Group South* to OKH, 6 Oct 41. in *KTB, H. Geb. Sued.* 16407/8.

[59] The *707th* and *339th Divs* had only two infantry regiments each.

[60] Hist Div, EUCOM, "Protection of Lines of Communication in the East," 21 Apr 47, p. 3. MS D-102. Foreign Studies Br., OCMH.

[61] Ltr, *Korueck 582* to *Ninth Army*, 22 Sep 41. 17326/15.

[62] *Bericht, H. Geb. Mitte, Nr. 940/41 geh., 5.X.41., Anl. 137 z. Anlagenband II z. KTB I, H. Geb. Mitte, 1.IX–31.XII.41.* 14684/3.

This was accentuated by the acute shortage of transport. In *Korueck 582* only a police battalion of three companies was motorized.[63] Other units were equally devoid of vehicles, although occasionally captured Russian trucks were supplied, generally without spare parts. In early October the *339th Infantry Division* was begging for 20 captured Soviet vehicles which had been "promised" it.[64]

On 7 October OKH authorized the recruiting of engineer units from Russian prisoners of Ukrainian and White Russian origin to alleviate the shortage of railway repair workers and furnish additional static guards along the lines.[65] In a further attempt to supplement these short hands, the army group rear areas were given permission to activate one trial Cossack squadron each from among prisoners of war for commitment against the bands. These squadrons were to be adequately armed, mounted, clothed, paid, and fed, and given missions against the partisans in definite areas under the command of their own officers. Detailed reports on the experiment were to be forwarded to OKW which would determine whether additional similar units would be formed.[66]

The manpower shortage was especially accented by the task of controlling the increasing number of Soviet prisoners as encirclement followed encirclement. With literally hundreds of thousands of Russians being cut off and surrendering, the security commands found themselves faced with an almost insoluble problem. Shorthanded as they were, groups of PW's as large as 1,000 were usually guarded by only two or three men, and in the heavy terrain those prisoners who wanted to escape could easily do so. Large numbers of them swarmed freely about the rear looking for food and shelter, under no control whatever, disappearing at will, and all at least possible recruits for irregular units. The inability of the Germans to provide sufficient food gave them an added incentive to escape and join the underground.[67]

By 1 October this situation had become so bad in the central sector that Von Bock issued stringent orders that all units taking prisoners, including armored forces, were to be responsible for their safe delivery to prisoner of war camps and that no excuses for failure to do so would be accepted. It was hoped that such a procedure would dry up a fruitful source of recruits for partisan units.[68]

With the closing of the Vyazma trap on an estimated 600,000 Red Army soldiers, the PW control problem was multiplied many times.

---

[63] Ltr, *Korueck 582* to *Ninth Army*, 22 Sep 41.   17326/15.
[64] *Bericht, H. Geb. Mitte, Nr. 940/41 geh., 5.X.41., Anl. 137 z. Anlagenband II z. KTB 1, H. Geb. Mitte, 1.IX–31.XII.41.*   14684/3.
[65] *Korpsbefehl Nr. 59, H. Geb. Mitte, Ia, 7.X.41., KTB, H. Geb. Mitte.*   16748/11.
[66] *OKH/Gen.St.d.H./GenQu., Az, Abt., K. Verw. (Qu4), Nr. 11/6878/41 geh., 6.X.41.* in *Bfh, H. Geb. Sued, Ia, Okt. 41–Nov. 43.*   75906.
[67] Gen. d. Inf. Walther von Unruh, "War Experiences in Russia," pp. 28, 29, 39, MS D–056.   Foreign Studies Br., OCMH.
[68] *Anl. 999 z. KTB, H. Gp. Mitte, 6.X.41.*   26974/10.

Large numbers of the Russians encircled there, having been told by the Soviet command that the Germans would let them starve to death, took advantage of the shortages of guards and slipped eastward through the front lines or joined the partisans.[69]

The Partisan Picture Begins To Change

The failure of the final German assault on Moscow and the rapid success of the Soviet counterattack brought about a distinct change in the bases of the Russian defense effort and marked a turning point for the partisan movement. For the first time the Red Army held the initiative, and with its units exploiting the advantage the situation in the German rear took on a new aspect. Not only was the spirit of the troops and the partisan bands improved but the morale of the natives whose support they needed was strongly bolstered. And as the early tactical gains promised to develop into strategical victories with Soviet units moving through and around the German divisions, the bands for the first time were given an opportunity to make a direct military contribution. It was a small contribution, perhaps, but it laid the foundation for a more telling one later.

Concurrent with the Soviet counteroffensive in December, the attacks of the partisans, which had begun to increase in November, reached an even higher peak, accompanied as they were by widespread propaganda and rumor mongering concerning the Russian successes.[70] The heaviest pressure remained behind the *Sixteenth Army* where the northern wing of the Russian attack had driven a breach in the line along the boundary between *Army Groups Center* and *North*. There the number of rail demolitions was steadily increasing. Train arrivals in the sector averaged 35 daily on 1 December but by 14 December dropped to an "alarming low" due to partisan activity.[71]

A similar situation existed in the central sector. During November the bands had begun to concentrate in the extensive forests about Bryansk. As the Soviet drive developed they began hitting sharply at the railroads from this base in addition to launching numerous raids on troop units and installations behind the overextended *Second Panzer Army* and keeping the natives in the surrounding countryside in a constant state of terror. By the first of the year their numbers had so increased and their organization so improved that they completely controlled 8 of the 10 *rayons* comprising the *Bryansk Agricultural Ad-*

[69] *Lagebericht, Ortskdtr, "Wyasma," 2.XI.41., KTB, Korueck 582.* 17326/11.
[70] *Lagebericht Nr. L Wi Kdo. Bryansk, 91.42., KTB. Bryansk, 17.XII.41.–31.III.42.* Wi/ID 2.84; *KTB, Korueck 580, 24.XII.41.* 16715/3.
[71] *Bericht, Wi Kdo. Pleskau, 27.XI.41., KTB, Wi Kdo. Pleskau, 1.X.–31.XII.41.* Wi/ID/2.189; *Bericht, Aussenstelle 51, 1.XII.41., KTB, Aussenstelle 51, 30.VIII.–31.XII.41.* Wi/ID 2.277. "Halder's Journal," *op. cit.,* VII, p. 220.

ministrative Area.[72] In the Ukraine, where natural cover was scarce, there were no bands of consequence in evidence outside the immediate Dnepr swamp area.

The persistent partisan emphasis was on the rail lines, although it never became overbearing during this period. The poor Russian roads had taken a terrific toll of Wehrmacht transport, and when the fall rains made all but the few paved highways virtually impassable it became impossible to move supplies by truck in any appreciable quantity. The result was an especially heavy load on the railroads. And then when the Russian rolling stock began breaking down for a lack of proper maintenance and the German engines, which had not been converted for operations at extremely low temperatures, failed to operate with anything like normal efficiency, the whole German supply system became particularly sensitive to any rail sabotage.[73]

A comparison of the German directives issued in the northern sector in July and late in December reflect the steadily increasing activity by the partisans aimed at the rail lines. On 12 July the *281st Security Division* was ordered to place guards on the rail bridge over the Niehen, at the tunnel near Kovno, in the area west of the rail bridge near Krustpils, on the rail bridge over the Dvina at Dvinsk, and on the rail bridge north of Dvinsk.[74] On 20 December the same division ordered that the lines Pskov-Ostrov-Rezekne and Pskov-Dno be secured with all available forces in such a manner as to insure uninterrupted service. All bridges and culverts less than 40 feet long were to have double sentries, longer structures to be guarded by a squad of one noncommissioned officer and six men. All stretches of rail in closed terrain were to have one sentry every 100 yards; in open terrain one sentry every 200 yards; sentries were to remain in sight of one another. Along all stretches where partisans had been or might be expected, additional guards were to be assigned. Each railroad yard was to be secured by at least one company and all yards were to have a cleared area at least 300 yards wide around them. This security schedule was not to be deviated from, even if the last man in the division was used.[75] Ten days later the same division was so jittery that it ordered the metropolitan area about Ostrov completely fortified by 15 January.[76]

It is probable that the danger was exaggerated by the Germans, their nerves strained by the rapidly deteriorating situation at the front.[77] At

---

[72] *Lagebericht 1, Wi Kdo. Bryansk, 9.I.42., KTB, Wi Kdo. Bryansk 17.XII.41.–31.III.42; Lagebericht 5, Wi Kdo. Bryansk, 23.III.42.* Wi/ID 284.
[73] See: MS P–041r, "OKH Transportation Services," ch. I, pp. 37–43. OCMH. Foreign Studies Br; "Halder's Journal," *op. cit.,* VII, p. 203.
[74] *Befehl, Bfh. H. Geb. Nord. 12.VII.41., KTB, 281 Sich. Div.* 15954/2.
[75] *281 Sich. Div., Ia, Nr. 714/41, 20.XII.41., KTB, 281 Sich. Div.* 15954/2.
[76] *281 Sich. Div., Ia. Nr. 740/41 geh., 30.XII.41., KTB, 281 Sich. Div.* 15954/2.
[77] See: Entries for period 20 Dec 41–1 Mar 42 in "Halder's Journal," *op. cit.* At times Halder showed the effect of the pressure as much as the commanders at the front.

least this seems to have been the case during December and the first three weeks of January, for during that period supply difficulties never became so acute that either OKH or the army groups ever considered using line units to protect communications. Matters at the front were far too desperate. Rather, on 30 December, OKH ordered security units pulled from the rear and committed at the front in an attempt to restore the situation there.[78] A month later OKH considered changing the gauge of the Smolensk-Vyazma line where partisan pressure was reported to be the heaviest.[79]

The Beginning of Partisan Cooperation With the Red Army

As the Red Army continued to press its advantage in the last days of January, the bands in the central sector came more boldly into the picture. With the temperature moderating somewhat—from −47° F. on 20 January to +5° ten days later—[80] they began moving northward out of their forest bases about Bryansk in some numbers and appearing between Smolensk and the rear of the *Fourth Army*. Here they joined forces with a number of Red Army parachute units dropped into the same area and were gradually pulled under the provisional command of General Belov, a Red Army cavalry corps commander who had broken through the German front with his divisions. Belov had established his headquarters at Dorogobuzh between Smolensk and Vyazma, and many of the bands set up their command posts in the vicinity. From this area a combined force of partisans, parachutists, and cavalry caused such disruption along the Smolensk-Vyazma rail line and highway, the principal supply line for the army group, that the Germans were forced to pull out elements of the *5th* and *11th Panzer Divisions* to right the situation.[81]

Belov, under orders from Moscow, constantly pressured these bands to increase their size and tighten up their organization in anticipation

---

[78] *Ibid.*, VII, p. 245.

[79] *Ibid.*, p. 263.

[80] These temperatures are overwritten in crayon on the OKH operations maps for the dates indicated. See: *Lage Ost. 20.I.42, and Lage Ost. 30.I.42.*

[81] "Halder's Journal," *op. cit.*, VII, p. 263; see also *Lage Ost. 20.I.42* and *Lage Ost. 1.II.42.* The thesis has been advanced that since these airborne units nowhere attacked in closed formations they were intended to serve as cadres for and to stiffen the morale of the partisan units as well as reinforce Russian ground troops who had broken through the German lines. See: MS P–116 "Russian Airborne Operations." (Hist Div, EUCOM). OCMH, Foreign Studies Br. The *Lage Ost* maps for the period bear out the fact that the airborne brigades were widely scattered in their drops. However, considering the very tenuous liaison between the Red Army and the partisans at the time it seems more reasonable that the scattering of the parachutists was due more to Russian inexperience with airborne operations than to a design to reinforce the irregulars. It is more probable that the partisans were ordered north to work with the airborne troops.

of campaigns to come. On his orders NKVD agents and Communist Party members recruited a number of irregular personnel to be flown from an air strip at Dorogobuzh to the Soviet rear for training in special partisan schools and then returned.[82] Belov was able to continue this control over the bands in his particular area until the late spring when the Germans with much difficulty drove him out.

In the northern sector, as the Soviets deepened the initial wedge they had driven between *Army Groups North* and *Center* and followed up with sharp attacks designed to isolate the German *II Corps* south of Lake Ilmen, the bands were able to lend material assistance in severing the north-south highway (*Rollbahn Nord*) and marooning the communications hub of Kholm. As the situation developed, a number of them operating in the rear of the *Sixteenth Army* were gradually brought under the control of a Red Army general officer who was working under directives of the headquarters of the Northwest Front.[83]

These two instances seem to have been the first of real cooperation between the bands and the Red Army, and the fact that in both cases the lead was taken by a Red Army officer is significant. Whether Belov and his colleague farther north made their initial contact and expanded their control over the partisans in their areas on orders from the Soviet high command as part of a prearranged plan or simply because they were far-thinking, aggressive leaders is unknown and can only be deduced from what the record reveals. The evidence seems to indicate Moscow's guiding hand.

The northward movement of the bands from Bryansk to the Dorogobuzh area at the same time numbers of Red Army parachutists were dropping into the latter region appears too well timed to have been accidental, and must have been ordered by the Central Staff, followed as it was by Belov's assumption of command on Moscow's orders. Also, coincident with the Red Army offensive, signal equipment and trained communications personnel had been dropped in some volume behind the German lines, and as the attack got under way, patrols on a number of occasions had penetrated the discontinuous German line carrying directives to the larger of the bands.[84] Then toward the latter part of January as the Soviet penetrations became deeper and the German rear more out of hand, instances of regular-irregular cooperation became more and more frequent. Cadres of Red Army officers and NCO's and heavy equipment were flown into the bands via airfields under partisan control. As a result, the attacks on Wehrmacht communica-

---

[82] The above was culled from a number of interrogations of partisan PW's and German intelligence estimates based on additional interrogations. See: *Tgb., 221 Inf. Div., 22.III.–17.VI.42.* 22639/6.

[83] Notes on conf between CofS, *Army Group North,* and CofS, *Sixteenth Army* 31 Jan 42, in *KTB, H. Gr. Nord, 18.I.–12.II.42.* 75128/6.

[84] *Meldung 156, Chef der Sicherheitspolizei und SD, EG "A," Krasnowardeisk 16.I.42.* 62/8; Fred Virski, *My Life in the Red Army* (New York, 1949), p. 198.

tions, supported by antitank guns, mortars, and occasionally even artillery, began to lose some of their hit-and-run characteristics.[85]

It was much the same behind the *Sixteenth Army*. There the bands almost from the first breaching of the German line worked in some sort of contact with the Russian regulars, and, as the drive developed and the Red Army general assumed direction of the action, joined actively with them in attempting to frustrate German efforts to relieve the Kholm hedgehog and reestablish control over their lateral communications.[86] In several instances the personnel of the bands were found mixed with Red Army soldiers who had come through the lines from the Soviet rear, and in at least one case a Red Army regiment furnished manpower to increase the striking power of a band.[87] So closely did the Red Army and the partisans seem to be working together that the Germans found reason to believe that the Soviet high command was attempting to raise several of the bands to the level and status of regular units.[88]

The success of this cooperative venture coupled with German transportation difficulties occasioned by the bitter winter weather began to tell and by 10 February the situation had deteriorated to such an extent behind the line south of Lake Ilmen that *Army Group North* admitted that unless it could stabilize the rear of the *Sixteenth Army* and regain control of the *Rollbahn Nord* all the troop units in that sector would have to be supplied by air.[89]

Early Use of the Bands as Intelligence Organs

As this early cooperation developed, Moscow saw that under close supervision valuable intelligence organs might be developed within the individual bands. With the Red Army now on the offensive the need for information of German dispositions and intentions was doubly acute. Consequently, during the winter guerrilla branches were installed in the intelligence divisions of all Red Army field headquarters to establish and maintain the closest possible liaison with the bands and work toward the establishment of a reliable information-gathering system within the over-all framework of the movement.[90] In this new role the bands were to work independently of and in addition to a number of small, specially trained espionage teams and Communist Party agent groups whose

---

[85] *Anl. 53 z. KTB. H. Geb. Nord. 1.I.–31.III.42.* 18320/6; *Bericht, Ic, Korueck 584. 3.II.42.. Anl. 52. z. KTB 3. Korueck.* 38998/2; rpt, 1430/42, Kluge to Halder, 24 Feb 42, in *KTB, Band Pz AOK 3, 1.II.–25.IV.42.* 20736/6.

[86] Notes on conf between CofS, *Army Group North*, and CofS, *Sixteenth Army* 31 Jan 42, in *KTB, H. Gr Nord, 18.I.–12.II.42.* 75128/6; *Anl. 53 z. KTB. H. Geb. Nord, 1.I.–31.III.42.* 18320/6.

[87] *Bericht, Ic, H. Geb. Nord, Maerz 42, Anl. 85 z. KTB 1. H. Geb. Nord.* 21287/1.

[88] *Bericht, Ic, H. Geb. Nord, Nr. 790/42, Mai 42, Anl. z. KTB 1, H. Geb. Nord.* 21287/1.

[89] "Halder's Journal," *op. cit.*, VII, p. 267; see also: Telephone conversation, CofS, *Sixteenth Army*, and CofS, *Army Group North*, 27 Feb 42, recorded in *Army Group North Hq Jnl* at 1904. *KTB, H. Gp Nord, 13.II.–12.III.42.* 75128/7.

[90] NKVD Document, *op. cit.*

primary mission was to reestablish the Soviet control in the overrun areas.[91]

To provide close supervision and aid in the espionage work, Moscow assigned Army political commissars to the bands with which liaison had been established and a senior commissar to each assault army for the express purpose of further controlling bands in the rear of the German units facing that army.[92] A large percentage of these commissars were NKVD personnel who, through what remained of the local police, fire fighting, and border guard organizations that had been under NKVD control prior to the war, were able to make at least a start toward setting up an espionage net.

Despite these efforts, for many months the bands played only minor roles as military intelligence agencies. The pressure of the Germans, who were still strong despite their winter set-backs, the lack of a dependable communications net, and general inexperience and lack of training as intelligence operatives precluded any real contribution on their part for some time to come. Further, there was the question of reliability of the information which they did send. Even the dependability of bands under close Communist Party scrutiny had to be proven.

Reorganization Within the Movement

The bands gained much through these first contacts with the Red Army. At least a portion of them were under Red Army control for a time and had the opportunity to work with regular units under experienced leadership. Their liaison with the Soviet rear improved somewhat. In several cases they had regular troops integrated in their ranks; some of their leaders were flown to the Soviet rear for training. Yet in almost all cases the partisan movement left much to be desired. The bands still lacked anything approaching uniformity in their organization at the unit level. Their leadership generally remained inept. Most important, they had no established chain of command and liaison with the Central Staff through which they could be brought into effective coordination with the Red Army and with each other.

It was with these deficiencies in mind that late in the winter the State Committee of Defense [93] sent groups of Red Army officers and cadre per-

---

[91] For information on these units, see: Rpt, "Notes on Conference by G–2, Army Group 'B'," no date, but after 25 Apr 42. 25124/2; statements by captured parachutists, Mar 42, in *Anl. 125 z. KTB 3, Korueck 584, 17.XII.41. 31.XII.42.* 38998/2; *Meldung 183, 20.III.42.* (doc. 3234) in *N.M.T., op. cit.* (Case 9).; *Chef der Sicherheitspolizei, H. Gr. Mitte, Nr. 1669/42 geh. Anl. 41 z. KTB Ic. 444 Sich. Div. 25.III.–31.XII.42.* 30260/2; *Bericht, 207 Sich. Div., 15.III.42., Anl. 67 z. KTB H. Geb. Nord.* 18320/6; *Anl. Ia, z. Tgb. Ic, 213 Sich. Div., 24.IV.42., 27358/4; Anl. 52 z. Tgb., Ic, Korueck 584, Ic, 3.II.42., Anl. z. KTB 3, Korueck 584.* 38998/2.
[92] Captured Soviet orders in *KTB, Ic, H. Gp Nord, 15.IX.41.–2.I.43.* 75131/93.
[93] This was the agency set up within the Central Committee of the Communist Party in Jul 41 to direct all the defenses of the nation; military, political and civilian. Its American counterpart today would be the National Security Council.

sonnel into the German rear to reorganize the partisan groups into more uniform military forces and raise the level of their leadership so as to enhance their value as tactical units.[94] At the same time they were to set up a practicable chain of liaison and command whereby partisan operations might be effectively controlled and tied in with the over-all strategy of the Russian armed forces.

As a result, before the end of spring, three distinct types of irregular units emerged: partisan brigades organized along strict military lines and commanded and staffed by Regular Army personnel; units composed exclusively of irregulars including commanders and staffs; and home guard detachments or "self-protection leagues."

The hard core of the brigades was made up of the Red Army enlisted cadres with the rank and file composed of troops that had been cut off in the German encirclements of the previous summer and fall, irregulars selected from existing partisan bands, and picked males of draft age who volunteered or were forcibly recruited locally. Each brigade had a total strength of 1,000 to 1,500 men, formed into battalions, companies, platoons, and squads. The brigades of a particular geographical area were loosely assigned for tactical control to a higher divisional staff operational group, commanded by a Red Army general, who coordinated their actions, maintained liaison with the assault armies opposite the German units in whose rear they operated, and served as sort of an inspector-general for the Central Staff.[95] Political control of individual units paralleled that of Red Army organizations of comparable size.

The units composed exclusively of irregulars were integrated into groups similar to the brigade—and later so designated—numbering as many as 1,500 men. The strength of the individual units comprising these varied from 30 to 300 men depending on the personality and leadership qualities of their commanders. Commissars sent from the Soviet rear exercised political control. The personnel were given some training and for the most part were adequately armed.

The normal missions of both the brigades and groups were sabotage, raids on German installations and convoys, attacks on state and collective farms, and the like. In addition, both were expected to operate as reconnaissance and intelligence organs for the Red Army. Each or-

---

[94] Unless otherwise noted, the material in this section is taken from: *Bericht ueber Unternehmen Vogelsang der 339 ID, Beilage zum KTB Pz AOK 2, Bericht Nr. 1505/42 g.*, 28499/58. The specific reorganization described below was that effected in the forest area about Bryansk in the rear of the *Second Panzer Army* of *Army Group Center.* However, there is excellent reason to believe that the same reorganization took place in other portions of the rear. See: *Bericht, Ic, Korueck 584. 22.VI.43., Anl. 158 z. KTB 3, Korueck 584.* 38998/2; "Report on the Effects of the Partisan Situation," *Anl. 52 z. KTB, Wirtschaftsinspektion Mitte, 1.IV.– 30.VI.42.* Wi/ID 2.53.

[95] See: *Bericht, Ic. Korueck 584, 22.VI.42., Anl. 1582, KTB 3, Korueck 584,* 38998/2; *Bericht 5, Ic, AOK 2, 15.IV.42., Anl. 362 z. KTB, AOK 2.* 23617/62.

ganization was assigned a Red Army intelligence section and a special unit of the counterintelligence agency OONKVD.[96]

The brigades and groups were normally designated by the names of Russian heroes past or present or by the geographical area in which they operated. The lower echelon units were generally known by the names of their respective commanders.

The home guard units were formed one for each village in partisan dominated areas, with all men, youths, and women liable for service. Through these the Soviets hoped to instigate popular armed risings.

It was during this same general period that Voroshilov was relieved as chief of the Central Staff and replaced by P. K. Ponomarenko, a high-ranking Communist Party official who prior to the war had been chairman of the Council of Ministers of the White Russian SSR.[97] Just what was behind this change of personalities is not clear. It appears to have been a measure designed to place the partisan movement under more rigid party—as opposed to Red Army—control, for at very nearly the same time the Central Committee of the Communist Party in Moscow was launching an all-out effort to reestablish the Communist Party in the German occupied areas, and in any series of steps taken to reassert Communist domination in the enemy rear prior to the return of the Red Army the bands would be a potent factor provided they could be adequately controlled.[98]

The Bands and Soviet Strategy

With these concurrent military and political moves, Soviet strategy with regard to the German rear began to take form. One principle overshadowed all others: the Communist regime was going to return. The bands were to lend tactical aid to the Red Army as fighting units; they were to gather information of long-range and immediate tactical value, continually attack the German lines of communication, breaking rails, blowing bridges, and raiding outposts, all in cooperation with the offensive or defensive moves of the regular units; they were to prevent enemy exploitation of the occupied territories through raids on economic installations and personnel and through a general terror campaign waged among the natives. The party agitators were to expand the party in the rear and prepare a Communist administration to take con-

---

[96] NKVD Document, *op. cit.*, pp. 7, 65, 66. This data was found in the instruction notes of a commissar of a brigade. The intelligence role of the bands was heavily emphasized in the partisan schools.

[97] *Ibid.*, p. 65. The exact date of Ponomarenko's assumption of command is unknown, but most sources, including WDGS, G–2, place it generally around 1 Aug 42.

[98] *Nachrichten ueber Bandenkrieg, Nr. 4, 10.IX.43., OKH/Fde. H. Ost. H 3/738.* This "News of Partisan Warfare" was a periodic summary of all available information concerning the partisan movement compiled and distributed down to division level and to the security commands by *Foreign Armies East.* As such, it constituted a digest of the best information available to the German command at the time.

trol of the natives the minute the Germans were driven out or even before, if circumstances permitted. Together with the bands they were to work to drive a wedge between the people and the enemy, undermine the enemy's control, and shorten his stay on Russian soil.[99]

Morale and Discipline in the Bands

Despite the progress made toward improving the organization of the bands and raising the quality of their leadership and the level of their operational efficiency, the unit commanders found themselves continually hampered by the same problems of morale and discipline inherent in any quasi-military force. Morale and discipline remained fairly good among the former Red Army personnel, who had with considerable reason come to fear the German prisoner of war camps, the convinced Communists, and those who had been with the bands any length of time. But with the less stable elements, the lazy, lawless individuals who can be found in any country and who join only for the opportunity to plunder, and particularly with those drafted from the rural areas, the desertion rate ran high, especially if an action was prolonged. German interrogation of such deserters indicated that many more would desert if they knew they would not be executed as guerrillas.[100]

The problem of morale was recognized in Moscow and received careful attention there. A propaganda campaign was projected with the objective of creating an *esprit de corps* in the bands and a definite sense of "belonging" to the national defense effort. The expression "partisan" was dropped from official usage and the expression "soldier of the Red Army in the rear of the enemy" substituted. Prior to the reorganization several of the larger bands were designated as armies "in the Rear of the Enemy."[101] Special decorations were authorized for outstanding partisan work.[102] Locally published propaganda newspapers extolling the exploits of outstanding irregulars were issued by political officers for consumption within the units, and the Moscow and Leningrad editions of *Pravda* were regularly received by air in many partisan-controlled areas.[103]

The better organized bands demonstrated a fair degree of combat discipline. They consistently refused to allow themselves to be trapped

[99] *Ibid.*
[100] *Bericht ueber Unternehmen Vogelsang der 339 ID, Beilage zum KTB Pz AOK 2, Bericht Nr. 1505/42 g., 28499/58.: Tgb., Ic. 221 Inf. Div., 22.III.–17.VI.42.* 22639; *Bericht, Ic. Korueck 584, 22.VI.42., Anl. 158 z. KTB 3, Korueck 584.* 38998/2.
[101] *Nachrichten ueber Bandenkrieg, Nr. 1, 3.V.43., OKH/Fde. H. Ost.* 3/738; *Bericht 4, Ic, AOK 2, 15.IV.42., Anl. 362 z. KTB, AOK 2, Band 4.* 23617/62.
[102] *Bericht 4, Ic, AOK 2, 15.IV.42., Anl. 362 z. KTB, AOK 2, Band 4.* 23617/62; "Top Leadership in the Soviet Ground Forces," Intelligence Research Project No. 6549, 24 Jul 51. G–2 Library.
[103] *Bericht, Ic, Korueck 584, 22.VI.42., Anl. 1582. KTB 3. Korueck 584.* 38998/2; *Bericht. Ia. H. Geb. Sued, 31.XII.41.–V.42.* 22571/17.

into a standup fight against superior forces, and when enemy pressure grew too strong they carried out their withdrawals in an orderly manner and generally according to preset plans, fighting their delaying and covering actions skillfully and tenaciously.[104]

Armament and Supply

The majority of the bands were set up under exceedingly loose tables of organization, and even after the reorganization the structure of the Red Army-led brigades and the irregular groups exhibited considerable variation. There were no tables of equipment as such. Each unit furnished its own basic needs from stock piles left by the Red Army in its 1941 retreat and from captured German materiel. These were basic weapons, rifles, machine guns, mortars, and occasional artillery pieces, and a few vehicles. The more specialized items such as automatic weapons, signal equipment, and a good portion of the ammunition other than that for small arms, were supplied by air from the Soviet rear. By the summer of 1942 all the better organized bands appear to have been well armed and supplied with ammunition.[105] Their materiel included light mortars, light and heavy machine guns, automatic rifles, bazookas, machine pistols, and grenades.[106]

Air supply seemed to have been fairly steady in the larger partisan-dominated areas. There were at least three operative air strips in the Lake Polisto sector behind the *Sixteenth Army* to which ammunition and specialized items were flown and from which casualties were evacuated on the return trip.[107] The bands in the Bryansk area were similarly supplied, and several of the brigades there operated their own planes.[108]

Some of the bands had Russian 76-mm guns and 45-mm antitank guns; a few had motor vehicles, and several operated reconnaissance cars, tanks, and even tank-recovery vehicles.[109] Whether they were able to maintain these vehicles in operating condition and supply them

---

[104] *Bericht ueber Unternehmen Vogelsang, der 339 ID, Beilage zum KTB Pz AOK 2, Bericht Nr. 1505/42 g.* 28499/58.

[105] Nearly all reports listing stocks captured from the partisans bear this out; there is no indication in the records that there were any such shortages as existed in 1941. See: *Bericht ueber Unternehmen Vogelsang der 339 ID, Beilage zum KTB Pz AOK 2, Bericht Nr. 1505/42 g.* 28499/58; *Bericht, Kdr., 703 Wach Bn., 7.VI.42., Band 2, Juni 42, Anl. I–III z. KTB Bfh, H. Geb. "B", 1.VI.–30.VI.42.* 25124/2.

[106] *Bericht, Ic, Korueck 584, 22.VI.42., Anl. 1582. KTB 3, Korueck 584.* 38998/2.

[107] *Ibid.*

[108] Five planes were captured from the partisans in Operation *VOGELSANG.* See: *Bericht ueber Unternehmen Vogelsang der 339 ID, Beilage zum KTB Pz AOK 2, Bericht Nr. 1505/42 g.* 28499/58.

[109] *Bericht ueber Unternehmen Vogelsang der 339 ID, Beilage zum KTB Pz AOK 2, Bericht Nr. 1505/42 g.* 28499/58; *Bericht, Kdr., 703 Wach Bn., 7.VI.42., Band 2, Juni 42, Anl. I–III z. KTB Bfh, H. Geb. "B", 1.VII.–30.VI.42.* 25124/2; *Bericht, Ic, Korueck 584, 22.VI.42., Bericht, Ic, Korueck 584, 22.VI.42., Anl. 582, KTB 3, Korueck 584.* 38998/2.

with fuel is unknown, but it appears doubtful. Several operated their own railroad trains.[110]

Land mines appeared to be in good supply in many of the bands, and were used in defensive positions around base camps and offensively along the roads and rail lines.[111]

As regards food, only such items as sugar, salt, coffee, and the like were brought in by air. The basic staples came from dumps left by the Red Army and raids upon German supply columns and outposts, or were requisitioned from the natives. In some areas herds of cattle were collected and held as a reserve for winter.[112]

The German Manpower Shortage, Spring, 1942

During the winter and spring of 1941–42 the German manpower situation in the East grew progressively worse. For the period of the campaign to 6 November 1941, the Army had lost 686,108 men in killed, wounded, and missing, and for the period 1 November 1941 to 1 April 1942, an additional 900,000 from all causes, or a total of 1,586,-108.[113] Even with returnees from hospitals OKH estimated that on 1 May the eastern army would be 625,000 men short.[114]

This shortage was even more obvious in the rear, since such a condition in the line armies virtually precluded the return of the security units pulled forward for duty at the front at the height of the Soviet counteroffensive. *Army Groups North* and *Center* had been particularly hard hit in this respect. In the northern sector, of 34 battalions originally assigned to the security command there for anti-partisan work, all but 4 had been pulled into the front lines, with the result that no forces were available for offensive operations against the bands and only native Baltic units for rail line guard and patrol.[115] Whereas previously all bridges behind the *Sixteenth Army* had been guarded, the security command there became so short of men that guard details were pulled off all spans less than 45 feet long, and 14 bridges totaling more than 500 yards, on which sentries were maintained, were covered with a total armament

---

[110] *Bericht, Bfh, H. Geb. "B", Nr. 195/42, 1. VI.–30.VI.42., Anl. z. KTB H. Geb. "B".* 25124/1. *Bericht ueber Unternehmen Vogelsang der 339 ID, Beilage zum KTB Pz AOK 2, Bericht Nr. 1505/42 g.,* 28499/58.

[111] *Bericht ueber Unternehmen Vogelsang der 339 ID, Beilage zum KTB Pz AOK 2, Bericht Nr. 1505/42 g.* 28499/58; *Bericht, Ic, Korueck 584, 22.VI.42., Bericht, Ic, Korueck 584, 22.VI.42., Anl. 1582. KTB 3, Korueck 584.* 38998/2.

[112] *Bericht, Ic, AOK 16, 4.VIII.42., KTB, H. Gr. Nord.* 75128/13; *Bericht, AOK 16, 13.IX.42., KTB, H. Gr. Nord.* 75128/14.

[113] "Halder's Journal," *op. cit.,* VII, p. 160; "A Study of the Employment of German Manpower, 1933–1945," app. 3. CRS, TAG.

[114] *Ibid.*

[115] *Lagebericht, Ic, Feb 42, Anl. 37 z. KTB, H. Geb. Nord. 1.I.–31.III.42.* 18320/6; *Lagebericht, Korueck 584, 22.I.42., Anl. 39 z. KTB 3, Korueck 584, 17.XII.41.–31.XII.42.* 38998/2.

of but 14 light machine guns.[116]   The situation was equally pinching behind *Army Group Center*.[117]

The few Baltic and Ukrainian volunteer battalions organized during the previous fall having proved reliable, OKH in January, as a partial solution to this security troop shortage, had recommended that additional native units be enlisted from among anti-Soviet inhabitants and reliable former prisoners of war.[118]   An enlistment campaign had then been initiated and a number of units of 100 to 150 men each, "Centuries" (*Hundertschaften*), were formed from among Baltic, Ukrainian, Cossack, and Tartar natives, many of whom had previously indicated their desire to enlist.[119]   They were cadred from experienced military police battalions and armed with captured Russian materiel. After training and some security work under close supervision, they were committed as rail line patrols and bridge guards, but not in areas where partisan pressure was heavy.[120]

Despite the fact that Berlin was fully aware of the state of affairs in the rear areas,[121] Hitler on 10 February ordered that no further native combat units were to be organized by the Army for antipartisan work, and that those already formed were not to be committed in active roles. He further directed that the ultimate control of the native units, even in the army group rear areas, was to lie with the higher SS and police chief (who was Himmler's representative) in each army group, and not with the Army Security Commands.[122]   This prohibition, however, did not apply to the enlistment of local civilians in police units in the *Reichskommissariate* where they would be under Himmler's direct control.[123]

OKH appealed this decision but was turned down, although combat and security units comprising Tartars, Caucasians, Georgians, Armenians, and Turkestani were specifically excepted from the prohibition, and units already enlisted and in service were allowed to continue.[124]

---

[116] *Befehl 19, Korueck 584, 4.II.42., Anl. 55 z. KTB 3, Korueck 584, 17.XII.41.–31.XII.42.* 38998/2; *Korueck 584 to Sixteenth Army*, 31 Jan 42, in *Anl. 49, z. KTB 3, Korueck 584, 17.XII.41.–31.XII.42.* 38998/2.

[117] *Bericht, H. Gr. Mitte, Nr. 1430/42 geh., 24.II.42., Anl. z. KTB, Ia, Pz AOK 3.* 20736/6.

[118] *OKH/Gen.St.d.H./Org. Abt., Nr. 213/42 geh., 9.I.42.* in *KTB, H. Gr. Nord.* 75131/94.

[119] *Bericht, Ic, 213 Sich. Div., 14.XI.41,* in *KTB, 213 Sich. Div.* 14424/4; *OKW/WFSt/Qu (II), Nr. 00738/42, 23.II.42.* in *KTB, H. Gr. Nord.* 75131/94; (doc. 628), prosecution document book in *N.M.T., op. cit.* (Case 9).

[120] *Korueck 584 to Sixteenth Army*, 8 Mar 42, in *Anl. 89 z. KTB 3, Korueck 584, 17.XII.41.–31.XII.42,* 38998/2.

[121] *The Goebbels Diaries*, ed. Louis P. Lochner (New York, 1948), p. 195.

[122] *OKH/Gen.St.d.H./Gen.Qu/Org. Abt. (II), Nr. 736/42 in KTB, H. Gr. Nord.* 75131/94.

[123] *OKW/WFSt/Qu (II), Nr. 00738/42, 23.II.42.* in *KTB, H. Gr. Nord.* 75131/94.

[124] *OKH/Gen.St.d.H./Gen.Qu/Org. Abt. (II), Nr. 1349/42 g. Kdos., 24.III.42.* in *KTB, H. Gr. Nord.* 75131/94.

The army groups, needing security troops badly, requested Himmler through OKH to release to them those native units under SS control in the *Reichskommissariate*, but they were rebuked.[125] Thus frustrated in its attempt to solve the manpower problem locally, OKH transferred two Hungarian security brigades from the southern sector to *Army Group Center Rear Area*. This move did little to restore matters, however, for some 30 percent of the personnel were untrained Carpatho-Ukrainians and the remainder second-rate reserves, the units were poorly equipped, and their indiscriminate looting and sharp repressive measures quickly turned the natives against them.[126] SS and SD units venturing into the rear areas from the *Reichskommissariate* were sometimes unceremoniously pressed into the fight; the forced enlistment of several SD intelligence and reconnaissance teams brought a sharp reaction from Himmler's headquarters.[127] Later several of the rear area commanders even went to the extreme of taking all draft age Germans working as civilians in administrative capacities in the *Reichskommissariat* and assigning them to alert forces or as leaders of native units.[128] As a further source of manpower *Army Group North* proposed that field training divisions of the *Replacement Army* be transferred from the Zone of the Interior to the east where they might complete their training in more realistic surroundings and at the same time release security and police forces from static employment for commitment against the bands.[129]

Even in the face of Hitler's pronouncement against the use of indigenous units, the rear area commanders continued to throw all available troops, native and German, into the fight against the bands. The performance of some of the "Centuries," especially Finnish, Estonian, and Russian, was generally good initially, but poor tactical employment and logistical support on the part of the security commands gradually began to impair their efficiency. Clothing, especially shoes, deteriorated during the bitter winter weather and was not replaced, and this combined with the lack of food other than the standard German emergency ration and the equipment necessary for preparing hot meals did much to lower their morale and operational value. Despite the fact that somewhat the same conditions were prevalent in all Wehrmacht units at the time, the indigenous troops felt forgotten and neglected and quickly tended to

---

[125] *OKH to Army Group North*, 23 Apr 42, in *KTB, H. Gr. Nord, 1.IV.–30.IV.42.* 75128/9.

[126] *Bericht 3, AOK 2, Ic, 30.III.42., Anl 331 z. KTB AOK 2, Ic, Band IV, 1.IV.–30.IV.42.* 23617/62.

[127] Entry for 26 May 42, in *KTB, 207 Sich. Div., 1.I.–31.XII.42.* 33300/1.

[128] *Bericht, H. Geb. Nord, 3.VIII.42.,* in *KTB, H. Gr. Nord, 1.VIII.–31.VIII.42., 3060.* 75128/13.

[129] *Army Group North to OKH*, 10 May 42, in *KTB, H. Gr. Nord. 1.V.–30.V.42,* p. 1998. 75128/10.

lose any sense of obligation they may have felt toward the German command.[130] Units were committed piecemeal and with inadequate training; nor was there provision made for casualty replacement. Some battalion commanders were without transportation of any sort, even animal, and frequently were out of contact with elements of their commands for long periods of time. There was no set chain of command, units being subordinated to any higher echelon in a hodge-podge fashion. Liaison with higher headquarters was generally inadequate.[131]

Fundamentally, the fault lay in the basic planning for the security of the occupied territories and in the breakdown of the whole Wehrmacht supply system during the winter. But the feeling ran through the rear area commands that since "Centuries" were ultimately under the command of the higher SS and police chiefs and might be pulled from under Wehrmacht jurisdiction at any time without notice, despite the fact that the Army had enlisted, equipped and trained them, they should be placed low on the logistical priority list.[132]

When the advent of the spring muddy period brought a slackening of irregular pressure, several of the *Koruecks* pulled their native units out for reorganization and short courses of intensive training. They relieved many unqualified officers and noncommissioned officers and made efforts to improve conditions of supply, pay and allowances.[133] This practice was not uniform throughout all the rear areas.

Late in the spring another factor entered the picture threatening to further weaken the security commands. Most of the native units had been mustered in on a short-term basis, and considering the generally low state of their morals it was feared they would quickly disintegrate when individual terms of service expired.[134] The Germans solved this problem, however, by summarily extending the enlistments for the duration of the war and making the personnel subject to the Articles of War and thus liable to death for desertion.[135]

---

[130] Tlg, CO, *Lith Security Bn* at Kovno, to CG, *Korueck 584*, 10 Mar 42, in *Anl. 92 z. KTB, Korueck 584, 17.XII.41.–31.XII.42.* 38998/2.

[131] Rpt on condition of the Lithuanian Security Bns, 3 May 42, in *Anl. 126 z. KTB 3, Korueck 584.* 38998/2; rpt of foreign units, 7 May 42, in *Anl. 825 z. KTB 1, Korueck 583.* 34735/2.

[132] *Ibid.*

[133] Rpt on the condition of the Lithuanian Security Bns, 3 May 42, in *Anl. 126 z. KTB 3, Korueck 584.* 38998/2.

[134] Ltr, CO, *Field Admin HQ 197*, to *Army Group South Rear Area*, 10 Jul 42, in *KTB, H. Geb. "B".* 25124/8; ltr, No. 465/42, *Army Group North Rear Area* to *Army Group North*, 15 Jun 42, in *KTB, H. Gr Nord.* 75131/94.

[135] *Tgb., Ic, 339 Inf. Div., 16.VIII.–21.VIII.42., Anl. 1 z. KTB 8, 339 Inf. Div., 26.VII.–31.XII.42.* 29087/20; *AOK 9, Nr. 4324/42, 26.IX.42., Landeseigene Verbende, Anlagenband IV, Armee Befehle und Verfuegungen, AOK 9, 1.IX.–7.X.42.* 26791/8.

About this time help came from another source. In the fall of 1941, as the Red Army fell back before the German October offensive, a violently anti-Communist Russian named Voskoboinikov had gathered a sizable group of anti-Soviet natives under his command and taken over control of a portion of the forest south of Bryansk. When the partisans began to concentrate in the region, Voskoboinikov came to the attention of Moscow, and Soviet agents were parachuted in who assassinated him. The leadership of the group then fell to Bronislav Kaminski, a Russian engineer of Polish extraction who had fallen from grace prior to the war and served a penal sentence in Siberia.[136] Kaminski, taking the lead from his predecessor, centered his aspirations on the overthrow of the Stalin regime and the founding of a new Russia under a Russian National Socialist Party in which there would be no collectives and the church would be free of political pressure.[137]

The first active German contact with the Kaminski organization was in January 1942 when railway repair troops, who were under constant pressure from the partisans, encountered a heavily armed group of Russians wearing white arm bands with a St. George's cross on them. A bitter enemy of the Red Army, Kaminski since assuming command had built an organization of some 1,400 well-armed men, and was waging a constant war against the partisans in his area. He controlled much of the territory south of Bryansk and during this first winter of the war aided the Germans in keeping the rail lines throughout the area operational.[138]

By the summer of 1942 his command had grown to a strength of more than 9,000 men, well-armed, with good transport, and under strict discipline. Although very jealous of his sovereign rights, he willingly cooperated with the German authorities in their fight with the bands. In the face of the growing partisan movement the Germans saw the obvious advantages to be gained from fostering Kaminski, and in July made him chief mayor (*Oberbuergermeister*) of the Autonomous Administration Lokot, an extensive jurisdiction comprising eight *rayons*, and brigade commander of the militia.[139]

---

[136] MS #P-123, "National Instinct and Governmental Institutions under German Occupation in Western Russia" (Hist Div, EUCOM), p. 34. OCMH, Foreign Studies Br; rpt, Dr. Guenzel, Ch. Adm Council, Mil Gov Sec, *Army Group Center*, on *Autonomous Administration Lokot*, 25 May 43. Filed in Rosenberg Collection. EAP 99/158.
[137] *Bericht 5, Ic, AOK 2, 15.IV.42., Anl. 362 z. KTB, Band IV, AOK 2*. 23617/62.
[138] *Ibid.*
[139] Guenzel, report, *op. cit.*; entry for 24 Aug 42, in *KTB 2, Teil 4, Pz AOK 2, 1.VII.–30.IX.42*. 28499/4.

The Rear Areas and the 1942 Offensive

German Preparation in the Rear [140]

The German Army's plan for the 1942 campaign stated that as a necessary prelude to the attack the entire length of the line in the east was to be re-formed and straightened in a number of limited offensives and the rear area mopped up immediately after the close of the muddy season.[141]

In the southern sector the only Soviet penetration during the winter had been contained and later successfully pinched off, but further to the north the situation was confused and far from bright. Hitler's rigid tactics had for the most part succeeded in denying the Soviets any gains of a strategic nature, but at the same time had opened the German rear to a number of deep penetrations and left the Wehrmacht with a difficult mop-up job.

Direct rail and road communication between *Army Group North* and *Army Group Center* had been completely severed and a deep wedge driven between the two. *Army Group North's* right flank, held by the *II* and *X Corps*, had been rolled up tight against Lake Ilmen, and the *II Corps* cut off. To the rear of these corps Red Army units and mixed groups of Red Army personnel and partisans in large part dominated the situation. In the middle of January a task force of the *XXXIX Corps* (*mot*) had opened a drive from the southwest to relieve the Kholm hedgehog on the *Rollbahn Nord* and reestablish control over the highway. To complement this attack, in February two other task forces (later replaced by the *Luftwaffe Division Meindl*) had attacked southward from the line of the Dno-Staraya-Russa railroad to clear the rear of the beleagured *II Corps* and close the breach in the *Sixteenth Army's* line. Kholm was relieved by 5 May and by 30 June the *Luftwaffe Division Meindl* had reestablished control of a sort along the *Rollbahn Nord*, though with a discontinuous line, while a *Landesschuetzen* regiment garrisoned the area just to the west. Still further to the west, the north-south Dno-Novosokolniki rail line, although under nominal German control remained open to interdiction along its entire length.

The situation in the rear of *Army Group Center* was hardly less difficult. Von Kluge's left flank had been rolled back on the *Ninth Army*, and several Soviet units had advanced from the north dangerously close to army group headquarters at Smolensk. At the time of the opening of the Caucasus offensive this portion of the line had not been wholly straightened, and direct communication with *Army Group North*, though reestablished, remained exceedingly tenuous.

---

[140] Unless otherwise stated, the material in this section is taken from *Lagen Ost. 10.I.–10.VII.42.*

[141] Directive No. 41, *OKW/WFSt Nr. 55616/42 g. K. Chefs., 5.V.42.*, in "Fuehrer Directives," *op. cit.*

As late as 1 April Belov with a strong mixed regular-irregular group still lay between the German front and Smolensk, threatening the Smolensk-Vyazma rail line from his base at Dorogobuzh. With the undermanned German security units concentrated in small perimeters along the railroads and highways, partisan units roamed the rear freely as far west as Borissov.

The danger posed by Belov's force was clear and as soon as the weather permitted, elements of two corps, aided by several security units, launched a concerted attack to clear it from the *Fourth Army* rear and secure communications there. Gradually, but with considerable difficulty, they drove Belov from his base, but despite an overwhelming superiority of numbers, including armor, they were unable to prevent his slipping eastward through the Soviet lines near Kirov with a good portion of his command.[142]

As a corollary operation, on 5 June the army group launched a large-scale antipartisan operation, code-named *VOGELSANG,* in the area about Bryansk to clear the forests there of partisans and scattered Red Army units and to secure the rail lines and highways supplying the *Second Panzer Army* and linking the central sector with the southern armies.[143] The action was concluded on schedule with some 1,200 irregulars counted dead, 500 captured, and large quantities of supplies and materiel taken. Despite the careful manner in which the action was planned and carried out, however, the bulk of the partisans withdrew from the area to the west in an orderly manner and according to a previously formulated plan, leaving specially designated personnel behind to reorganize the region once the Germans had moved through. At no point were any large groups brought to bay.[144]

Taken as a whole, these efforts to bring the rear area under control fell somewhat short of the mark. They did clear the *Rollbahn Nord* and drive the bands in the immediate rear of the *Sixteenth Army* to the west, eliminate the threat of the Belov group, and temporarily break up the partisan concentrations in the Bryansk forest area. But they failed to even approach a permanent solution. In combing out these areas the Germans scattered a number of bands, but nowhere were they able to trap and annihilate any sizable groups. Under pressure, the partisans merely dispersed, slipped through the attacking lines, and reassembled elsewhere. As a result, all during the spring months, and even while the German clearing actions were in progress, they continued their activity.

---

[142] See: "Halder's Journal," *op cit.,* VII, pp. 316–28; *Anl. 19, 75, 76, z. Tgb Ic, 221 Sich. Div., 22.III.–17.VI.42.* 22639/6.

[143] *Bericht ueber Unternehmen Vogelsang der 339 Inf. Div., Nr. 1505 11.VII.42., Anl. z. KTB Pz AOK 2.* 28499/58.

[144] *Ibid.*

Passive Measures

These limited offensives represented the maximum direct pressure the Germans could bring to bear on the bands at the time. Beyond this, in a purely military sense, they could only garrison or outpost certain selected localities, guard their installations, and screen their primary supply lines against major interruptions, leaving the initiative with the enemy. They well knew that such measures alone could never crush the movement or even contain it. Yet they knew equally well that it had to be contained before it grew into a really open menace, and that the support of the people was the key to the problem.

The Russian winter successes had done much to destroy the confidence of the population in the Germans. Unprotected all winter from the terror tactics of the partisans and still exposed to their pressure at the end of the muddy season, the natives had begun to see that their "liberators" too often could not control the vast areas they had overrun. And taking the line of least resistance they began to support the bands more and more, sometimes under duress, though more often voluntarily.[145]

Recognizing this shift of popular sentiment for the hazard it was and realizing that Germany was in danger of losing completely the only popular support it had ever enjoyed in any country invaded to date, the Army, in conjunction with the antipartisan drives, attempted to counter the threat by modifying its policy of reprisals and collective punitive actions. These had heretofore been standard practice as retaliation for raids by the bands and to prevent the natives from aiding them. Experience had shown, however, that such measures had not had the desired effect and in many cases had driven sizable blocks of the people into active cooperation with the bands. At the same time they had fed raw material into the Soviet propaganda machine.[146] Accordingly, OKH directed that retaliatory measures be taken only when absolutely necessary to maintain German authority, and only after the reasons for such were carefully explained to the people.[147]

Experience gained during subsequent antipartisan offensives not only bore out the soundness of this change of policy but also indicated additional measures which might further undermine the strength of the bands. Captured documents and interrogations of partisan prisoners conclusively demonstrated that while reprisals as a means of weaning

---

[145] *Monatsbericht, Juni 42, 201 Sich. Div., Anl. z. KTB, Ia, 201 Sich. Div., 1.IV.–31.XII.42.*, 29196/2; *Army Group North* to *Army Group North Rear Area*, 19 Jun 42, in *KTB, H. Gr Nord, 1.VI.–30.VI.42.* 75128/11.

[146] Entry for 11 Aug 42 in *KTB, H. Gr Nord*, p. 3164. 75128/13; evaluation rpt, *Corps Rear Area 447*, in *Evakuierungen z. KTB 2, Pz AOK 2, 23.V.–5.IX.42.* 28499/72; *OKH/Gen. St. d. H./Gen. Qu. Nr. 3033/42, 7.V.42., Anl. z. KTB, Ia, H. Geb. B, 1.VI.–30.VI.42.* 25124/1.

[147] *Ibid.; OKH/Gen. St. d. H./Gen. Qu. Nr. 3033/42, 7.V.42., Anl. z. KTB, Ia, H. Geb. B, 1.VI.–30.VI.42.* 25124/1.

the people away from the bands, and thus weakening the support of the latter, were generally ineffective, the evacuation of all natives from partisan-infested areas and the destruction of all farms, villages, and buildings in the areas following the evacuations did much to slow up the growth of the movement and sap its strength.[148]

Several thousand civilians had been evacuated from the Bryansk forests during the antipartisan operations in May and June, and the practice was continued during the summer in areas which could not be properly supervised.[149]

Several other passive measures were considered. The *Second Panzer Army* strongly recommended that a 6 mile wide strip immediately behind the front be completely cleared of all but Wehrmacht personnel to prevent natives from passing information on German dispositions to the bands for transmission to the Soviet rear.[150] Somewhat later the same unit directed that all teenage boys in partisan-endangered areas be conscripted into a "Reconstruction Service" where they might be reeducated along National Socialist lines and trained as cadres for native units, lest they be drawn into the partisan units.[151]

Partisan Reaction to the Offensive

The Soviets had considerable advance notice concerning the German 1942 offensive. The direction of the attack and some idea of the weight, if not the actual timing, was known to them as early as the middle of May.[152] To what extent they planned to use the partisans to help counter the thrust is unknown, but during the latter part of May a number of bands, several under orders to avoid a stand-up fight to conserve their strength for other operations, were noted moving into the rear of *Army Group B* from the Bryansk forest area and the Pripyat Marshes.[153] During the same period the few active bands in the Ukraine began to step up their activity against the rail lines there, especially the east-west double-tracked line from Kiev to Kursk.[154]

---

[148] Entry for 11 Aug 42, *KTB, H. Gr. Nord*, p. 3164. 75128/13; *Bericht ueber Unternehmen Vogelsang der 339 ID, Beilage zum KTB Pz AOK 2, Bericht Nr. 1505/42 g.*, 28499/58.

[149] *Pz AOK 2, Ia, Nr. 1013/42 geh., 9.VI.42., Anl. z. KTB 2, Pz AOK 2, 23.V.– 5.IX.42.* 28499/72; *Bericht, 15.X.42., Pz AOK 2, Anl. z. KTB 2, Teil 5, Ia, Pz AOK 2, 1.X.–31.XII.42.* 28499/5.

[150] Note, CofS, *Second Panzer Army*, to *Army Group Center*, 5 Sep 42. No. 02640/42 in *Anl. z. KTB 2, Pz AOK 2, 23.V.–5.IX.42.* 28499/72.

[151] Entry for 3 Nov 42, in *KTB 2, Teil 5, Pz AOK 2, 1.X.–31.XII.42.* 28499/5.

[152] See: DA Pamphlet 20–261a, *The German Campaign in Russia, op. cit.*, ch. 9.

[153] *Bericht ueber Unternehmen Vogelsang der 339 ID, Beilage zum KTB Pz AOK 2, Bericht Nr. 1505/42 g.*, 28499/58. *Lagebericht, Hoeherer SS und Polizeifuehrer, Ukraine, 27.XII.42.* 51/10; *Bericht, H. Geb. B. Nr. 195/42, Anl. z. KTB H. Geb. B, 1–30.VI.42.* 25124/1.

[154] *Bericht, H. Geb. B. Nr. 195/42, Anl. z. KTB H. Geb. B. 1–30.VI.42.,* 25124/1.

Similarly in the northern sector the partisans intensified their raiding. During the first 20 days of June attacks of all kinds, on small Wehrmacht units, on rail and highway bridges, and military installations, rose almost 40 percent over May.[155] Behind the *Sixteenth Army* alone between 1 May and 31 July the partisans blew 30 bridges, broke rails in 84 places, and damaged or destroyed 20 locomotives and 113 railroad cars, causing a total of 1,129 hours interruption in service.[156]

Behind *Army Group Center* the situation was similar, attempts to blow the rail lines rising more than 100 percent from May to the end of July.[157]

Still, despite these attempts to embarrass them, the Germans moved to the Volga and the foothills of the Caucasus without undue interference with their supply. It is possible that Operation *VOGELSANG* caught a number of southward-bound bands in transit and scattered them or robbed them of much of their striking power. Certainly the partisans found the lack of cover in the steppes a serious handicap, for it was not until late August that there was any report of sabotage on the lines of communication there.[158] Indeed, by the first week in September they were reported moving back north again toward their Bryansk stronghold without having touched the east-west Kiev-Kursk line which was the primary logistical trunk feeding the attack.[159] During the same period there were no reports of interference by bands which had been identified in the Konotop area east of Kiev.

As for the demolitions in the northern and central sectors, they had no visible effect on the main course of events. The figures themselves are misleading. The nearly 40 percent increase in partisan attacks in the northern sector for the first 20 days in June, it must be remembered, included attacks of all kinds, large and small, successful and unsuccessful and of the rail damage there, 75 percent occurred on the north-south Dno-Novosokolniki line which although important was never a primary supply link.[160] Similarly, in the *Army Group Center* rear where rail demolitions rose more than 100 percent in three months the actual count was 71 charges successfully detonated on the lines with varying effect as against 31 unsuccessful attempts in May and 145 successful

---

[155] CG, *Army Group North Rear Area,* to *Army Group North,* 24 June 42, in *KTB H. Gr. Nord.* 75128/11.

[156] *Anlagenband W–VI, Partisanen-Sonderakten, 1.VIII.–31.VIII.42., Teil 5 z., KTB 5, AOK 16.* 36588/60.

[157] *Kdr. Gen. der Sicherungstruppen und Bfh. im H. Geb. Mitte, Ia, Br. B. Nr. 2051/43 geh., 9.VII.43., Anl. z. KTB, H. Gr. Mitte, 11.VI.–31.VII.43.* 65002/22.

[158] Entries for 23 Aug 42 and 16 Sep 42 in *KTB 2, Teil 4, Ia, 1.VII.–30.IX.42., Pz AOK 2.* 28499/4.

[159] *Lagebericht, Ia, Pz AOK 2, Nr. 1838/42, 6.IX.42. and 11.XI.42, Anl. z. KTB, Pz AOK 2, 16.VIII.42.–28.II.42.* 37075/90.

[160] *Anlagenband W–VI, Partisanen-Sonderakten, 1.VIII–31.VIII.42., Teil 5 z. KTB 5, AOK 16.* 36588/60.

attempts as against 91 unsuccessful in July,[161] and this against weak opposition. In July the *Second Panzer Army Rear Area,* whose area of responsibility included the Bryansk forest region where a large number of the bands had their bases of operations, reported that it had but 3,763 security troops to protect 855 kilometers of roads and 730 kilometers of rail lines considered operationally important to the Army.[162]

During June and July Romanian units in the Crimea made almost daily reports of partisan action in the peninsula,[163] but there is no evidence that this activity in any way affected the movement of elements of the *Eleventh Army* across the Kerch Straits into the Caucasus.

In other sectors the bands appeared equally unable to affect the tactical situation. On 30 July the Red Army launched a heavy attack on the *Ninth Army* in the central sector which by 4 August had effected wide and deep penetrations. Yet there were no irregular attacks launched in conjunction with it. Similarly, when the *Second Panzer Army* in August launched an attack designed to pinch off the Russian salient in the Suchinichi area, there was no perceptible partisan reaction.[164] In fact, all along the front there was a conspicuous absence of positive interference with communications. On 17 August, 299 trains were unloaded along the entire eastern front, 71 of them troop trains. This was a new record for the campaign in the east.[165]

It was not until later in the fall that the bands behind the southern armies hit the rail lines with anything resembling a coordinated attack. On 13 October a large partisan unit struck the north-south railroad between Bryansk and Dmitryev and virtually destroyed an entire 12 mile section. After they had removed some miles of telephone line, the irregulars simultaneously attacked all guard details along the stretch and blew the tracks at 178 different points, demolishing some 2,400 continuous sections of trackage.[166] No other attacks were made in conjunction with this one, nor was it followed up. Later in October three

---

[161] *Kdr, Gen. der Sicherungstruppen und Bfh. im H. Geb. Mitte, Ia, Nr. 2051/43 geh., 9.VII.43., Anl. z. KTB, H. Gr. Mitte, 11.VI.–31.VII.43.* 65002/22.

[162] Entry for 23 July, *KTB, Ia, Pz AOK 2, Teil 4, 1.VII.–30.IX.42.* 28499/4.

[163] See: Rpts, *Eleventh Army* in *KTB, H. Gr. "A", Band 1, Teil 1, 22.IV.–31.VII. 42.* 75126/1.

[164] Unfortunately, this has to be based on negative evidence. Neither Halder nor Greiner, the custodian of the War Diary in Hitler's headquarters, makes any mention of irregular activity in connection with either the Russian assault in the *Ninth Army* sector or the *Second Panzer Army's* attack, although considerable concern over both these operations was expressed in OKW and OKH. See: "Halder's Journal," *op. cit.,* VII, entries for 30 Jul–18 Aug; and MS C–065a, Helmuth Greiner, "Notes on the Situation Reports and Discussions at Hitler's Headquarters from 12 August 1942 to 17 March 1943" (Hist. Div. EUCOM), p. 4 ff. OCMH, Foreign Studies Br.

[165] Greiner, "Notes on the Situation . . . 12 August 1942 to 17 March 1943," *op. cit.,* p. 21.

[166] Entry for 13 Oct 42 in *KTB 2, Teil 5, Ia, Pz AOK 2, 1.X.–31.XII.42.* 28499/5.

brigades under leaders just returned from Moscow training centers were reported moving south from the Bryansk area to the Ukraine toward a junction with an irregular group which had moved eastward from the southern portion of the Pipyat Marshes.[167] It is likely that this latter concentration was ordered in conjunction with the preparations for the Soviet counterattack at Stalingrad, for after the Red Army had successfully isolated the *Sixth Army* in the city, the Central Staff directed a number of bands in the Ukraine to strike at German installations and communications as far to the rear as the Dnepr River and to make detailed reports on German troop strengths, in an attempt to embarrass German efforts to relieve the Stalingrad garrison.[168] The results of this maneuver are unknown.

In November four partisan brigades estimated at an aggregate strength of 19,000 men were reported in the Bryansk area behind the *Second Panzer Army*.[169] Still, in spite of this strength and despite continued weakness of the security command there they mounted no effective offensive action. The rail lines remained open and demolitions dropped appreciably.[170]

Further to the west in the Vitebsk-Polotsk-Nevel area of White Russia where their strength was on the rise, the partisans demonstrated a similar lack of aggressiveness toward German communications. They did hamper the work of the economic authorities which could not be given adequate protection because of manpower limitations within the security command, and they did much to turn the natives further away from the occupation, but they raided the communication lines only sporadically, and never in a concerted offensive.[171] Raids continued, but in no great volume. Demolitions set off on the rail lines in the entire *Army Group Center Rear Area* numbered 235 for September, 203 for October, 162 for November, and dropped to 147 for December.[172]

---

[167] Entry for 25 Oct 42, in *ibid.; Bericht, Hoeherer SS und Polizeifuehrer, Ukraine, 27.XII.42.* 51/10.

[168] See: Captured Soviet directive, dated 28 Nov 42, in *Anl. z. Bfh. H. Geb. "B", Ia, Nr. 12001/42 g., 16.XII.42., KTB, Ia, H. Geb. Sued, VIII.41.–XII.42.* 75905.

[169] *Lagebericht Nr. 1838/42, Ia, Pz AOK 2, 6.IX.42., Anl. 77 z KTB Pz AOK 2, 16.VIII.42.–28.II.43 and 11.XI.42.* 37075/90.

[170] *Bericht, H. Geb. Mitte, Ia. Nr. 2051/43, 9.VII.43., Anl. z. KTB, H. Gr. Mitte, 11.VI.–31.VII.43., Teil XXII, Band 10.* 65002/22.

[171] *Berichte, 201 Sich. Div., Okt, Nov, Dez 42, Anl. z. KTB 2, 201 Sich. Div., 1.IV.–31.XII.42.* 29196/2.

[172] *Bericht, H. Geb. Mitte, Ia, Nr. 2051/43, 9.VII.43., Anl. z. KTB, H. Gr. Mitte, 11.VI.–31.VII.43., Teil XXII, Band 10.* 65002/22.

CHAPTER 6

THE OCCUPATION FALTERS

Political Aspects

By the end of the summer of 1942 the Germans had all but squandered their opportunity to establish a workable administration in Russia. And in so doing they had lost their chance to crush the growing partisan movement, for large blocks of the Russian people had turned from them almost to a man. Those natives who in 1941 had been pro-"liberator" had turned apathetic, and those once apathetic had turned back to the Soviets. In Great Russia where Communist influence had always been heavy there had never been any serious question of allegiance. Many large areas there had quickly gone under partisan control and the German Army had not the troop strength to contest the loss. Elsewhere many of the natives still worked for or with the invaders, but the seeds of doubt and disappointment had been planted in their minds. Even if it had been possible to solve the manpower problem in the rear and retain all the security units for occupational duty and antipartisan operations, the deterioration of popular morale and the consequent loss of native support could hardly have been prevented, for the problem went far deeper than a mere question of armed strength.

Hitler had sent the Wehrmacht into Russia to establish and enforce a policy of blindly negative self-interest:

> Germany wages war in the east for self-preservation, that is, in order to gain the necessary living space for the German people, and in order to improve the basis for a secure food supply for Europe, but particularly for the German nation. It is not the purpose of this war to lead the people of the Soviet Union to a happier future, or to give them full freedom or political independence.[1]

When the Russian, who had welcomed or at least acquiesced in the invasion became aware of this attitude and of German plans for the future, he slowly, and in many cases regretfully, turned away.

General Thomas, the chief of the Armed Forces Economic Office, Von Weizsaecker, State Secretary in the German Foreign Office, and Rosenberg, the Reich Minister for the Occupied Eastern Territories had all believed that the ultimate success of the war effort in the east would hinge on the actions of the population, and all three had very nearly been

---

[1] *OKW/WPr, "Grundlagen der Propaganda gegen Wehrmacht und Voelker der Sowjetunion," 23.III.42., in Heeresgruppe Nord, Propaganda Befehle.* 75131/104.

proven correct in the space of 12 months. This is not to say that the eastern campaign was lost in the rear areas—partisans do not win wars; at best they only help prevent others from winning them. In the last analysis, the real issue was decided in the snows before Moscow and on the banks of the Volga at Stalingrad. But German negativism in the occupied territories went far toward uniting a shattered and divided nation against an invader and it certainly gave the partisan movement the strength and popular support it needed to develop into both a potent weapon in its own right and a valuable adjunct to the Red Army in the over-all Soviet defense picture.

Basically, the failure of the occupation was the Germans' failure to understand the eastern peoples, to treat them as human beings, and admit them as equals into the new order being created; the failure to outline a definite program which took into consideration the most basic desires of the people, to broadcast it with an effective propaganda line, and to carry it out; and the failure to provide a standard of living and set up a system of social justice at least equal to that formerly provided by the Soviet Government.

The power of resistance of the entire nation would have begun to crumble the moment the individual Russian became convinced that Germany offered him a better life than was possible under the Soviet regime. The emptiness of German promises was not immediately evident to the Soviet people. They had been discontented with their lot and were weary of Bolshevism, but, with the exception of the peoples in the Polish border areas, they were not imbued with as intense a hatred of Stalinist leadership as the Germans had assumed. The vague and generalized promises of liberation were at first accepted and sufficed to hold popular sympathies.[2] As time went on, however, the people began to see through the fiction of the "liberation" theme. Slowly but surely they came to realize that the Nazis did not regard them as partners to be admitted into a new society on an equal basis, but only as a group to be exploited according to alien economic and political aims, and they saw that the "liberation" slogan was only a pretext to enslave them according to Nazi methods. Rather than being treated as coequals in a new venture, they found themselves regarded as *Untermenschen*, subhumans, and told that the Germans were a superior race destined to rule the world.

---

[2] For initial acceptance of the "liberation" theme in the Ukraine, see staff study on propaganda, *H. Gr. Sued, 4.XII.41, Propaganda Angelegenheiten, 3.XII.42.* OKW/635. For confirmation of this point as far as the northern and central sectors were concerned, see: Final Report Commission in White Russia to Minister for the Occupied Eastern Territories, 31 Aug 44. EAP 161–b–12/14.

The common Russian's knowledge of the Germans, based only on what he had heard of their high organizational and cultural reputation and the negative Soviet propaganda which had been dinned into his ears for years, was at best vague. Still, in many areas he had placed high hopes on their coming, and his realization of the true tenor of their policy disillusioned him greatly, for in the last analysis he asked for nothing more than a reasonable life and a recognition of his human dignity.[3] It was fear of the future and a vague desire for security which drove him back into the arms of Bolshevism; the absence of any positive German policy for the future, coupled with the fact that Soviet propaganda was too often substantiated by German actions. "What do you want with us, if not slavery?" became the stereotyped question.[4] "We are ready to sacrifice everything for this common battle, but first we want to know distinctly and clearly what [we] will get out of it." [5]

It is amazing how many of the Nazi hierarchy understood the neutralizing force of this negative approach, saw how surely it was driving the Russian people into a common front with the Soviets, and yet were unable or unwlling to try to influence the deteriorating course of events. "It would have been better if we had promised them nothing," wrote Von Homeyer to Rosenberg.[6] "We have hit the Russians . . . too hard on the head in our manner of dealing with them," diaried even so ardent a Nazi as Goebbels.[7] One of Rosenberg's deputies went even deeper and saw the real wreckage created by Hitler's steadfast negativism: "The power of resistance of the Red Army and the strength of the partisan movement has mounted in the same degree as the population realized our true opinion of them." [8]

Land Reform

Throughout modern Russian history, the greatest domestic bone of contention had always revolved around the question of the emancipation of the serfs and its complement—the breaking up of the great landed estates and the distribution of the acreage to the peasants. The wave of liberalism which swept over western Europe during the 19th century crept slowly into Russia, bringing emancipation in 1861 and a gradual process of acquisition of land by the liberated serfs. With

---

[3] *Aufzeichnung, Berlin, den 25.X.42., gez. Braeutigam,* in *I.M.T., op. cit.,* XXV, pp. 331–42.

[4] *OKH/Fde. H. Ost. Studien, Ia, Nr, 3220/42, 25.XI.42. _H 3/468.2.*

[5] Latvian Propaganda leaflet, found 23 Feb 42, in rpt 178, 9 Mar 42 (doc. 3241), in *N.M.T., op. cit.* (Case 9).

[6] Ltr, Von Homeyer [an unidentified occupation official] to Rosenberg, 30 Dec 42. EAP 99/40, in Rosenberg collection.

[7] *The Goebbels Diaries, op. cit.,* pp. 184–85, entry for 25 Apr 42.

[8] *Aufzeichnung, Berlin, den 25.X.42., gez. Braeutigam,* in *I.M.T., op. cit.,* XXV, pp. 331–42.

the revolution the last of the great holdings of the nobility disappeared. The Soviet collectivization of the 1930's, however, which was so bitterly resented by the peasants, voided the gains of 70 years, and at the time of the German entry into the Soviet Union the decisive question with the rural population was still ownership of land. In few cases did the peasant thought process go beyond this basic issue.

In planning *BARBAROSSA*, the needs of the Four-Year Plan dictated that the *Kolkhozes* [9] be retained intact at least for the duration of the war despite the insistence of Rosenberg's office that they be broken up and an individual agrarian economy introduced. Propaganda units were to impress on the people that immediate changes in the economic set-up would harm everyone and serve only to increase the disruption of economic life occasioned by the war. [10]

However, when the maintenance of the collective economy was found to be impossible due to the widespread Soviet destruction and removal of farm machinery and when any resort to individual farming impractical because the necessary small tools were lacking, the *Wehrmacht Propaganda Division* was authorized to tell the people that the collectives were to be transformed into communal farms with the peasant retaining taxfree his cottage and certain small plots of land as his own property. Further, individual efficiency and initiative were to be rewarded with additional grants of land. [11] On 3 October 1941, however, there came a sudden policy shift which brought the question of land reform to a halt and prohibited any further discussion of the return of the land to the people. [12]

The reasons for this about-face during a critical period are unknown. It is possible that it was indirectly the work of Erich Koch, the *Reichskommissar Ukraine,* who was a strong opponent of the agrarian policy and thought Rosenberg far too liberal in his policies. More likely the decision was Goering's as head of the exploitation program. In any event, the effect was to postpone a solution until the Soviet successes in the winter of 1941–42 cut deeply into the popular support the Germans had enjoyed. When the new land policy was finally announced much of the effect was lost.

The land reform order, "the Restitution Law" (*Reprivatisierungsgesetz*), put into effect on 16 February 1942, was "to pave the way for a gradual and orderly transition from Bolshevistic production on a col-

---

[9] *Kolkhozes:* Soviet collective farms; *Sovkhozes:* Soviet State farms.
[10] "Directive for Handling Propaganda for *Operation BARBAROSSA*," *OKW Nr. 144/41, g. Kdos, Chefs, WFSt/WPr., VI.41.,* in "Fuehrer Directives," *op. cit.*
[11] Annex to Propaganda Dir, 21 Aug 41 in *OKW/486/4, WFSt/WPr;* also: Oral testimony of Riecke in *I.M.T., op. cit.,* XI, pp. 590–91.
[12] Dir, *OKW/WPr, 3.X.41.,* in *OKW/WPr, Propaganda-Angelegenheiten aller Art, X.–XII.41.* OKW/634.

lective basis to individual production on a cooperative or independent basis." The *Kolkhozes* were to be changed to cooperative establishments to be farmed on a communalistic basis with compulsory collaboration, each collaborator retaining for his own use, tax-free, a strip of land belonging wholly to him.[13]

Actually, the German political leadership had no intention of carrying out a real land reform and returning the soil to the peasants. One month after the publication of the land decree Hitler assured his advisers that it was only natural that the occupied east, rather than Germany, should pay for the war.

> The predominant part of the agricultural soil in those territories must, . . . remain the property of the state, as before; thus the profits from the agricultural production of these enormous state-owned lands will . . . accrue exclusively to the [German] State, and may be used for the liquidation of the internal war debt. . . .[14]

Almost from the very beginning the result of the failure to alter the system at an earlier date and to propagandize the change was evident. The expansion of the partisan movement with a resultant increase in terror raids on the natives in the rural areas made even preparatory work for executing the new measures difficult, and in some areas brought it completely to a halt. *Rayons* which in February 1942 had been clear of the bands and in which it had been planned to institute the first land reform were so infested with irregulars by March that the entire civil and economic administration was unable to function. Further, due to the partisan activity and the absence of effective German counteraction a good portion of the population behind *Army Group Center* so feared reprisals by the bands that they refused to take advantage of the proffered opportunity.[15]

But only a small percent of the collectives were converted, and then generally only by the Wehrmacht administration and not by the *Reichskommissariate*.[16] Koch was avowedly against giving the people anything,[17] and even though the agrarian policy had originally been the idea of his superior, Rosenberg, he consistently refused to put it into

---

[13] *Die neue Agrarordnung, Erl. des Reichsministers fuer die besetzten Ostgebiete v. 16/2/42* in Dr. Alfred Meyer, *Das Recht der besetzten Ostgebiete, Teil Ostland, Wirtschaft, Ernaehrung und Landwirtschaft,* Landwirtschaft. O III, D66.

[14] Ltr, Bormann (on behalf of Hitler) 25 May 42, in *Hitler's Tischgespraeche im Fuehrerhauptquartier 1941–42,* Henry Picker, ed. (Bonn, 1951), 136.

[15] *Lagebericht 4, 23.III.42., Wi Kommando Bryansk, KTB, 17.XII.42.—31.III.42.* Wi/ID 2.84.

[16] See: *Bericht, Ortskommandantur Taganrog, 6.VIII.42., Anl. z. KTB, Lageberichte, H. Geb. "B," 18.V.42.–16.I.43.; II Aufzeichnung gez. Braeutigam, 25.X.42,* in *I.M.T., op. cit.,* XXV, pp. 331–42.

[17] See Koch's speech to agricultural officials at Rovno, 28 Aug 42. 99/456, Rosenberg Collection.

effect and Rosenberg was unable to enforce his orders.[18]   Behind *Army Group North* there seems to have been as little action on the land question, for late in September 1942 the people were still waiting for the much-publicized farm grants.[19]   As for those farms actually changed over, a Rosenberg deputy described them as "bad, miserable copies of Soviet forms of organization from which partly the names have been taken over unchanged." [20]

In the last analysis, this view was essentially correct.   Nothing disappointed the rural population as much as the agrarian reform.   The liberation of the peasants from the collective economy was stressed to the limit by German propaganda as one of the main points of the German program in the east.   And indeed, the promise to restore the property of the farmer was well designed to win the sympathies of the entire rural population.   Generally the first distributions were enthusiastically received and plots were diligently worked right up to the front lines.[21]   In the long run, however, it worked out quite differently.   It was a far cry from collective farms via cooperatives to agricultural unions.   Too often the simple Russian peasant was unable to discern the difference between the collective on the one hand and the cooperative and agricultural union on the other.   The soil which had been the common property of all Russian people now became the common property of the members of the cooperative.   This theoretical distinction had no practical value, since it failed to give the new owners any tangible benefits or rights.   Organization, management, quotas, and routine remained unchanged.   The plot of ground was his, but he could not sell it.   Taxes were shifted from the land to the products of the land.   Farmers were promised extra acreage for outstanding performance, but it was made equally plain that substandard performance could result in the loss of a man's plot.   In the villages from which laborers were taken for shipment to Germany, the people said: "The Germans cannot possibly be serious about land reform if they send the formers to work in Germany."   When a plot was assigned to a peasant, 50 rubles had to be paid by the farmer for surveying costs and 20 percent of the yield had to be delivered to the Germans, whereas under the Soviet regime such land assignments were tax- and requisition-free.[22]   In the end the peasant came to the conclusion that actually there was little change in comparison with former Soviet conditions.[23]

---

[18] See: Oral testimony of Lammers, in I.M.T., op. cit., XI. pp. 48–9.
[19] Rpt, *Korueck 584* to *Sixteenth Army,* 26 Oct 42, in *Anl. 216 z. KTB 3, Korueck 584.*   38998/2.
[20] Ltr, Von Homeyer to Rosenberg, 30 Dec 42.   EAP 99/40, Rosenberg Collection.
[21] *Bericht, Wi Stab Ost, 16.IV.–15.V.42.*   Wi/ID 2.346.
[22] *Ibid.*
[23] *Army Group "A" Rear Area,* "Final Report of the Activity of Military Government in the Eastern Theater of War," undtd (approx end of 44).   75156/1; see also: Buchsbaum MS, *op. cit.*

Religion

In the matter of religion, from the very first the Germans were offered a unique opportunity to unite a large segment of the Russian people against the avowedly anti-Christian Soviet Government and win them to their "liberation" cause. But again their negativism and tardiness in taking any sort of a stand on the question of the reopening of the churches merely added another item to their long list of lost opportunities. In the same manner in which they feared revival of nationalism, they feared the unifying effect of the reestablishment of a large religious organization and firm church leadership.

Although the question of religion was never of as great moment with the Russian people as the abolition of the collective farms, the reopening of the churches under German sponsorship would not have been lost on a people who basically were intensely religious, and would certainly have brought over the influential Orthodox clergy on a collaborationist basis. In the last analysis, it was Moscow that grasped the opportunity, spreading rumors and propaganda to the effect that Stalin had proclaimed religious freedom for the entire USSR.

It was in the fear of a nationalistic revival that Hitler originally refused to allow the churches to reopen. Jodl reflected the official attitude: "A religious organization based on a unifying Russian church is just as much against the interests of Germany as a political unification of the peoples of the Soviet Union." [24] But when the natives spontaneously reinstituted worship services in the wake of the Wehrmacht advance, thus facing the Germans with a *fait accompli*, the proscription was relaxed to the extent of tolerating, but never encouraging, religious worship. No foreign priests were to enter the occupied areas and all priests were to refrain from any political leanings.[25] Wehrmacht chaplains were forbidden to conduct services for the natives.[26]

Even after the Russians had opened their churches and the Germans had acquiesced but not helped, they took an obstructive attitude. The SD closed the theological seminary in Volna with the explanation that it had aided subversive elements.[27]

Rosenberg had originally planned to announce the return of religious freeedom ceremoniously, but Hitler decided that on the basis of toleration only it should merely be allowed to come into existence as quietly as possible. Consequently, all possible propaganda effect was lost.[28] Rosenberg admitted that his only reason for wanting religious freedom was

---

[24] *OKW/WPr, Grundlagen der Propaganda gegen Wehrmacht und Voelker der Sowjetunion, 23.III.42.*, in H. Gr. Nord, Propaganda Befehl.   75131/104.

[25] *Propaganda Befehl, OKW/WPr, 21.VIII.41.*   OKW/1938.

[26] See: Oral testimony of Von Brauchitsch, in *I.M.T., op. cit.*, XX, p. 578.

[27] Ltr, *OKW to Eighteenth Army*, 10 Apr 42 in *H. Gr. Nord, Propaganda Befehl.* 75131/104.

[28] *Aufzeichnung gez. Braeutigam, 25.X.42*, in *I.M.T., op. cit.*, XXV, pp. 331–42.

to counteract Soviet propaganda, appease the local population, and gain
an effective theme for German propaganda in the rear areas.[29]   And
even Goebbels saw the need for a clearly drawn church policy and
understood its propaganda value.[30]

In the campaigns prior to *BARBAROSSA,* the Army had restored
churches to religious uses when desired by the populace and German
chaplains had frequently held services for the people.   In Russia, however, there was the strange picture of Hungarian, Romanian, and Italian
chaplains holding services for the natives when the German chaplains
were not allowed to do so.[31]

Education

Hitler flatly ordered that the people of the occupied territories be
denied all but the most rudimentary education.   Anything higher, he
said, was under no circumstances to be permitted, for a knowledge of
reading and writing would enable the eastern peoples to acquire some
historical background which might lead them to nationalism and opposition to German rule.[32]

All in all, it is extremely doubtful that the average Russian ever
became overly perturbed about this matter of schooling, despite the fact
the USSR had provided free education and the opportunity for un-
limited advancement for the younger generation within the framework
of the state.   In executing such a policy, however, certainly the Germans lost a valuable propaganda medium, and one the Soviets had
always made maximum use of.   Probably the most detrimental effect
of the whole business was the propaganda opening it gave the Communists who used it to the fullest.   "The Germans need land and slaves;
slaves must be kept dumb, so they close the schools," was a typical
approach.[33]   For the Germans, it was just another lost opportunity.

Food Shortages

While in a general sense the decline of native morale stemmed from
the German failure to provide positive answers to many burning problems, more immediately felt and direct in its effect on the population

---

[29] Ltr, Rosenberg to Reich Commissioners for Ostland and Ukraine, 13 Mar 42.
EAP 99/40 in Rosenberg files.

[30] *The Goebbels Diaries,* op. cit., p. 225, entry for 22 May 42.

[31] See: Oral testimony of Von Brauchitsch, in *I.M.T.,* op. cit., XX, p. 578.

[32] Picker, op. cit., pp. 73, 116–17; for additional German views on the educational
policy, see: Himmler's speech, 16 Sep 42, in *Persoenl Stab RFSS.* 161–b–12/154;
ltr, Von Homeyer to Rosenberg, 30 Dec 42.   EAP 99/40, in Rosenberg Collection.

[33] Soviet propaganda quoted in "Urgent Questions of Partisan Warfare and Recruitment of Local Volunteers," in *OKH/Fde. H. Ost, Nr. 3220/42, 25.XI.42.*
H 3/468.2.

was the steady deterioration of the food situation. Nowhere during 1942 was there an adequate food supply: while the shortage was more acutely felt in the cities than in the rural districts there was a general retrogression of morale in all areas because of it. Even in the Baltic States and the Ukraine, where popular discontent was not as evident as in the central sector, the short supply of basic food stuffs and the continuous German requisitions steadily deepened the general disappointment of the workers in the occupation administration.

In the urban areas the shortage was most acutely felt. In Stalino, which had a population of 248,000, with all food under a strict rationing system, some 70,000 people had no ration cards.[34] In another large city, Rostov, the ration distribution was so uneven that some two-thirds of the people received no food through the German administration.[35] Black market prices were impossibly high and the wide differential between all prices and the wages paid by the occupation soon robbed money of the little value it had and forced the urban dwellers into a barter system, carting their household furnishings into the countryside to trade with the peasants for enough food to survive. Even in the farm districts the heavy forced requisitions of cattle and grain lowered agricultural stocks far below the existence minimum and went far toward demoralizing the very peasants who had been promised so much.[36]

Suppression of Indigenous Administrations

In the border areas of western Russia there was one factor affecting morale which was peculiar to that part of the USSR. The natives in the western Ukraine, White Russia, and the Baltic States were in large measure of non-Russian extraction and generally anti-Soviet in feeling, and the cold and suppressive German attitude toward the numerous anti-Bolshevik separatist groups created widespread disappointment in the many circles that had hoped for national expression. As the months passed following the opening of the campaign, the obvious lack of any positive German policy for the future led the people to ask the question: "What is to be our political future? What do you really want with us, if not slavery? What will our people get out of this?" [37]

---

[34] Bericht, Oberfeldkommandantur Donets, 20.XI.42., Anl. z. KTB, H. Geb. Sued, 16.V.42.–18.I.43.   27089.

[35] Ibid.

[36] Ltr, Von Homeyer to Rosenberg, 30 Dec 42.   EAP 99/40, in Rosenberg Collection, OKW/WPr., Lageberichte, 1.VIII.–15.VIII.42., KTB, OKW/WPr., 12.II.–12.XII.42.   OKW/793.

[37] Ltr, Soviet defector [sic] to Ch, Wehrmacht Propaganda Division, 1 Nov 41, in Propaganda-Angelegenheiten aller Art. Okt–Dez 41.   OKW/634; "Urgent Questions of Partisan Warfare and Recruitment of Local Volunteers," in OKH/Fde, H. Ost, Nr. 3220/42, 25.XI.42.   H 3/468.2; op cit rpt # 178, 9 Mar 42 (doc. 3241) prosecution document book in N. M. T., op. cit. (Case 9).

Leaders in the nationalist circles pointedly indicated to the occupation
administrators that these questions had to be answered if the people
were to be won over, and they desperately tried to demonstrate to
them that the establishment of native provisional authorities would
form the nerve centers of a strong central government and would lead
directly to civil war and the collapse of all pro-Soviet sentiment in the
western districts without further German efforts.[38]

As was the case in all the errors of German policy, Hitler and his
advisers were adamant in their refusal to veer one degree from their set
path. Certainly their blindness was of their own making, for they were
amply advised by those who had been on the scene. The operating
armies saw the efficacy of setting up and supporting indigenous administrations, as in the case of the Kaminski group. Although their basic
reason for so doing was to enlist native aid in the antipartisan fight, in
the case of Kaminski they made no effort to limit his actions to the tactical
field. The *Fourth Panzer Army* reported that the non-Soviet population in its rear openly sought a centrum or a symbol of a countergovern-
ment under German leadership, opposed to the Soviets and made up of
true Russians, to which they might look for help. As late as January
1942 such expressions as "we have prayed to God to bring us war so
that you may come to us and that we, with your help, may drive off the
Soviets. We will serve you loyally and honorably . . ." were continually heard in the cities, villages, and prisoner of war camps.[39] *Foreign Armies East* urged OKW to give the natives the opportunity to
cooperate voluntarily in the governmental structure as the last remaining
means of coping with the backsliding of the once collaborative population and thus stabilize the deteriorating partisan situation.[40] One of
Rosenberg's deputies clearly saw how the policy of using the Ukraine
as a counterweight against Great Russia had broken on the same rock-
bound program of negation,[41] and even Goebbels saw the crux of the
question and reasoned that a series of puppet governments might be
used as a camouflage for unpopular measures in order to hold proper
confidence.[42] But the Fuehrer and his deputies continued in their same
line of thinking and only when it was far too late was the Vlassov movement half-heartedly launched.

---

[38] Ltr, Soviet defector [*sic*] to Ch, *Wehrmacht Propaganda Division,* 1 Nov 41, in
Propaganda-Angelegenheiten aller Art, Okt–Dez 41. OKW/634; Shigunov Interrogation, pp. 175, 844–46. EAP 3–a–11/2.
[39] Rpt of interpreter, Lt Col Von Blankenhagen, in rpt, *Fourth Panzer Army* to
Army Group Center, 7 Jan 42. EAP 99/480.
[40] "Urgent Questions of Partisan Warfare and Recruitment of Local Volunteers,"
in *OKH/Fde. H. Ost, Nr. 3220/42, 25.XI.42.* 3/468.2.
[41] *Aufzeichnung gez. Braeutigam, 25.X.42.,* in *I. M. T., op. cit.,* XXV, pp. 331–42.
[42] *The Goebbels Diaries, op. cit.,* p. 225, entry for 22 May 42.

The Forced Labor Program and Its Effect on the Partisan Movement

Granting the detrimental effect of the abortively handled land problem, the question of churches, and the general shortage of food in the occupied territories, the German labor program as instituted in the late winter of 1941–42 probably contributed more to the ultimate frustration of the German war effort in the rear areas than any one other policy. Not only did it have the effect of turning the native population further away from the German cause—and this was particularly important in the case of the Ukraine whence the largest proportion of the workers were to be taken and where the people originally were least in sympathy with Soviet policies and institutions—but also of driving tens of thousands of hitherto peaceful citizens into active collaboration with the mushrooming partisan movement.

The 1941 campaign and the winter stalemate had so depleted German manpower reserves that new sources had to be tapped. This meant that thousands of workers would have to be drawn from war industry and agriculture, while at the same time the output of the armaments industry had not only to be maintained but sharply increased to make good the enormous materiel losses of the fall and winter. To replace the workers thus lost to industry, Hitler ordered the integration of 6,000,000 workers from the occupied countries into the German economy, of which 1,600,000 were to come from the east, 1,200,000 of these from the Ukraine.[43] Fritz Sauckel, Plenipotentiary for the Allocation of Labor under the Four-Year Plan, was placed in charge of the program, with the authority to issue instructions to all top authorities in the Reich and in the occupied territories.[44] All prisoners of war were to be integrated into the armament and nutrition industries, and additional workers were to be brought in from the occupied countries. As far as possible these civilian workers were to be recruited on a voluntary basis. If quotas could not be filled in this manner, a program of forced labor "in its severest form" would be instituted. In addition to this manpower for industry, 400,000 to 500,000 young girls were to be sent from the east for domestic duties in German homes.[45] The keynote for the treatment of these workers was struck in Sauckel's original program. They were to be "fed, sheltered, and treated in such a way as to exploit them to the highest possible extent at the lowest conceivable degree of expenditure."[46]

---

[43] Quoted by Sauckel in speech to officials of the *Generalkommissariat Kiev*, 27 May 42, in *KTB Ruestungskommando Kiev*. Wi/ID 2.1297.
[44] See: Oral testimony of Rosenberg in *I.M.T.*, *op. cit.*, XI, p. 485.
[45] *Der Beauftragte fuer den Vierjahresplan, Des Arbeitseinsatzes*, 20.IV.42., in *I.M.T.*, *op. cit.*, XXV, pp. 55–71; ltr, Sauckel to *Reichskommissare*, 31 Mar 42 in *ibid.*, XV, p. 168.
[46] *Das Programm des Arbeitseinsatzes, 20.IV.42.* in *I.M.T.*, *op. cit.*, XXV, pp. 56–71.

Although volunteers were originally called for, almost immediately the local administrations were put under considerable pressure to fill minimum quotas as quickly as possible. This led to numerous abuses almost from the start. Both male and female workers were literally pulled from their beds or picked off the streets and assembled without being allowed time to pack clothing, blankets, or food. Families were indiscriminately split up. Many were marched long distances in severe weather and then crowded into cattle cars and locked in without adequate provision for feeding or sanitation. Many, drafted without regard for physical qualifications and unfit for labor services from the beginning, were returned from the Reich in deplorable condition. Such a practice had a very depressing effect on the morale of both the drafted workers and the population left behind.[47] This feeling was intensified by the spectacle of public beatings and the burning of whole villages for failure to comply with demands for filled labor quotas.[48] Families were held in ransom for conscripted workers who escaped to the forests. The entire population became widely stirred up and quickly came to regard the transports to the Reich as similar to exile by the Soviets to Siberia.[49] Fear soon gripped large areas of the Ukraine, and numbers of the natives left their villages for the forest country seeking the protection of the partisans, greatly increasing and strengthening the bands.[50] Soviet propaganda gave wide play to the whole program and the open German substantiation had an almost immediately visible effect of cutting volunteering to near zero and increasing the powers of resistance of both the Red Army and the irregulars.[51]

With this added strength the bands extended their control over larger and larger areas with the result, in the rear of *Army Group Center* at least, of cutting heavily into German attempts to fill their labor quotas there. Against a monthly quota of 30,000, in February 1942 the labor draft authorities there obtained 5,588 workers, the volume growing to a high of 25,000 in July, then dropping sharply to 6,034 in September, and further to 1,191 in January 1943.[52]

---

[47] *Facharbeitersammellager Charkow an Bfh. Heeresgebiet B., Abt. VII. betreff, Uebelstaende in der Behandlung ukrainischer Facharbeiter*, 15.IX.42., in *I.M.T., op. cit.*, XXV, pp. 103–12. For a comprehensive picture of the abuses in the conscription and treatment of forced laborers from the occupied eastern territories, see: "*Gegenwaertiger Stand der Ostarbeiter-Frage,*" *Zentralstelle fuer Angehoerige der Ostvoelker*, 30.IX.42., in *ibid.*, pp. 161–79.

[48] *Der Reichsminister fuer die besetzten Ostgebiete* [Rosenberg] *an den Gauleiter Fritz Sauckel*, 21.XII.42., Nr. 02926/42., in *ibid.*, pp. 74–79.

[49] *Der Generalkommissar, Shitomir, den 30.VI.43., geheim, Muendlicher Lagebericht des Generalkommissar Leyser ueber den Generalbezirk Shitomir, gehalten in einer Dienstbesprechung vor dem Herrn Reichsminister Rosenberg in Winniza am 17.VI.43.*, in *ibid.*, pp. 319–23.

[50] *Der Reichsminister fuer die besetzten Ostgebiete an Sauckel*, 21.XII.42., Nr. 02926/42., in *ibid.*, pp. 74–79.

[51] *Gegenwaertiger Stand der Ostarbeiter-Frage, Zentralstelle fuer Angehoerige der Ostvoelker*, 30.IX.42., in *ibid.*, pp. 161–79.

[52] *Anl. 52 z. KTB, Wirtschaftsinspektion Mitte, 1.IV.–30.VI.43.* Wi/ID 2.53.

As the program continued with its devastating effect on popular morale, the occupation administration began to feel the over-all effect more and more acutely. The economic program was especially hard hit by the rise in partisan activity.[53] Rosenberg became concerned about the effect on his occupational set-up and remonstrated sharply with Sauckel. The large increase in the bands, he wrote, was largely due to the methods of procuring laborers, the result of which could only be a strengthening of the number and fighting spirit of the irregulars and a danger to all German activities in the eastern areas.[54]

Despite the obviously harmful consequences of the draft, the quotas were raised even higher, 225,000 being demanded from the Ukraine alone between 5 October and 31 December, and 225,000 more by 1 May 1943.[55] To aid in the draft, the labor officials began calling up workers by age groups, both male and female. With this intensification rather than mitigation of the program, it became more and more obvious that the ruling group in Berlin was completely unaware of the rocks onto which this blind policy was driving the entire eastern war effort.

Treatment of Prisoners of War [56]

The German treatment of Red Army prisoners of war also exercised a deep and lasting effect on the entire Soviet defense effort. It only indirectly touched the natives and influenced them to no such degree as the land reform question which for decades had been their end-all in life. But it did serve to substantiate Communist propaganda, their disappointment and disgust with "liberation" policies, and it heightened and drove them even further away from the "liberators." The effect on the will of the Red Army to resist and the growth of the partisan movement was much greater.

The German position regarding the treatment to be accorded prisoners of war was clear and explicit: "The regulations of the Hague Rules of Land Warfare . . . are not valid since the USSR is dissolved." [57] ". . . [therefore] the Geneva Convention for the Treatment of Prisoners

---

[53] For the effect on the economic program, see: "Report on the Effects of the Partisan Situation," 30 Jun 43, in *ibid.*

[54] *Der Reichsminister fuer die besetzten Ostgebiete* [Rosenberg] *an den Gauleiter Fritz Sauckel, 21.XII.42., Nr. 02926/42, in Facharbeitersammellager Charkow an Bfh. Heeresgebiet B., Abt. VII, betreff, Uebelstaende in der Behandlung ukrainischer Facharbeiter, 15.IX.42.,* in *I.M.T., op. cit.,* XXV, pp. 74–79.

[55] *Der Generalbevollmaechtigte fuer den Arbeitseinsatz* [Sauckel] *an den Herrn Reichsminister fuer die besetzten Ostgebiete* [Rosenberg], *VA Nr. 5780.28/4265, 3.X.42.,* in *ibid.,* pp. 72–73.

[56] Unless otherwise noted, the material in this section is taken from: *Rosenberg an den Herrn Chef des Oberkommandos des Wehrmacht, betr.: Kriegsgefangene 28.II. 42.,* in *I.M.T., op. cit.,* XXV, pp. 156–61.

[57] *Erster Abschnitt: Die Organisation der Verwaltung in den besetzten Ostgebieten* in *I.M.T., op. cit.,* XXVI, pp. 592–609.

of War is not binding in the relationship between Germany and the USSR. . . ." [58]

In carrying out this policy, the Germans ignored the fact that the Russians, in contrast to the peoples of western Europe who made no attempt to conceal their enmity, initially at least were happy over their liberation and defected and surrendered in large numbers only to find themselves more contemptibly treated than the people of the west. Numbers of them were allowed to starve or die from exposure or typhus. Many of those lagging on marches to the rear because of exhaustion were summarily shot before the eyes of the civilian population. In many cases the natives were forbidden to feed the prisoners. Various ethnic groups were screened out and executed by the *Einsatzgruppen*. Those prisoners who actually reached Germany were so underfed and poorly sheltered that by February 1942 only several hundred thousand of some 3,600,000 [59] taken were alive or able to work. Despite the promises on millions of propaganda leaflets and surrender passes dropped behind Red Army lines encouraging Red soldiers to desert, no difference was made between those who deserted as a result of these promises and those who were forced to surrender. As a natural consequence the will to defect became paralyzed and was replaced by a deadly fear of German captivity.

The knowledge that surrender to the Wehrmacht meant almost certain death was not long in coming to the Russian rank and file, not only by rumor but also through the stories of refugees and escaped prisoners and by what the troops saw for themselves when they reoccupied certain areas in the central sector during the winter counteroffensive. This was all in confirmation of Soviet propaganda. Surrenders practically came to a halt when the troops became convinced that fighting to the death in a losing battle was preferable to capture by the Germans. Once eyewitness accounts and personal observations, reinforced by propaganda, had established the facts of enemy behavior, there was nothing left but to persevere to the end. [60]

---

[58] *"Anordnung fuer die Behandlung sowjetischer Kriegsgefangener,"* Amt Ausl/ Abw., Nr. 9731/41 geh. Chef Ausl., 15.IX.41., in I.M.T., op. cit., XXXVI, pp. 317–27.

[59] The source of this figure of Rosenberg's is unknown, and it seems abnormally high. Still the number of prisoners taken during the first months of the war was tremendous. Wehrmacht tabulations, which in round numbers appear more reasonably correct, place the figure closer to two or two and one-quarter millions.

[60] Study, Col Bushmenov on propaganda questions, incl. in rpt, Representative of the Ministry for the Occupied Eastern Territories with *Army Group Center Rear Area* to the Ministry in Berlin, undated (early in 1942). EAP 99/480: *The Soviet Army* ("Service Conditions and Morale in the Soviet Armed Forces: A Pilot Study," vol I, [Washington, 25 Aug 51]) (S), pp. 37, 42, 74. This is the aggregate view of a number of Red Army soldiers who were under arms during the first year of the war.

This growing fear of German captivity provided a large pool of trained leaders and personnel for the partisan movement during the formative period when they were most needed. Russian officers, commissars, and soldiers when irretrievably cut off from their own lines disappeared into the forests singly or in groups and joined or formed bands, giving the movement the professional touch which it sorely lacked at the time, and without which it might never have grown into an effective agency of the Soviet war effort.

The Failure of the German Propaganda Effort [61]

The efforts of the *Wehrmacht Propaganda Division* to counter this steady loss of native support was woefully inadequate, and ended in failure. It was a losing fight from the start. Closely restricted by shortsighted OKW policy as to what it could and could not tell the people, and opposed by well-executed Soviet counterpropaganda which cleverly exploited almost every aspect of German negativism and almost every German mistake, the *Propaganda Division* never had a real chance to accomplish its mission once the true German war aims were revealed.

The responsibility for the failure was at the OKW level, for the *Propaganda Division* was an operational agency only and worked entirely within the scope of directives handed it from above. Not only were these directives generally vague in content, but they placed sharp limitations on subject matter. So few were the permissible propaganda themes given it that in the last analysis the only positive point offered during the crucial first months of the campaign was that of liberation from Bolshevik oppression, while the population awaited the answers to many vital questions which were studiously avoided. This silence on important basic questions was widely exploited by the Soviets. Added to this was the strong psychological effect of the obvious German inability to either protect the pro-German segments of the population from the partisans or bring an end to the murdering of mayors and village elders and the indiscriminate looting by the irregulars.[62]

Prisoners of war, defecting Red Army officers, and native intelligence agents all testified to the poorly conceived and executed German propaganda. All agreed that it was based too much on the German viewpoint and demonstrated a complete lack of understanding of the Russian thought process. The Russian People, and probably a good portion of the Red Army, could have been won over, they believed, if definite promises had been made and a definite program outlined for the political

---

[61] For a detailed treatment of German propaganda in the eastern campaign, see: Buchsbaum, *op. cit.* Unless otherwise stated, the factual material in this section is drawn from this manuscript.

[62] *Bericht, H. Geb. Nord, Nr. 930/42, 4.VI.42., Anl. 150 z. KTB 1, H. Geb. Nord.* 21287/1.

and economic future of the USSR.[63]   As early as January 1942 *Army Group Center* saw how much damage had been done and believed that the time was past when even a general revision of the whole propaganda campaign could attain any decisive success, especially in the face of the Russian winter successes. Still the situation might be partially retrieved, Von Kluge told OKH, if the general policies regarding the occupied territories and the propaganda approach were radically overhauled. Then the Red Army's will to fight might be considerably lessened and the deteriorating situation in the rear brought at least partially under control.[64]

Equally as shortsighted was Berlin's ignorance of the true nature and power of the common Russian's love for his native land, a side of the Russian mentality to which the Soviets constantly appealed in an effort to stem the German tide. It was not based on any political consideration, but on love of the soil and on a pride in Russian nationality which had lasted throughout many wars and famines. It was never a product of defiant defensiveness, as is sometimes the case in other cultures, nor did it seem under ordinary circumstances to impose any special norms of behavior on individuals. It was simply a national pride, completely apolitical, and was effective in the fight against Hitler because Hitler was a foreign tyrant.[65]

Following the initial German attack, the Soviet propagandists had quickly dropped the standard Communist slogans and placed heavy emphasis on patriotism, playing up "The Great Patriotic War" and the "fatherland." The masthead on *Pravda* was changed from "Workers of the World, Unite!" to "Death to the German Invader." The old czarist heroes were dragged out and the Russian victory over Napoleon in 1812 was given wide play.[66] In answer to this, the Germans could offer little more than their "liberation" theme, now worn somewhat thin.

To make a bad situation even more difficult, the civilian and paramilitary agencies which followed on the heels of the operating armies, the *Reichskommissariate,* the SS and police units, and the economic and labor organizations, all instituted separate propaganda programs with the result that the entire propaganda effort grew into a maze of independent, unrelated, and uncoordinated projects.[67]

----

[63] Study, Col Bushmenov on propaganda questions, incl. in rpt, Representative of the Ministry for the Occupied Eastern Territories with *Army Group Center Rear Area* to the Ministry in Berlin, undated (early in 1942). EAP 99/480.

[64] Rpt, *Army Group Center* to *OKH* on propaganda, 31 Jan 42. EAP 99/480.

[65] Study, Col. Bushmenov on propaganda questions, incl. in rpt, Representative of the Ministry for the Occupied Eastern Territories with *Army Group Center Rear Area* to the Ministry in Berlin, undated (early in 1942). EAP 99/480; *The Soviet Army* ("Service Conditions and Morale in the Soviet Armed Forces: A Pilot Study," vol. I, [Washington, 25 Aug 51]) (S), pp. 37, 42, 74.

[66] *Ibid.*

[67] See: Buchsbaum, *op. cit.*

The Partisans and the German Economic Program

Although the bands based within several hundred miles of the front were probably given first priority in the reorganization because they were easily reached and controlled, those in the deeper rear were by no means neglected. As early as May well-led brigades had begun to appear far to the west in White Russia, and under directives from the Central Staff had started working intensively against the German occupation, especially the economic program.[68] The Germans had made no secret of their intention to milk the Soviet Union dry economically, and the action of the partisans in this sphere must have been part of a Moscow-directed campaign to counter this exploitation.

It was not a difficult campaign to wage. By the spring of 1942 German manpower in the rear was so short that the security commands were forced to use all available security units to guarantee the continued supply of the divisions at the front. Since there was never enough of these even for adequate rail line and highway security, large portions of the countryside went unprotected and rapidly fell under partisan control.[69]

By the beginning of the summer the partisans had paralyzed many phases of the economy in the outlying areas of White Russia and threatened to cause the Germans to lose a large portion of the grain crop which was nearing harvest. Several of the economic inspectorates were completely in their hands. They concentrated on the isolated state and collective farms and dairies and destroyed dozens of them with all their cattle and agricultural stocks. Much the same conditions existed in northwest Russia and some parts of the Baltic States.[70]

As the summer progressed the situation deteriorated still further. Inability of the security commands to control much of the rear beyond the corridors along the major communication axes and the larger population centers made the work of the economic inspectors almost impossible. By July, 50 percent of the *rayons* in White Russia were under partisan domination, complete losses not only economically but as sources of labor.[71]

---

[68] *Monatsbericht, Wi-Stab Ost, Juni 42, KTB, Wi-Stab Ost, 1.V.–30.IX.42.*, Wi/ID 2.346; "Report on the Effects of the Partisan Situation," 30 Jun 43. Wi/ID 2.53.

[69] *Monatsberichte, Mai, Juni, Juli 42, KTB, Wi-Stab Ost. 1.V.–30.IX.42.* Wi/ID 2.346.

[70] Ltr, *Generalkommissar* for White Ruthenia to *Reichskommissar Ostland*, 18 Sep 42. EAP 99/96, Rosenberg Collection; *Monatsbericht, Wi-Stab Ost, Mai 42, KTB, Wi-Stab Ost, 1.V.–30.IX.42.* Wi/ID 2.346.

[71] *Monatsbericht, Wi-Stab Ost. Juni 42; Monatsbericht, Wi-Stab Ost, Mai 42, KTB, Wi-Stab Ost, 1.V.–30.IX.42.* Wi/ID 2.346.

During the agricultural year 1941–1942—the agricultural year ran from June through the following May—losses of quotas set for meat, grain, and lard were heavy due to partisan action:

Product	White Russia		Baltic States and Northwest Russia	
	Percentage	Tons	Percentage	Tons
Meat.............	65	16, 000	40	1, 200
Grain.............	60	55, 000	40	20, 000
Lard.............	55	1, 700	16	*340

*Para. 11 of rpt, "Partisan Effect" in *Geschichte des Wirtschaftstabes Ost.* This report is not further identifiable at source. It was apparently compiled in late 1944 or 1945 from a number of reports over the period 1941–45. This was the personal copy of a Dr. Barth. Wi/ID 2.1345.

Even considering the possibility that the Germans had set the quotas so high as to be impossible to achieve without any interference, partisan or other, and the probability that all losses were not caused by the bands, although so reported to Berlin, the figures are significant in that they reveal the extent of the development of the partisan movement in the central sector and the intent of the Soviets to strike at all aspects of the German war effort.   In striking at the state and collective farms and at the dairies, the partisans not only denied a source of food to the Germans and at the same time built up ration stocks for themselves, but they created a food shortage among the civilian population which the Germans were unable to solve.

Even harder hit than food production at this early date was the timber industry.   Lumbering was a perfect target for the bands because it was very difficult to protect and because an adequate supply of rough-finished lumber was essential to the armies for the construction and maintenance of bridges over the many Russian rivers and logs were needed for corduroy roads through the extensive swamps.   The forests were the natural haunts of the bands, and from such cover they easily interrupted cutting and milling operations.   In August of 1941 only some 10 percent of the forests were partisan-infested.   By April 1942 this figure had risen to 40 percent, by October to 75 percent.[72]   Numbers of forestry officials, both Russian and German, were murdered on the job, and the natives became so terrified of the partisans that they had to be forced to work. As a result, often only narrow strips along the rail lines that were pro-

[72] "Effects of Partisan Activity on Forestry," *Anl. 4 z. Anl. 52 z. KTB, Wirtschafts-inspektion Mitte, 1.IV.–30.VI.43;* "Report on the Effects of the Partisan Situation," 30 Jun 43.   Wi/ID 2.53.

tected by the security commands and tracts in close proximity to military strong points could be cut. Sawmills were raided regularly and many were destroyed, while log floating was brought almost to a standstill.[73] By hiring additional experts and importing sawmill machinery, the lumber output was stepped up despite the partisans. Still, because of their pressure, only 58 percent of the potential output of all the mills in operation could be exploited.[74]

The peat industry was also hard hit. The significance of maintaining an adequate supply of peat lay in its connection with electric power and its importance as the primary source of domestic heat for the population. Behind *Army Group Center,* due to the absence of rapids in the rivers, there were no hydroelectric plants, nor was there any adequate source of coal. Peat was the only fuel available in large quantities for the generation of electricity and any interruption in its production curtailed the power needed for military installations and did much to lower popular morale in the urban areas in much the same way as the food shortage. During 1941 sufficiently large stocks were left over from the previous year to satisfy demands. In 1942, however, some 30,000 workers cut only half that needed, due in large part to the physical and mental threat posed by the partisans.[75] Actual production totaled only 50 percent of a potential of some 850,000 tons.[76]

---

[73] *Monatsberichte, 1.X.42.–28.II.43, Wi-Stab Ost.* Wi/ID 2.336.

[74] "Report of the Effects of the Partisan Situation," 30 Jun 43. Wi/ID 2.53.

[75] *Monatsberichte, Wi-Stab Ost, Juni–Okt 42.* Wi/ID 2.346; "Report on the Effects of the Partisan Situation," 30 Jun 43. Wi/ID 2.53.

[76] *Anl. 5,* to "Report on the Effects of the Partisan Situation," 30 Jun 43. Wi/ID 2.53.

CHAPTER 7

THE GERMANS CHANGE THEIR TACTICS

During the winter and spring months there had been no question in the minds of the Army of the most effective way to deal with the partisan groups and eliminate them permanently. The proper tactic, as they saw it, was an active offense by sufficient first-line troops to carry the fight to them in their own strongholds, destroy their camps and bases, and never relax the pressure long enough to allow them to reconstitute. And they had to be denied the passive as well as the active support of the people. A strictly passive defense with garrisons, outposts, and patrols was not the answer, they knew, for such would leave the initiative with the insurgents and play directly into their hands.[1]

In the spring OKH had made a sound move toward pulling the natives away from the partisans when it modified the then standard practice of using reprisals and collective punitive measures to prevent the people from aiding or joining the bands. Then in August, in the more active sphere, it went a long way toward placing all aspects of the antipartisan campaign on a firmer and more centralized military basis when it announced that thereafter all actions against the insurgents would be conducted like normal combat operations at the front, with the operations section of OKH determining the general policy and handling all coordination, and similar questions at lower echelon levels being handled by the operations section of the headquarters concerned.[2]

The New OKW Antipartisan Policy

During the days just prior to the launching of the attack toward the Caucasus in June of 1942, Hitler himself, for the first time in months, had begun to show a renewed interest in the Soviet partisans. Both in Russia and in the Balkans irregular resistance had been increasing, and with the opening of the summer campaign drawing near he iterated his "get tough" prescription as the surest means of ridding the rear areas of all insurgent threats and securing communications.[3]

---

[1] "Report on Effects of the Partisan Situation," 30 Jun 43. Wi/ID 2.53; entry for 4 Nov 42 in *KTB 2. Teil 2, Pz AOK 2.* 28499/5; *Bandenlage, 16.VIII.42.–28.II.43., Anl. 77 z. KTB, Ia, Pz AOK 2.* 37075/90.

[2] See: *H. Gr. Mitte, Ia, Partisanenbekaempfung, 10.VIII.42., Anl. z. KTB, Ia, Pz AOK 2.* 37075/91.

[3] *KTB, Ob. d. Wehrmacht, 1.IV.–30.VI.42.* X-126. OCMH, Foreign Studies Br.

Sometime between June and the first part of August, however, his advisers must have acquainted him with the facts relating to the failure of the unrestricted punitive measures to curb partisan activities and the reaction the same policy was having on the native population. Furthermore they must have persuaded him that the basic changes ordered by the Army were the sounder course, for he drastically changed his tune. On 18 August 1942, OKW issued a new directive on antipartisan warfare which as it was carried out represented an almost complete reversal of views held earlier as to the strategy to be used to suppress irregular activity and indicated a much clearer understanding on the part of Berlin than heretofore as to just what the movement was and how best to combat it and undermine its bases.[4] This was the first comprehensive order concerning antipartisan strategy issued by the Wehrmacht high command since the repressive directives of 23 July and 16 September 1941.[5]

The war against the bands was to be considered as much a part of general operations as the moves of the front line armies against the Red Army, the directive stated. All means of politics, economics, and propaganda were to be brought to bear. The destruction of the bands required vigorous, offensive action by all available military, SS and police units, which could be released for the purpose, and the "harshest measures" against both active and passive adherents to the movement. The natives' confidence in German leadership was to be restored and their cooperation solicited by fair and above-board treatment and by the assurance of sufficient food.

Himmler was designated the central authority for the collection and evaluation of all information relating to the bands and in addition was given sole responsibility for all antipartisan operations in the *Reichskommissariate,* with the *Wehrmachtbefehlshaber* subordinated to him. In the combat zone and the army group rear areas, however, the Army retained control, with all police forces in the area subordinated to it.

The forces available for antipartisan operations were to be augmented in every possible way. The police and SS units in the rear areas were to be used in active rather than passive roles. They were to be reinforced by the transfer of other organizations subordinate to Himmler to the areas endangered by the partisans. Security units then assigned to the armies and committed in the front lines, but which were indispensable for antipartisan operations, were to be relieved by the Army as

---

[4] Dir No. 46, "General Directions for the Intensified Fight Against Banditry in the East," *OKW/WFSt, Op. Nr. 2821/42 g. Kdos., 18.VIII.42.* in "Fuehrer Directives," *op. cit.*

[5] *OKW/WFSt/Abt. L (I Op.). Nr. 442254/41 g.K. Chefs.* in "Fuehrer Directives," *op. cit.; OKW/WFSt/Abt. L (IV/Qu), Nr. 2060/41 g. Kdos., 16.IX.41.* in *I.M.T., op. cit.,* XXXIV, pp. 501–04.

soon as possible. Army training and school units and Luftwaffe ground organizations were to be shifted to areas under partisan pressure, either in the *Reichskommissariate* or the army group rear areas. As a further reinforcement the prohibition against the formation and use of native security units by the Army (which had frequently been ignored) was lifted. However, it was specifically forbidden to commit these units in the front lines. There were to be "no Germans left in the bandit-infested regions who [were] not engaged either actively or passively in the anti-partisan campaign." In addition, OKW ordered that the term "partisan" (*Partisanen*), which had been found to mean "fighter for freedom" in Russian terminology, no longer be used, and the term "bandit" (*Banditen*) substituted in referring to the insurgents.[6]

OKH passed these provisions along to the Army almost verbatim and without elaboration, since the more pertinent ones were already in effect in the operations zone.[7] Himmler was much more specific and went into considerable detail,[8] borrowing much from the experience of the security commands. He emphasized the importance of the population's regaining a feeling of security and receiving fair treatment from the occupation administration. Punitive measures, acts of violence, and the like could be justified only in cases where the subjective collaboration of the population with the partisans was clearly established, his directive stated. Where the people supported the bands only under pressure, the bands alone were to be punished. Experience had shown that the people often fled to the forests in fear of reprisals and there became prey to the bands who forcibly recruited the men into the irregular ranks. When collective punitive measures had to be exacted, it was highly important that the reasons for so doing be carefully explained to the people. This latter was considered especially pertinent. Further, the people were to be made to realize that the partisans, following instructions from Moscow, often deliberately attempted to place them, even though innocent, in a position where the Germans would take reprisals—as firing on German troops from a village and then escaping, thus leaving the inhabitants to face the penalties which the Germans might lawfully impose—in order to turn them away from the invaders and into the ranks of the irregulars.

Continuing, Himmler outlined his general tactical concepts relating to antipartisan warfare which varied little from those drawn up by the security units of the army group rear areas. To attempt to meet the partisan's clever, swift and often well-disguised activity with traditional

---

[6] See: Entry for 26 Aug 42 in *KTB, H. Gr. Nord.* 75128/13.

[7] *Gen.St.d.H.-Op Abt. (I) Nr. 10990/42 g. Kdos., OKH, 23.8.42.* NOKW–1635.

[8] *Bandenbekaempfung, Prs. St. RFSS, Sep 42.* A photostatic copy of this pamphlet is located in CRS, TAG, and is not further identifiable. The translation is that of the Army Security Agency and is confidential.

forms of defense was to court disaster. Passive defense and purely defensive measures only played into the hands of the bands and gave them control of the situation. The objective should always be to seize the initiative and throw the enemy on the defensive, to separate him from the population, to deprive him of supplies from the countryside, to limit his freedom of action, to encircle him, break him up, and pursue him until he has been eliminated. The object was to destroy the bands, not scatter or drive them away.

The first prerequisite for success was accurate information, and highest priority was to be given to the establishment of an adequate intelligence net. All sources of information were to be carefully and fully exploited. A general information net composed of local inhabitants and village officials was to be set up and exploited, a confidential agent service established, and all prisoners carefully interrogated. After the intelligence network was established definite preventive measures were to be taken to limit the activity of the bands.

All residents were to be listed and nonresidents registered and carefully controlled; a dependable communication system was to be established; a number of strong support points were to be set up in the vicinity of important installations both as defense against partisan raids and to bolster the morale of the population; all protective cover which might be utilized by the partisans as defensive strong points or as a mask for an attack was to be eliminated.

Following the establishment of an information net and a system of passive defense, the bands were to be attacked. Antipartisan action was always to be taken only on the basis of sound intelligence, and was to be swift, surprising, enveloping, and mobile. The main thrust whenever possible was to be made against the camp of the partisan leaders, for once the bands were deprived of their commanders, they generally were easily broken up. This type of action presupposed trained shock troops equipped with all necessary weapons.

The organization of "counter" or "dummy" bands was recommended. They were to be made up of units from the security police and the security service and of the *Ordnungspolizei,* with a number of reliable natives, and committed in partisan-dominated areas in the manner of a genuine partisan unit. In this manner they would be able to keep a constant check on the sentiments of the population, make contact with irregular units, and often quietly eliminate partisan leaders.[9]

Hitler's renewed interest in the security of the rear areas and the growing anti-German sentiments of the natives did not stop with his directive of 18 August. On 26 August, OKW issued a supplementary

---

[9] For results of this, see: *OKH/Gen.St.d.H., FdeH/Ost, Nr. 2460/43 geh., 3.V.43.,* in *Kdr. Gen. d. Sich. Tr. Sued Ia, Anl. 37, 30.IV.—1.VIII.43., Abw. Nachr. OKH, Befh. H. Geb. Sued.* 39502/41.

order for distribution to all lower echelons stating that Hitler had directed a comprehensive procedural guide for antipartisan warfare be drawn up on the basis of after-action reports and recommendations of units which had been in actual contact with the bands. All organizations assigned to rear area security duties were ordered to forward detailed reports on their practical experience with the irregulars along with any suggestions such experience might indicate. In these reports, especial emphasis was to be placed on reconnaissance and intelligence, tactics, propaganda directed at both the partisans and the civil populace, treatment of captured irregulars and of the people at large, area control, supervision and security of communication lines, and the commitment of indigenous security formations.[10]

Reports submitted to OKW generally bore out the soundness of the contents of the 18 August directive.[11]   On the basis of these experiences and recommendations, OKW drew up and issued on 11 November 1942 a "Directive for Anti-Partisan Warfare in the East"[12] which elaborated on the general policy relative to the treatment of the civilian population previously established and gave official sanction to the preferential treatment for certain classes of partisan prisoners that several of the line armies and security commands had been granting for some time.[13]

In general, policy relating to captured partisans and to civilians, including women, found to have actively participated in combat remained unchanged: such persons were to be shot or hanged.   Likewise, anyone who harbored, fed, concealed, or otherwise aided partisans was to be executed.   Partisan deserters, "depending on circumstances," were to be treated as prisoners of war.   Captured partisans who could prove that they had been pressed into the movement and who were able to work were to be sent to punitive work details and be considered for labor service in Germany.   Collective measures were to be taken against communities in which the partisans received aid of any kind.   These measures, however, were to be in relation to the graveness of the offense and might consist of anything from an increase of quotas of requisitioned materials to the destruction of an entire village.   Such reprisals were to be exacted only where the inhabitants voluntarily aided the irregulars. The population was not to be placed in a position where it was threatened

[10] *Bandenbekaempfung (O.Qu), OKW/WFSt, Nr. 2391/42, 26.VIII.42.*, in *Anl. Band 6–11, KTB 6, Ia, AOK 2, 1.VII.42.–31.V.43.*   37418/109.
[11] See: *AOK 16, Ia, Nr. 4462/42, 11.IX.42., Anl. 49 z. KTB 5, W/IV, AOK 16, 26.VI.–30.XI.42.*   36588/68.
[12] *Kampfanweisung fuer die Bandenbekaempfung im Osten, 11.XI.42., Anlage 2 to H. Dv. Ia.,* in *Anlage f to KTB, Ia, Kdr, Gen. der Sicherungstruppen, Heeresgebiet Sued, 1943.*   39502/45.
[13] On this latter, see: app. 2 to ltr, *Second Panzer Army* to *Army Group Center, 2 Nov 42,* in *KTB, Pz AOK 2.*   28499/67; *Bericht, AOK 16, Nr. 4462/42, 11.IX.42., Anl. 49 z. KTB 5, AOK 16.*   36588/68; *Anl. 67 z. KTB 221 Sich. Div., 12.IX.42.* 29380/9.

with destruction by both sides. In every case where collective measures were taken, it was of the utmost importance that the people be made to understand the reasons. Through propaganda media the partisans were to be informed that as deserters they would be well treated, as prisoners they would be executed. "A different approach [than heretofore used]," the directive concluded "must be used toward the population under partisan oppression."[14]

Too Little Too Late

There is much to be said for this change of policy. Militarily it was sound, based as it was on the sum total of German experience against the bands. But it was impracticable in that it presupposed manpower which the Germans simply did not have. Put into practice in the fall of 1941 when the security divisions were full strength rather than mere skeletons, it might have nipped the movement in the bud. In the fall of 1942 there was little chance for it to work.

The bands were to be hit and hit again with strong offensive strikes. Yet there was not enough manpower available to give adequate static coverage to the lines of communication. Security regiments which had been drawn into the front lines during the winter crisis were not returned to the rear area commands,[15] while line units which had helped mop up the rear in the late spring reverted to their parent commands at the conclusion of their missions.[16] The transfer of six training divisions from the *Wehrkreise* to the *Reichskommissariate*, where they were to assume some static guard duties while completing their basic training, afforded some relief and released a few security units for more active employment in the operations zone.[17] These latter small gains to the security commands, however, were more than offset by the loss of training time by the divisions to the ultimate detriment of the armies at the front. All of them were so stripped of detachments up to regimental size for full-time antipartisan work that their training was badly disrupted and in several cases brought to a virtual standstill.[18]

Then again, when occasionally a force of sufficient numerical strength for a limited offensive sweep against the bands could be assembled by

---

[14] *Kampfanweisung fuer die Bandenbekaempfung im Osten, 11.XI.42., Anlage 2* to *H. Dv. Ia.*, in *Anlage f* to *KTB, Ia, Kdr, Gen. der Sicherungstruppen, Heeresgebiet Sued, 1943.* 39502/45.

[45] *KTB, H. Gr. Nord. 31.VIII.42.* 75138/13.

[16] *KTB, H. Gr. Nord, 12.IX.42.* 75128/14; *Lage Ost, 20.IX.42.*

[17] MS # C–065a, *op. cit.,* p. 37; *KTB, H. Gr. Nord, 17.IX.42., 18.IX.42.* 75128/14; *OKW/WFSt., Op. Nr. 2821/42 g. Kdos., F. H. Qu., 18.VIII.42.,* in "Fuehrer Directives," *op. cit.; Gen. Kdo. LXII. Res. K., Ia. Tgb. Heimat-Russland. 9.IX.42.–31.III.43.* 29483; *Gen. Kdo. LXI Res. Korps, Tgb., Ia. 14.IX.42.– 31.III.43.* 30500/1.

[18] *Gen. Kdo. LXI Res. Korps, Tgb., Ia. 14.IX.42.–31.III.43.* 30500/1.

literally scraping the bottom of the manpower barrel, almost invariably it comprised such a miscellany of units that effective tactical coordination proved nearly impossible, and as a consequence objectives were rarely attained. Static defense forces were often of similar makeup.[19]

Despite these difficulties, superior German organization and planning in the main served to offset any advantage the partisans might have gained at the time. The bands were growing in strength and experience, but they were still building, spreading their influence, and reorganizing, and they still lacked the aggressiveness to be more than a threat for months to come. Yet their potential as an effective military force was good and they would have to be hit hard again and again if they were to be prevented from attaining it.

The changes of policy designed to undermine the movement by weaning away its external support by the people and weakening it from within by granting preferential treatment to partisan deserters were likewise "too little too late." While they were a distinct improvement, the time had since passed when the mass of the people could be brought over into the German camp. Then also, these changes applied only to agencies actively engaged in the antipartisan fight. The civilian administrators of the *Reichskommissariate,* among them those who filled Sauckel's labor quotas and the officials of the economic administration, remained outside their application and served to offset any gains made by other agencies in this sphere.

---

[19] See: *Bericht, Korueck 584, 27.VII.42., Anl. 159 z. KTB 3, Korueck 584.* 38998/2; *KTB 2, Teil 5, Pz AOK 2, 4.X.42.* 28499/5.

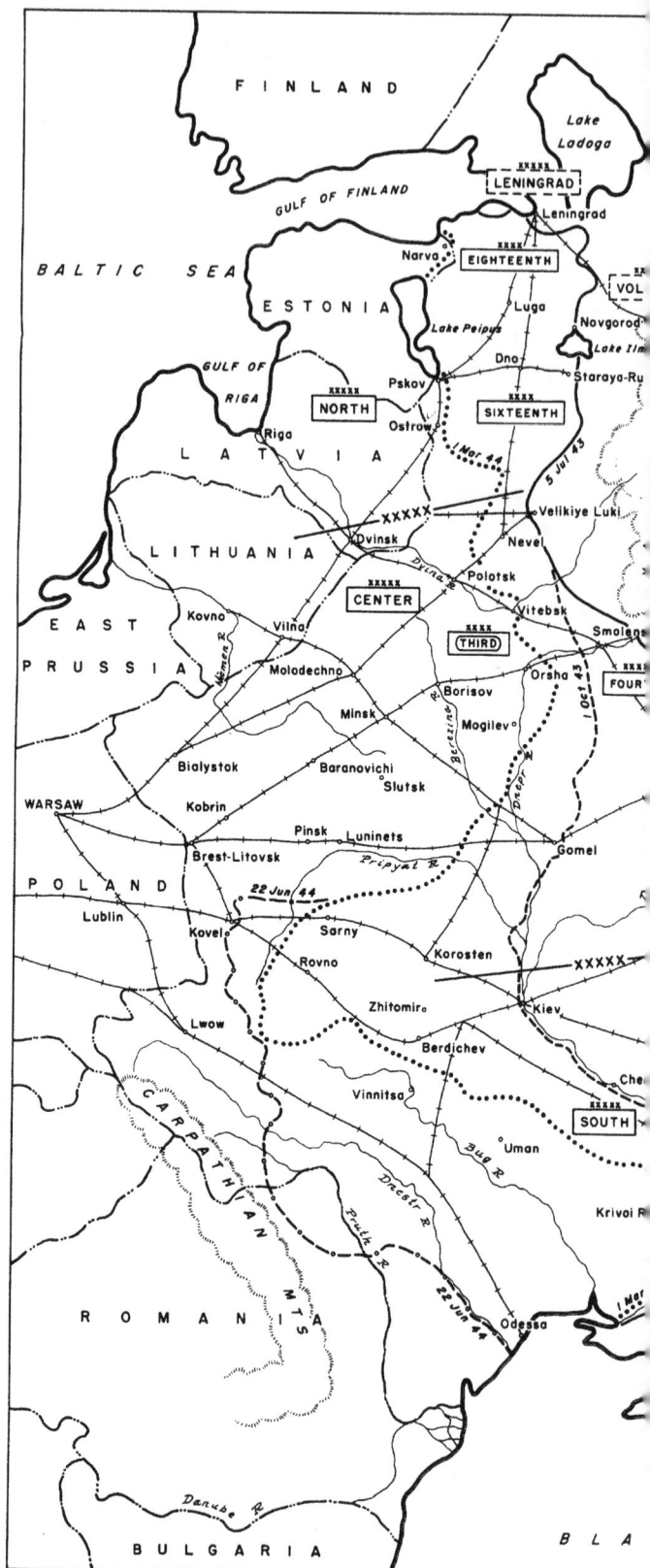

Map 4. *Period of Soviet Offensives, 1943–1944.*

Map 4

D OF SOVIET OFFENSIVES, 1943-1944

ITH FRONT INDICATED AS OF

———— 5 July 1943
– – – 1 October 1943
•••••• 1 March 1944
—o— 22 June 1944
+–+–+ Railways
▭ German
▱ Russian

50   0   100
MILES

ORDER OF BATTLE
RUSSIAN

Leningrad Front – Govorov
Volkhov Front – Meretskov
Kalinin Front – Yeremenko
West Front – Sokolovski
Bryansk Front – Popov
Center Front – Rokossovski
Voronezh Front – Vatutin
Steppes Front – Konev
Southwest Front – Malinovski
South Front – Tolbukhin
North Caucasus Front – Petrov

GERMAN

Army Group North – Von Kuechler
Army Group Center – Von Kluge
Army Group South – Von Manstein
Army Group A – Von Kleist

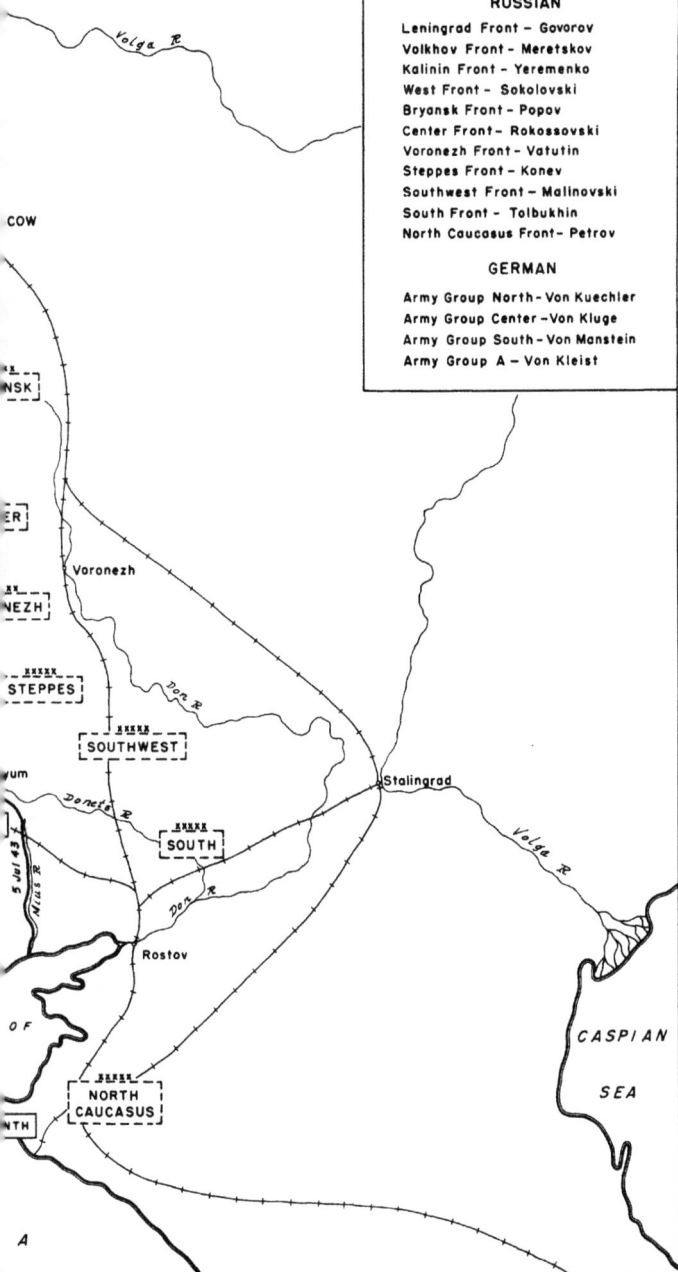

COW

Volga R.

NSK

ER

Voronezh

NEZH

STEPPES

Don R.

SOUTHWEST

yum

Donets R.

Stalingrad

SOUTH

Volga R.

Don R.

Rostov

NORTH
CAUCASUS

NTH

O F

CASPIAN

SEA

A

PART THREE

1943–1944: THE PERIOD OF SOVIET OFFENSIVES

CHAPTER 8

GERMAN-RUSSIAN OPERATIONS FOLLOWING THE FALL OF STALINGRAD

The Soviet Offensive, Early 1943

Following the fall of Stalingrad and Von Kleist's withdrawal from the Caucasus in January and February of 1943, the Germans attempted to set up their defenses along the line of the Donets River. In a reorganization of the southern command, the *Second Army* was returned to the control of *Army Group Center* while *Army Group South* was reconstituted to consolidate the units of *Army Group B* and *Army Group Don* under Von Manstein's command. Von Kleist remained in the Crimea and the foothold across the Kerch Straits with his *Army Group A*. Von Manstein's major units were the *First* and *Fourth Panzer Armies* and two *Armeeabteilungen*,[1] comprising a total of 32 divisions of which 12 were armored. Von Kleist's command consisted of the *Seventeenth Army* and a miscellany of satellite organizations. Many of these latter were no longer effective fighting units.

The Red Army was in no wise content with its victories on the Volga and in the southeast. While the Germans were striving to extricate their units from Stalingrad and the Caucasus, the Soviet offensive had spread further. On 15 January troops of Gen. F. I. Golikov's Voronezh Front[2] attacked across the Don in the northern part of the sector and quickly routed the Italians at Rossosh and Valuiki. On 23 January they captured Voronezh. They continued the assault and by the end of the month opened the road to Kursk whence the German summer offensive had started.

Meanwhile, in the Don basin, units of Gen. N. F. Vatutin's Southwest Front had closed up along the lower Oskol River and by 2 February held a bridgehead over the Donets below Voroshilovgrad. Several days previously Gen. A. I. Yeremenko had made a crossing at the confluence of

---

[1] A provisional army the size of an overstrength corps, commanded by a corps commander with a corps staff.

[2] A Red Army "front" was roughly equivalent to a German army, a Russian army to a German corps.

the Don and the Donets. These two springboards placed the Russians in an excellent position to continue their assault after Von Kleist's escape through Rostov. Keeping the offensive rolling, they continued the attack both north and southeast of Kharkov. On 5 February Vatutin crossed the Donets in heavy force in the Izyum area, and before the middle of the month cut the main rail lines running into the Donets bend area and forced Von Manstein to withdraw westward to the old Mius River positions. Farther to the north Golikov captured Kursk on 7 February and then swung to the south and took Belgorod two days later. Continuing, he pushed further south toward the rear of Kharkov while Vatutin attacked the city from the east and south. The city fell on 16 February, breaking the entire German position on the upper Donets. The situation of the Wehrmacht appeared precarious with the Russians threatening to go clear to the Dnepr and trap all German forces east of the river.

At this point, however, the Russian attack slowed almost to a stop. The Soviets' communications lines were badly overstretched and their front in the south had almost doubled in length. This combined with a sudden unseasonal thaw served to give the Germans a breathing spell and an opportunity to consolidate their defensive positions and reorganize. Von Manstein quickly took advantage of his opportunity. Regrouping his armor and aided by reinforcements from other sectors and theaters he struck back at the dangerous salient which had been driven around Kharkov. Starting on 21 February, his *First* and *Fourth Panzer Armies* counterattacked north and south of the city and by 15 March cleared the line of the Donets as far up as Belgorod. In the meantime, however, Golikov had deepened the bulge he had driven around Kursk. By the end of March operations had bogged down in the spring thaw generally along the line the Germans held in the spring of 1942.

In the northern and central sectors operations were on a more limited and less spectacular scale. On the Leningrad front the Soviets in the middle of January launched a limited offensive which in five days cut through a 10-mile wide corridor south of Lake Ladoga. This reopened land communication with Leningrad which had been cut off for over 500 days. During the same period, units of Gen. V. D. Sokolovski's Kalinin Front, which for months had slowly been pushing westward between *Army Groups North* and *Center,* finally occupied Velikiye-Luki, but failed in an attempt to take the Nevel hedgehog and cut the north-south Dno-Nevel rail line. The only other change of note in the north was a voluntary German withdrawal from the exposed Demyansk salient below Lake Ilmen. In the central sector the Germans shortened and straightened their front by withdrawing the *Ninth Army* from the Rzhev salient. This line remained unchanged until July.

The 1942 operating year had started as the greatest in German military history. The summer offensive had driven rapidly to the Volga and deep into the Caucasus, but the end of the campaigning season found the Wehrmacht generally back where it had started in June. In addition, the Germans had been forced out of the Rzhev-Vyazma salient which threatened Moscow, and the Red Army had been able to drive and hold a deep position in the Kursk area which threatened to sever communications between the southern and central groups of armies. These reverses, resulting as they did in huge and irreplaceable losses in men and materiel, combined with the defeat in Tunisia, brought an end to the period of sustained German offensives.

The Red Army in 1943

The Soviet Army which faced the Germans in the summer of 1943 had little in common with the hordes who had fled in confusion before the Wehrmacht in the first months of the war. Reorganized throughout, it had a paper strength of some 500 divisions, a good number of which were well equipped with modern weapons. The high command had carefully studied the reverses of 1941 and 1942 and assimilated the lessons, as the careful preparations and well-directed execution of the November counterblow at Stalingrad demonstrated. New combat regulations had been drawn up, military discipline had been tightened; insignia of rank had reappeared on Red Army uniforms; and the power of the political commissars had been curtailed, the military becoming wholly responsible for operations. Ample supplies of new weapons were coming off the production lines of plants relocated far to the east in the Ural Mountains, and lend-lease from the United States and Britain was beginning to make itself felt. Even more important was the improvement of morale among the common soldiers. The collapse of the myth of Wehrmacht invincibility combined with the revival of the past glories of Russian arms and a hate of the enemy engendered by the inept German occupation policy and treatment of prisoners of war went far toward making a new fighting man of the Red soldier.

German Strategy in 1943

Compared with former years, Hitler's strategic plan for the summer campaign of 1943 was anything but optimistic and, for once, indicated an awareness of the adverse state of German affairs in the east. His former buoyant aggressiveness was completely lacking and for the first time he talked in terms of a general defensive. He expected the Red Army to continue its heavy attacks at the close of the muddy season and reasoned that if he were to dictate Soviet actions anywhere he had to take the initiative at several points along the front before the Russians struck. The point of greatest danger, according to his reasoning, and the spot at which the Wehrmacht should strike before the Red Army resumed its offensive was the deep salient in the Kursk area which lay like a sore

between *Army Groups Center* and *South.* The two army groups were
to ready strong armored forces to the north and south of the salient so
that they could attack before the enemy mounted his expected offensive.[3] Zeitzler, who had proposed the operation, believed that if
successful it would destroy a large number of Red Army divisions, thus
decisively weakening the offensive strength of the Soviets, and leave
the Germans in a more favorable position for continuing the war in
the east.[4] Elsewhere along the eastern front the Army was to remain
on the defensive in heavily fortified positions.[5] The controversy among
the ranking Army leaders over this operation was in reality a dispute
over the future conduct of the entire war effort in the east. Many of
the generals saw that they could not win and thought that their only
prospect of avoiding defeat in Russia was to shorten the line and wear
down the Red Army's offensive power by a strategic, or elastic, defense.
They contended that the muddy season stalemate following on Von
Manstein's successful counterblow in the Kharkov sector offered them
an opportunity to consolidate and rebuild their strength to the point
where they might hold the Soviets at bay with strong tank forces held
in the rear as mobile reserves for rapid movement to any threatened
point. Such an operation as Zeitzler envisioned, they argued, was sure
to cause severe tank losses and make impossible such an elastic defense.
Zeitzler, supported by Von Kluge, insisted that through this operation, in which he proposed to use the latest model tanks, he could regain
the initiative. Generaloberst Walter Model, commanding the *Ninth
Army,* raised violent objections. Arguing on the basis of extensive aerial
reconnaissance, he claimed that the Soviets, in expectation of just such
an attack at the most obvious spot in the line, had prepared very strong
antitank defenses many miles in depth in the localities of possible breakthroughs and had withdrawn the mass of their mobile units far to the
rear. He proposed that a fresh tactical approach be found or else
that the whole idea be dropped. Guderian, then Inspector of Panzer
Troops, also opposed the operation, calling it foolish from a strategical
point of view. He pointed out that the eastern front had just been reorganized and reequipped to the point where a successful strategic
defensive fight might be made, but that the tank losses which he felt
certain would result from the attack could not be replaced in 1943 and
would make such a defense impossible. He argued further that such
losses would also greatly hinder defensive preparations for the invasion
which was sure to come in the west.[6]

---

[3] Opns Order 5, *OKH/Gen.St.d.H./Op.Abt.* (*vorg.St.*), *Nr. 430163/43 g. Kdos.
Chefs., 13.III.43.* in "Fuehrer Directives," *op. cit.*
[4] Heinz Guderian, *Panzer Leader,* (New York, 1952), p. 306.
[5] Opns Order 5, *OKH/Gen.St.d.H./Op Abt.* (*vorg.St.*),*Nr. 430163/43 g. Kdos.
Chefs., 13.III.43* in "Fuehrer Directives," *op. cit.*
[6] Hart, *op. cit.,* pp. 210–13; Guderian, *op. cit.,* pp. 306–07.

These controversies indicated more clearly than at any other time the differences in thinking between Hitler and his immediate advisers on the one hand and the majority of the Army commanders on the other. The latter argued in favor of shortening the line in keeping with German manpower limitations and conserving armored strength for a mobile defense, while Hitler steadfastly clung to the rigid policy of holding the line as far from the Reich as possible.[7]

Despite the arguments of his ranking Army leaders, Hitler adopted Zeitzler's views and ordered that the attack, code-named Operation *ZITADELLE*, be scheduled for early execution.

The Battle for Kursk and Kharkov

The Russian forces facing the Germans along the eastern front as the operating season opened in July consisted of some 45 armies organized into 12 fronts.[8] To oppose these the Wehrmacht had 161 divisions organized into 11 armies and 4 army groups. The disparity of strength, however, was far wider than the number of units would indicate on paper. Russian strength had been building up steadily while the Germans remained unable to replace their extremely heavy losses. Battle casualties alone since the start of the campaign totaled more than 2,500,000 men, and the German nation simply had not the manpower to replace them.[9]

Operation *ZITADELLE* began on 5 July. The plan called for the same tactics the Germans had used many times before and with which the Russians were more than familiar. Model was to send his *Ninth Army*—seven panzer, two panzergrenadier,[10] and nine infantry divisions—against the northern face of the salient, while Von Manstein attacked from the south in the vicinity of Belgorod with ten panzer, one panzergrenadier, and seven infantry divisions. Additional elements of the *Ninth Army* were to drive to the southeast to protect Model's left flank, while *Armeeabteilung Kempf* covered the right of Von Manstein's effort. No particular care was taken to conceal the directions of the main efforts, and as a result the Russians knew what to expect and where.

From the first hours of the attack it was clearly evident that Model and Guderian had been correct and that the Russians were ready and

---

[7] United States Strategic Bombing Survey, Keitel interrogation report, 27 Jun 45. Shuster Collection. Foreign Studies Br, OCMH.

[8] See: *Lage Ost, 5.VII.43.*

[9] *Gefechtsausfaelle Sowjetfeldzug, vom 22.VI.41. bis 10.VII.43., Der Heeresarzt b. Obdh/GenQu, Nr. I/4451/43 g. Kdos., OKH, den 14.VII.43.* H 17/189. Losses to 10 Jul 43 totaled 2,614,039 enlisted men and 75,084 officers killed, wounded, and missing. This figure does not include medical and accident casualties or satellite casualties. Nor does it include the number of convalescents returned to duty.

[10] A *Panzergrenadier* division was made up of armored infantry and motorized infantry supported by several units of assault guns.

waiting. The Soviet defenses proved even more formidable than air reconnaissance had predicted. The defense zone ran to a depth of more than 60 miles partitioned into a series of prepared positions, the whole liberally sowed with mines.

The *Ninth Army* made little headway from the start. By 8 July its attack had spent itself after a maximum penetration of but six miles. Tank losses were very high. In the south Von Manstein made somewhat greater progress, but by 16 July he had been forced over to the defensive after losing the majority of his panzers. By 23 July both attacking forces had been pushed back almost to their jump-off positions.

Thus the offensive ended as Guderian had predicted with the eastern army virtually stripped of the armor sorely needed for a balanced defense and with no mobile reserves and no replacements. More serious was the fact that the losses left the entire eastern front highly vulnerable to Russian massed armored attacks.

As the German attack was brought to a halt, the Soviets made their move. On 12 July, following up their attacks on the shoulders of the German pincer, they launched a general offensive on both sides of the salient. Sokolovski and Gen. M. M. Popov, as they drove back Model's attack group, struck simultaneously at Orel from the north and east, while Vatutin and Gen. I. S. Konev hit hard into Von Manstein's divisions further south. The pressure was irresistible and the Germans, with their armor all but dissipated, were forced back rapidly. Orel, for two years the central anchor of the whole German line in the east, fell to Popov on 4 August, while Vatutin entered Belgorod the same day, breaking the German hold on the northern face of the salient about Kharkov. The Soviets never relaxed their pressure, but opened an assault on Kharkov itself. Hitler threw what tank strength he had left into this battle for the city, but was able to delay the inevitable only a few days. Despite fanatical resistance, the city fell on 23 August and the last German stronghold in the southcentral sector east of the Dnepr was gone.

The Germans faced literal disaster. Their losses in Operation *ZITADELLE* and in the defensive battles for Orel and Kharkov had been staggering. In the first five days of *ZITADELLE* they lost 2,268 armored vehicles of all types including assault guns,[11] and by 20 July had but 828 serviceable panzers in all of *Army Groups South* and *Center* to oppose an estimated 3,992 Russian tanks in the line and an additional 2,051 in reserve.[12] Losses in personnel were nearly as great. Dur-

---

[11] *Panzerausfaelle ZITADELLE, Stand: 5.—10.VI.43., g. Kdos.,* in *Pz.-Lage "S".* H 16/237.

[12] *Kraeftegegenueberstellung, Stand vom 20.VII.43., Fremde Heere Ost (11c).* H 3/119. Unfortunately the extant figures on German tank strength and losses for this period are fragmentary, but such as are available give an idea of the seriousness of the German situation as regarded armor during the period.

ing the period 10 July through 10 August the two army groups lost 163,158 officers and men killed, wounded, or missing.[13]

During the latter part of August other sectors of the front also became active. In the extreme south Gen. F. I. Tolbukhin with his Fourth Ukrainian Front attacked the Mius River positions and forced a breakthrough in the area of the reconstituted *Sixth Army*. Taganrog, at the mouth of the Mius River and the southernmost anchor of the German line, fell on 30 August, while Gen. R. Ya. Malinovski with his Third Ukrainian Front forced a large bridgehead over the Donets east of Izyum. In the meantime, Gen. K. K. Rokossovski continued his offensive west of Kursk and Orel. With the elimination of the Orel and Kharkov salients and the forcing of the German southern defenses along the Mius and the Donets, the Russians were in excellent position for a concerted drive all along the front.

The Drive Across the Dnepr

With their line broken at three strategic points, Orel, Kharkov, and in the Donets bend, and with the Red Army moving powerfully with seven army fronts from the Smolensk area to the Sea of Azov, the Germans had no choice but to withdraw from the Ukraine and to attempt to stabilize the situation at the line of the Dnepr. Driving relentlessly, by mid-September Malinovski and Tolbukhin had forced the Germans to completely abandon the Donets line and before the end of the month were attacking Melitopol and Zaporozhye on the Dnepr. Vatutin and Konev quickly exploited their breakthrough at Kharkov and, despite a desperate counterattack by Von Manstein to cover his bridgehead at Kremenchug over which his units were trying to withdraw, reached the river on 28 September. Two days later Vatutin put units over the river near the mouth of Pripyat and below Kiev, Konev was across southeast of Kremenchug, and Malinovski had a bridgehead south of Dnepropetrovsk. Meanwhile Rokossovski had continued his drive in the Orel-Kursk sector. By 1 October he had reached the upper Dnepr, and was threatening the German strong point at Gomel. With the few German reserves concentrated in the south, Sokolovski opened a strong offensive in the central sector aimed at the key city of Smolensk. Using nine armies on a front of some 110 miles he broke through strong German fortifications in the face of desperate resistance by the *Fourth Army* and entered Smolensk and Roslavl on 25 September. Under this pressure Von Kluge pulled back his line to defensive positions east of Orsha and Vitebsk and held there.

In the south, the Soviets, never relaxing their pressure, gave the Germans no time to consolidate any sort of a line along the Dnepr. The

---

[13] *Gefechtsausfaelle Sowjetfeldzug, ObdH/GenQu, vom 22.VI.41. bis 10.VII.43., Der Heeresarzt b. Nr. I/4451/43 g. Kdos., OKH, den 14.VII.43.* H 17/189.

four fronts between the Crimea and the southern edge of the Pripyat
Marshes had been redesignated the First, Second, Third, and Fourth
Ukrainian Fronts, and during the first week in October these fronts
immediately began exploiting the river crossings they had seized. Taking Zaporozhye on 16 October and Melitopol a week later, they broke the
Sixth Army's line from the Dnepr bend to the Sea of Azov and pushed
on. By the end of October Tolbukhin had cut off the Crimea and had
closed up along the river except at Kherson and Nikopol where the
Germans held onto small bridgeheads. On 17 October Konev attacked
out of his bridgehead at Kremenchug and swung to the south toward
the iron ore center at Krivoi Rog and the main rail line into the Dnepr
bend from the west. This threat forced the Germans to give up
Dnepropetrovsk, but the *First Panzer Army* was able to hold in front of
Krivoi Rog.

During October there was little Russian activity in the vicinity of Kiev
as the Soviets enlarged their crossing north of the city and gathered their
strength to assault it. Then early in November Vatutin broke his First
Ukrainian Front out of the bridgehead and attacked the city from the
north and west. Von Manstein, seeing his position was hopeless, evacuated the stronghold and pulled back to the west. Exploiting his advantage, Vatutin continued to drive. On 12 November he captured
Zhitomir, and five days later entered Korosten, a key communications
center on both lateral and east-west rail lines. Stung by this loss of
rail facilities, Von Manstein countered and before the end of the month
retook both cities.

During this same period the Soviets were able to make much less
impression on Von Kluge's defensive line in the central sector where the
Fourth Army contained five successive offensives along the Smolensk-
Minsk highway toward Orsha. Rokossovski was also repulsed before
Gomel, and only by placing tremendous pressure on the city was he
finally able to force the Germans to evacuate on 12 October.

On 3 October Yeremenko, with his Kalinin Front, had captured
Nevel on the northern edge of the sector and driven a 30 mile wide
salient between Nevel and Vitebsk, the anchor of the upper Dnepr line.
In conjunction with this attack, Sokolovski, continuing his offensive west
of Smolensk, made repeated attacks on Vitebsk in an attempt to envelop
it from the south. But the Germans hung on tenaciously, and despite
continued Soviet pressure, forced the fight into a stalemate. In January,
the Russians, balked by the stubborn defense and the difficult terrain
which heavily favored the Germans and which never froze over in an
unusually mild winter, abandoned the assault and attempted no further
major operations in the central sector during the remainder of the
winter.

During the first days of December Konev resumed his attacks in the south, taking Cherkassy in the rear on 14 December and driving on to Kirovo, which he entered on 7 January. The effect of this penetration was to seriously threaten the rear of the German units in the Nikopol area as well as that of the *Eighth Army* above Cherkassy on the Dnepr.

While these probing attacks were in progress, the main effort was in preparation in the Kiev sector. During the first part of December Von Manstein had continued his counterattacks east of Korosten and Zhitomir, but on Christmas Eve Vatutin launched a new, large-scale offensive which by 4 January had driven the Germans out of those two cities and crossed the old Polish border south of the Pripyat Marshes.

The Winter Battles

In January 1944 the Red Army facing the Germans comprised 10 fronts. From north to south opposite *Army Group North* were Gen-L. A. Govorov's Leningrad Front, Gen. K. A. Meretskov's Volkhov Front, and Popov's Second Baltic Front; facing *Army Group Center* across the upper Dnepr line Gen. I. Kh. Bagramyan's First Baltic Front, Sokolovski's Second White Russian Front, and Rokossovski's First White Russian Front; and driving against *Army Group South* were the First, Second, Third, and Fourth Ukrainian Fronts under Vatutin, Konev, Malinovski, and Tolbukhin respectively. The German order of battle remained unchanged, with Von Kuechler commanding in the northern sector, Busch in the center, and Von Manstein in the south.

The Soviets struck the first blow of the winter campaign against the *Eighteenth Army* on the left flank of the *Army Group North.* With the exception of the Russian attack to reopen land communication with Leningrad the previous January, this 200 mile sector of the eastern line had remained static for two and one-half years along the Volkhov River and the Leningrad perimeter. The *Eighteenth Army* at this time comprised the equivalent of 20 divisions including five Luftwaffe field divisions,[14] two brigades of Latvian volunteers, and the *Spanish Legion.* It had few reserves available, having transferred three infantry divisions to *Army Group Center* in December to help contain the attacks in the Nevel-Vitebsk area. Opposite these units the Russians had concentrated the six armies of the Leningrad and Volkhov Fronts.

Looking at the map, the most likely point of attack for the Red Army seemed the salient the Germans held directly south of Lake Ladoga, since it furnished the principal cover for the rail net feeding the line before Leningrad. The Soviets, however, had other ideas. For some

---

[14] Divisions of Luftwaffe personnel fighting as ground troops. Officered from the Luftwaffe, they were inadequately trained for ground combat and were deficient in heavy weapons and artillery.

time Govorov had been moving strong elements of his command, including heavy masses of artillery, across the frozen Gulf of Finland into the
Russian-held beachhead west of the old Czarist capital. By the middle
of January the streams, lakes, and swamps to the south were frozen solid
and suitable for maneuver. On 14 January he launched his attack, the
artillery blasting paths through the prepared German defenses. German counteraction was weak and disorganized, and in four days his
units had opened a sizable gap and gained operational freedom.

On the same day, Meretskov launched a surprise attack against the
army's right flank. Ignoring the bridgehead he held over the Volkhov
River just north of Novogorod, he struck across the upper end of the
frozen Lake Ilmen and took the strong German defenses along the river
in reverse. Novogorod, the anchor of the line, fell four days later.

With both flanks turned, the commander of the *Eighteenth Army,*
Generaloberst Georg Lindemann, had no choice but to withdraw to the
south to prevent the larger part of his force being cut off. Momentarily
he was able to outdistance his pursuers, and for a few days managed
to maintain a line between the lakes in the vicinity of Luga. But Meretskov's pressure on his right soon made this new position untenable and
he was forced to pull back again, this time all the way to the Baltic
States border. The *Sixteenth Army,* with its right flank thus thrown
in the air, was then forced to withdraw westward, and by 1 March the
whole of *Army Group North* had taken up a new line extending from
Narva on the Gulf of Finland to a junction with *Army Group Center*
near Polotsk. From this position the Germans were able to beat off
further assaults, and, with the spring thaws approaching, all movement
came to a halt until summer.

In the south, Vatutin's attacks of early January, which had overrun
Korosten, Zhitomir, and Kazatin and placed the best of the rail net
west of the Dnepr in Russian hands, had left *Army Group South* in a
difficult position. Only one rail line, the Lwow-Proskurov-Odessa,
remained open, and the Red divisions stood less than 90 miles from it at
Kazatin. In addition, the *Sixth and Eighth Armies* lay exposed to
envelopment from the north. Under such pressure, Von Manstein was
compelled to shift much of his strength to the center of his line around
Vinnitsa at the expense of weakening his left. He was thus able to
screen his last remaining supply link and at the same time lend support
to his two armies further south. In so doing, however, he was forced
to spread his defenses so thin that he was unable to halt the Soviets who
were moving along the lower edge of the Pripyat Marshes, cutting his
last lateral link with *Army Group Center.*

On 29 January the First and Second Ukrainian Fronts launched a
coordinated attack from the north and east on the *Eighth Army* below
Kiev and in less than three weeks cut off and destroyed eight German

divisions. Simultaneously, Malinovski and Tolbukhin with their Third and Fourth Ukrainian Fronts struck convergently at the *Sixth Army* in the Dnepr bend area and by 2 February took Nikopol and Krivoi Rog, the two defensive anchors in that portion of the sector.

Meanwhile from the Sarny area Vatutin continued against Von Manstein's now weakened left and quickly took Rovno. On 3 February he occupied Lutsk and pushed on toward Dubno and Lwow. The retention of this latter city was highly important to *Army Group South* as its loss would have cut the last rail line from Poland and forced the use of the poor Romanian net. The *Fourth Panzer Army* was rushed to the trouble spot and the drive brought to a halt.

After a short period for regrouping, on 4 March the offensive again began to roll along the whole southern front. Gen. G. Zhukov, now commanding the First Ukrainian Front, opened the assault with an attack on a 105-mile front between Dubno and Vinnitsa, with the main effort toward Tarnopol. In the first two days he drove 40 miles between the *First* and *Fourth Panzer Armies*, cutting the Lwow-Odessa line and forcing Von Manstein to pull the *First Panzer Army* from the vicinity of Uman to halt the attack across his rear. On 6 March, Konev struck southwestward with his Second Ukrainian Front and on 10 March captured Uman, which had been uncovered to stop Zhukov. Continuing to push, he reached and crossed the Bug River on 12 March and cut the Lwow-Odessa line three days later. On 19 March he crossed the Dnestr River and a week later, against little opposition, reached the Prutt River on a 125-mile front.

Meanwhile Zhukov, making little headway against the *Fourth Panzer Army* guarding the entrance to Poland along the line Kovel-Lwow-Tarnopol, turned the weight of his attack to the south and took Vinnitsa on 22 March. On 25 March he reached the Dnestr, and three days later captured Cernauti in the foothills of the Carpathian Mountains.

Coordinating his movement with Zhukov, Malinovski broke through the *Sixth Army* defenses toward the lower Dnestr, and on 13 March took Kherson. Three days later he reached the Bug River. Pressing on, he forced the evacuation of Odessa on 10 April and on 12 April reached the Dnestr throughout the length of his front.

Then with the Russians feeling the effect of their overstretched supply lines and the spring thaws upon them, the southern front quieted down, the Red divisions standing virtually along the Polish border of 1941.

The Final Drives

In June of 1944 the end was clearly in sight for Hitler's Reich. After five years of war Germany was at last beginning to feel the full fury of its enemies. With the Normandy landings on 6 June the Wehrmacht became actively. engaged in operations on three fronts against vastly superior forces, and because of Hitler's refusal to shorten his eastern line there was no strategic reserve. German divisions were so scattered that everywhere they were forced to fight at an increasing disadvantage. The U-boat campaign had been brought under control in 1943 in the Battle of the Atlantic; and Allied bombing was beginning to take heavy toll of German industrial output. With the approach of summer campaigning weather in the east, Wehrmacht prospects were never darker.

At the start of the summer battles almost every consideration indicated that the Soviets would strike their next major blow against *Army Group Center*. The German hold in the center of the line constituted a huge salient overhanging the Red Armies in the south which to the methodical Russian mind had to be eliminated. The Russian forces there had not been in serious action since the first of the year. Their supply line to the great logistical center at Moscow was relatively short compared to the overextended axes in the south, and, unlike the forces in the Ukraine, they had had opportunity during a quiet winter to rehabilitate the rail lines and build up large stocks near the front.

Nonetheless the Germans, with Hitler dominating almost every plan and disposition, clung to the belief that the major Soviet blow of the summer would be a continuation of the attack in the south, and disposed their divisions accordingly: 37 infantry divisions, 11 panzer divisions, and a miscellany of Romanian and Hungarian units in the south; one panzer and 33 infantry divisions in the center. Strategic reserves in the latter sector comprised the one panzer division, an infantry division, and a panzer group made up of a number of miscellaneous motorized units.

On 23 June the Soviets struck, and against *Army Group Center*. The First Baltic and the three White Russian Fronts [15] launched a general offensive on a 360-mile front from Velikiye-Luki to the lower Pripyat behind a preparation fired by some 380 artillery pieces and mortars per mile of line. The preparation inflicted heavy casualties on the German front line troops and enabled the Red infantry to quickly open a number of holes through which the armored brigades poured. Almost immediately the German situation was desperate. There was no second line of defense to fall back on, and the two reserve divisions were quickly committed and almost as quickly destroyed. Chernyakovski with his Third White Russian Front quickly surrounded Vitebsk and sent his mobile reserves into the fight through a 25 mile gap south of the city. One of his columns reached the Minsk-Smolensk rail line and highway

---

[15] Rokossovski continued to command the First White Russian Front, but Sokolovski's old Second White Russian Front was reorganized as the Second and Third White Russian Fronts with Gen F. D. Zakharov and Gen I. D. Chernyakovski as commanders.

on 25 June, cutting the *Fourth Army's* principal line of retreat. At the same time Rokossovski broke his armored units into the Germans' rear through a 20-mile hole in the *Ninth Army's* front, one column swinging north to encircle Bobruysk, the other driving on to the west. On 27 June he surrounded Bobruysk and trapped some 70,000 German troops. Both Orsha and Vitebsk fell on 27 June, and Mogilev the next day. The loss of these anchors of the line split the front into three segments and brought an end to defensive action on an army group basis. Thereafter, German opposition deteriorated rapidly.

There was no letup in the attack, however, with Gen. I. Kh. Bagramyan's First Baltic Front units driving on Polotsk and Chernyakovski and Rokossovski's right wing enveloping Minsk from the north and south. The fall of the latter city on 4 July trapped almost the entire *Fourth Army* which was fighting some miles to the southeast. In just 10 days the Red Army had completely obliterated the Dnepr line between Polotsk and the Pripyat River and destroyed 25 German divisions. During the next week the pace continued with Baranovichi falling on 8 July and Vilna surrounded on 10 July.

In the southern sector Konev and Rokossovski's left wing launched their summer offensive on 14 July. By 25 July Konev had surrounded Lwow while Rokossovski, swinging more to the northwest to maintain contact with his right wing, took Lublin on 22 July. Two days later he reached the Vistula and on 31 July his units stood only some 12 miles from Warsaw. With the drive through White Russia continuing, by the end of the first week in August the fight in the central and southern sectors had passed over the western boundary of the Soviet Union, whence *BARBAROSSA* had been launched more than three years before.

Further to the north, Yeremenko, now commanding the Second Baltic Front had joined the general offensive on 13 July, attacking along an 80-mile front from Ostrov to the Dvina River. Model, then commanding *Army Group Center,* had foreseen just such an attack in the north and two days before it was launched had suggested that *Army Group North* withdraw from Estonia and northern Latvia to below the Dvina in order that its divisions might be used to stabilize the fast deteriorating situation in the central sector, but Hitler turned down the proposal. The Germans facing Yeremenko were strongly entrenched, but their position was without depth, and when Opochka, the central anchor of the line, fell on 15 July they were forced to pull back to positions along the Dvinsk-Pskov rail line and re-form.

Gen. I. I. Maslennikov now joined the fight with his Third Baltic Front just below Lake Peipus, taking Ostrov on 21 July and Pskov two days later. On 25 July Yeremenko cut the road from Dvinsk to Riga, and the next day captured Dvinsk itself, forcing the Germans back further still. Here they were able to reestablish their line and hold. At the same time Narva on the Gulf of Finland fell to units of the Leningrad Front.

Meanwhile, Bagramyan had taken Polotsk the same day Minsk fell and then swung his attack to the northwest between Kovno and the Dvina. By 15 July he had driven open a 30-mile gap in the front at that point. Then, almost unopposed, he sent his armor racing on toward Riga. On 1 August he stood but 20 miles from the sea, virtually isolating both the *Sixteenth* and *Eighteenth Armies.* Generaloberst Ferdinand Schoerner, newly in command of *Army Group North,* then launched a series of local counterattacks and managed to stabilize his contracted line for a time as the rest of the eastern front quieted down.

In six weeks the Red Army had driven more than 400 miles from the Dnepr to the Vistula; it had virtually destroyed *Army Group Center,* it had isolated *Army Group North* in the Baltic States, and in the south had driven the last German from Soviet soil except in the southern portion of Bessarabia.

After a short pause, Maslennikov continued to push just south of Lake Peipus. By 15 August he achieved a breakthrough and then turned northward into Estonia. Chernyakovski, Bagramyan, and Yeremenko maintained their pressure but, continually checked by stubborn German resistance from a series of defense positions prepared in depth, were unable to break away.

The capitulation of Finland early in September freed a number of troop units to the Leningrad Front and their added pressure forced Schoerner to evacuate Estonia through the narrow escape corridor along the southern shore of the Gulf of Riga which, using the last of his armor, he had been able to maintain in the face of all attacks. When Bagramyan found himself unable to cut through this last life line, he switched his main effort further to the south in a final drive to the coast. By 10 October he reached the Baltic Sea between Liepaja and Klaipeda. The remnants of Schoerner's armies were trapped in northern Latvia, and the Baltic campaign was at an end.

CHAPTER 9

THE PARTISAN MOVEMENT REACHES MATURITY

With the failure of the *Sixth Army* before Stalingrad in November 1943 the entire course of the war in the east changed abruptly. The period of sustained German drives came to an end and the Red Army, going over to the offensive along most of the front, gained the initiative from the Gulf of Finland to the Black Sea.

For the partisan movement the change was highly significant. During the 18 months of its existence, the period of its infancy and growth, it had been pitted against the strength of a winning army. Now, as it approached maturity, it could strike at the rear of a retreating, weakening enemy. It was a promising opportunity.

The reorganization within the movement which had started the previous spring had been only a beginning. During the fall of 1942 and on through the winter and into the spring of 1943 the rebuilding continued. Where the earlier stress had been on the individual partisan units, the emphasis was now placed on a reorganization of the movement as a whole along lines which would make it an efficient auxiliary of the entire Soviet war effort.

Completion of the Reorganization

The new Central Staff of the Partisan Movement that emerged was in effect a fourth armed service, standing on a level with the Red Army, the Red Air Force, and the Red Navy. Despite the fact that it was designed as a ground combat command whose primary mission was to support and aid and abet the operations of the Red Army, its ultimate control was political, not military, descending directly from the Central Committee of the Communist Party through the State Defense Committee, to Ponomarenko, himself a member of the latter agency.

Its structure [see *chart 2*] was similar to that of the Red Army and was organized along conventional general staff lines, with sections for personnel, intelligence, operations, and supply. In addition, there was a political security section headed by a high-ranking NKVD officer, and several special staff sections for such matters as cryptography, transportation, and the like.[1]

Directly below the Central Staff were the territorial commands. These were executive partisan staffs for the Karelo-Finnish Soviet So-

---

[1] *"Nachrichten ueber Bandenkrieg, Nr. 3," OKH/Gen.St.d.H/ABt. Frde. H. Ost (I/Bd), Nr. 5632/43 g. Kdos., 28.VII.43.* H 3/748.

cialist Republic (SSR), the Leningrad area, Estonia, Latvia, Lithuania, the Kalinin Front, the White Russian SSR, the Russian Socialist Federated Soviet Republic (including the Kursk, Orel, and Smolensk areas), the Ukrainian SSR, the Crimean SSR, and the Caucasus. With but one exception, the chiefs of these staffs were Communist Party or NKVD officers, often officials of the former government of the areas. The exact function of these territorial commands is unknown. They did not constitute an echelon in the chain of command.

The lower echelon command organs were grouped laterally according to the Red Army front sectors. Below the Central Staff there were partisan staffs with each front command, exercising control through operating groups set up at the headquarters of each army of the front. Beyond the main line of resistance and under the control of each of these latter were "Operations Groups in the Enemy's Rear" which exercised immediate command of the partisan brigades [see *chart 3*], battalions, and lesser units. These operational groups issued orders to the brigades and separate battalions on the basis of directives from the higher staffs and headquarters; oversaw recruiting training; required regular reports on results of missions, unit strengths, and positions; and strove in every way to maintain and improve discipline.[2]

Although they were to cooperate closely with their respective front and army commands, the staffs and operating groups were not under military direction. The chain of command was clear: the partisans were to work with and in support of the Red Army, but they were to take their orders from the Central Staff. They were not to allow themselves to be absorbed by the Red Army in the event of a successful offensive. On the contrary, they were under orders to move westward before such an advance so as to remain in the rear of the enemy and under political control. To ensure a continuation of this control under all circumstances, when the political commissar in the Red Army was divested of the greater part of his power he remained secure in his old position in the partisan units coequal with the tactical commander. Furthermore, the Central Staff retained the authority to alter the partisan organization or insert special task groups into the enemy rear without reference to any military agency.[3]

It was sometime during the latter period of this reorganization that the distinction between the Red Army-led partisan brigades and the purely partisan groups, that had formerly been so marked, disappeared, with the latter being raised to or assuming the level of the former.[4]

---

[2] *Ibid.*

[3] Captured partisan directive, incl. to: *OKW/WFSt/WOr, (I/IV). Nr. 4630/43g. 24.VII.43.* in *H. Gr. Nord. Ic/AO, Propaganda, 24.VIII.–24.X.43.* 75131/108.

[4] See: *Bandenlisten, Februar bis September 43, H. Gr. Mitte, Ic/AO (Abw.).* 65003/4.

ORGANIZATION OF THE PARTISAN MOVEMENT AND THE COMMUNIST PARTY IN THE GERMAN REAR WITH

RELATION TO THE RED ARMY: 1943 *

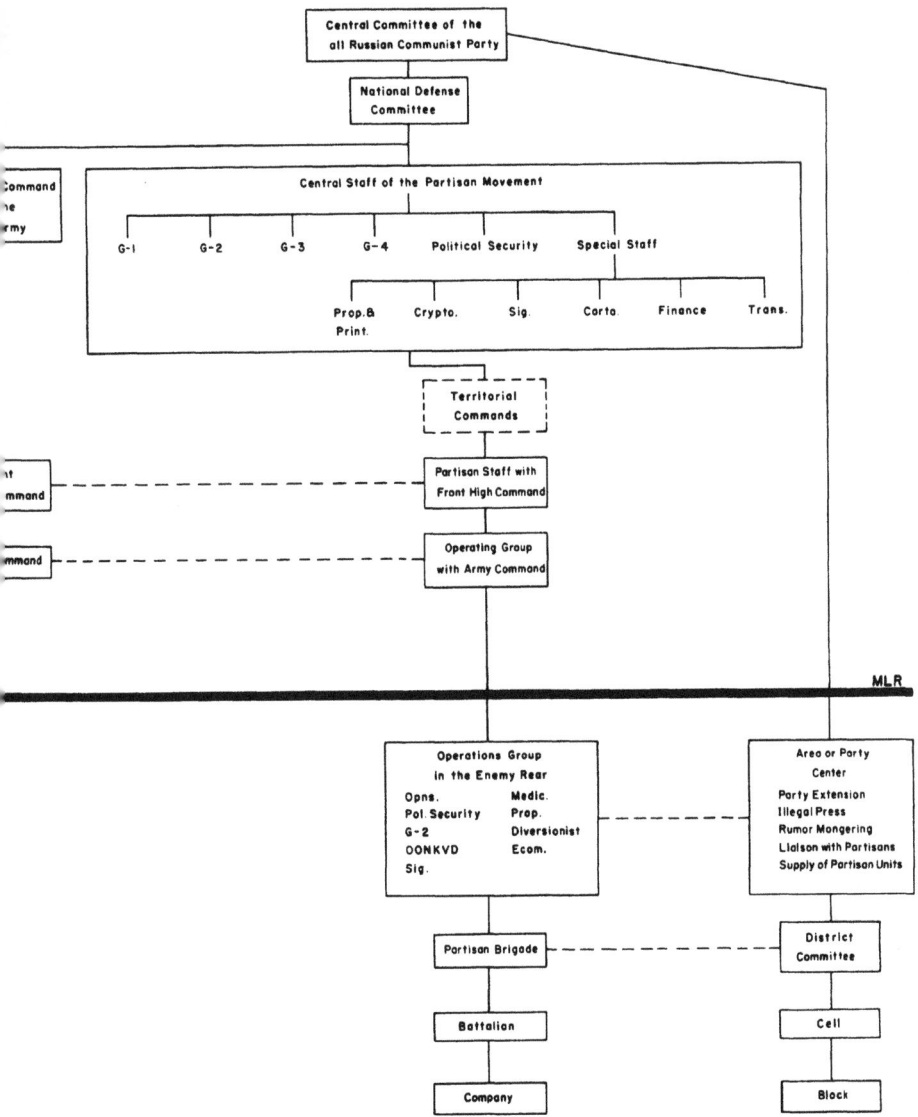

Central Committee of the
all Russian Communist Party

National Defense
Committee

Central Staff of the Partisan Movement

| G-I | G-2 | G-3 | G-4 | Political Security | Special Staff |

Prop. & Crypto. Sig. Carto. Finance Trans.
Print.

Command
ne
rmy

Territorial
Commands

Partisan Staff with
Front High Command

Operating Group
with Army Command

nt
mmand

mmand

MLR

Operations Group
in the Enemy Rear

Opns.	Medic.
Pol. Security	Prop.
G-2	Diversionist
OONKVD	Ecom.
Sig.	

Area or Party
Center

Party Extension
Illegal Press
Rumor Mongering
Liaison with Partisans
Supply of Partisan Units

Partisan Brigade

District
Committee

Battalion

Cell

Company

Block

Nachrichten ueber Bandenkrieg Nr.3" OKH/Gen Std H/Abt. Frde H Ost, Nr. 5632/43, geh., 28.VII.43. (H3/748).

388413 O - 56 - (Face p . 138)

Chart No. 2.   Organization of the Partisan Movement.

Chart 3

ORGANIZATION OF A PARTISAN BRIGADE *

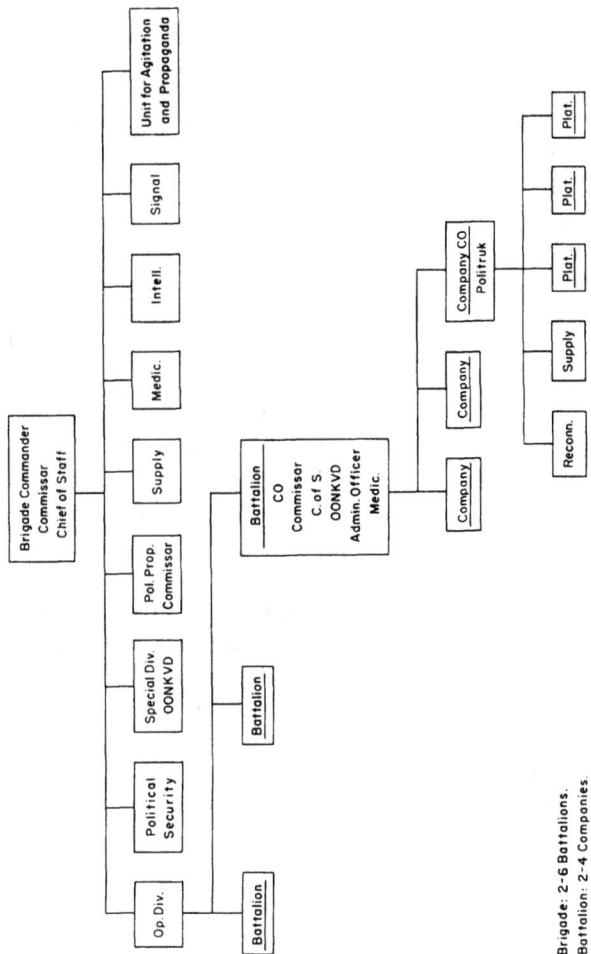

Brigade Commander
Commissar
Chief of Staff

Op. Div.

Political
Security

Special Div.
OONKVD

Pol. Prop.
Commissar

Supply

Medic.

Intell.

Signal

Unit for Agitation
and Propaganda

Battalion

Battalion

Battalion

Battalion
CO
Commissar
C. of S.
OONKVD
Admin. Officer
Medic.

Company

Company

Company

Company CO
Politruk

Recon.

Supply

Plat.

Plat.

Plat.

Brigade: 2-6 Battalions.
Battalion: 2-4 Companies.

* Anl 3 z."Nachrichten ueber Bandenkrieg, Nr. 3", op. cit.

Chart No. 3. Organization of the Partisan Brigade.

Such was the organization, on paper at least. How well it was ever actually established throughout the whole German rear is impossible to say. In the Ukraine, for instance, where no really serious partisan resistance ever developed, it must have remained rather embryonic. In portions of the central and northern sectors, however, to judge by subsequent events, it must have reached a fairly high stage of development.

Leadership and Personnel

Despite the predomininantly political control of the movement, by the spring of 1943 the actual leadership of a good proportion of the bands was in the hands of the Red Army officers, a number of whom had been trained in partisan schools. The political functionaries who in many cases had formed or taken command of bands in the earlier stages of the war became the commissars of the units, and, although retaining their positions as "cocommanders," primarily concerned themselves with political security within their particular unit and with Communist propaganda in their areas of operation. In addition, they often served dually as secretaries of illegal district party committees.[5]

Manpower for the bands continued to be drawn from a variety of sources. Escaped prisoners of war still drifted into the partisan ranks, but in no such numbers as formerly. German occupation policies caused many civilians to volunteer. But by and large, as the movement expanded, the larger proportion of the personnel was drafted from the native populace, forcibly when necessary, although during this period fear of the German forced labor draft and overbearing economic requisitions coupled with the general military situation and widespread Soviet propaganda generally made the use of pressure unnecessary. The Central Staff constantly advised the lower echelons to foster the best possible relations with the natives as a means of facilitating such recruiting.[6] In some areas recruits were taken systematically by age groups, and at times even women were drafted.[7] Special attention was paid to recruiting members of the Komsomolsk, the communist youth organization. These young Bolsheviks were highly desirable as combat men or political activists because of their fanaticism.[8]

In partisan-dominated areas recruits were put through a training course. Generally they spent several weeks on probation to prevent

[5] "Nachrichten ueber Bandenkrieg, Nr. 6," OKH/Gen.St.d.H./Abt. Frde. H. Ost. H 3/738.

[6] "Nachrichten ueber Bandenkrieg, Nr. 3," OKH/Gen.St.d.H./Abt. Frde. H. Ost (I/Bd), Nr. 5632/43 g. Kdos., 28.VII.43. H 3/748.

[7] Korueck 532, Ic. Br. Tgb. Nr. 442/43 geh., 30.I.43., Feindlage im Korueckgebiet, Stand: 36.I.43., in Anlageheft 2 zu KTB Korueck 559, Ia, Unternehmen "Klette 2," 5.I.–19.I.43. 44404/3.

[8] "Nachrichten ueber Bandenkrieg, Nr. 3," OKH/Gen.St.d.H./Abt. Frde. H. Ost (I/Bd), Nr. 5632/43 g. Kdos., 28.VII.43. H 3/748.

escape or defection of those forcibly drafted and to give attached NKVD agents an opportunity to check their backgrounds against the possibility of infiltration of agents in German pay. Through informants within the units the commissars also kept a constant check on all personnel.[9] Desertions of individual partisans were reported to the Central Staff, and their families, if they could be reached, were sent to labor camps in Siberia. If a defector was apprehended, the NKVD both passed and executed sentence.[10] In a number of cases the NKVD terrorized German collaborators into doubledealing by forcing them under threat of death to sign oaths of loyalty to the Soviet regime and then threatening to have the oath delivered to the occupation authorities should the individual fail to cooperate with the partisans.[11]

Demolition, intelligence, and communication specialists were flown in to the bands both as regularly assigned personnel and as special assistants on training. The radio operators were particularly well trained in their field. They adhered closely to standard procedures and demonstrated far better communications discipline than the average Red Army operators.[12] The better established units were often inspected by Red Army personnel, and high-ranking Soviet officers, both military and political, were frequently flown in to partisan centers for conferences.[13]

Targets

In February the Central Staff issued a directive designating in order of priority the targets the partisans were to attack. At the top of the list were roads, rail lines, bridges, and enemy vehicles and rolling stock. Secondary targets comprised telephone and telegraph lines and supply depots. The bands were to take offensive action against German guard posts, patrols, and other small units only when they had a definite superiority in numbers.[14]

---

[9] Rpt, *Cav Regt Center*, to Hq *Army Group Center, 23, VI.43.*, H Gr Mitte, Ia, Nr. 6810/43, in Anl z. KTB H Gr Mitte, Fuehrungsabt., Akte XXII, Heft 10, 11.VI.–31.VII.43. 65002/22.

[10] Anl. 3 z. "Nachrichten ueber Bandenkrieg, Nr. 1," OKH/Gen.St.d.H/Abt. Frde Heere Ost, 3 May 43. H. 3/738.

[11] AOK 4, Feindnachrichtenblaetter Nr. 1, 2.II.43. in KTB, AOK 4, Ic. 2.II.–28.XI.43. 48448/6.

[12] MS P–038, "German Radio Intelligence," (Hist. Div. EUCOM), p. 209 (S). OCMH, Foreign Studies Br; Anl. 3 z. "Nachrichten ueber Bandenkrieg, Nr. 1," OKH/Gen.St.d.H./Abt. Frde Heere Ost, 3 May 43. H. 3/738.

[13] Anl. 3 z. "Nachrichten ueber Bandenkrieg, Nr. 1." OKH/Gen.St.d.H./Abt. Frde Heere Ost, 3 May 43. H. 3/738; tlg, Army Group Center to OKH, 26 Apr 43, in Anl. z. KTB, H. Gr. Mitte, Fuehrungsabt., Akte XXII, Bandenbekaempfung, Heft 8, 6.IV.–15.V.43. 65002/20.

[14] No copy of this directive is extant. It is referred to several times as the Stalin Order of 25 Feb 43. See: Anl. 3 z. "Nachrichten ueber Bandenkrieg, Nr. 1," OKH/Gen.St.d.H./Abt. Frde Heere Ost, 3 May 43. H 3/738.

The Bands as Intelligence Organs

Although in 1942 a start had been made toward utilizing the bands as information-gathering agencies, little was actually accomplished in this regard prior to the completion of the reorganization in the spring of 1943. With the establishment of the partisan staffs and operating groups within the Red Army field commands and with the operations groups in over-all command of irregular units behind the German lines, both RO and OONKVD [15] sections were attached to the various partisan staffs [see *chart 4*], down to and including brigades, to control all Soviet intelligence activities in the occupied areas. Generally the assignment of these sections was espionage for the Red Army and for the party committees in the immediate sector; reconnaissance in line with combat missions and the security of bases and installations; and political espionage for the Central Committee of the Communist Party in Moscow.

To guide and control this work, a deputy chief for Reconnaissance and Information was attached to each operations group, and manuals such as a "Guide for Political Espionage" and a "Guide Book for the Partisan Intelligence Agent," were issued to the lower echelons.[16] A supplement to the latter covered in detail the scope of the information desired, both military and political. It contained altogether 172 questions in 21 fields and covered almost every aspect of the situation in the German-occupied areas. From German occupation agencies and administrative measures to native working and living conditions, edution, religion, public health, and political attitude, the list went on to Wehrmacht morale, antipartisan measures and tactics, organization of native police, and a very detailed list on German use of native troops, including nationalities involved, social and economic background, methods of recruiting, inducements offered, morale, and political attitude.[17] The brigade RO's and the commissars of the smaller bands worked to provide answers to these questions through local agent informer nets they set up and through de-briefing sessions with the partisans themselves following an operation. Missions assigned to the bands were often dual-purpose. A brigade working opposite the Leningrad Front received orders to set demolitions along a specified section of rail line, attack an outlying enemy air field, and reconnoiter for German troop strength and dispositions, all in the same mission.[18]

---

[15] *Ossobyj Odtel*-NKVD intelligence, i. e. Soviet counterintelligence.
[16] *Anl. 9 z. "Nachrichten ueber Bandenkrieg, Nr. 3," OKH/Gen.St.d.H./Abt. Frde. H. Ost (I/Bd), Nr. 5632/43 g. Kdos., 28.VII.43. H 3/748; Anl. 3 z. "Nachrichten ueber Bandenkrieg, Nr. 1."; "Nachrichten ueber Bandenkrieg, Nr. 4," OKH/Gen. St.d.H./Abt. Frde. H. Ost.* H 3/738.
[17] Annex 1 to *"Nachrichten ueber Bandenkrieg, Nr. 4," OKH/Gen.St.d.H./Abt. Frde. H. Ost.* H 3/738.
[18] Captured partisan order in *Anl. 3 z. "Nachrichten ueber Bandenkrieg, Nr. 1," OKH/Gen.St.d.H./Abt. Frde Heere Ost, 3 May 43.* H 3/738.

Chart 4

THE PARTISANS AND SOVIET INTELLIGENCE

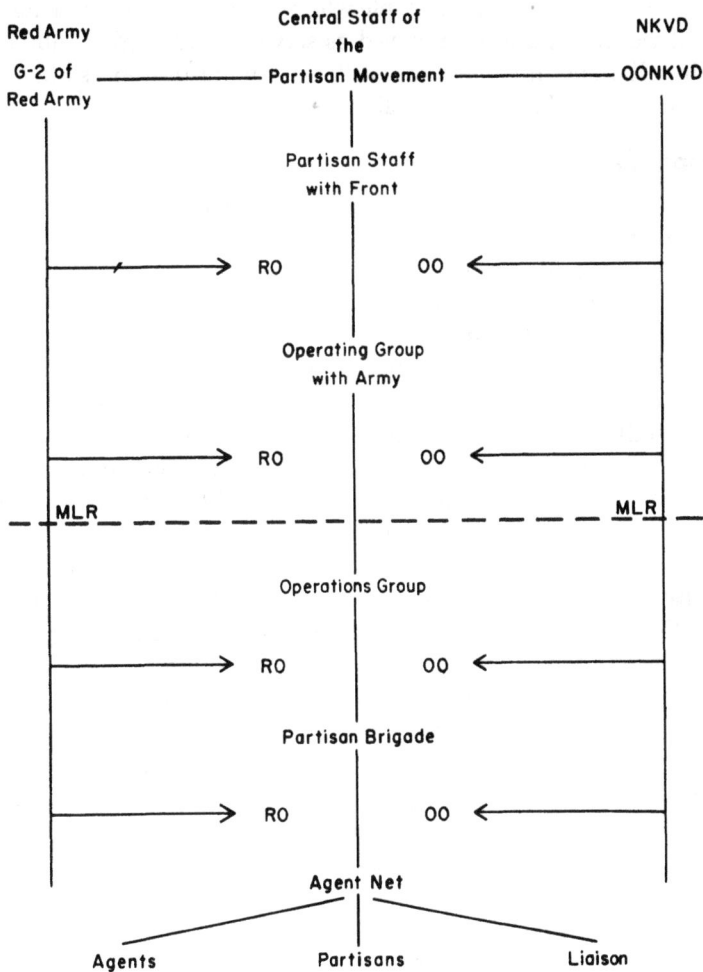

Red Army	Central Staff of the	NKVD
G-2 of Red Army ———————	Partisan Movement ———————	OONKVD

Partisan Staff
with Front

RO   OO ←

Operating Group
with Army

RO   OO ←

MLR — MLR —

Operations Group

RO   OO ←

Partisan Brigade

RO   OO ←

Agent Net

Agents   Partisans   Liaison

RO: Intelligence (Army)
OO (NKVD): Counter-Intelligence

Chart No. 4. The Partisans and Soviet Intelligence.

Although some excellent information was obtained in this manner, in the long run the informer nets proved the more reliable source. These informers were wives or relatives of Red Army men, local party members or candidates for party membership anxious to qualify themselves, village mayors or elders, and people who worked for occupation agencies, railroad workers, natives employed as servants and workers about German installations, members of the local administration established by the Germans, and local native police.[19]

Partisan Propaganda

Some of the bands from their earliest days had directed a crude sort of propaganda at the natives in the German rear in an attempt to wean them away from the occupation. Then late in 1942, coincident with the reorganization of the movement, Moscow moved to increase such efforts and bring all propaganda under its control. In the revamped partisan command structure special propaganda and press divisions were created not only within the Central Staff, but in the territorial staffs and the staffs and operating groups with the fronts and armies.

Units for Agitation and Propaganda were established in brigades and smaller independent units and in the Communist Party centers and district committees in the German rear. Training schools for propaganda editors, writers, printers, and art layout men were set up, and graduates were distributed throughout the movement.[20] Depending on their size, the partisan units and Communist Party groups were supplied with large or small field presses, operators, and sometimes editors. Often the editorial work was done by the commissar of the band or the secretary of a local illegal party committee. Raw propaganda material was broadcast regularly to the units over the partisan or party radio net.[21]

Under this centralized setup, the Soviets made every possible emotional appeal and attempted to expose every weakness exhibited by the occupation. Taken *in toto* it appears to have been very effective with a population which long before had begun to waver. The subject matter was the same old standardized material: the success of the Red Army and the partisans; the Allied second front; German intentions to reduce Russia to colonial status; German failure to abolish the collective farms; the fact that taxes and economic requisitions were higher under the Germans than they had been under the Soviet system; stories of German atrocities; the German slave labor program; hints that the Soviets would

[19] *"Nachrichten ueber Bandenkrieg, Nr. 4,"* OKH/Gen.St.d.H./Abt. Frde. H. Ost. H 3/738.
[20] See: Stalin Order of December 1942, quoted in *ibid.; "Nachrichten ueber Bandenkrieg, Nr. 7,"* OKH/Gen.St.d.H./Abt Frde Heere Ost. H 3/738.
[21] *Feindnachrichtenblaetter, Bandenlage, AOK 16, III.43.,* in AOK 16, Ic, TB Ic/AO, z. KTB # 5, Teil VI, 1.I.–31.III.43. 36588/142; *"Nachrichten ueber Bandenkrieg, Nr. 4,"* OKH/Gen.St.d.H./Abt. Frde. H. Ost. H 3/738.

correct the social mistakes of the past; and, again and again, the promise that the Red Army and the strong hand of the party would return.[22]

In some areas the partisans distributed the land to the natives, setting the agricultural quotas considerably lower than those in the German-controlled sectors.[23]   In the rear of the *Second Army* they even went to the extreme of distributing religious printed matter and holding church services for the populace.[24]

The indigenous native units in German service were primary targets for this propaganda, and by late spring it had not only scored considerable success but visibly hampered German security operations.[25]

Reestablishment of the Communist Party in the Rear [26]

Coincident with the reorganization of the partisan movement, Moscow took measures to regenerate the Communist Party in the German rear on a similar centrally directed and uniform basis.   The early attempts to revive the party in the overrun areas had been desultory and uncoordinated, patterned after the prewar political setup.   Early in 1943, however, this underground organization was completely revised and realigned in accordance with the Red Army order of battle along the front and paralleling the new partisan structure.

Area or party centers—Central Committees of the Communist Party in the Rear Areas,—political counterparts of the partisan operations groups, were established as working headquarters opposite each Red Army front without regard to former administrative divisions.   As such, these centers with their command channel running direct from the Central Committee of the Communist Party in Moscow had over-all control of all party organizations and activities in their respective sectors. They exercised their jurisdiction through a number of district committees.   The district committees which were responsible for certain well-defined areas of strategic significance as agricultural or industrial districts were broken down into cells made up of a number of blocks, these latter the real germ cells of the party.   A block generally comprised a village, a part of a town, a collective or state farm, a small factory, or similar unit.

---

[22] *Ibid., Anlage 52 z. KTB Wirtschaftsinspektion Mitte, 1.IV.–30.VI.43.*   Wi/ID 2.53.

[23] *Anl. 3 z. "Nachrichten ueber Bandenkrieg, Nr. 1," OKH/Gen.St.d.H./Abt. Frde Heere Ost, 3 May 43.* H 3/738.

[24] *Bandennachrichtenblatt Nr. 1, Korueck 580, 2.VII.43., Anl. z. KTB 25a, Korueck 580, Teil 7, 1.VII.–15.VII.43.*   37516/1.

[25] *Reichskommissar fuer die Ukraine, V–I–7422, Tgb. Nr. 378/43 geh., 25.VI.43.* Footlocker 50, folder 4; *Bandennachrichtenblatt Nr. 1, Korueck 580, 2.VII.43., Anl. z. KTB 25a, Korueck 580, Teil 7, 1.VII.–15.VII.43.*   37516/1.

[26] Unless otherwise noted, the material in this section is taken from: "Working Plan and Program of the Communist Party (of the Bolsheviks) of the Rear Area, 1943," *Anlage 1 z. "Nachrichten ueber Bandenkrieg, Nr. 6," OKH/Gen.St.d.H./Abt. Frde Heere Ost.* H 3/738.

This "Party in the Rear Areas" was to bend every effort to loosen the German hold on Soviet territory by setting up a tight Communist administration wherever it could and at the same time giving all possible aid to the partisan movement. This it was to do by creating and closely controlling Young Communist groups on the farms, in the villages, and in the existent partisan units; by keeping close watch on and exploiting the temper of the natives; through propaganda; through leadership in the partisan movement; and through general preparation for an armed revolt. In this work the party centers were to cooperate closely with the partisan operations groups. The actual connection between the two extended to the procurement of recruits for the bands, the assignment of combat missions to the bands by the district committees in the event of interruption of communications between the bands and the operating groups with the armies, district committee approval of appointments or dismissals in the ranks of the political leadership of the brigades and lesser units, and the procurement of food, clothing, and means of transportation for the bands.[27]

---

[27] "Nachrichten ueber Bandenkrieg, Nr. 4," OKH/Gen.St.d.H./Abt. Frde. H. Ost. H 3/738.

CHAPTER 10

THE PARTISANS AND THE CAMPAIGN OF 1943

Beginning with the campaigns of the summer of 1943, the story of the partisan movement became in great part the story of the offensive and defensive moves of the Wehrmacht and the Soviet armed forces, and so continued as long as the fighting remained on Soviet territory. Before the opening of the German *ZITADELLE* offensive in July, the reorganization of the partisan movement was complete and the bands, greatly increased in numbers and operationally much improved over their 1941–1942 counterparts, were ready to take over with some authority the clearly defined role assigned them in the Soviet war effort. As in the previous two years, their operations were for the most part confined to the central and northern sectors where the terrain was favorable.

The Winter Period, January to May

Partisan Forces

At the beginning of 1943 the heaviest concentrations of partisans lay in three regions of the *Army Group Center Rear Area*, the wooded Orel-Bryansk area, the Pripyat Marshes, and the White Russian forests west of Mogilev-Orsha-Vitebsk.[1]   In the rear of *Army Group North* there were several sizeable groups behind the *Sixteenth Army* west of the Dno-Nevel rail line along the army group boundary and straddling the Velikiye Luki-Rezekne railroad.[2]   Other irregular units were scattered through the occupied areas from the region between Lakes Ilmen and Peipus behind the *Eighteenth Army* to the Yaila Mountains in the Crimea, but for the most part they were weak and ineffective.

Before the middle of February the concentrations in the Central sector had expanded considerably with the appearance of additional bands, a number of which had crossed over into the German rear through gaps in the front lines.[3]   By the end of March they constituted an almost solid block from Bryansk-Orel through Gomel and Bobruysk and thence north through the area west of Orsha and Vitebsk where they

---

[1] *Bandenlage im Bereich d. H. Gr. Mitte, Stand: 28.II.43., Anl. 2, Bandenlisten, Februar bis September 43, H. Gr. Mitte.* 65003/4.

[2] *Feindnachrichtenblaetter, Bandenlage, usw., AOK 16, Tgb., Ic/AO z. KTB 5, Teil VI, 1.I.–31.III.43.* 36588/142.

[3] *Feindnachrichtenblaetter, Bandenlage, usw., AOK 16, Tgb., Ic/AO z. KTB 5, Teil VI, 1.I.–31.III.43.* 36588/142; *201 Sich Div. Ia. KTB 4a, ueber grosse Bandenunternehmungen, SCHNEEHASE, 24.I.–12.II.43., Bericht 15.II.43.* 38204/2.

linked up with the bands behind the *Sixteenth Army* in the Nevel region.[4]

In the territory between Orel and Gomel the German security commands by 1 March had identified 34 separate partisan units totaling an estimated 28,000 men. Nine of these were of brigade size comprising more than 500 men each. In the Pripyat west of Gomel were 26 smaller bands totaling 7,500 men, and behind the *Third Panzer Army* in the Orsha-Vitebsk-Nevel region 37 bands totaling some 21,000 men. In the rear of the *Ninth* and *Second Armies* were smaller groupings totaling an estimated 2,900 in each case.[5] West of the Dnepr in the southern edge of the Pripyat there were estimated to be some 12,500 additional partisans in units as yet unidentified.[6] On 15 March according to German estimate the number of partisans in organized units totaled 77,800, of which 3,000 were east of the Dnepr in the more immediate rear of *Army Group South*, 57,800 behind *Army Group Center*, 4,500 in the rear of *Army Group North*, and 12,500 in that portion of the Pripyat Marshes just south of the *Army Group Center* boundary.

German Forces

Facing these, the Germans had a heterogeneous force of German security units, satellite security brigades and divisions, *Ostbataillone* or native security units, the *Einwohner Kampf Abteilungen* (EKA) or local volunteer units, the *Hilfswillige* (*Hiwis*) or foreign labor auxiliaries, and the *Volkswehr* or anti-Soviet people's defense units.

Although on paper such a force appeared rather formidable, in practice it fell far below the standards necessary to even contain the growing bands. This was true as regarded both the quantity and quality of the troops concerned. The strength of the security commands was built around the German security units, but where these had formerly been of division size, because of continued withdrawals to plug gaps in the front lines or furnish replacements for shattered line organizations, they now represented but a number of scattered and understrength Landesschuetzen battalions. Not only were they insufficiently trained and equipped for their missions, but their personnel were too old for the exacting physical task of all-weather operations in forests and swamps. There was no provision for regular replacement of losses, and combat strengths remained low. The satellite units were of very doubtful quality. The native units, made up variously of Estonians, Latvians, Lithuanians, Russians, Ukrainians, Armenians, Azerbaijanians, Tartars, Cossacks, and others, as a whole represented a very low combat value.

---

[4] *Bandenlage in Bereich d. H. Gr. Mitte, Stand: 31.III.43., 28.II.43., Anl. 2, Bandenlisten, Februar bis September 43, H. Gr. Mitte.* 65003/4.

[5] *Zusammenstellung ueber Bandenlage mit Stand vom 28.II.43., Okdo der H. Gr. Mitte, Abt. Ic/AO Nr. 2475/43 geh., 16.III.43. in Bandenlisten, Februar bis September 43, H. Gr. Mitte/Ic/AO (Abw.).* 65003/4.

[6] *Entwicklung der Bandenstaerke (Ostfront), Anlage 5, z. Bandenlage im Osten, Anlagen, OKH/Gen.St.d.H./GenQu. Abt. II, g. Kdos.* H 3/749.

Not only were they poorly trained, armed, and equipped, but they were beginning to show definite signs of unreliability as the Red Army continued its offensive westward. Defections to the partisans were numerous.[7] The *Kaminski Volkswehr Brigade* was an exception and almost to the end of the war continued to give a good account of itself. Of the German administrative units which might have been tapped for security service, only the personnel of the post office and veterinary service groups were available, all men of the supply services as well as railroad troops and engineers and medical unit personnel having been exempted from antipartisan work.[8]

Partisan Activities

The activity of the bands, which had been stepped up during the last weeks of 1942 as the coming of frost ended the fall muddy season, continued as the winter wore on and increased somewhat with the approach of spring. Objectives were much the same as before: attacks on the German lines of communication, terror raids on the native communities, recruiting among the local inhabitants, forage raids, espionage, and attacks designed to hamper the German economic program. At times the pressure they exerted was heavy, but never did it become in any sense overpowering, and in the aggregate it had little effect on the tactical situation at the front. Combined with the reorganization of the movement going on at the time, however, it did presage improvement in the partisan effort for the days to come.

The rail lines continued to be their primary target. The number of raids they made on them was not great, however, and taken in total never represented a really serious effort. During February they blew trackage in 24 places in the rear of the *Sixteenth Army* and in the central sector broke rails in 94 places in 170 attempts.[9] On one single night, that of 15 April, they temporarily interrupted all rail lines leading out of Bryansk.[10] They also struck rather sharply at rail bridges. During February they successfully damaged or destroyed 12 behind the *Sixteenth Army*, and in March in the Bryansk area on orders from the Central

---

[7] *Bericht des rueckw, Armeegebiets der Pz AOK 2, Br, B. Nr. 1100/43 geh., 20.V.43.* 37075/91; *Bericht, Unternehmen DONNERKEIL, 21.III.–21.IV.43., Anl. z. KTB 4a, 201 Sich, Div.* 38204/2; *Reichskommissar fuer die Ukraine z. Reichsminister Rosenberg, 25.VI.43.* Footlocker 50, folder 4.; see also: entries for 6 Jan and 25 Feb 43 in *KTB 3, Pz AOK 2, Ia, Band 1, 1.I.–28.II.43.*, 37075/11.

[8] *Pz AOK 2, Ia, KTB 3, Band 2, 1.III.–31.V.43.* 37075/12.

[9] *Bericht z. Abwehroffizier beim Kdr. Gen. d. Sicherungstruppen u. Bfh. H. Geb. Nord. Abt. Ic/AO, Tgb. Nr. 226/43 g., 27.II.43., Anl. 1 z. KTB 1, H. Geb. Nord, 1.I.–31.III.43.* 30809/1; *Kdr. Gen. d. Sicherungstruppen u. Bfh. H. Geb. Mitte z. H. Gr. Mitte, Ia. Br. B. Nr. 2051/43 geh., 9.VII.43., Anl. z. Ktb, H. Gr. Mitte, Fuehrungsabt., Heft 10, 11.VI.–31.VII.43.* 65002/22.

[10] Entry for 16 Apr 43, in *KTB 3, Band 2, Ia, Pz AOK 2, 1.III.–31.V.43.* 37075/12.

Staff attacked 5 in force (4 of them important ones) and successfully blew 3, one the span over the Desna River at Wygonitschi on the Bryansk-Gomel line.[11]

The success of this latter-mentioned attack was attributable directly to the German practice of pulling troop units off security duty in the rear for commitment at the front. For some time a battalion of the *747th Grenadier Regiment* had been guarding the section of track which included the Wygonitschi bridge with good success. The first part of March this unit was transferred to the front and replaced with the *974th Security Battalion,* an understrength *Landesschuetzen* outfit new to the area. Before the latter had been in position two weeks the region was out of control and the bridge attacked and destroyed.[12]

Although these attacks interfered with the supply of the forward units for a time and at one point temporarily delayed the arrival of replacements, their over-all effect on the situation at the front was negligible. The *Second Panzer Army* which at the time was heavily engaged with the right wing of the Red Army drive on Kursk reported that while the interruptions were "disagreeable" they in no wise served to weaken the defenses of Orel, although such had been expected and the attacking bands had appeared well-organized, -armed, and -led.[13] In the Vitebsk-Nevel sector the situation was similar. Despite increased pressure on the supply lines by the partisans, who were in radio contact with Sokolovski's West Front then attacking in the Velikiye Luki area, the German defenses were hampered little if at all.[14]

Taken all in all, during this period the bands seldom demonstrated any sustained aggressiveness. The relatively small number of raids of any size is witness to this. Although they had good communication with the Soviet rear and often with each other, and at times, at least, operated under directives from the Central Staff, their attacks were sporadic and

[11] *Bericht z. Abwehroffizier, H. Geb. Nord, Ic/AO, Tgb. Nr. 226/43g., 27.II.43., Anl. 1 z. KTB 1, H. Geb. Nord, 1.I.–31.III.43.* 30809/1; *KTB 3, Band 2, Pz AOK 2, Ia, 1.III.–31.V.43.* 37075/12; annex 1a to *Bericht des Kdr. Gen. des Rueckw. Armeegebiets des Pz AOK 2, Nr. 1100/43 geh. z. Pz AOK 2, 20.V.43., Anl. 14. z. Anl. Bd. 78, Bandenlage II, Pz AOK 2, 11.VIII.42.–1.VII.43.* 37075/91.

[12] Annex 1a to *Bericht des Kdr. Gen. des Rueckw. Armeegebiets des Pz AOK 2, Nr. 1100/43 geh. z. Pz AOK 2, 20.V.43., Anl. 14 z. Anl. Bd. 78, Bandenlage II, Pz AOK 2, 11.VIII.42.–1.VII.43.* 37075/91.

[13] *Anl. Bd. 77, Bandenlage, Pz AOK 2, Ia. Februar–Maerz 43.* 37075/90; entries for 15–17 Feb 43, in *Bandenlage, Pz AOK 2, Ia, KTB 3, 1.I.–28.II.43.* 37075/11; *Bandenlage, Maerz 43, Anl. Bd. 78, Bandenlage, Pz AOK 2, Ia. 11.VIII.42.–1.VII. 43.* 37075/91; *Pz AOK 2, Ia, KTB 3, Band 2, 1.III.–31.V.43.* 37075/12.

[14] *Bericht, der Feldpolizeidirektor beim Kdr. Gen. d. Sicherungstruppen u. Bfh. H. Geb. Nord, Tgb. Nr. 42/42. 11.I.43., Anl 1 z. KTB 1, Bfh. H. Geb. Nord. 1.I.– 31.III.43.* 30809/1; *201 Sich. Div. Ia. KTB 4a, ueber grosse Bandenunternehmungen, "DONNERKEIL", 21.III.–2.IV.43.* 38204/2.

scattered, and appeared to conform to no set pattern.[15] And when they did strike, as in the case of the rail bridges in the Bryansk area, they attempted neither to follow up their advantage nor to exploit the confusion they created.[16] There is no evidence that the Central Staff intended them to operate differently. Either too few of them had reached a level of training which Moscow thought high enough to successfully cope with the German defenses, or they were deliberately held back for bigger things, meanwhile operating only extensively enough to keep the Germans close to their supply axes and out of the partisan concentration areas where they might interrupt the reorganization still in progress. This latter seems the more logical explanation, for with the spring muddy season approaching, which would sharply curtail all movement—German and Soviet alike—there was little to be gained by operations which were certain to have few positive results and heavy casualties. All possible strength would be needed in the summer campaigns ahead, for the Red Army was sure to continue its heavy attacks all along the line.

Accordingly, the bands appeared to pay more attention to completing their reorganization and to feeding themselves than to anything else. They expended much time and energy on drafting and training recruits to fill out their ranks and form new units, and often gave recruiting drives precedence over all other activity.[17] In addition, they foraged extensively. Whereas arms and ammunition were supplied by air from the Soviet rear, they were expected to live off the land. With their numbers increasing rapidly, the problem of feeding this force grew more acute daily, and as the winter wore on they more and more turned from sabotage to raiding for their own needs.[18]

---

[15] *201 Sich. Div., Ia, KTB ra, ueber grosse Bandenunternehmungen, DONNER-KEIL, 21.III.–2.IV.43., Bericht 12.III.43.* 38204/2; annex 1 to *Bericht des Kdr. Gen. des Armeegebiets des Pz AOK 2, Nr. 1100/43 geh., Bandenlage II, Pz AOK 2, 11.VIII.42.–1.VII.43.* 37075/91; *Feindnachrichtenblatt ueber die Bandenlage im Bereich des Pz AOK 3, Stand: 1.IV.–1.VII.43.* 35568/50; order to partisan Bn Cmdr, Troop No. 00105, signed Burkov, in *213 Sich. Div., Anl. z. KTB, Feindlagen-karten, 16.V.–31.VII.43.* 35307/4.

[16] See entries for 1 Mar–7 Apr 43 in *KTB 3, Band 2, Pz AOK 2, Ia. 1.III.–31.V.43.* 37075/12.

[17] *Feindnachrichtenblatt ueber die Bandenlage im Bereich des Pz AOK 3, Stand: 2.III.43.* in Pz AOK 3, Ic/AO, Anl. Bd. E. z. Tgb. 8, 22.I–30.VI.43. 35568/50; *Bandenlage im Bereich des AOK 16, Februar 43,* in AOK 16, Ic, Tgb. Ic/AO z. KTB 5, Teil VI. 1.I.–31.III.43. 36588/142.

[18] *Bandenlage, Februar, Mai 43, Pz AOK 2, Ia, Anl. Bd. 77, 78, 11.VIII.43.* 37075/90, 37075/91; *Bericht, Korueck 532, Ic, Br. Tgb. Nr. 442/43 geh., 30.I.43., Feindlage im Korueck–Gebiet, Stand: 26.I.43., Anlagenheft 2, z. KTB Korueck 559, Ia. Unternehmen "KLETTE 2", 5.I.–19.I.43.* 44404/3; *Feindnachrichtenblatt ueber die Bandenlage im Bereich des Pz AOK 3, Stand: 1.VII.43.,* in Pz AOK 3, Ic/AO, Anl. Bd. E. z. Tgb. 8, 22.I.–30.VI.43. 35568/50; Hq. H. Gp. Mitte, Ia, Nr. 6810/43, 23.VI.43., Anl. z. KTB H. Gp. Mitte, Fuehrungsabt, Akte XXII, Heft 10, 11.VI.–31.VII.43. 65002/22.

German Countermeasures

Then too, the character of the opposition they faced cannot be overlooked. Although the German security commands were badly handicapped by a shortage of manpower, by making judicious use of what strength they did have they were able in large measure to curtail any offensive tendencies the bands showed. Keeping in view their primary mission, the uninterrupted supply of the field armies, they drew themselves in defensively on their lines of communication and installations and then mounted what offensive actions they could. When troops were available from the front lines, they launched large-scale drives. In between times they sent out a steady stream of raiding parties and small combat teams to probe for and strike at the bands and keep their concentration areas in a continual state of flux. They also employed "dummy bands," made up of Russian-speaking German officers and NCO's and native volunteers passing themselves off as partisan units, to seek out the more virulent pro-Soviet elements of the population and mark them for roundup and evacuation.[19]

As far as achieving permanent results was concerned, the larger-scale operations had little success. When attacked in force, the bands simply pulled back and dispersed and later regrouped in the same area. Time and again the security commands reported they had annihilated a large concentration or permanently cleared an area only to discover that their enemy had merely slipped away until the opposition lessened. But combined with the smaller actions which kept the bands under constant pressure and possibly deceived them as to the low level of German security strength,[20] these larger-scale operations gave good results and showed the security commands just what they could really achieve with the manpower available. Although reports of operations repeatedly carried the notation "band only dispersed," "partisans escaped encirclement," or "no contact made," the Germans saw that every raid brought some relief; that the temporary dispersion of a band meant that several weeks would pass before it could be operative again; and that even failure to make contact indicated that the band had gotten wind of the operation ahead of time and had left its normal stamping grounds and bases. They saw further that driving the partisans from an area gave an opportunity to destroy their cantonments, airfields, and defensive installations

---

[19] Special appendix to *Nachrichten ueber Bandenkrieg, Nr. 1. OKH/Gen.St.d.H. Fde H. Ost (II/Bd), Nr. 2460/43 geh., 3.V.43.,* in *Kdr Gen. d. Sich. Tr. Sued, Ia. Anl. Bd. 37, 30.IV.–1.VIII.43.* 39502/41; *OKH/Gen.St.d.H./GenQu. Abt. Kriegsverw. (Qu. 4), 10.IV.43.,* to *Op. Abt. Fde H Ost. Gen. d. Osttruppen OKW/Wpr., Auszug aus SD-Bericht Ost, Nr. 48, 2.IV.43.* OKW 734.

[20] For operations of these smaller groups, see: annexes 3b and 3c to *Bericht des Kdr. Gen. des Rueckw. Armeegebiets des Pz AOK 2, Nr. 1100/43 geh. z. Pz AOK 2, 20.V.43., Anl. 14. z. Anl. Bd. 78, Bandenlage II, Pz AOK 2, 11.VIII.42.–1.VII.43.* 37075/91.

THE PARTISANS AND THE CAMPAIGN OF 1943   **153**

and to evacuate the natives if the sector had been a particularly trouble-some one. Indeed, if enough pressure was applied the bands often burned their own camps and supply depots before withdrawing.[21] Thus, with this strategy of keeping the irregulars off balance and forcing them to stay almost continually on the move, they were able, as they said, "to prevent the bands from gaining a foothold in the country and attracting sizeable numbers of the population, and at the same time to provide general protection for the movement of army supplies."[22]

As a supplement to this expedient of doing what they could with what they had, which they admitted was no more than a half measure, the Germans modified their policy regarding the treatment of punishable offenses committed by civilians and the treatment of partisan deserters in an effort to loosen the hold of the bands on their personnel and on the natives. In the areas under Army jurisdiction the death penalty was retained for "serious" cases of rebellion and other "serious crimes" as attacks on German personnel or sabotage. But since public hangings for such offenses had not had the desired effect—in fact they were generally looked on as sensations by the natives—and had given the Soviets ready-made propaganda material, culprits were ordered shot rather than sent to the gallows. For less serious crimes persons might be confined at hard labor for a maximum of six months. Corporal punishment was prohibited.[23]

In regard to partisan deserters, the 1942 policy of according them prisoner of war status was somewhat amplified. Following a directive by Hitler which ordered that all Red Army deserters were to be classed as enemies of the Soviet state and treated preferentially as such in special deserter camps with extra rations and certain luxury items, OKH passed the order that defectors from the bands, individuals or groups, were to be accorded similar treatment.[24] Although this was broadcast widely, it brought few positive results.[25] The partisans simply did not believe the

[21] *AOK 4, Ic. Feindnachrichtenblaetter Nr. 6, 6.VI.43., Bericht, Mai 43.* 48448/6.
[22] *Bericht des Kdr. Gen. des Rueckw. Armeegebiets des Pz AOK 2, Nr. 1100/43 geh. z. Pz. AOK 2, 20.V.43., Anl. 14. z. Anl. Bd. 78, Bandenlage II, Pz AOK 2, 11.VIII.42.–1.VII.43.* 37075/91; also see antipartisan actions in: *Bandenlage, Pz AOK 2, Ia, Anl. Bd. 77, 78, 11.VIII.42.–1.VII.43.* 37075/90, 37075/91; *Feind-nachrichtenblatt ueber die Bandenlage im Bereich des Pz AOK 3*, in *Pz AOK 3, Ic/AO, Anl. Bd. E z. Taetigkeitsbericht 8, 22.I.–30.VI.43.* 35568/50; *201 Sich Div. Ia. KTB, 4a, ueber gross Bandenunternehmungen, 24.I.–2.IV.43.* 38204/2; *AOK 2, Ia. Anl. 104, 106, z. KTB, Bandenbekaempfung, Apr–Jun 43.* 37418/107, 37418/109.
[23] *Ltr, OKH Nr. 5/43. g. Kdos., to Heeresgruppen, AOK's usw., 6.II.43.*, in *Pz AOK 2, Ia. Anl. Bd. 94, 3.III.43.–16.VII.43.* 37075/107.
[24] *Ltr, OKH/GenStdH/Fde H Ost*, "Deserter Propaganda in Partisan Infested Areas," 16 May 43. H 3/746: also: Basic Order 13, "Treatment of Deserters," *OKH/GenStdH/Fde H Ost. Nr. II/2310/43 geh., 20.IV.43.* H 1/403.
[25] *Pz AOK 3, Ic/AO, Anl. Bd. G. z. Tgb. 8, 22.I.–30.V.43.* 35568/52.

Germans and preferred to take their chances, dubious as they were, with the Soviets, whether they disliked the Bolshevik regime or not.[26]

Preliminary Operations, May–June

With the end of the muddy season and the approach of good campaigning weather, the Red Army could be expected to continue its heavy attacks toward the west all along the eastern line. The most sensitive points in the front and those sure to feel the earliest brunt of the Soviet attack were the Kharkov-Belgorod area, which Von Manstein had retaken in his March counterattack, and the Bryansk-Orel sector. Both of these positions could be hit hard in the flank from the 60 x 110 miles salient the Soviets held about Kursk. A successful push to the southwest through the Kharkov area would turn the German defenses in the south, making the entire eastern Ukraine untenable, and open up the flat, treeless steppes to Soviet armor. At the same time, a reduction of the German-held Bryansk-Orel bulge by a two-pronged attack from Kursk and the smaller salient at Kirov just to the north would at once protect the Red Army drive to the southwest and unhinge the whole central sector. A strong secondary attack could be expected in the Velikiye Luki-Nevel sector where the Soviets had driven a deep wedge between *Army Groups Center* and *North.*

Partisan Concentration Areas and the Rail Lines

The Orel defenses were supplied for the most part over two rail lines, both of which passed through Bryansk: the Smolensk-Roslavl-Bryansk-Lgov link and the east-west Minsk-Gomel-Bryansk line. As of 1 May a 50 mile stretch of the Roslavl-Bryansk line was under constant pressure from five partisan brigades totaling some 7,000 men, the Bryansk-Lgov link between Bryansk and a point just south of Lokot, another 50 mile stretch, was continually threatened by six brigades totaling more than 6,500 irregulars, while some 5,000 additional partisans lay astride the Bryansk-Gomel link.[27] In equally great danger were the seven highly important temporary bridges built over the the Desna River south of Bryansk for use in the event of a forced withdrawal to the intermediate defense line west of the stream.[28] Further west the danger of paralysis of rail traffic was even greater. The Minsk-Gomel line, which carried much of *Army Group South's* supply traffic as well as that of the *Second Army* and *Second Panzer Army,* ran directly through the eastern portion of

---

[26] See statement of captured partisan battalion commander in *Amt Ausland/Abw., Befehlsstab Walli/Abw. III, Br. B. Nr. D 1138/43g (Ausw. 69). 23.II.43.* in *Abt. Wehrmacht Propaganda, I.XI.42–31.II.43.* OKW 639.

[27] *Bandenlage im Bereich d. Obkds, d. H. Gr. Mitte, Stand: 30.IV.43.* in *H. Gr. Mitte Ic/AO (Abw.). Bandenlisten, Februar bis September 43.* 65003/4.

[28] See: *Lage Ost. Stand: 16.VI.43.* Oddly enough, these bridges were attacked by the bands.

the Pripyat and lay highly vulnerable to attack by more than 10,000 irregulars.[29]

In the Velikiye Luki-Nevel-Vitebsk area, the situation was little better. To supply its defenses there, the *Third Panzer Army* and the *Fourth Army* had the east-west Velikiye Luki-Rezekne and Vitebsk-Polotsk-Dvinsk lines to Latvia and Lithuania and the lateral Nevel-Vitebsk-Orsha link connecting with the army group's major supply route, Brest-Litovsk-Minsk-Smolensk. The lateral line, being near the front, remained generally free of interference, but the two east-west lines ran through an area dominated by some 18 partisan units comprising more than 11,000 men and the Brest-Litovsk-Smolensk line was under continual pressure from another group of bands totaling 8,000 to 9,000.[30]

A number of other bands were concentrated in the southernmost portion of the army group rear directly west of Kursk and north of the Kursk-Kiev rail line. Although they totaled more than 8,000 men, they were constrained by the more open terrain and remained generally quiet during the spring and early summer.[31]   As of 1 May by German estimate there were some 62,000 partisans in identified units in the central sector, with an additional 40,000 in bands as yet unidentified.[32]

For the most part these were a far cry from the semi-independent bands of 1942 and early 1943. Under the leadership of the operations groups the organization and offensive potential of many of them had been vastly improved. Their loose concentrations had gradually been pulled together into tight-knit commands, with individual units assigned set areas as bases of operations, the operations groups exercising control through well-developed communications systems. This was especially true in the Bryansk and Nevel sectors. The organization in the Rosonno area west of Nevel had progressed to the point where the operations group there had divided the units under its control into two subcommands with separate staffs for each.[33]

---

[29] *Bandenlage im Bereich d. Obkds. d. H. Gr. Mitte, Stand: 30.IV.43.*, in *H. Gr. Mitte Ic/AO (Abw.), Bandenlisten, Februar bis September 43.* 65003/4.

[30] *Ibid.*

[31] *Bericht Mai, Juni 43, Anl. 104 z. KTB, Bandenbekaempfung, AOK 2, Ia.* 37418/107.

[32] These figures include the *Reichskommissariat Ostland.* See: *Entwicklung der Bandenstaerke (Ostfront). Anl. 5., z. Bandenlage im Osten, Anlagen, OKH/Gen StdH/GenQu. Abt. II, g. Kdos. H 3/749; Bandenlage im Bereich d. Obkds. d. H. Gr. Mitte, Stand: 30.IV.43.*, in *H. Gr. Mitte Ic/AO (Abw.), Bandenlisten, Februar bis September 43.* 65003/4.

[33] *Bandenlage im Bereich d. H. Gr. Mitte, Stand: 30.VI.43., 30.VII.43.*, in *H. Gr. Mitte Ic/AO (Abw.), Bandenlisten, Februar bis September 43.* 65003/4; *Stand: 1.IV.–1.VII.43., Feindnachrichtenblatt ueber die Bandenlage im Bereich des Pz AOK 3*, in *Pz AOK 3, Ic/AO, Anl. Bd. E z. Taetigkeitsbericht 8, 22.I.–30.VI.43.* 35568/50.

Strategic Significance of the Concentrations

The strategic significance of these concentrations was plain. The disposition of the bands was such that their first action in the event of a Soviet general offensive would be to cut the rail lines, thus shutting of supplies to the German forward units and slowing the shifting of reserves and the arrival of replacements, and to then attack the Germans as they attempted to withdraw to the west over the inadequate road net. It is true that throughout the sector these concentrations largely conformed to the terrain, being heaviest where the cover was most favorable, but it also happened that the cover was most favorable behind the two most critical points in the sector—the Bryansk forests and the woods and swamps of White Russia. In the rear of the *Fourth* and *Ninth Armies*, where the terrain was anything but open, there were few bands in evidence. Once in their areas the bands were told to stay there in the face of all opposition,[34] and although they dispersed when hit they always returned within a matter of days.

Certainly the opportunity offered them was excellent. Their great increase in strength and improvement in organization combined with the Germans' strategy of pulling their security forces back to their supply lines had by the end of spring virtually turned the countryside, apart from the railroads and primary highways and the population centers, over to their control. The natives were badly demoralized and more and more looked to the bands for leadership. Some maintained a wait-and-see attitude, but many others became so convinced of the return of the Red Army in the near future or were so in terror of the bands that they dared not even report raids to the Germans. They became progressively susceptible to Soviet propaganda and rumor mongering and increasingly impervious to German counterpropaganda.[35] Even in the *Army Group South Rear Area* where the bands were almost nonexistent the morale of the people was low. Their belief in a German victory seemed completely shattered and their almost every act appeared to be determined by the feeling that the Red Army would return shortly. They were turning away from the Germans in increasingly large numbers, and many aided the Soviet cause in any way they were able.[36] This condition did much to facilitate the reestablishment of Communist Party control in these areas, and thus virtually assured a complete disintegration of all pro-German sentiment which the Wehrmacht, now on a desperate defensive, so badly needed.

---

[34] Entry for 7 Apr 43, in *Pz AOK 2, Ia. KTB 3, Bd. 2, 1.III.–31.V.43.* 37075/12.
[35] *Stand: Mai–Juni 43, Feindnachrichtenblatt ueber die Bandenlage im Bereich des Pz AOK 3,* in *Pz AOK 3, Ic/AO, Anl. Bd. E z. Taetigkeitsbericht 8, 22.I.–30.IV.43.* 35568/50.
[36] *Bericht, Mai, Juni, Pz AOK 1, Ic, Tgb., AO, 1.V.–31.VIII.43.* 36835/7.

GERMAN ANTIPARTISAN OPERATIONS
IN THE BRYANSK AREA
MAY-JUNE 1943

1	Operation ZIGEUNERBARON
2	Operation FREISCHUETZ
3	Operation NACHBARHILFE
4	Operation TANNHAEUSER
5	Operation OSTEREI

Limits of Operations

(100) Partisan Concentrations

10 5 0   10   20   30   40
MILES

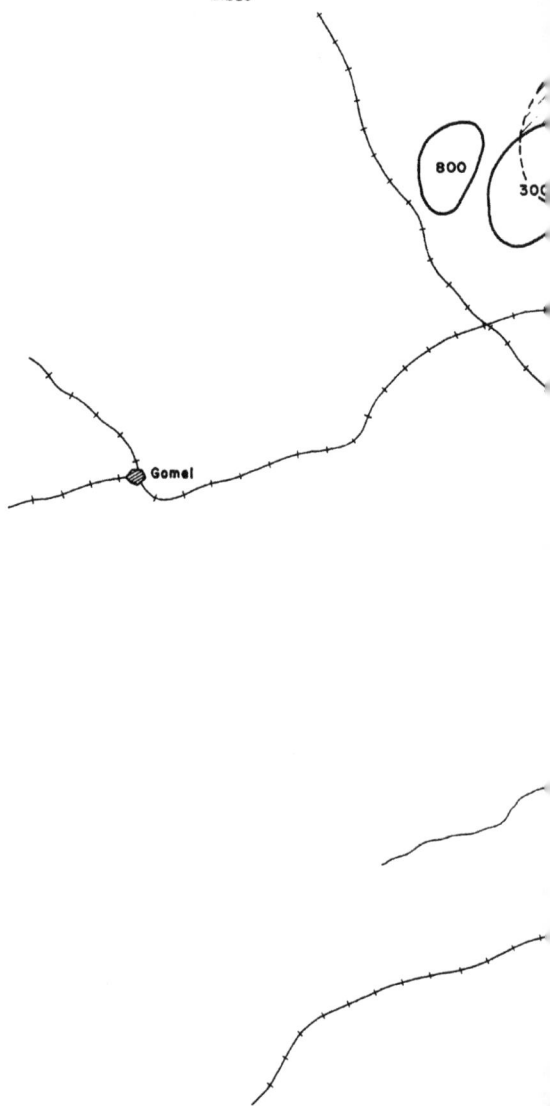

800

300

Gomel

Map 5. German Antipartisan Operations in the Bryansk Area, May–

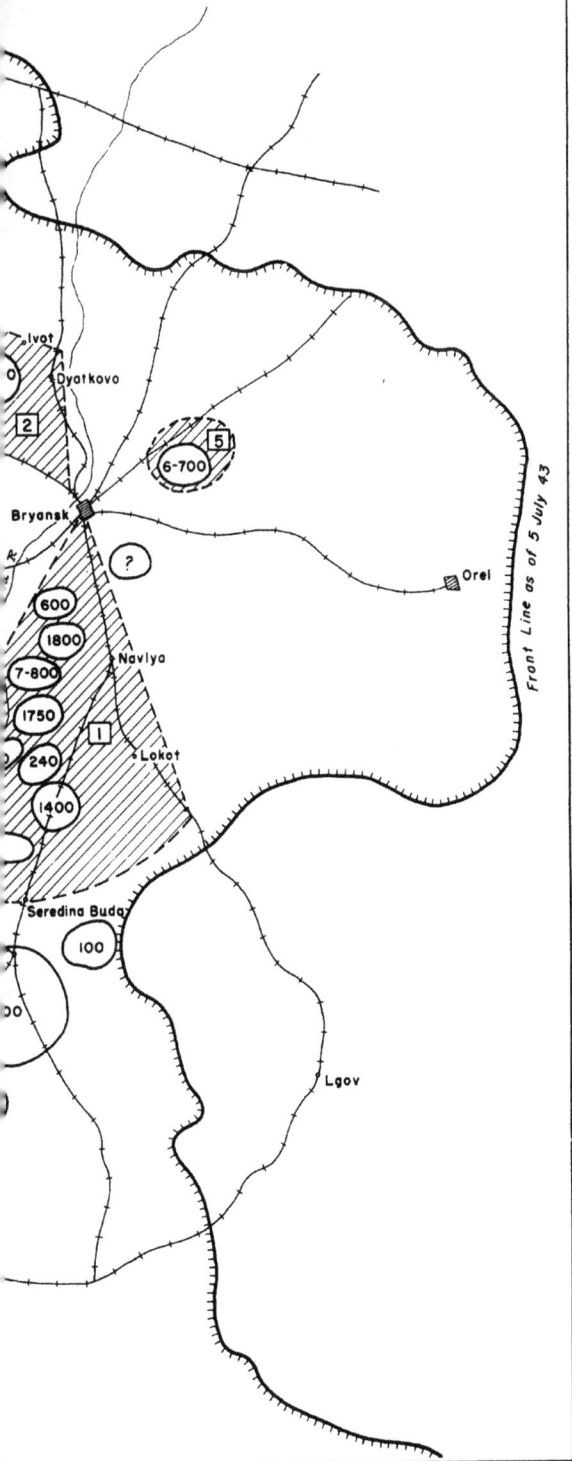

Map 5

Ivot

Dyatkovo

2

5

6-700

Bryansk

?

Orel

Front Line as of 5 July 43

600

1800

7-800

Navlya

1750

240

Lokot

1

1400

Seredina Buda

100

Lgov

Soviet Plans

The Soviet high command assigned the bands a prominent role in its plans for the 1943 campaign. The Germans had made no particular effort to conceal their buildup for Operation *ZITADELLE;* as a result the Russians knew what to expect and where and were well prepared. The Soviet strategy was to allow the German armored columns to batter themselves to pieces against the deep, prepared defenses of the Kursk salient and then launch a general counteroffensive when their strength had been spent.

The bands were to support this counterblow, and plans for coordinating their actions with the moves of the Red Army were made well in advance. The plan was to hold them in readiness until *ZITADELLE* had been stopped and the Germans were in the midst of a general withdrawal, and then order them to strike all the rail lines at once, blocking the *Second Panzer* and *Ninth Armies* in the forward areas without prepared defenses where they might be cut off and destroyed. The railroads were to be their principal target. Throughout the whole of the central sector they were to strike at the rail lines "simultaneously" on signal from Moscow and follow up "continuously" and "systematically." Individual bands were assigned specific sections of trackage and told how many rails they were expected to break in the first blow.[37] Special manuals on rail demolition technique were distributed and mines and bulk explosives were air-landed well in advance. Air supply was stepped up tremendously, for the first two weeks of May almost 1,000 percent over February.[38]

German Counteraction

Although the Germans had no detailed foreknowledge of Soviet intentions, they were aided by their nets of native informers and their highly efficient signal intelligence [39] and were thus able to read the implications of the bands' dispositions correctly. Unless they could take effective preventive actions beforehand, they saw, the first move of the partisans in the event of a Soviet general offensive would be to cut their lines of communications and then attack from the rear.[40] At army level and

---

[37] Order of the Central Staff of the Partisan Movement No. 006, 17 Jul 43, in *KTB, General der Eisenbahntruppen.* H 14/14; see also: *Bericht Mai, Juni 43, Pz AOK 3, Ic/AO, Anl. Bd. E z. Tgb. 8, 22.I.–30.VI.43.* 35568/50.

[38] *Bericht Mai, Juni 43, Pz AOK 3, Ic/AO, Anl. Bd. E z. Tgb. 8, 22.I.–30.VI.43.* 35568/50; *Anl. 4 z. Bandenlage im Osten, Anlagen, OKH/Gen.St.d.H./GenQu. Abt. II.* H 3/749.

[39] See: MS # P–038, "German Radio Intelligence," (S), pp. 206–12. Foreign Studies Br. OCMH; *Bericht Mai, Juni 43, Pz AOK 3, Ic/AO, Anl. Bd. E z. Tgb. 8, 22.I.–30.VI.43.* 35568/50.

[40] *Ibid.; Feindnachrichtenblatt ueber die Bandenlage im Bereich des Pz AOK 3, Mai–Juni 43, Pz 3, Ic/AO, Anl. Bd. E z. Tgb 8, 22.I.–30.VI.43.* 35568/50.

below there were few illusions as to the possibility of regaining the initiative with Operation *ZITADELLE* or even of conducting a successful defensive along the front as it then stood. The lines of communication thus assumed added importance as routes of withdrawal, and the possibility of their loss at the same time the Soviets were attacking was a very real danger.

The answer was obvious: the concentrations had to be broken up and scattered by a series of large-scale offensive strikes by first-line forces prior to any moves by the Red Army.[41]   Here the Germans faced a dilemma.   Antipartisan operations such as they had mounted during the winter could never hold the bands should they strike with their full strength, and, with the summer battles impending, they could not spare the manpower to clear the whole rear or even a good portion of it. Again they would have to do what they could with what they had, that is, make a concerted effort to clear at least temporarily the rear of the most critical point in the line, the Bryansk-Orel sector, where the first Soviet blow seemed sure to fall, and let the rest go for the present.

Accordingly, when a postponement of *ZITADELLE* gave promise of the loan of several line divisions, plans for clearing the entire Bryansk region with a series of offensive sweeps were drawn up for execution in late May and June.   Priority was given to Operations *FREISCHUETZ* and *OSTEREI*, the actions north of Bryansk designed to secure the rear of the more thinly held northern flank of the *Second Panzer Army*. Operation *ZIGEUNERBARON*, projected to clear a large pocket south of Bryansk between the Desna River and the Bryansk-Lgov railroad which had been extremely active during the winter, was to follow. Operation *NACHBARHILFE* was to be another attempt to eliminate an exceptionally strong concentration between the Bryansk-Roslavl and Bryansk-Gomel rail lines.   A smaller operation, *TANNHAEUSER*, was planned to eliminate a troublesome pocket southeast of Pochep on the Bryansk-Gomel line.[42]

OSTEREI and *FREISCHUETZ* were launched almost simultaneously.   The former, a relatively small-scale action by security units alone, had as its mission the destruction of an especially active partisan battalion of some 600 to 700 men just to the north and east of Bryansk which had been blocking the Bryansk-Dudorovsky rail line, a feeder link used to supply *LV Corps*. The mission was accomplished to the extent of dis-

---

[41] See entry for 7 Apr 43, in *Pz AOK 2, Ia, KTB 3, Bd. 2, 1.III.–31.V.43.* 37075/12.

[42] See: *H. Gr. Mitte/Ia. 4875/43 g.K. Chefs. z. OKH, 7.V.43., H. Gr. Mitte/Ia. Anl. z. KTB. Besondere Bandenunternehmungen, Mai–Juni 43.*   65002/26.

persing the irregulars.⁴³ *FREISCHUETZ* was conducted on a considerably larger scale by the *LV Corps*. The task force assembled for the operation, consisting of elements of the *Sixth Infantry* and *Fifth Panzer Divisions* and a miscellany of security and native volunteer units, had the mission of enveloping and destroying a group estimated at 4,000 to 6,000 men. The attack was carefully planned as an encirclement to be launched from blocking lines with phase lines set as limits for each day's progress. Starting on 21 May and concluded 10 days later, the operation was considered successful, although the partisans were driven from the area rather than annihilated. This was due, the task force commander believed, to the extremely heavy terrain, the weather (which was rainy throughout), and the relatively small force committed considering the size of the area to be covered.⁴⁴ Before the end of June 1,800 irregulars in three groups were reported back in the area.⁴⁵

ZIGEUNERBARON, which had been scheduled for early spring only to be canceled because of a shortage of troops, was mounted on 16 May under the direction of the *XLVII Panzer Corps*. The task force comprised elements of three infantry divisions, two panzer divisions, a Hungarian light division, and a number of security, *Ost,* and *Volkswehr* units, and faced an estimated 6,000 partisans in an extensive and deeply wooded area which they had had ample time to fortify. The action was launched as a driving operation with a majority of the task force units "beating" the area from east to west in an attempt to pin the bands against the Desna River held as blocking line by the remainder of the force. It was concluded on 6 June with the bands dispersed but nowhere destroyed. Partisan casualties were listed as 1,584 killed, 1,568 prisoners, and 869 deserters; 207 camps were destroyed along with 2,930 bunkers and dugouts. Captured armament included 1,128 small arms.⁴⁶

Although the task force command considered the action generally successful, it attributed the failure to destroy rather than disperse the bands to the insufficient number of men assigned the operation. The divisions, each comprising but seven infantry battalions (and these very probably under strength), had to comb sectors 20 miles wide, despite the fact that experience had shown that in dense forests and swamps one

---

⁴³ *Bericht, Mai 43, Pz AOK 2, Ia. Anl. Bd. 78, Bandenlage, 11.VIII.42.–1.VII.43.,* 37075/91. *Stand: 30.V.43.,* in *Bandenlage im Bereich d. Obkds. d. H. Gr. Mitte, Stand: 28.II.43., Anl. 2, Bandenlisten, Februar bis September 43, H. Gr. Mitte.* 65003/4.

⁴⁴ Originally the *10th Div (mot)* and a reinforced regiment of the *31st Div* had been assigned to the force, but were pulled off at the last minute.

⁴⁵ *Stand: 30.IV.43., 30.V.43., 30.VII.43., Bandenlage im Bereich d. Obkds. d. H. Gr. Mitte, Stand: 28.II.43., Anl. 2, Bandenlisten, Februar bis September 43, H. Gr. Mitte.* 65003/4; *H. Gr. Mitte, Abt. Ia. Anl. 2 z. KTB, Bericht Ueber Unternehmen FREISCHUETZ, Juni–Juli 43, Gen. Kdo, LV AK, Abt., Ia. Nr. 1560/43 geh. v, 7.VI.43.* 65002/28.

⁴⁶ *Gen. Kdo. XXXXVII Pz Korps, Ia. Nr. 2100/43 geh., 2.VII.43.,* in *Pz AOK 2, Ia. Anl. Bd. 47. 7.V.–4.VI.43., ZIGEUNERBARON.* 37075/60.

battalion could cover and thoroughly search but 1.2 miles of front. Further, the command felt that that attack had been mounted on too short notice—three days—and had been pushed too fast from the start.[47] These appreciations were borne out by the rapid reconstitution of the partisan structure in the area immediately following the German withdrawal. By the end of June more than 3,000 irregulars were estimated to have returned and before the end of July had been reorganized into at least eight units under the control of an operations group.[48]

Operation *NACHBARHILFE,* designed to relieve pressure on the Roslavl-Bryansk railroad by destruction of an estimated 3,700 partisans in the area south of the line, had the same general pattern of results. Launched on 19 May by the *98th Infantry Division,* reinforced by elements of the *221st Security Division* and *Ost* and *Volkswehr* units, the action was successful insofar as it dispersed the bands and forced them to destroy their camps, supply dumps, and air fields, but proved again, as one report stated, that an encirclement in heavily wooded terrain was seldom successful. In this case, a large number of the partisans withdrew to the west before the attack was launched, apparently forewarned of German intentions.[49]

Operation *TANNHAEUSER* was concluded on 23 June without enemy contact, the partisans having retired with their organization intact.[50]

The Germans obtained generally the same results from all five operations: the bands were dispersed or driven out of their camps and away from their bases and sources of supply. Nowhere, however, did these results give any promise of being permanent. Indeed, the Germans, because of their failure to destroy the bands and especially their staffs and their inability to garrison the areas cleared, expected no lasting benefit. Four of the five operations were unsuccessful in trapping and destroying the bands because of the inability of the army command to allot sufficient troop strength for the scope of the action. In two, the enemy was apparently forewarned and thus enabled to escape. Throughout all five operations the bands demonstrated their general reluctance to fight when they could avoid it as well as their ability to slip out of relatively tight encirclements. That Moscow was determined to keep the bands active in such critical areas was evidenced in a noticeable increase in air supply to the bands almost immediately following the opera-

---

[47] *Ibid.*

[48] *Stand: 30.VI., 30.VII.43., Bandenlage im Bereich d. H. Gr. Mitte, Stand: 28.II.43., Anl. 2, Bandenlisten, Februar bis September 43, H. Gr. Mitte.* 65003/4.

[49] *AOK 4, Ic. Feindnachrichtenblaetter 16, 6.VI.43.* 48448/6; *Abschlussmeldung ueber Unternehmen "NACHBARHILFE", 19.VI.43., Anlagenheft 7 z. KTB Korueck 559, Ia. 13.V.–20.VI.43.* 44404/8.

[50] Entry for 23 Jun 43, *Pz AOK 2, Ia. KTB 3, Bd. 3, 1.VI.–13.VIII.43.* 37075/13.

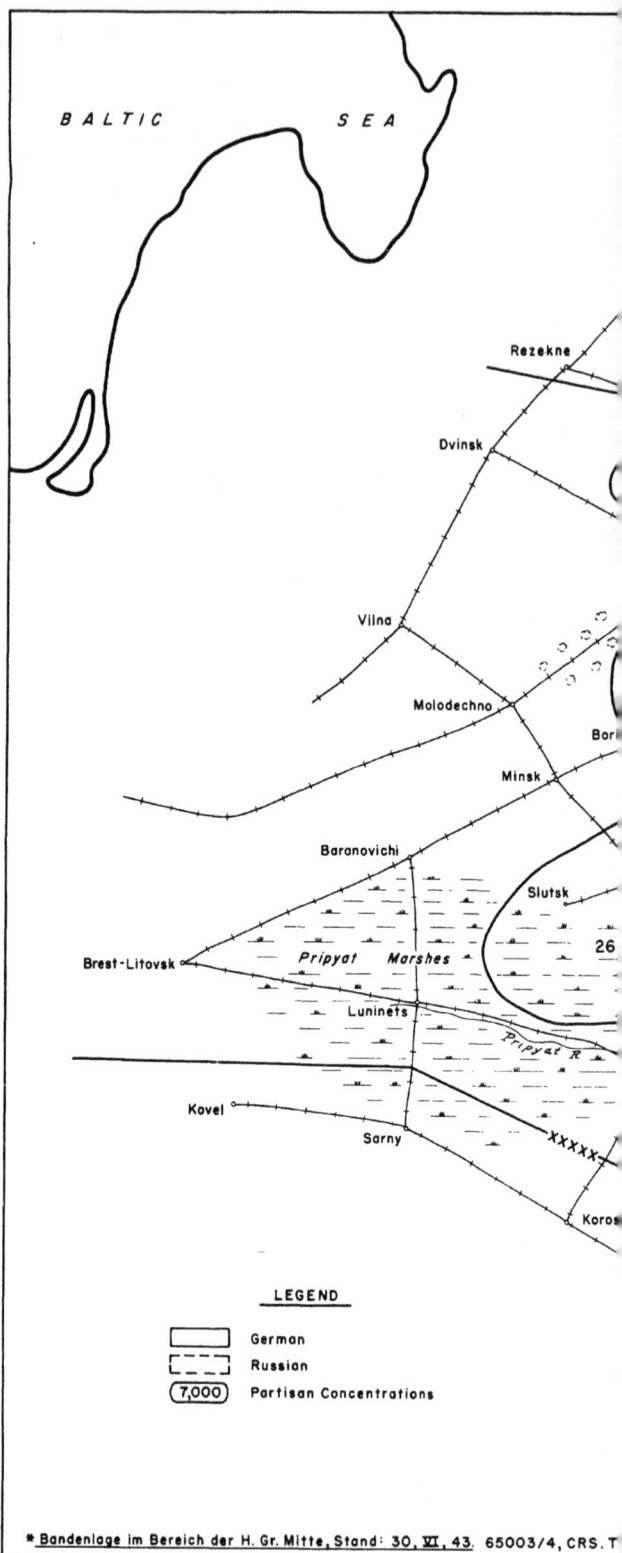

BALTIC   SEA

Rezekne

Dvinsk

Vilna

Molodechno

Bor

Minsk

Baranovichi

Slutsk

Brest-Litovsk   Pripyat   Marshes

26

Luninets

Pripyat R.

Kovel

Sarny

XXXXX

Koros

LEGEND

German
Russian
7,000   Partisan Concentrations

*Bandenlage im Bereich der H. Gr. Mitte, Stand: 30, VI, 43. 65003/4, CRS.T

Map 6.   Partisan Concentrations in Sector of Army Group Center as of

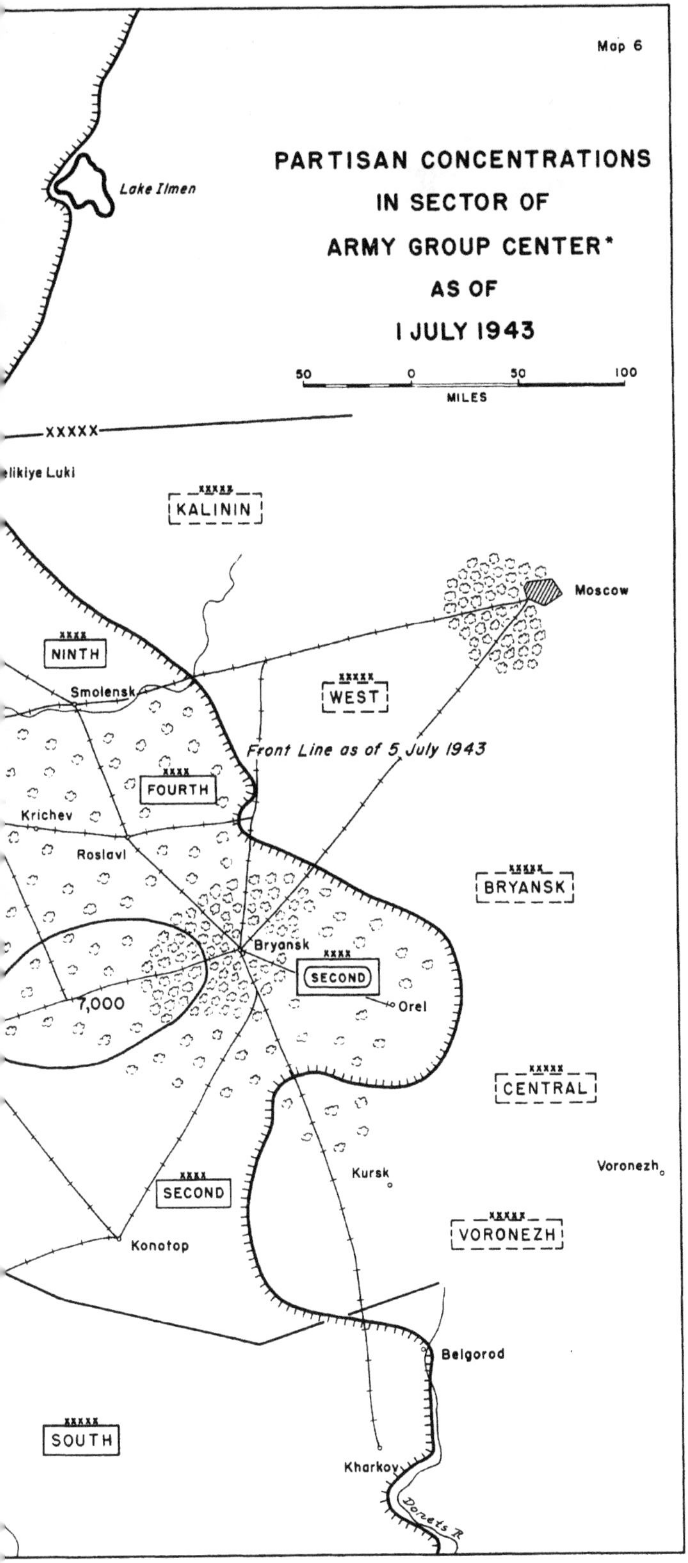

Map 6

PARTISAN CONCENTRATIONS
IN SECTOR OF
ARMY GROUP CENTER*
AS OF
I JULY 1943

Lake Ilmen

50   0   50   100

MILES

—xxxxx—

elikiye Luki

KALININ

Moscow

NINTH

Smolensk

WEST

Front Line as of 5 July 1943

FOURTH

Krichev

Roslavl

BRYANSK

Bryansk

SECOND

7,000

Orel

CENTRAL

Voronezh

Kursk

SECOND

VORONEZH

Konotop

Belgorod

SOUTH

Kharkov

Donets R.

388413 O - 56 - (Face p.161)

tions.[51] No effort was made to coordinate the operations or to tie them together tactically. Indeed, two were mounted on very short notice. Yet they did what they were designed to do: relieve the pressure on the supply lines when such relief was most needed.

In the Nevel-Vitebsk area, which the Germans believed to be of secondary importance in Soviet plans, only one antipartisan action was launched during this period. This was Operation *KOTTBUS* executed by a mixed force of Army, SS, SD, and native volunteer units under the command of the Higher SS and Police Leader of *Army Group Center* in the area west and south of Vitebsk. Launched in late April and not concluded until 21 June, the drive moved methodically through the forests and swamps and kept the partisans concentrated there in a constant state of flux. Similar to the actions in the Bryansk area, the operation did little beyond keeping the bands off balance for the duration of the drive and forcing them to scatter temporarily.[52]

Despite these operations, which temporarily cleared the immediate Bryansk area and to some extent weakened the hold of the bands on the region west and southwest of Vitebsk, the partisans still remained strong in a number of areas. As of 1 July there were some 7,000 astride the Bryansk-Gomel line, some 26,000 in a number of units in the Pripyat generally centered about Bobruysk, 11,000 in the area west of Orsha-Vitebsk, and 12,000 west of Nevel, with an additional 3,500 just to the north of the Velikiye Luki-Rezekne line.[53]

The Summer Battles in the Central Sector

Operation *ZITADELLE* was launched on 5 July. By 8 July the northern wing of the attack had been stopped cold with heavy losses and thrown back on the defensive. On 17 July the Soviets, having driven the German divisions back to their jumpoff line, launched their counterblow with two fronts, hitting concentrically from above and below Orel.

The bands did not react immediately to either the German attack or the Russian counter. On 4 July 300 partisans supported by Red Air Force planes had raided several points along the rail lines near Bryansk, and on 6 July a band raided Malzevo, again with air support. But these attacks were isolated and not followed up, and gave

[51] *Bericht, Juni 43, Pz AOK 2, Anl. Bd. 78, Bandenlage, 11.VIII.42.–1.VII.43.* 37075/91; *Abschlussmeldung ueber NACHBARHILFE, 19.VI.43., Anlagenheft 7 z. KTB Korueck 559, Ia. NACHBARHILFE, 13.V.–20.VI.43.* 44404/8; *AOK 4, Ic. Feindnachrichtenblaetter Nr. 7, 9.VII.43.* 48448/6.
[52] *Gefechtsbericht ueber das Unternehmen KOTTBUS, 28.VI.43., Anl. 53 z. KTB 286 Sich. Div., Ia. 1.I.–4.VII.43.* 38424/2; *Stand: 30.IV.43., 30.VI.43., Bandenlage im Bereich d. H. Gr. Mitte, Stand: 28.II.43., Anl. 2, Bandenlisten, Februar bis September 43, H. Gr. Mitte.* 65003/4.
[53] *Bandenlage im Bereich der H. Gr. Mitte, Stand: 30.VI.43., H. Gr. Mitte, Ic/AO (Abw.), Bandenlisten, Feb. bis Sept. 43.* 65003/4.

no evidence of any plan for concerted action.[54]   Even the abrupt German switch to the defensive, which caused a considerable increase in troop movements through the Bryansk area, brought no untoward response from the irregulars, the *Second Panzer Army* reporting only a few widely spread rail demolitions in its rear.[55]

Even further to the rear in the heavy terrain of the Pripyat there was little change in the sabotage picture from June. For the 20-day period ending 21 July the *203d Security Division* in the area about Bobruysk, which included the highly vulnerable Minsk-Bobruysk-Gomel line, recorded a total 101 demolitions which caused damage, 39 which resulted in no harm to trackage, and 140 charges removed prior to explosion, only a slight increase over the preceding 20 days.[56]

By 27 July the Germans realized that the Bryansk-Orel salient was no longer tenable and passed the order to withdraw to a defense line just east of the Desna River. Almost coincident with this German decision the tempo of partisan activity changed abruptly.

On 22 July, bands which had been forced westward out of the forests south of Bryansk hit very hard at the north-south Bryansk-Konotop line, which was used primarily for shuttling troops between the central and southern sectors, and set off demolitions on the tracks at 430 places, blocking all traffic for 48 hours. In many of these demolitions and those which followed in the next weeks, they used a small, newly designed mine set in chains of up to 500 at one demolition site.[57] The same day, a mine which had been attached to a railroad car detonated in the station at Osipovichi, on the main line between Minsk and Gomel, blowing up two ammunition trains and one fuel train as well as a trainload of badly needed "Tiger" tanks.[58] This increase in sabotage continued the remainder of the month, totaling 1,114 for the entire month (an average of 36 demolitions per day), and including over 400 raids on targets other than the rail lines and more than 30 bridges blown in the area of the *203d Security Division* alone.[59] Still, despite this increased interference

---

[54] See entries for 4 Jul–13 Jul 43 in *Pz AOK 2, Ia. KTB 3, Band 3, 1.VI.–13.VIII. 43.* 37075/13.

[55] Actually the only report of rail demolitions was on 14 July when nine track breaks were recorded for the preceding 24 hours. See *ibid.,* entry for 14 July.

[56] *Anlagen 99, 100 z. KTB 203 Sich. Div., 1.I–3.VIII.43., Zehntagebericht.* 35950/2. The respective totals for the preceding twenty day period were 75, 55, and 133. See *Anlagen 83, 87 in ibid.*

[57] *Ibid.* See also: Hermann Teske, *Die Silbernen Spiegel* (Heidelberg, 1952), p. 192; Hermann Teske, "Railroad Transportation Operation *ZITADELLE* (1943)." MS # D–369. Foreign Studies Br., OCMH.

[58] Hermann Teske, "Railroad Transportation Operation *ZITADELLE* (1943)." MS # D–369. Foreign Studies Br., OCMH.

[59] Herman Teske, "Railroad Transportation Operation *ZITADELLE* (1943)." MS # D–369, Foreign Studies Br., OCMH: *Anlagen 99, 100, 101, z. KTB 203 Sich. Div., 1.I–31.VIII.43., Zehntagebericht.* 35950/2; Teske, *op. cit.,* p. 192. Actually the total of bridges and culverts blown in the *203d Security Division* area for the period 2 July through 3 August totaled 57, with 34 in the last 10-day period. However, this last period included the mass attacks of the night 2–3 August and thus only an estimated fraction of the 38 can be included for July.

on the rail lines and the attacks of the Red Air Force, the Germans successfully moved 2,932 troop and supply trains in the sector during the month.[60] This step-up in sabotage ahead of the northern wing of the Soviet attack was reflected only to a lesser degree in the rest of the sector. In the rear of the *Second Army*, which was defending along the western edge of the Kursk salient, there was no appreciable change during July, although a slight increase in partisan activity was noted for the latter half of the month. There were few bands of any size in the area, although several estimated to comprise as many as 500 men were dispersed attempting to infiltrate eastward from the Pripyat. A number of attempts to blow the rail lines were made using magnetic mines with time fuzes. These were apparently designed to detonate in the middle of a train, rather than under the flat cars loaded with rocks usually pushed ahead of trains. Few were effective.[61] In the rear of the *Fourth Army* the bands for the most part were quiet, making but 28 attempts on the railroads mostly aimed at the Roslavl-Bryansk link.[62]

The *Third Panzer Army's* rear remained similarly quiet until Soviet pressure forced the withdrawal of two line divisions which had been covering the Nevel-Vitebsk and Vitebsk-Smolensk rail links for commitment on the Orel front. Following their replacement by but three security battalions on 20 July, the bands almost immediately reappeared and began raiding throughout the countryside, setting several chain demolitions on both lines.[63] The area directly west of Vitebsk-Orsha remained the critical sector. There, despite the presence of the *223d Infantry Division*, the bands continued to concentrate to such an extent that the army command believed a complete clearing of the area prior to the fall muddy season necessary for a successful winter defense. It was estimated that six to seven line divisions would be necessary to do the job.[64]

Early in August the real blows fell. Once the German withdrawal from Orel was well under way, Moscow ordered the bands to attack, and on the night of 2–3 August they struck, "simultaneously," as directed. During that one night they set 10,900 demolition charges and mines

---

[60] Hermann Teske, "Railroad Transportation Operation *ZITADELLE* (1943)," p. 16. MS # D–369. Foreign Studies Br, OCMH. This total includes supply trains carrying ammunition, fuel, and rations, hospital trains, troop trains for the army, Luftwaffe, railroad engineers, salvage platoons, and furlough traffic, and trains for the *Reichskommissariat* and the economic administration.

[61] *AOK 2, Ia. Anl z. KTB, Bandenbekaempfung, Juli 43.* 37418/108. *Korueck 580, Ic. Tgb. Nr. 2722/43 geh., 31.VII.43., KTB 26a, Teil 7.* 37516/4.

[62] *Korueck 559, Ic. Tgb. Nr. 2952/43 geh., 31.VII.43., KTB Heft 3, Anl. 1–17.* 45668/4.

[63] *Pz AOK 3, Ia. Nr. 6592/43 geh., 16.VIII.43., in H. Gr. Mitte, Bandenbekaempfung, Akte XXII, Heft 11, 1.VIII.–30.IX.43.* 65002/23.

[64] *Ibid; Bericht, Juli, Pz AOK 3, Ic/AO, Anl. Bd. 2, Tgb. 9, 1.VIII.–30.IX.43.* 40252/7.

on the rail lines of the central sector, 8,422 of which detonated, the Germans discovering and disarming the remainder prior to explosion. Many of these charges were set in chains.[65] Throughout the rest of the month, these attacks on railroads continued, but in no such volume as in the initial assault. The total for the 31-day period was 15,977 demolitions. Included in these were 345 set in chains containing more than 10 charges each. An additional 4,528 were removed by the Germans.[66]

After the initial attacks the partisans expanded their sabotage to include all railroad facilities and installations. They damaged or demolished 266 locomotives and 1,378 cars, and destroyed extensive stocks of railroad construction and maintenance material, including 500,000 linear feet of spare rails and hundreds of ties. The loss of the latter, in view of the long sections of trackage rendered unserviceable by the chain demolitions, placed an added burden on the German repair crews. In many instances in order to get rails to repair one line, one set of tracks of a double track line had to be torn up.[67] They raided numbers of water towers, switching points, and stations, and in a number of instances attacked trains which had been blocked by broken rails.[68]

The more concentrated chain demolitions seem to have been executed in large part by a number of specially organized Red Army engineer demolition teams flown into the German rear for this particular series of attacks. These teams comprising some 30 men and 1 officer were landed in the vicinity of particular bands with which they were to work and which were to furnish necessary reconnaissance and security details.[69]

---

[65] Hermann Teske, "Railroad Transportation Operation *ZITADELLE* (1943)," p. 12. MS # D–369. Foreign Studies Br, OCMH. These figures are for the combined *Army Group Center Rear Area* and the political occupation zone, the *Generalkommissariat Weissruthenien*. The *Army Group Center Rear Area* listed 6,519 successful and 2,086 unsuccessful for the same date. See: *H. Gr. Mitte, Ia. Nr. 9842/43 g. Kdos., 5.IX.43., Anl. z. KTB, H. Gr. Mitte, Fuehrungsabt., Akte XXII, Heft 11, 1.VII.–30.IX.43.* 65002/23. In this particular series of attacks the Germans listed demolitions by the partisans (literally "demolition sites"—*Sprengstellen*) as "successful" or "unsuccessful"; "successful" when the mine or charge actually detonated, irrespective of the damage done, "unsuccessful" when it was discovered and disarmed prior to detonation.
[66] See: *H. Gr. Mitte, Ia, Nr. 9842/43 g. Kdos., 5.IX.43., Anl. z. KTB, H. Gr. Mitte, Fuehrungsabt., Akte XXII, Heft 11, 1.VII.–30.IX.43.* 65002/23. *Army Group Center Rear Area* listed 12,717 successful demolitions and 3,011 charges deactivated in its rear for the same period.
[67] *Ibid.;* Teske, *op. cit.,* pp. 194–95; *Bericht, August 43, Pz AOK 3, Tgb. 9, Ic/AO.* 1/0252/7.
[68] *AOK 9, Anl. 2, KTB 9, Fuehrungsabt. II. Tagesmeldungen, 19.VIII.–15.X.43.* 52535/2; *Bericht, Korueck 559, Ic. Nr. 4313/43 geh., 30.VIII.43.,* in *KTB Korueck 559, Ic, Heft 3, Anl. 1–17, 5.VII.–28.XII.43.* 45668/4.
[69] *Nachrichten ueber Bandenkrieg, Nr. 4, OKH/GenStdH. Fde H Ost (II/Bd), Nr. 2460/43 geh. 3.V.43.,* in *Kdr Gen d. Sich. Tr. Sued., Ia, Anl. Bd. 37, 30.IV.–1.VIII.43.* 39502/41; *H. Gr. Mitte, Ia, Nr. 9842/43 g. Kdos., 5.IX.43., Anl. z. Ktb, H. Gr. Mitte, Fuehrungsabt., Akte XXII, Heft 11, 1.VIII.–30.IX.43.,* 65002/23; *Korueck 559, Ic. Nachrichten, 15.X.43.,* in *Anl. 1–17, der Abt. Ic. z. KTB Korueck 559/Ia. fuer die Zeit, v. 5.VII.–28.XII.43.* 45668/4.

Much of the sabotage along the rail lines, other than the demolitions, was committed by native railroad employees and deserting members of *Ost* security units guarding the lines. On 17 August a native unit of 600 men went over to the partisans in a body, attacking a sizeable railroad station and doing considerable damage.[70]

The effect of these interruptions, while never disastrous, was considerable, and only through an outstanding performance by the German railway personnel and the rail transportation command were both the continued supply of the troops and the successive withdrawal movements carried out. Through a series of expedients as shuttles over lateral lines, reductions in speed, travel by daylight only and then with trains operating within sight of one another, they were able to meet the demands made of them regarding supply and the shifting of reserves, as well as the evacuation of wounded and materiel. A total of 2,951 supply and troop trains was successfully moved during the month.[71]

This increase in successful raids on the rail lines was due, in part at least, to heavy pressure of the Red Army forcing *Army Group Center* to pull many of the German security battalions out of the rear and commit them in the line. When this practice was brought to a halt by an OKW directive, the chain demolitions decreased and the raids lost much of their sting although the number of single rail demolitions continued to rise.[72]

The bands accompanied this campaign against the railroads with an increase in raids on other communication facilities. They mined a number of highways, especially in the Pripyat and repeatedly attacked truck convoys, raided German-occupied towns and supply depots in considerable strength, destroyed several telephone relay trains, and cut the important Minsk-Smolensk cable in a number of places. Their raids on economic installations increased and caused great damage. And they committed many deliberate acts of terror against the families of indigenous railway personnel and natives serving in the locally recruited security battalions which served to increase the already sizeable number of desertions from these units and further lowered native morale.

---

[70] *Korueck 559, Ic. Nachrichten, 15.X.43.*, in *Anl. 1–17, der Abt. Ic. z. KTB Korueck 559/Ia. fuer die Zeit. v. 5.VII.–28.XII.43.* 45668/4. Teske, *op. cit.*, p. 195; *KTB Heft 3, Anl. 1–17.* 45668/4; entry for 20 Aug 43 in *AOK 9, Anl. 2, KTB 9, 19.VIII.–15.X.43., Fuehrungsabt. II, Tagesmeldungen.* 52535/2.

[71] Hermann Teske, "Railroad Transportation Operation *ZITADELLE* (1943)," pp. 13, 16–17. MS # D–369. Foreign Studies Br, OCMH.

[72] No copy of this OKW directive appears to be extant. It is referred to as Fuehrer Order No. 9 in *H Gr Mitte, Ia, Nr. 9842/43 g. Kdos., 5.IX.43., Anl. z. KTB, H Gr Mitte, Fuehrungsabt., Akte XXII, Heft 11, 1.VIII.–30.IX.43.* 65002/23.

Soviet propaganda aimed at the civil populace increased both in volume and in quality.[73]

Before the withdrawal to the positions east of the Desna was complete the Soviet attack shifted with such violence to the front of the *Fourth Army* defending the Smolensk sector and along the boundary between *Army Groups South* and *Center* in the area of the *Fourth Panzer* and *Second Armies* directly east of Kursk that a proper balancing of forces was found to be no longer possible. A new withdrawal became necessary, this time of the entire army group, to positions paralleling the line upper Dnepr-Orsha-Vitebsk-Nevel and some 30 miles to the east. This withdrawal continued throughout September and was completed on 1 October.

Throughout all of September the transport situation in the central sector remained serious due to partisan action, and, although the distance to the front grew progressively less and supply and troop movements from the Zone of the Interior decreased proportionately, the difficulties caused by the bands were greater than during the previous withdrawal because this time the whole army group was involved. In actual volume partisan activity decreased from the previous month, but was generally more effective. Although the rear area was slowly compressed and the total mileage of communication lines was steadily cut down by the retrograde movement, this was far more than offset by the continued heavy pressure of the Red Army and the fact that so many of the German security units were either fighting at the front or on the move to areas further west. As news of the succeeding German reverses spread the increasing number of desertions of local railway personnel and of whole companies and battalions of indigenous units (the latter units often killing the German cadres) added further difficulties. The general military and political situation drove increasing numbers of heretofore neutral civilians into the bands, and in some cases these civilians, incensed by rumors and Soviet propaganda, made heavy armed raids on German-occupied villages. Others withdrawing with the German divisions went over to the bands because of their fear of the forced labor draft.[74]

---

[73] *Ibid.; Bericht, Korueck 559, Ic, Tgb. Nr. 2952/43 geh., 31.VII.43., KTB Heft 3, Anl. 1–17.* 45668/4. Hermann Teske, "Railroad Transportation Operation *ZITADELLE* (1943)," pp. 12–13. MS # D–369. Foreign Studies Br, OCMH.; *AOK 9, Anl. 2, KTB 9, 19.VIII.–15.X.43., Fuehrungsabt, II, Tagesmeldungen.* 52535/2.

[74] *H. Gr. Mitte, Ia. Nr. 11822/43 g. Kdos., 17.X.43., Anl. z. KTB, H. Gr. Mitte, Fuehrungsabt., Akte XXIII, Heft 12, 1.X.–31.XII.43.* 65002/24; *Bericht, September 43, Pz AOK 3, Anl. Bd. 2, Tgb. 9, Ic/AO, 1.VII.–30.IX.43.* 40252/7; *Bericht, September 43, AOK 2, Ia, Anl z. KTB Russland, Schriftwechsel Banden-bekaempfung III, 21.VI.–29.X.43.* 60311/21; Hermann Teske, "Railroad Transportation Operation *ZITADELLE* (1943)," pp. 13–14. MS # D–369. Foreign Studies Br, OCMH. Teske, *op. cit.,* pp. 195–97.

Generally the situation remained fluid. Because so many partisan raids went unreported due to the natives' fear of the bands and because many mayors and village elders defected or were murdered and many of those remaining in office were afraid to carry out their duties, the Germans found it increasingly impossible to get a clear picture of just what was happening in their rear and of the extent of the disruption there.[75]

During the first days of the month, there was a lull in the attacks, especially in the chain demolitions, due, as the Germans thought, to a shortage of explosives following the heavy sabotage of the preceding weeks.[76] The emphasis, however, remained on the rail lines, and by the middle of the month the bands again started operating on a large scale with chain attempts. On the night of 18–19 September they set 3,250 demolitions and on the night of 25–26 September 4,240, more than 50 percent of which were successful.[77] Raids on the lines in the army group rear area totaled 1,256 for the month with an aggregate of 4,257 successful demolitions, of which 72 were of the chain variety comprising 3,800, with nearly half again as many in the *Generalkommissariat Weissruthenien*.[78] In 255 cases lines were cut for more than 12 hours, in 18 cases for more than 24 hours.[79] Rolling stock continued to suffer heavily with 109 locomotives and 600 cars damaged or destroyed. Many water towers were demolished and some 30 miles of spare rails ruined. In addition, the Minsk-Smolensk "U" cable was cut 40 times in 14 days.[80]

The focus of these September raids was in the northeastern edge of the Pripyat behind the *Second Army* and directly in line with the heaviest Soviet attack. Here, where the terrain was the most formidable in the eastern theater and for the most part had been in the hands of the bands for many months, travel became very difficult, with the partisans exerting extremely heavy pressure on the rail lines, mining the few roads, and striking at the bridges. The Minsk-Gomel and Mogilev-Zhlobin

[75] Dir. *Hq. AOK 2, O. Qu/Qu 2, 29.IX.43.*, in *KTB Russland AOK 2, Ia. Schriftwechsel Bandenbekaempfung, III, 21.VI.–29.X.43.* 60311/21; *Bandenlage im September, Korueck 559, Ic. Tgb. Nr. 3735/43 geh., 25.IX.43.*, in *KTB Korueck 559/Ia fuer die Zeit v. 5.VII.–28.XII.43.* 45668/4.
[76] *Bericht Sept. 43, Pz AOK 3, Anl. Bd. 2, Tgb. 9.* 40252/7.
[77] *H. Gr. Mitte, Ia. Nr. 11822/43 g.Kdos., 17.X.43., Anl. z. KTB. H. Gr. Mitte, Fuehrungsabt., Akte XXIII, Heft 12, 1.X.–31.XII.43.* 65002/24; Hermann Teske, "Railroad Transportation Operation *ZITADELLE* (1943)," p. 15. MS # D–369. Foreign Studies Br, OCMH.
[78] *Ibid.; H. Gr. Mitte, Ia. Nr. 11822/43 g.Kdos., 17.X.43., Anl. z. KTB, Mitte, Fuehrungsabt., Akte XXIII, Heft 12, 1.X.–31.XII.43.* 65002/24. *Wehrmachtsbefehlshaber Ostland, Ia. Nr. 2360/43 geh., vom 1 Okt, 43, Anl. 1, 19.IX.–27.IX.43.* 65002/24.
[79] Teske, *op. cit.*, p. 197.
[80] *Ibid.; H. Gr. Mitte, Ia. Nr. 11822/43 g.Kdos., 17.X.43., Anl. z. KTB. Mitte, Fuehrungsabt., Akte XXIII, Heft 12, 1.X.–31.XII.43.* 65002/24.

lines continued to be the hardest hit in the whole central sector, the former suffering 643 demolitions in one 30 mile stretch between Zhlobin and Bobruysk, the latter 580 in 40 miles.[81] Travel between Gomel and Zhlobin finally became so difficult that the Germans, in a desperate attempt to curb the raids, unloaded replacements along that particular stretch and placed them at 20 foot intervals as static track guards. Yet the demolitions continued.[82]

For several days following the mass demolitions of 18–19 September, the majority of which occurred in the Pripyat west of Gomel, the rail traffic situation in the vicinity of that city was quite critical. Due to the large number of track breaks caused by the bands and raids by the Red Air Force and the unusually great traffic demands occasioned by the withdrawal, 130 evacuation trains became blocked in the marshalling yards there with the Red Army attacking but a few miles to the east. The failure of the bands to follow up their first assaults prior to 25–26 September, however, gave the transportation command an opportunity to bring the situation under control, and none of the 130 was lost.[83]

OKH became so worried over these continued demolitions in the Pripyat area that *Foreign Armies East* for a while seriously considered entering the radio nets of the bands there and simulating orders from Moscow to halt the attacks. The Germans were very familiar with the partisan nets and had monitored their traffic for some time. The plan was finally dropped, however, in the fear that the bands might discover the subterfuge and alter their codes and procedures and thus deny the German command a valuable source of intelligence.[84]

As the withdrawal progressed, the bands were gradually forced westward into new areas by the retreating Germans. But they went reluctantly, in some cases forcing Wehrmacht units to fight their way back to the new positions.[85]

By 1 October the Germans had occupied their Dnepr line, and the pressure of the Red Army attacks began to ease as the Soviets paused to regroup. During September the transportation command successfully moved a total of 2,029 trains in the central sector, 713 of them evacuation trains. This brought the total of rail movements since the opening of

[81] *Bandenanschlaege im Monat Sept. 43*, Anl. z. KTB, H. Gr. Mitte, Ia. Nr. 11822/43 g.Kdos. 17.X.43. 65002/24; Hermann Teske, "Railroad Transportation Operation *ZITADELLE* (1943)," p. 15. MS # D–369. Foreign Studies Br, OCMH.

[82] Teske, *op. cit.*, p. 197.

[83] Hermann Teske, "Railroad Transportation Operation *ZITADELLE* (1943)," p. 15. MS # D–369. Foreign Studies Br, OCMH.

[84] *Funktaeuschung der Banden, Fde. H. Ost* (I/Bd), Nr. 2488/43 g.Kdos., 4.X.43. H 3/193.

[85] *Befehl, Hq, AOK 2, 1.X.43.* 60311/21.

ZITADELLE to 7,912.[86] During the same period the partisans had successfully set off some 21,348 rail demolitions in more than 26,000 attempts, in addition to other extensive sabotage. In spite of these efforts and the tremendous pressure exerted by the Red Army, the Germans had executed their two successive withdrawal movements on schedule, with a minimum loss of troop and supply trains, and at all times under their own control.[87]

The Northern and Southern Sectors During the Summer and Fall

In the northern sector the partisans were not overly active. Due to the more stable situation along the front there, the rear area commands had not been weakened by withdrawals of security units for service in the line and were generally able to hold them in check by constant patrolling and occasional raids.[88]

In the rear of the *Sixteenth Army* sabotage activity, especially on the rail lines, increased somewhat during August in connection with the Soviet assaults on the Staraya-Russa front, but never assumed any such proportions as behind *Army Group Center*. Although the partisans there set some chain demolitions, using as many as several hundred mines on occasion, the fact that their units were small and not well established in the area precluded their exercising any real effect on the tactical situation.[89] A similar situation existed in the rear of the *Eighteenth Army* between Lake Ilmen and Lake Peipus.[90] During September the partisans broke rails at but 81 places and damaged but 7 bridges in the whole sector, in addition to some small-scale raiding and pillaging and occasional clashes with security patrols.[91]

Under the surface of this comparative quiet, however, lay a definite threat for the future. All during the summer the natives in the sector had been growing increasingly hostile to the occupation, and by September they were no longer cooperating in reporting raids or the whereabouts of partisans. This deprived the security commands of a valuable source of information. To cap this, the bands were steadily growing in

---

[86] See: Hermann Teske, "Railroad Transportation Operation *ZITADELLE* (1943)," pp. 14, 16–17. MS # D–369. Foreign Studies Br, OCMH.

[87] *Ibid.; H. Gr. Mitte, Ia. Nr. 11822/43 g. Kdos., 17.X.43., Anl. z. KTB. H. Gr. Mitte, Fuehrungsabt., Akte XXIII, Heft 12, 1.X.–31.XII.43.* 65002/24; see also: *Lagen Ost* for the period.

[88] *Bandenlage, Kurze Beurteilung der Feindlage, OKH/Fde. H. Ost (I), 1.IX.–31.X.43.* H 3/204; *Bericht, September 43, AOK 16, Ia. KTB 5, Teil VII, Bandenakten, 1.VII.–31.XII.43.* 44185/69.

[89] *Bericht, August 43, AOK 16, Ia. KTB 5, Teil VII, Bandenakten, 1.VII.–31.XII.43.* 44185/69.

[90] *Banden, Sept. 43. in H. Gr. Nord. Ic/AO, KTB Bandenlagekarten, Jan. bis Sept. 43.* 75131/40; *285 Sich. Div., Anl. z. KTB 3, Ic. u. IIa, 1.II.–30.VI.43., 1.VII.–31.XII.43.* 35155/4, 43060/4.

[91] *H. Gr. Nord, Ic/AO, KTB, Bandenlagekarten, Jan. bis Sep 43.* 75131/40.

size and number, recruiting successfully among the more dissident elements of the population and being reinforced both from the Soviet rear and by desertions from the *Ost* units.[92]

This situation was considerably worsened late in September when 150,000 civilians—men, women, and children—were ordered evacuated from the area between Lake Ilmen and Lake Peipus "on foot."[93] The *Eighteenth Army,* in protesting, reported that there were no facilities for caring for the evacuees on the march and no camps suitable for housing them within 90 miles, and that even while the move was only in process of organization the details of the plan became widely known and large numbers of the natives began going over to the partisans in self-defense.   Such open mistreatment, the report continued, presaged a great intensification of partisan activity and a complete breakdown of morale and discipline in the indigenous units with resultant disaffection and desertion to the bands.[94]

In the southern sector, sabotage increased somewhat during July, but was not generally aimed at the German lines of communication.   The few larger bands there remained quiet, but during the month a number of small units of 8 to 10 men, apparently under some sort of central control, appeared in the northern portion of the area hitting sharply at harvesting machinery and grain storage facilities.[95]   Rather obviously the Soviet high command, if indeed it had control of these groups, did not intend that the Germans make any harvest or carry any surplus food stocks with them in their withdrawal.

In August coincident with the Red Army attack in the central sector, there was a considerable increase in partisan activity along the traffic arteries leading into Kiev, especially west of the Dnepr River.   Although this caused a number of short interruptions in traffic and was generally "a great nuisance," it caused no critical delays in supply for the front.[96] As the fighting moved steadily westward, most of the bands east of the Dnepr moved across the river into the lower edges of the Pripyat Marsh. This general westward movement of the whole war in the south brought

---

[92] *Bericht, Sept, 43, AOK 16, Ia. KTB 5, Teil VII, Bandenakten, 1.VII.–31.XII.43.* 44185/69.

[93] The origin of this order is unknown. See: *Bericht, AOK 18* to *Gen. der Ostruppen, H. Gr. Nord. 7.X.43., AOK 18, Ia, Nachreichungen d. Abt. Ic/AO, 43–45.* 64847. This is not the directive, but a report by the *Eighteenth Army* giving the provisions of the order and protesting.

[94] *Ibid.*

[95] *H. Geb. Sued, Ic. Nr. 182/43g., 4.VIII.43., KTB, H. Geb. Sued, Juli 43.* 39502/1.

[96] "The German Military Transport System in Southern Russia, Romania, and Hungary from 24 November 1942 to 25 March 1945," p. 14. MS # D–139. Foreign Studies Br, OCMH; *Bandenlage, August 43, Korueck 585, Anl. z. KTB. 10.IX.–17.X.43.* 44172/3; *OKH/Fde. H. Ost (I), Kurze Beurteilung der Feindlage, 1.IX.–31.X.43.* H 3/204.

Map 7

PARTISAN SITUATION
IN REAR OF
ARMY GROUP CENTER *

1 OCTOBER 1943

German
Russian
200   Partisan Concentrations

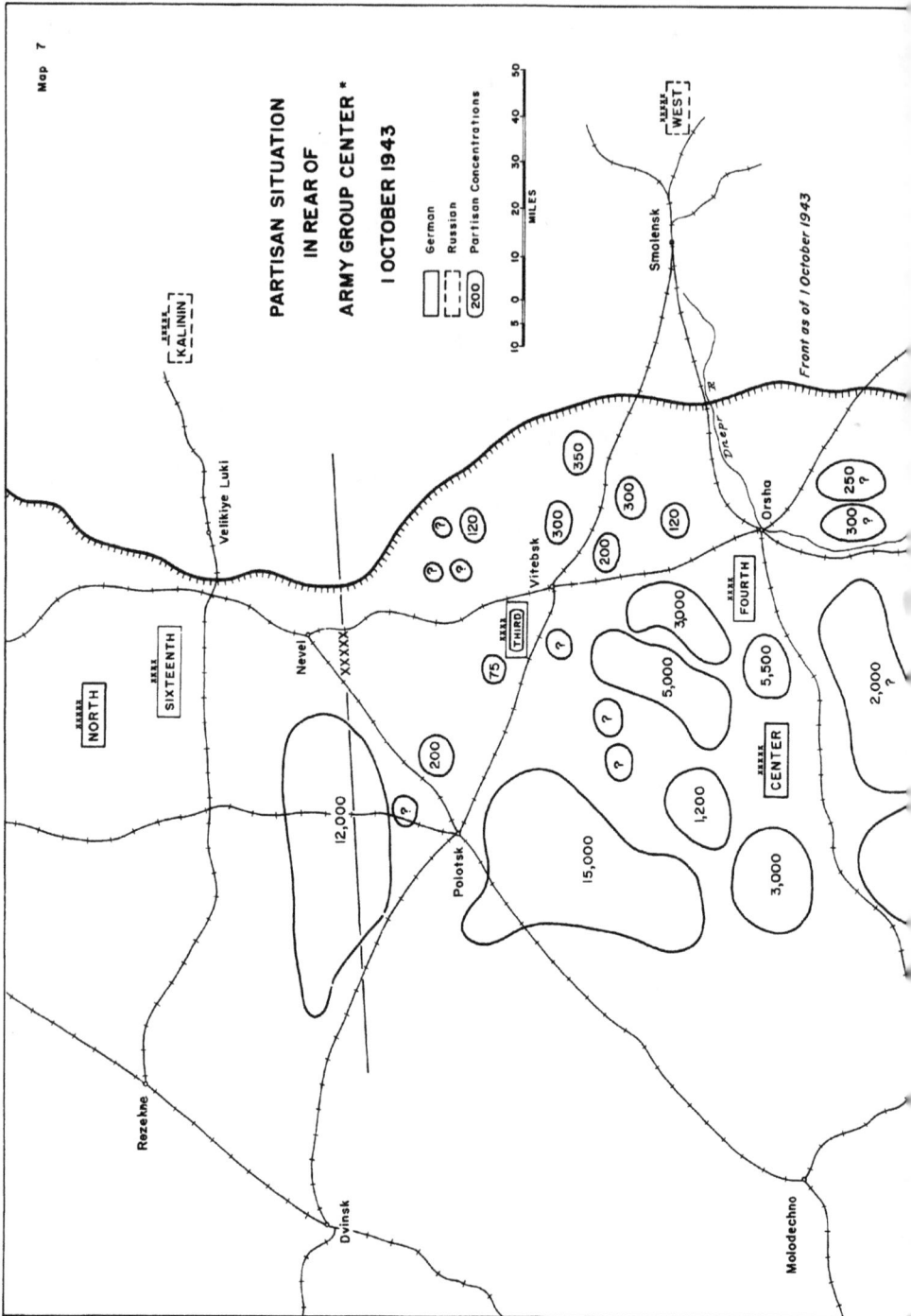

0 5 10 20 30 40 50
MILES

Front as of 1 October 1943

KALININ

NORTH

SIXTEENTH

Velikiye Luki

Nevel

XXXX

THIRD

Vitebsk

Smolensk

WEST

Dnepr R

Orsha

FOURTH

CENTER

Rezekne

Polotsk

Dvinsk

Molodechno

12,000

200

15,000

3,000

1,200

5,000

3,000

5,500

2,000

75

120

350

300

300

200

120

250

300

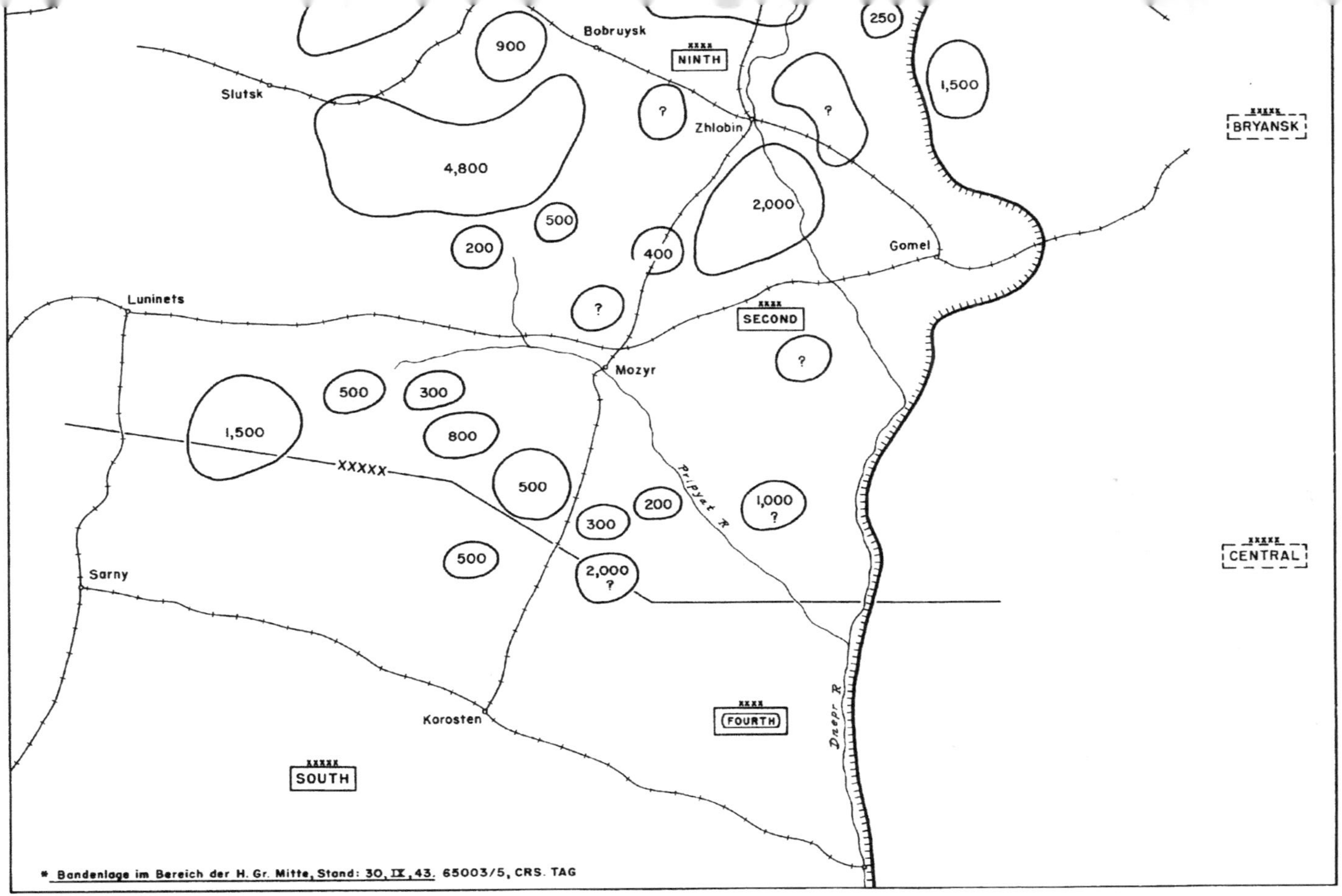

Map 7. Partisan Situation in Rear of Army Group Center, 1 October 1943.

* Bandenlage im Bereich der H. Gr. Mitte, Stand: 30. IX. 43. 65003/5, CRS. TAG

388413 O - 56 (Face p. 171)

out a number of Ukrainian nationalist bands in force, and in the Sarny-Korosten area they fought several pitched battles with partisan units.[97] The same pattern continued throughout the fall months. Although the bands showed some increase in size and numbers, for the most part they remained inactive, avoiding clashes with the German security units and steering clear of the increasing number of line divisions in the region. In September, a typical month, they blew the rail lines at but 36 places, with no mass demolitions, and attacked economic installations but 40 times.[98]

As in the central and northern sectors, popular morale took a sharp drop during the summer as the Wehrmacht withdrawal continued. In the areas still in German hands panic mounted over fear of a scorched-earth campaign. Many natives went over to the bands, and in some areas, for the first time since the invasion in June 1941, the Germans became the object of unconcealed hatred because of the general devastation of the civilian property that the war had occasioned.[99]

The Central Sector, October–December

On 1 October, the eastern front ran, at least momentarily, from Melitopol on the Sea of Azov to the head of the Dnepr bend at Zaporozhe and thence up the west bank of the river, continuing on in the central and northern sectors generally from the confluence of the Dnepr and Pripyat Rivers through Gomel north along the prepared defenses just east of the line upper Dnepr-Orsha-Vitebsk-Nevel, and thence to Lake Ilmen and down the course of the Volkhov River to the old Leningrad perimeter.

Partisan Concentrations

Despite the presence of an increasing number of bands behind the length of this line, the focus of the partisan effort remained in the rear of *Army Group Center.* There the areas of heaviest partisan concentration, with the exception of the territory abandoned during the summer withdrawals, remained unchanged from the spring and summer, albeit considerably reinforced by local levies and bands forced westward by the retrogression of the front. In the Rossono area west of Nevel and north of Polotsk were approximately 12,000 irregulars; in the Senno-Lepel-Ushachi area, some 60 miles west of Vitebsk-Orsha, above 30,000; and in the general region bounded Minsk-Orsha-Gomel-Slutsk and centered about Bobruysk, 28,000. In addition, there were a number

---

[97] *OKH/Fde. H. Ost I, Kurze Beurteilung der Feindlage, 1.IX.–31.X.43.* H 3/204.

[98] *Kdr. d. H. Geb. Sued, Ic. Nr. 395/43g., 3.X.43., KTB, Ia. Kdr. G. d. Sich. Tr. Sued. Monat Okt. u. Nov 43, mit Anl.* 39502/4.

[99] *Bericht, Sept 43, Pz AOK 1, Beilage 6 z. Tgb., Ic/AO, 1.IX.–31.XII.43.* 45393/19.

of bands concentrated in the Pripyat south of the Gomel-Luninets railroad whose strength the Germans had not determined.[100]

The Security Commands

The sector, including the *Generalkommissariat Weissruthenien*, at this time comprised something more than 90,000 square miles, roughly twice the size of the state of Pennsylvania. In the area were 2,300 miles of railroads and 1,700 miles of roads which the Germans considered important enough to require security. For all security tasks, including the coverage of these lines of communication, the combined Wehrmacht and political security commands had an assigned strength of 163 miscellaneous battalions, of which two-thirds were German, two were French and the remainder Hungarian and native.

On the basis of experience which had shown that one German security battalion with a strength of 350 men could "barely" provide static security for 25 kilometers of railroad or 50 kilometers of road, 210 German security battalions were required for these traffic routes alone, making a paper deficit of 47. The actual deficit, however, was much greater, for the 163 needed more than 14,000 replacements to bring them up to a strength of 350 per unit, 15 of the total were in the front lines, and the Hungarian and indigenous units were of such poor quality that their combat effectiveness was considered to be less than one-half that of their German counterparts. The aggregate effect was to reduce the true strength of the combined security commands to no more than 100 battalions, enough for static security of one-half the roads and rail lines, and nothing for anything else.[101]

This critical shortage of security forces was due in no small part to the widespread defections of the personnel of the native volunteer units. The morale of these natives had never been of the best, and during the summer months they had proved unable to withstand the psychological effects of the continuing German reverses and the terror campaign waged by the partisans against their families. The upshot of it was that all indigenous units became suspect and most were removed from partisan-endangered areas.

In September the whole question of the reliability of the *Osttruppen* was reviewed by OKH [102] and the decision was made to exchange *Ost* units from the east for German units in France on the basis of two *Ost*

---

[100] *Bandenlage im Bereich der H. Gr. Mitte, Stand: 30.IX.43.*, H. Gr. Mitte, Ic/AO (Abw.), Bandenlisten, Sept. bis Dez. 43.   65003/5.
[101] *Bandenlage, Okt. 43,* H. Gr. Mitte, Ia. Nr. 13097/43 g. Kdos., 9.XI.43., Anl. z. KTB, H. Gr. Mitte, Fuehrungsabt., Akte XXIII, Heft 12, 1.X.–31.XII.43. 65002/24.
[102] See: Folder, *Osttruppen,* OKH/Org. Abt., Nr. II/12593/43, II/12595/43. Foreign Studies Br, OCMH.

battalions for one German battalion.[103] During September and October about 45 were transferred to the west. In October the continued Red Army pressure caused a modification of the original ratio to the advantage of the eastern theater. At that time it was planned to exchange 32 additional *Ost* battalions for 26 German battalions.[104] There is no evidence that these German battalions were to be utilized in security roles rather than in the tottering front lines. Contrarily, OKH's announcement that 25,000 additional *Osttruppen* would be trained in November and December would seem to indicate that such was not the case.[105]

In any event, the problem of desertions from the *Ostbataillone* was not solved as far as those remaining in the east were concerned, for the basic causes of defection were not removed.[106] Desertions continued, often by platoon and company, and ceased only when the units were transferred. The newly activated units appeared to be more trustworthy, especially when committed in danger spots, but the German unit commanders reported that it would be some time before they could accurately estimate their reliability and combat worth.[107]

Sabotage in October

Both the increase in partisan strength and this manpower shortage were evidenced in continued raids and sabotage by the bands, proportionate to be sure to the decrease in the extent of the rear. As in previous months, they concentrated their efforts against the German communications. During October they hit railroad installations with 1,093 raids and set off demolitions along the tracks at 5,456 places. In addition, they destroyed or damaged sizeable stores of railway construction and maintenance materials and a number of engines and cars. They also paid special attention to signal communication facilities, breaking the Orsha-Minsk-Brest-Litovsk cable more than 100 times and cutting down 1,472 telephone poles.[108] Often they waited in ambush in the vicinity of these breaks for the German repair details and caused them heavy casualties over a period of time.[109] So heavy did the attrition of signal

[103] *OKW/WFSt. KTB 1, 1.IX.–31.XII.43., 25.IX.43.*, quoted in Gordon A. Harrison, *Cross Channel Attack* in UNITED STATES ARMY IN WORLD WAR II (Washington 1951), p. 146.
[104] *OKH/Op. Abt., Kraefte Westen, Allgemein, Band III, 24.VII.42.–1.XI.43.*, quoted in Harrison, *op. cit.*, p. 146.
[105] *Ibid.*
[106] For these causes, see: Folder, *Osttruppen, OKH/Org. Abt., Nr. II/12593/43, II/12595/43.* Foreign Studies Br, OCMH.
[107] *Bericht, Oktober 43, AOK 16, Ia. KTB 5, Teil VII, Qu. 1. Bandenakten, 1.VII.–31.XII.43.* 44185/69; *Bericht, Oktober 43, 2.XI.43., AOK 2, Ia. Bandenbekaempfung IV, 1.IX.43.–30.I.44.* 52701/107; *Korueck 559, Ia. Nr. 5891/43 geh., Heft 2, Anl. 94–126 z. KTB Korueck 559, Ia. fuer die Zeit v. 5.XI.–30.XII.43.* 45668/3.
[108] *Bandenlage, Okt. 43, H. Gr. Mitte, Ia. Nr. 13097/43 g. Kdos., 9.XI.43., Anl. z. KTB. H. Gr. Mitte, Fuehrungsabt., Akte XXIII, Heft 12, 1.X.–31.XII.43.* 65002/24.
[109] MS # P–038, "German Radio Intelligence" (S). Foreign Studies Br, OCMH.

facilities become that before the end of the year the copper requirements to rebuild lines destroyed by the partisans had risen 700 percent over those of 1942.[110] They also continued to mine the roads, both primary and secondary, although with much less success than in the case of the rail lines. The *Second Army*, whose rear was particularly harassed, reported that it was able to locate and disarm two-thirds of the charges, so poorly were they laid, and recommended to its security command that details of civilians drafted from nearby villages be forced to plow and grade the roads with their own horses in an effort to neutralize the remainder of the mines.[111]

The focus of these raids hit much deeper into the German rear than ever before, spilling well over into the extreme western portions of the political occupation zone, which heretofore had suffered little damage, and even on occasion across the Polish border. Raids on the Brest-Litovsk-Baranowicze line increased 50 percent, on the Volkovsk-Lida 200 percent; the Gomel-Luninets-Brest-Litovsk link bisecting the Pripyat suffered 1,600 demolitions during the month, over 1,200 west of Luninets. Conversely, attacks on the much assaulted Gomel-Zhlobin-Minsk line, now close to the front, dropped more than 300 percent.[112]

Much of this rise in sabotage in the Generalkommissariat was attributed by the political occupation authorities to the vicious methods of the police and SS units securing the sector. Villages were burned without cause; cattle were ruthlessly shot lest they fall into the hands of the partisans; and in many cases adults were forcibly evacuated and their children left to fend for themselves. The natives became so antagonized that Organization Todt [113] found itself unable to operate due to an almost complete refusal of the people to work.[114]

[110] *Entwicklung der Bandenlage, Bandentaetigkeit u. Auswirkungen auf die Wirtschaft, 1.IX.43.* H 3/519.

[111] *Monatsbericht Okt. 43, Korueck 580, Ic. Nr. 4307/43 geh., KTB 28a, Korueck 580, 16.X.–31.X.43.* 41217/2; *Befehl, AOK 2, O. Qu/Qu 2, 29.IX.43., Anl. z. KTB Russland, AOK 2, Ia. 21.VI.–29.X.43.* 60311/21.

[112] *Bandenlage, Okt. 43. H. Gr. Mitte, Ia. Nr. 13097/43 g. Kdos., 9.XI.43., Anl. z. KTB. H. Gr. Mitte, Fuehrungsabt., Akte XXIII, Heft 12, 1.X.–31.XII.43.* 65002/24; *Eisenbahnsprengungen, Monat Sept. 43, Anl. z. Fde. H. Ost (I/Bd.), Nr. 2488/43 g. Kdos., 4.X.43.* H 3/193; *Bandenanschlaege im Monat Sept., Okt. 43, Anl. z. KTB, H. Gr. Mitte, Ia. Nr. 11822/43 g. Kdos. 17.X.43.* 65002/24.

[113] The Organization Todt was a paramilitary organization of the Nazi Party Auxiliary to the Wehrmacht. Named after its founder, Dr. Todt, it comprised a cadre of engineers and was expanded as necessary by the use of hired, conscript, or foreign labor.

[114] Sit rpt, *Reichskommissar Ostland* to Reichsminister for the Occupied Eastern Territory, 14 Oct 43. EAP 99/62; Oral testimony of Von dem Bach-Zolewski in *I.M.T., op. cit.,* IV, pp. 475–96.

The Pressure Eases Momentarily

During the latter half of October the security commands, by literally scraping the bottom of the manpower barrel and by abandoning the protection of several roads and population centers and the construction of one section of railroad,[115] were able to mount several medium-scale antipartisan operations, thus causing a noticeable drop in sabotage before the first of November.[116] A sharp decrease in airborne supply from the Soviet rear was also a material factor in this drop, flights shrinking from the high of more than 2,000 for the first two weeks of May to 315 for the last two weeks of October.[117]

Also affecting the volume of raids and sabotage during this period was the need for the bands to stockpile food supplies for the coming winter. With their numbers constantly increasing, they more and more were forced to turn their energies to extensive foraging and looting of civilian stores. Too often mindful only of their own requirements, they indiscriminately struck in any locality where food was to be had, irrespective of the political sentiments of the inhabitants, seizing quantities of grain and large numbers of cattle, sometimes as many as 200 in a single raid.[118]

The looting finally assumed such proportions and created such ill feeling among the natives against both the bands and the Soviet high command that the Central Staff issued a directive that food could be requisitioned only in daylight and then through negotiation with the village elders, and that all taken was to be signed for. Pillaging and foraging at night were forbidden and all caught so doing were ordered to be shot.[119]

Despite the cut in air supply, Moscow made it clear that the bands were in no wise being abandoned and showed itself both willing and able to aid them when the occasion demanded. During October one German antipartisan unit succeeded in isolating the 2,500-man *Polk Grischin* in the Pripyat Marshes behind the *Ninth Army*. This *Polk*

---

[115] *H. Gr. Mitte, Ia, Nr. 13097/43 g. Kdos., 9.XI.43., Bandenlage, Okt. 43, Anl. z. KTB, H. Gr. Mitte, Fuehrungsabt., Akte XXIII, Heft 12, 1.X.–31.XII.43.* 65002/24.

[116] *Monatsbericht, Okt. 43, Korueck 580, Ic, Nr. 4307/43 geh., 28.X.43., KTB 28a, Korueck 580, 16.X.–31.X.43.* 41217/2; *Bericht, Okt. 43, AOK 2, Ia. Bandenbekaempfung IV, 1.XI.43.–30.I.44., 52701/107;* see also: *Bandenlage im Bereich der H. Gr. Mitte, Stand: 30.IX.43., Anl. z. KTB H. Gr. Mitte.* 65002/24.

[117] See: *Anl. 4 z. Bandenlage im Osten, Anlagen.* H 3/749; *Feindeinfluege vom 1.X.–15.X.43., H. Gr. Mitte, Ia. Nr. 13097/43 g. Kdos., Anl. 4.5 z. KTB, H. Gr. Mitte.* 65002/24.

[118] *Monatsbericht, Okt. 43, Korueck 559, Ic. Nr. 4424/43 geh., Heft 3, Anl. 1–17 z. KTB, Ic. Korueck 559, 5.VII.–28.XII.43.* 45668/4.

[119] *Bandenlage, Okt. 43, im Bereich des Korueck 585, Anl. z. KTB, Korueck 585, 11.X.–1.XII.43.* 44172/4; captured partisan directive, *Anl. z. KTB, H. Gr. Mitte, Bandenmeldungen, Nov. 43–Maerz 44.* 65002/69.

since early 1942 had been one of the most aggressive and effective partisan units in the central sector, and was something of a favorite with the Central Staff. When Grischin saw the critical nature of the situation, he radioed for additional arms and ammunition, which Moscow promptly dispatched in 10 Soviet cargo aircraft.[120]

Cooperation With the Red Army Again

Then in the first days of November the partisan effort, especially behind the *Third Panzer* and *Second Armies,* appeared to take on more purpose. When the Red Army had resumed its offensive in the middle of October, it had placed its heaviest pressure on the wings of the sector. In the Nevel area the Red divisions had struck hard along the boundary between *Army Groups Center* and *North* and by 15 November had driven a sizeable salient in the German line north of Vitebsk. At the same time in the south they had pushed the *Second Army* back across the Dnepr west of Gomel and forced a breakthrough in the Pripyat Marshes which threatened to parallel the Soviet successes against *Army Group South.*[121] Although both penetrations were eventually contained, they gave added impetus to the activity of the bands, especially those west of the points of Soviet main effort, and in large measure dictated their offensive actions for the remainder of the year.

Sometime prior to the attack on the northern wing of the sector, Moscow had ordered the bands in the area west of Nevel-Vitebsk to hold the region for the arrival of the Red Army and, if possible, to force a breach in the rear of the German defenses in conjunction with the Soviet attack, withdrawing only if faced by superior German forces.[122] A copy of this directive fell into German hands prior to the attack, and OKH, seeing the danger of a breakthrough in an area where freezing weather would in large part overcome any terrain difficulties and thus turn it into a gateway to Lithuania, quickly organized a large antipartisan operation as a preventive measure. The action was to be launched in late October by two *Kampfgruppen* (task forces) of police and SS units from the *Reichskommissariat Ostland* totaling 29 battalions. This was Operation *HEINRICH.*[123]

Before these units could do more than move into position, however, the critical nature of the Red Army penetration there forced them over to the defensive under army group command. As a result, although the mere presence of German troops in the area caused a number of the

---

[120] Entry for 11 Oct 43, in *Anl. 2 z. KTB 9, AOK 9, Fuehrungsabt. II, Tagesmeld-ungen, 11.VIII.–15.X.43.* 52535/2.

[121] For these operational developments along the front, see *Lagen Ost* for the period.

[122] Referred to in *Bandenlage im Bereich des Pz AOK 3, Nov. 43, Pz AOK 3, Anl. Bd. z. Tgb. 10, Ic/AO, 1.X.–31.XII.43.* 49113/37.

[123] *Ibid.; Lagen Ost* for period 20 Oct–16 Nov. 43.

bands to withdraw to the west, a good portion of the partisans were able to breach the German line from the rear, and only aggressive action by the *Kampfgruppen* averted a really serious breakthrough toward Dvinsk.[124]

Behind the *Second Army* the partisans, spurred by the Red Army successes, reinfiltrated the areas from which they had been driven by the German actions of October and regrouped under the leadership of a number of regular officers dropped into the area for the purpose, forming a solid block of some 7,000 men directly in the path of the Soviet penetration.[125]

Somewhat farther to the west and south of the Pripyat River, where the partisan situation had not previously been clear, a large block of bands extending longitudinally toward Brest-Litovsk appeared under a headquarters the Germans believed to be on the level of an army command.[126] This latter development forced the security command to pull a number of Hungarian units out of the threatened area southwest of Gomel and spread them out as far west as the Polish border to protect the Gomel-Luminets-Brest-Litovsk rail line.[127]

Sabotage Continues

Despite a further drop in air supply, 167 supply flights for November as against 886 in October, the partisans continued their attacks on the supply lines throughout the sector. Although some of the damage in the area west of Vitebsk, especially on the Vitebsk-Polotsk line, was obviously done by Red Army units before the penetration there was contained, the bands generally maintained the pace they set the previous month. Demolitions were set off on the tracks at 5,290 places and railway installations were hit with over 900 damaging raids. Fifty-six bridges were damaged.[128] In the central and southern portions of the sector the emphasis of the attacks continued to shift to the west. Demolitions on the Luninets-Baranovichi and Lida-Baranovichi lines rose 100 percent

---

[124] *Ibid.; H. Gr. Mitte, Ia, Nr. 14550/43 g. Kdos., 8.XII.43., Anl. z. KTB, H. Gr. Mitte, Fuehrungsabt., Akte XXIII, Heft 12, 1.X.–31.XII.43.* 65002/24.

[125] *Bericht, Nov. 43, AOK 2, Ia. Bandenbekaempfung IV, 1.XI.43.–30.I.44.* 52701/107; *Bandenlage im Bereich der H. Gr. Mitte, Stand: 30.XI.43., H. Gr. Mitte, Ic/AO (Abw.) Bandenlisten, Sept. bis Dez. 43.* 65003/5.

[126] *Bandenlage im Bereich der H. Gr. Mitte, Stand: 30.XI.43., H. Gr. Mitte, Ic/AO (Abw.) Bandenlisten, Sept. bis Dez. 43.* 65003/5; *H. Gr. Mitte, Ia, Nr. 14550/43 g. Kdos., 8.XII.43., Anl. z. KTB, H. Gr. Mitte, Fuehrungsabt., Akte XXIII, Heft 12, 1.X.–31.XII.43.* 65002/24. Evidence indicates that the Germans were mistaken in this, and that the command organization believed to be an army headquarters was merely an operations group heretofore unidentified.

[127] See *Lagen Ost* for this period.

[128] *H. Gr. Mitte, Ia, Nr. 14550/43 g. Kdos., 8.XII.43., Anl. z. KTB, H. Gr. Mitte, Fuehrungsabt., Akte XXIII, Heft 12, 1.X.–31.XII.43.* 65002/24; *Bandenanschlaege im Monat Nov. 43, Anl. 7 z. Schreiben Gen. d. Trspw., in KTB, H. Gr. Mitte, Ia, 1.X.–31.XII.43.* 65002/24.

over the previous month, and for the first time there were demolitions west of Lida, Brest-Litovsk, and Vilna.[129] The incidence of other sabotage went up. There was a large increase in damage to signal facilities: the Orsha-Minsk "U" cable was broken in 296 places, an increase of 195 percent, and 7,163 telephone poles representing a length of more than 200 miles of line were cut down. Valuable ration and agricultural stocks were destroyed in raids or by arson, one dump of 300 tons of rations and another containing 1,800 tons of potatoes and 170 tons of grain being burned. Deserters from the indigenous units aided the bands in many of these raids.[130]

German Attempts To Curb the Sabotage

With the German manpower situation what it was, only an extraordinary effort by the security commands and a number of protective innovations held the damage to this level. The replacement battalions of the *1st Ski Brigade,* totaling 3,000 men, were temporarily pulled out of the pipeline and committed as track guards along the Minsk-Brest-Litovsk line west of Baranovichi with an immediate reduction in sabotage. Listening posts tied in with an alarm system were set up for trial in one area. The use of searchlights along especially endangered stretches of road reduced mine laying, as did the resumption of armor-guarded convoys maintained on a frequent schedule, the vehicles running with bright lights. Antipersonnel mines were laid along trails known to be used by partisans with emergency warning systems attached. In the protection of signal facilities, alarm signals and "protective strip illumination" attached to the lines themselves proved of great value. Demolition charges were attached to telephone poles and were rigged to explode when the partisans attempted to cut them down. These proved very effective until the partisans forced women and children to do the actual cutting for them. Bicycle "trolleys" were constructed for patrolling along the rail lines and the more rapid commitment of offensive units. Whenever the manpower was available, even temporarily, "alert" forces were organized to deal with sudden emergencies and vigorous patrolling was the order of the day for all security commands that could scrape together a handful of men over

---

[129] *Ibid.*
[130] *H. Gr. Mitte, Ia, Nr. 14550/43 g. Kdos., 8.XII.43., Anl. z. KTB, H. Gr. Mitte, Fuehrungsabt., Akte XXIII, Heft 12, 1.X.–31.XII.43.* 65002/24; *Korueck 559, Ic. Tgb., Nr. 5103/43 geh., 27.XI.43., Korueck 559, Ia, 5.VII.–28.XII.43.* 45668/4; *Anl. 99, 6.XI.43., KTB Korueck 559, 5.XI.–30.XII.43.* 45668/3.

and above their static guard commitments. At night native scouts were widely employed, but with limited success.[131] The need for such innovations was clearly emphasized when in late November the continued Red Army pressure on the flanks of the sector and a newly opened assault on Orsha forced *Army Group Center* to draw off more and more units from the security commands for service at the front. The quieter portions of the rear were especially hard hit in this respect. The *Fourth Army Rear Area*, where the bands were less active for the moment, lost a total of 4,366 men, all Germans and all combat troops, to army and corps units during November alone.[132] Accentuating this was the loss to security command control of the SS and police battalions originally committed in Operation *HEINRICH*. Before the end of the month the situation became so bad that *Army Group Center* advised OKH that it could mount no antipartisan operations until the situation at the front warranted returning these troops to their parent commands or they were replaced from the Zone of the Interior.[133] The indigenous units which had been recruited to replace those transferred to France were of little help in this situation. Although they were proving more reliable than their predecessors, due, so the Germans believed, to the Wehrmacht success in the defensive battles, they still could not be trusted on other than the most routine security assignments in quiet areas.[134]

The Long-Range Partisan Strategy

Although during the last weeks of the year the bands continued their raids on the roads and railroads and especially on the telephone and cable lines, the attacks lacked cohesion, and on the whole they appeared more intent on expanding and consolidating their areas of concentration than disrupting the German supply axes. In the country paralleling these axes, they worked steadily at forming continuous, solid areas where they might completely dominate every phase of the situation; they no longer conformed their dispositions to billeting and forage possibilities or to the proximity of other bands. More and more their primary aim seemed to be a strategic redistribution of their centers of strength. This became so marked before the end of the year that the Germans believed they were subordinating all activity to preparations for a coordinated attack on

---

[131] *H. Gr. Mitte, Ia, Nr. 14550/43 g. Kdos., 8.XII.43., Anl. z. KTB, H. Gr. Mitte, Fuehrungsabt., Akte XXIII, Heft 12, 1.X.–31.XII.43.* 65002/24. MS # P–132, "Signal Communications in the East," pp. 219–20. Foreign Studies Br., OCMH; *Bericht, Korueck 559, Ia. Nr. 5216/43 geh., KTB, Korueck 559, Ia, 5.XI.–30.XII.43.* 45668/3.

[132] *Bericht, Korueck 559, Ia. Nr. 5216/43 geh., KTB, Korueck 559, Ia, 5.XI.–30.XII.43.* 45668/3.

[133] *H. Gr. Mitte, Ia. Nr. 14550/43 g. Kdos., 8.XII.43., Anl. z. KTB, H. Gr. Mitte, Fuehrungsabt., Akte XXIII, Heft 12, 1.X.–31.XII.43.* 65002/24.

[134] *Korueck 559, Ia. Nr. 5216/43 geh. 29.XI.43., Bericht, Korueck 559, Ia. Nr. 5216/43 geh., KTB, Korueck 559, Ia. 5.XI.–30.XII.43.* 45668/3,

German communications and routes of withdrawal in support of a general Red Army offensive.[135]

The bands lacked neither the manpower nor the popular support to execute this mission. As of 1 January 1944 the number of men in bands in the central sector that had been identified by the Germans was slightly in excess of 140,000,[136] nor was there any dearth of fillers for the expanding ranks. With the critical nature of the German situation an established fact, the natives flocked to them in such numbers that all could not be armed and many had to be sluiced eastward through gaps in the front for duty with the Red Army.[137]

In like manner the Soviets extended their political control. As the partisans consolidated their hold on the countryside, the Communist Party advanced side by side with them, conforming closely to their lateral administrative organization and establishing itself in such a manner as to be able to throw its whole weight into the fight when needed.[138]

---

[135] *Korueck 559, Ic. Tgb. Nr. 5899/43 geh., 28.XII.43., Heft 3, Anl. 1–17, Ic. z. KTB Korueck 559/Ia. 5.VII.–28.XII.43.*   45668/4; *Korueck 559/Ia. Nr. 5891/43 geh., 30.XII.43., Heft 2, Anl. 94–126 z. KTB Korueck 559/Ia. 5.XI.–30.XII.43.* 45668/3; *Meldung, Dez. 43, 3.I.44., AOK 2, Ia. Bandenbekaempfung IV, 1.XI.43.– 30.I.44.*   52701/107; *H. Gr. Mitte, Ia, Nr. 279/44 g. Kdos., 8.I.44., Anl. z. KTB H. Gr. Mitte, Akte XXII, Heft 13, 1.I.–31.III.44.*   65002/48; *H. Gr. Mitte, Ic/AO (Abw.) Nr. 63/44 geh., 3.I.44., Anl. z. KTB, H. Gr. Mitte, Bandenmeldungen, Nov 43–Mar 44.*   65002/69.

[136] *Bandenlage im Bereich der H. Gr. Mitte, Stand: 1.I.44., Bandenlisten, H. Gr. Mitte, Ic/AO (Abw.), Sept.–Dez. 43.*   65003/5.

[137] *Ibid.; H. Gr. Mitte, Ia, Nr. 279/44 g. Kdos., 8.I.44., Anl. z. KTB H. Gr. Mitte, Akte XXII, Heft 13, 1.I.–31.III.44.*   65002/48.

[138] *H. Gr. Mitte, Ic/AO (Abw.), Nr. 63/44 geh., 3.I.44., Anl. z. KTB, H. Gr. Mitte, Bandenmeldungen, Nov 43–Mar 44.*   65002/69; *"Nachrichten ueber Bandenkrieg Nr. 6," OKH GenStdH. Fde H. Ost.* H 3/738.

CHAPTER 11

THE DECISIVE MONTHS: JANUARY-JUNE 1944

The Northern Sector

In the *Army Group North Rear Area* the partisan situation had steadily worsened toward the end of 1943. Throughout the year the bands there had increased in size and especially in strength, although to no such degree as in the central sector. In many areas they reigned almost supreme, and in at least two *rayons* behind the *Sixteenth Army* operated a wholly Soviet administration.[1] Despite their improved position, however, they were not overly active, and throughout the sector seemed more interested in biding their time and hoarding their strength than in raiding German installations. Although only 250 of the 1,200-odd miles of railroad in the 60,000 square mile sector [2] had German security units permanently stationed along them, they set off but 439 rail demolitions in 575 attempts during December.[3]

Whether they refrained from more extensive operations on orders from the Central Staff, conserving their strength until the Red Army should launch a general offensive, or whether they were held in check by the security commands is unknown. Their reaction to subsequent Soviet moves, however, seemed to indicate Moscow's guiding hand.[4] At the beginning of 1944 these bands comprised some 27,000 partisans, in sharp contrast to the 140,000-plus behind *Army Group Center*. Roughly 14,000 were in the rear of the *Sixteenth Army*, for the most part concentrated in the area west and northwest of Nevel. The remainder were in the *Eighteenth Army* rear between Lake Ilmen and Lake Peipus.[5] The terrain definitely favored their operations. Almost the entire sector was covered with dense forests and swamps interspersed with numbers of small lakes, and was passable for heavy traffic only

---

[1] *Meldung, Nov. 43, Korueck 584, AOK 16, Ia, Anl. Bd. IV, Allgemein, 4.XI.43.–24.V.44.* 54321/6.

[2] This was exclusive of the Baltic States which were under a political administration and where the partisans had never been a factor.

[3] *Sicherungstruppen und Bandenlage im Bereich der H. Gr. Nord. Dezember 43; Bandenanschlaege auf Eisenbahnen und wichtige Strassenbruecken, Dezember 43, im Bereich der H. Gr. Nord.* Both in OCMH files.

[4] See: *KTB, H. Gr. Nord. Ia. 12.I.–10.II.44.* 75128/31, 75128/32, 75128/34.

[5] *OKH/Fde.H.Ost/Abt. (I/Bd.). 29.II.44.* H 3/361; *Bandenlage im Bereich der H. Gr. Mitte, Stand: 1.I.44., H. Gr. Mitte, Ic/AO (Abw.), Bandenlisten, Sep.–Dez. 43.* 65003/5; *Bandenlage, Dez. 43, H. Gr. Nord, Ic/AO, KTB, Bandenlagekarten, Dez. 43.* 75131/41.

over the rail lines and one primary highway, the Dvinsk-Pskov-Luga-Leningrad. The secondary net consisted of unimproved roads and trails.

The Offensive Against the Eighteenth Army [6]

The 13,000-odd partisans in the *Eighteenth Army* sector were rather evenly distributed on either side of the Pskov-Luga-Leningrad railroad and highway, with the heaviest concentrations just west of Lake Ilmen and Novogorod and south of the Narva-Gatchina rail line.[7]   The army saw this latter concentration as the greatest danger to its rear should the Soviets launch a full-dress offensive.   Since the beginning of the war the bands had remained in the swamp wastes east of Lake Peipus, lying undisturbed and free to develop as they wished, and since early January the army had been looking for the means to clear them out.   No concern was expressed over the bands grouped west of Lake Ilmen.[8]

On 14 January the Red Army launched its drive to free Leningrad and clear the area between the lakes, striking with a two-pronged attack out of the Gulf of Finland beachhead and across the ice on Lake Ilmen below Novogorod.   Following on the heels of the Army in a series of closely coordinated moves, the bands descended on selected sections of the German lines of communication.

The offensive seemed to have been planned as a double envelopment to trap the *Eighteenth Army* against the Russian defenses before Leningrad and the Volkhov River, with the bands complementing the attack by interdicting the principal north-south traffic axes.   This latter would not only make a withdrawal by the Germans doubly difficult, but would cut them off from reinforcement and resupply and at the same time cover the exposed Soviet left flank.

The partisans struck after the initial assaults of the regular units when the situation had become somewhat clarified and the necessity for security had passed.   By thus delaying their attacks, they induced the Germans, in the face of the heavy Russian assaults, to commit many of their security units in the front lines almost immediately, leaving sizeable portions of the rear undefended.

Contrary to German expectations, the partisans concentrated south of the Narva-Gatchina railroad made no major effort to disrupt the immediate rear of the divisions defending against the northern wing of the Red Army drive.   Rather, almost directly after the attack started,

---

[6] Unless otherwise noted, the material in this section is taken from *KTB, H. Gr. Nord, 12.I.–28.I.44., 24.I.–31.I.44., 1.II.–10.II.44.*   75128/31, 32, 34.

[7] *Bandenlage, Dez. 43, H. Gr. Nord, Ic/AO, KTB, Bandenlagekarten Dez. 43.* 75131/41.

[8] See entries for 2, 3, 6, 7, and 8 Jan 44 in *KTB, H. Gr. Nord, Ia, 1.I.–11.I.44.* 75128/30.

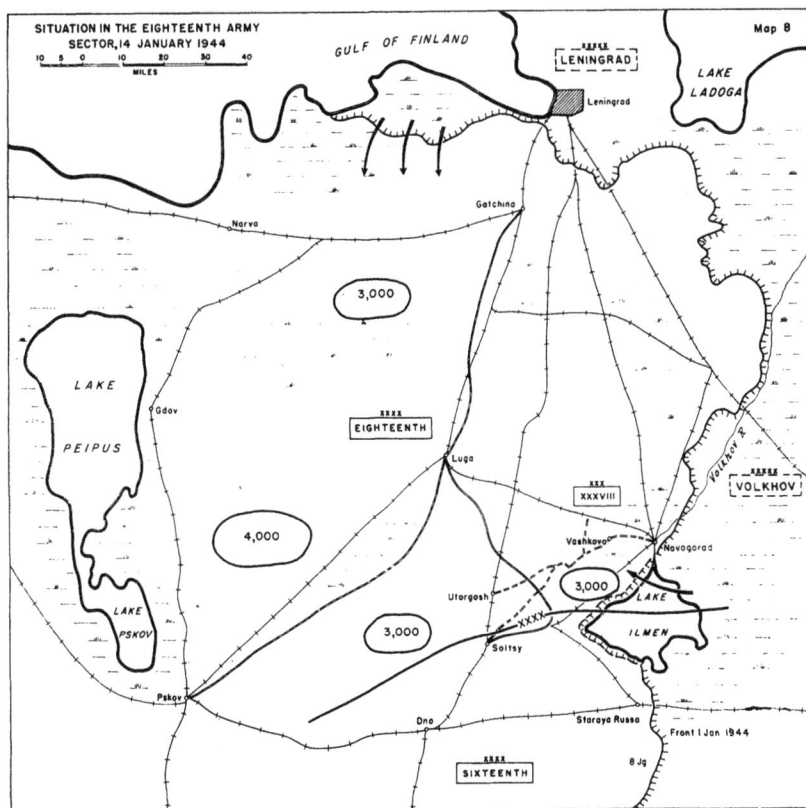

Map 8.   *Situation in the Eighteenth Army Sector, 14 January 1944.*

they moved to the south and threw their weight at the primary axis of the sector, the Pskov-Luga-Leningrad rail line and highway, while those just west of Lake Ilmen moved against the Dno-Soltsy-Leningrad line and the lateral feeders into Novogorod and the Volkhov area. They made themselves almost immediately felt by the German defenses. As early as 15 January both the security units and the local reserves shifting to meet the attacks were running into heavy firefights with "superior" partisan organization; by noon of the 16th *Army Group North* reported to OKH that all security units in the *Eighteenth Army* sector had been committed and requested immediate reinforcement by six security battalions from *Army Group Center* which were badly needed in a "partisan situation [even then considered] very dangerous." Then came the demolitions.

On the evening of the 16th a large band struck a railroad station and switching point some 20 miles north of Luga, destroying all station installations and blowing a number of difficult to replace switches while inflicting heavy casualties on the defending force. This attack was followed on the night of 17–18 by a general assault on all rail lines in the sector and by open attacks on security strong points and garrisons. The Dno-Soltsy-Leningrad line, which was feeding reinforcements into the *XXXVIII Corps* defending against the assaults across Lake Ilmen, was blown in more than 300 places in a 25-mile stretch on either side of Soltsy, while the Pskov-Luga line was broken in 157 places in 15 miles.[9] By the evening of the 19th all reinforcements sent into the Lake Ilmen sector were forced to move to the front on foot because of the "tense railroad situation." More demolitions followed in the next 24 hours, and repair operations were repeatedly interrupted by attacks on repair crews. By noon of the 20th the Dno-Soltsy line was "completely paralyzed." Additional attacks elsewhere throughout the sector were executed so aggressively and in such strength that all forces available for security duties were forced over to a static defensive, and several regiments of reinforcements had to be halted in transit and retained in the rear, even though they were badly needed at the front, in order that supply traffic move at all. When on the 20th the Red Army started to exploit the penetrations it had made in the German line, the partisans stepped up their raiding against the rail lines "tremendously." As a result, supply and troop movements for the whole army were curtailed almost immediately.

The double assault by the Volkhov and Leningrad Fronts could hardly have failed either with or without the virtual isolation of the battle area by the partisans. The Germans were simply too weak at the points of attack and had no strategic reserves in the sector. Yet these attacks

---

[9] *Banden-Einzelkarte, Januar 1944, H. Gr. Nord, Ic/AO, KTB Bandenlagekarten.* 75131/42.

by the bands played particular havoc with all operational and logistical movement in the whole army area and had the effect of at least hastening the decision by some days.   The attempt to reinforce the Novogorod sector is illustrative.

In a desperate attempt to seal off the penetration below that anchor of the line and reinforce the garrison there, OKH on 17 January ordered the *8th Jaeger* [Light] *Division* from the left flank of the *Sixteenth Army* to the aid of the hard-pressed *XXXVIII Corps*. The route of travel for the division was by rail from Staraya-Russa west to Dno and thence north over the Dno-Soltsy line, a total distance of 110 miles of which no more than half was subject to partisan attack at that time.   Excerpts from the *Army Group North* war diary tell the story:

18 Jan 44

(1800) Chief of transportation reports that *8th Jaeger Division* is being transported in nine trains.   Four leave today and will arrive Novogorod area tomorrow if track stays open.   Remaining will arrive 24 hours later if everything goes smoothly.

(2400) *Korueck 583* reports attack by strong partisan bands on line Bateskaya-Soltsy north and south of station at Utorgozh. [11 miles north of Soltsy]   About 140 demolitions.

19 Jan 44

(1100) Arrival of *8th Jaeger Division* cannot be predicted due to numerous demolitions.

(1245) Forces in Novogorod can only get out to the southwest. Unless *8th Jaeger Division* is committed now, enemy tanks will be in Luga [54 miles west of Novogorod] tomorrow.   G–3 says that *8th Jaeger Division* is moving by truck but will arrive at earliest tomorrow.

(1347) *Eighteenth Army* reports to OKH that *8th Jaeger Division* much delayed by railroad demolitions.   Numerous demolitions on other rail lines.

(1800) CG, *Army Group North* reports that *8th Jaeger Division* arriving in army group sector only in small increments due to extensive railroad demolitions.

20 Jan 44

(0040) Staff of *8th Jaeger Division* arrives in *Eighteenth Army Area*.

(0945) *8th Jaeger Division* has to detrain in Utorgozh due to railroad demolitions.   Arrival still uncertain.   [Entry of 19 Jan at 1925 states: Arriving units have to go on foot from Utorgozh (to *XXXVIII Corps* sector) via Medved to Vashkovo.   (Thirty-eight miles over unimproved roads.)]

388413—56——14

(1205) Only one battalion of *8th Jaeger Division* has arrived in army sector; another by tonight via foot and truck. The railroad is completely paralyzed.

21 Jan 44

(0010) The Novogorod garrison withdrew, fighting its way out.

(1235) Only one battalion of *8th Jaeger Division* has reached Vashkovo. Another is expected.

(2400) Numerous demolitions by partisans, especially on all supply routes of *Eighteenth Army*. Partisans attacked railroad stations and installations.

22 Jan 44

(2400) Many partisan attacks against railroads, especially the Dno-Soltsy Line.

Other reinforcements moving in to bolster the line were similarly delayed by rail demolitions and convoy ambushes when they were most needed at the front. The *12th Panzer Division,* which had been ordered north from *Army Group Center,* became stalled in transit when its advance elements were halted at Luga on 23 January by chain demolitions north of the city, and more than 24 hours later was still immobilized there by additional attacks on the rail line. It was not until the 28th that sufficient of its elements had arrived for it to join the battle above the city and then it had to swing to the southeast to plug a gap developing between the *Eighteenth* and *Sixteenth Armies* because another reinforcing unit, the *58th Infantry Division,* did not arrive due to blocked rail lines and raids on convoys.[10] This latter division, which had been routed north through Estonia to Narva because of the state of the Pskov-Luga line, was forced to move southward on foot through the frozen swamps east of Lake Peipus where it was constantly under direct partisan attack. Often it had to fight its way through, and, forced to furnish security for its own line of communications, it lost heavily in transport. At one point the partisans had so wrecked the route by blowing bridges and destroying corduroy roads that the column was forced to go across country in very difficult terrain.[11] Then as the *12th Panzer Division* was moving up to its jumpoff position, partisans made a night raid on its column as it moved forward through forest and swamps and destroyed a number of vehicles, halting the entire division on the road for some time.[12]

As the Germans continued their withdrawals to the south and west, the bands shifted their areas of operations accordingly. A number of

---

[10] Entries for 24, 28, and 30 Jan 44 in *KTB, H. Gr. Nord. 24.I.–31.I.44.* 75128/32.

[11] Entries for 30, 31 Jan and 5, 7 Feb 44 in *ibid.*

[12] Entry for 8 Feb 44 in *ibid.*

them, holding to their sectors east of Lake Peipus, were overrun and absorbed by the advancing Soviets, while others, greatly strengthened by large numbers of civilians evading forced evacuation by the enemy, moved south of Luga into the heavy terrain on either side of the Pskov-Luga rail line and highway whence they increased their pressure on the few avenues of march left to the German units. To add to this, several large bands moved northward from the *Sixteenth Army* rear and brought additional pressure to bear, especially on the Pskov-Dno and Pskov-Ostrov lines.[13]

At the end of the first week in February, by German estimate there were some 10,000 irregulars astride or in close vicinity to the Pskov-Luga connections, with another 3,000 close enough to be dangerous. In addition, there were 5,000–6,000, just below the Pskov-Dno line.[14] The Germans considered the combat effectiveness of these to be 40 percent that of Wehrmacht line units, which when added to their familiarity with the terrain and their ability to move through it almost at will made them a formidable force to contend with in a withdrawal.

To make matters even more serious, by the end of January these bands were working in much closer cooperation with the Red Army than ever before, and were operating almost exclusively according to specific directives from the Soviet rear under the supervision of a number of Red Army and NKVD officers newly sent to them to improve liaison. In the area west of the Pskov-Luga line, the cooperation was especially close, with the partisans scouting for advancing Russian units and passing to them a steady stream of information on German movements and dispositions. In several instances they gave direct aid by massing in fortified villages astride the German line of retreat.[15]

As a result of this increased aggressiveness, the German transport situation continued to deteriorate, and the supply of the Army suffered accordingly. Although the partisans were never able to completely paralyze the few lines remaining, on several occasions they did knock out sizeable sections of trackage for as much as 24 to 48 hours. Such blows as these combined with the normal traffic demands finally made it almost impossible to evacuate rolling stock. To make the situation even worse, as the battle area became more restricted the bands began hitting at the few roads capable of carrying motor traffic. The Pskov-Luga artery, the only primary highway in the army sector, was cut for 40 hours when the partisans blew 5 bridges, just at the time the Germans were trying to stabilize a line south of Luga. In a number of instances convoys found themselves stopped on the road by log road blocks manned by partisans and protected by mine fields. One regiment of reserves mov-

---

[13] *Bandenlage, Januar 1944, H. Gr. Nord. Ic/AO, KTB, Bandenlagekarten.* 75131/42.
[14] *Ibid.*
[15] *Anl. 43 z. KTB, H. Gr. Nord. 14.II.–10.III.44.* 75128/48.

ing up to the line ran into an extensive mine field across their route of march which was cleared without engineer aid and at the expense of a number of casualties. Then early in February the bands began cutting telephone lines so extensively that the Germans were often forced to depend exclusively on radio. At times the radio failed and thus interrupted command functions; at other times the partisans were found to be tapping the lines and monitoring traffic.

As the Germans continued to shorten their front, however, they were able to free some units for static road guard. Although there were never enough units for offensive action against the bands, those available were able to prevent complete paralysis from settling over the lines remaining to them and hold down sabotage "to a bearable degree." [16]

While the German withdrawal to the south was still in progress, Moscow initiated steps to broaden the base of the partisan effort in the northern sector. The Baltic States, and especially Estonia, throughout the war had been singularly free of partisan interference because of the general antipathy of the populance for the Soviet regime. When it became obvious that the Germans were going to be unable to stabilize their front east of the Narva-Pskov-Vitebsk line, the Soviets began dropping numbers of Red Army and NKVD officers into the Estonia-Latvia area in an attempt to organize partisan units even under the adverse political conditions existing.[17] Apparently the first drops were discovered and their mission correctly interpreted by the Germans. As early as 23 January the army group had committed one battalion of security troops along the straits between Lake Peipus and Lake Pskov with the specific mission of preventing partisans from crossing over into Estonia, and five days later the security command was requesting three regiments of SS-trained native troops for the same purpose.[18] Several days later the soundness of these precautions was borne out when a radio message from Moscow ordering one band to reconnoiter and report on ice conditions on both lakes was intercepted.[19]

These attempts at infiltration also alerted the security command in the *Reichskommissariat Ostland,* and on 28 January the Higher SS and Police Leader *Ostland* requested the immediate drafting of 15,000 Estonians, 30,000–33,000 Latvians, and an additional 5,000 Lithuanians to be formed into security units for antipartisan operations.[20] Apparently balked by the prompt German blocking of the narrows between the lakes, several bands retired southward before the Wehr-

---

[16] Entry for 6 Mar 44 in *KTB, H. Gr. Nord. 1.III.–15.III.44.* 75128/38.

[17] *Ibid.; OKH/Abt. Frd. H. Ost (I/Bd),* 29.II.44. H 3/361; *Bandenlagebericht, 15.I.–31.I.44., OKH/Frd. H. Ost (I/Bd).* EAP IV-38–x/7.

[18] Entry for 23 Jan in *KTB H. Gr. Nord, 12.I.–28.I.44.* 75128/31; entry for 28 Jan in *KTB, H. Gr. Nord, 24.I.–31.I.44.* 75128/32.

[19] Entry for 4 Feb in *KTB, H. Gr. Nord. 1.II.–10.II.44.* 75128/34.

[20] Entry for 28 Jan in *KTB, H. Gr. Nord. 24.I.–31.I.44.* 75128/32.

macht withdrawal, and as early as 15 February began crossing into Latvia and Estonia below Pskov. One such unit was identified as the 8th Leningrad Brigade. Other bands slipped through the lines in the Narva area.[21] This was in no sense an attempt at wholesale evacuation to the west, for few bands actually ever appeared, especially in Estonia, and these were quickly scattered by the security command. On the whole the attempt of the agents dropped there to step up a resistance movement failed. A majority of them were quickly picked up by the local Estonian militia, and although the few who escaped detection carried out an active propaganda campaign, they committed little sabotage.[22]

During the last days of February the *Eighteenth Army* under continuing heavy pressure slowly pulled back to a line just east of the Baltic States border. This retrograde movement at the same time threw the left flank of the *Sixteenth Army* in the air and forced it into a similar withdrawal, and on 1 March the line of the entire army group ran substantially Narva-Lake Peipus-Pskov-Ostrov-Polotsk-Vitebsk. Then with the spring muddy season coming on early after an unusually mild winter, the front quieted down and so remained until June.

The Baltic States, March–June

While the big battle raged along and behind the *Eighteenth Army* front, the rest of the army group rear had remained generally quiet. On 10 January the right flank of the *Sixteenth Army* had been extended southward to include the old partisan concentration area about Rosonno and the rail junction of Polotsk. But due to the losses the bands there had suffered when they joined the Red Army in its attempted envelopment of Vitebsk in November and December and to the success of an antipartisan operation launched just at the turn of the year by an SS and police combat team, the area had lost much of its sting. A number of the units there were scattered or driven to the east through the Soviet lines and their bases destroyed.[23]

The Baltic States, which were under the jurisdiction of the *Reichskommissariat Ostland,* were also quiet during January and February. Estonia and Lithuania continued free of sabotage, with only a scattering of isolated bands being reported. Latvia, which prior to the German attack in 1941 had had a larger element of Communists in her population than her sister states, suffered some 50 rail demolitions concurrent with the Soviet assaults against the *Eighteenth Army,* all in the eastern

[21] Entries for 15, 22 Feb in *KTB, H. Gr. Nord. 10.II.–21.II.44, 22.II.–29.II.44.* 75128/34, 36; *Anl. 463 z. Anl 43 z. KTB, H. Gr. Nord, 14.II.* 75128/48.
[22] *Anl. 374 z. Anl. 44 z. KTB H. Gr. Nord, 11.III.–30.IV.44.* 75128/49.
[23] On this antipartisan operation, see: *Pz AOK 3, Entwicklung d. Bandenlage, 1.II.44.,* in *Pz AOK 3, Anl. Bd. E z. Tgb. 11, 1.–30.VI.44.* 62587/12; entry for 3 Jan 44 in *KTB, H. Gr. Nord. Ia. 1.I.–11.I.44.* 75128/30.

border area, and some scattered lootings and dynamiting of public buildings which the Germans attributed more to Communist Party agents than to organized partisan action.[24] From the first days of March following the occupation of the positions along the Baltic States border the quiet in the rear of the sector continued. There were few bands of any size in evidence except behind the right flank of the *Sixteenth Army* in the vicinity of Polotsk and in the woods in the Opochka area. Even in the region north of Polotsk where the partisans had once been so strong there was little open opposition. But there were indications that the bands scattered by Operation *HEINRICH*, and rescattered in late December, were moving back into the area south of the Polotsk-Dvinsk rail line and were rebuilding their strength by recruiting and training. Probing attacks by small antipartisan units kept many of these on the move, however, and served to keep the supply lines relatively clear. Still, their mere presence there constituted a very real threat, especially with the certainty of a continuation of Red Army attacks with the coming of dry weather.[25]

Almost immediately on settling themselves in their new positions [26] the Germans, determined to have no repetition of their experience of January and February between Lake Ilmen and Lake Peipus, increased their efforts to neutralize any attempt of the Soviets to build up a new partisan front behind them. Constantly prodded by army group headquarters the security commands made good use of the increased number of security units available following the shortening of the line and the activation of new native units. They constantly patrolled the supply axes and probed the wooded areas, meanwhile keeping sharp watch against infiltration from the Soviet rear. SS-recruited native units destroyed several bands attempting to enter northern Estonia via Lake Peipus, one of which included over 200 Red Army officers and enlisted men apparently intended as cadre personnel for bands to be raised.

To intensify the antipartisan effort, early in April OKH opened a school for antipartisan warfare for all the armed forces and civilian agencies in the east. Although the school introduced nothing new in the way of operations against the bands, the greatest emphasis in the course was placed on uniformity of method and the utilization of all possible sources of manpower in case of a widespread irregular outbreak.

During April and May the quiet continued, partisan activity being restricted to small-scale ambushes in the southern part of the sector and sporadic forage raids in the center and north. Even behind the *Sixteenth Army* where the partisan units were more numerous, there was

---

[24] Anl 240, 344, z. Anl. 42 z. KTB, H. Gr. Nord. 11.I.–13.II.44. 75128/47;
Anl. 498, 617 z. Anl. 43 z. KTB H. Gr. Nord. 14.II.–10.III.44. 75128/48.
[25] *Anl. 374 z. Anl. 44 z. KTB. H. Gr. Nord. 11.III.–30.IV.44.* 75128/49.
[26] Unless otherwise noted, the material in this section is taken from: *KTB, H. Gr.
Nord. 1.III.–15.III.44.* 75128/38; *KTB, H. Gr. Nord. 1.IV.–14.IV.44.* 75128/41a.

little sabotage. Here, the bands working on orders from the Central Staff,[27] carried out no raids in force, but confined themselves to making felt the silent threat of their presence in strength. They continued to be amply supplied with weapons and ammunition by air, while food and clothing were obtained from the population.

Even more dangerous than the threat to the supply lines was the very active espionage net which the partisans had set up during the winter. For the first time the Germans found themselves faced with a situation where they believed all their dispositions and movements were regularly reported to the Red Army, and, although they saw it as a danger which could have the most serious consequences for them in the coming campaigns, they felt helpless to combat it.[28] These fears were further confirmed in May by an almost complete cessation of sabotage of the highly vulnerable signal facilities, due, the Germans thought, to the fact that the lines were being tapped and the traffic monitored.

In late May and June the bands appeared to give up sabotage almost entirely and confined their efforts to general reconnaissance and espionage. In this work they operated through and with Soviet strategic intelligence teams, the latter directing the efforts and utilizing the agent nets previously established. The largest percentage of these agents was concentrated behind the junction of the northern and central sectors.[29] The information thus gained was supplemented by reconnaissance by small partisan groups working up close to the front, and the whole forwarded to the Soviet rear either by the intelligence teams direct or via the partisan radio net.[30]

The raids which were made against the rail net were confined almost exclusively to the southern flank of the army group. They were infrequent and unconcerted and made no serious inroad on German supply. The demolition techniques used were poor, and 50 to 75 percent of the charges placed were disarmed by security patrols.[31] The morale of the population had been lowered by the expectation of a continuation of the Red Army offensive with the coming of dry weather and the continued forced labor drafts, but there was no open anti-German feeling, rather a strictly neutral wait-and-see attitude.[32]

---

[27] One such order issued by the Lepel Partisan Brigade Stalin on 4 March directed the unit to continue its expansion and organizational efforts in order to tie down as many German troop units as possible on security missions and to hold and expand its area of influence until the arrival of the Red Army. See: *Bericht, April 44, 1.V.44., AOK 16, Ic/AO, Fnb., Bandenlage, 1.IV.–15.VII.44.* 54323/8.

[28] *Bericht, April 44 in AOK 16, Ic/AO, Fnb., Bandenlage, 1.IV.–15.VII.44.* 54323/8.

[29] See: *Schwerpunkte des Sowj. Agenteneinsatzes im Operationsgebiet Ost. Februar 1944.* OKW 1941b.

[30] *Bericht, Mai 44 in AOK 16, Ic/AO, Fnb. Bandenlage, 1.IX.–15.VII.44* 54323/8; *Bericht, Juni 44 in ibid.*

[31] *Bericht, Mai, Juni 44 in ibid.*

[32] *Bericht, Mai 44, 22.VI.44., OKH Gen.St.d.H./GenQu. Abt. Kriegsverw (Qu4).* H 3/476.

During June continued small-scale antipartisan operations in the area about Opochka and north of Polotsk kept some of the bands on the move, but because of their restricted scope they achieved no permanent results. Further north the sector remained quiet with only scattered small bands in evidence.[33]

The Southern Sector [34]

Following the shattering of the German front along the Dnepr in the late fall of 1943, the Soviets for the first time began making an effort to build up a partisan front behind the retreating German divisions in the western Ukraine. This effort never assumed sizeable proportions and it never exercised any real effect on what was left of the German occupation or on the main course of Wehrmacht operations. But the manner in which it was done and the varied missions given the bands in the attempt are interesting.

The rapid Soviet advances in the lower Pripyat area during December, January, and February freed considerable numbers of partisans who were concentrated in the area south of the Pripyat River as far west as Brest-Litovsk for activity in other areas. Some of these moved directly to the west along the line Kovel-Lublin, even into Poland, in what was obviously an attempt to build up an irregular ring about the Brest-Litovsk rail hub, while others, under the leadership of several experienced commanders including Sidor Kolpak, Fedorov, and Naumov[35] moved to the south and southwest. The majority of these latter concentrated in the Lwow-Kovel-Vinnitsa sector behind the *Fourth Panzer Army* rather than farther south where they had much less maneuver room and stood the chance of being pinned against the Carpathians.

Communication between these bands and the Soviet rear was consistently good, and their varied operations took form along ordered lines. Kolpak, who was one of the most experienced and successful of the partisan commanders[36] and whom the Germans had identified as the leader of several large irregular units, kept his command generally behind Von Manstein's left flank in the Kovel-Dubno area. He com-

[33] See entries for period 6 May–19 Jun 44 in *KTB, H. Gr. Nord. 1.V.–31.V.44., 1.VI.–15.VI.44.* 75128/44a, 75128/45b; *AOK 18, KTB, Teil Ag, Zusammenfassungen 1.I.–15.VII.44.* 52614/1.

[34] Unless otherwise noted, the material in this section is taken from notes compiled and translated by 1st Lt. Larry Wolff, "The Partisan Situation in Army Group South, 1 January to 30 June 1944." OCMH files.

[35] These three partisan commanders had been known to the Germans for some time, although the record gives no details of their previous operations. See: *Pz AOK, Ia, KTB 2, Teil 5, 1.X.–31.XII.42.* 28499/5; *Bandenlage im Monat Februar 1944, Pz AOK 4, 1.III.44.* 52981/28.

[36] According to Soviet sources, Sidor Kolpak (Kovpak) was a major general and twice a Hero of the Soviet Union. See: *USSR Information Bulletin* (Washington, D. C.) 9 Dec 49. He was frequently mentioned in German situation reports.

mitted some of his units in the front line alongside Red Army organizations. Others he sent against the rail lines radiating out of Kovel. Federov operated farther to the south, having moved across the Soviet rear and through the front line via a gap between the German *XIII* and *LIX Corps*. He was under orders to set up his base of operations in the Gaisin area some 60 miles southwest of Vinnitsa with the mission of developing a partisan concentration area there and working against German communications. Naumov moved into the Tarnopol region and began to operate against the Lwow-Odessa railroad. All three bands were reported well armed with light artillery and automatic weapons and to have Red Army officers among their officer personnel. Several other bands were identified in the line alongside the Russian I and VI Guards Corps opposite the *Fourth Panzer Army*. Additional units were occasionally reported operating exclusively against the Ukrainian nationalist organizations, others were recruiting civilians for the Red Army ranks and waging local terror campaigns to dissuade the natives from working for the Germans on their defensive positions.

Taken all in all, the efforts of these groups had little effect on German operations. During February in the rear of the *Fourth Panzer Army,* which was holding the most critical sector of the line, they carried out but 49 raids, clashed with security units 65 times, and set demolitions on the rail lines at but 113 places.

With the fight moving south and west into the sub-Carpathians and Galicia, the various groups of anti-Soviet Ukrainian separatists, organizations again came into the picture, but without visible effect on the tactical situation. Many of these groups appeared hesitant to declare their sympathies, seeming content to await developments at the front. Although some had their doubts as to the efficacy of opposing the high-riding Soviets, all of them appear to have had one common goal, the expulsion of all ethnic Poles from the Ukrainian nationalist stronghold in Galicia. One group, the Ukrainian Insurgent Army (*Ukrainska Povstancha Armia*—UPA) attacked the partisans almost as soon as they moved in from the northeast, and suffered such heavy losses initially that it was forced to withdraw from the picture for a time. One unconfirmed rumor had the UPA ordering several of its smaller units into the Soviet rear to attack Red Army communications.

During this period the Soviets made a curious move in an attempt to undermine a part of the German security command. Behind the left flank of *Army Group South* and the extreme southern wing of *Army Group Center* there were elements of nine Hungarian security divisions in two corps. The morale and combat efficiency of these units was low and the Germans consistently felt that they could be counted on for little effective action, even against the partisans. Perhaps knowing this and hoping to even further lower their fighting spirit and induce them to defect as units, the Soviet high command sometime after the first of the year issued a directive to both the Red Army and those partisan organizations currently in the area that the Hungarian units were not to be attacked. If fired on by them, the Soviets were to bypass them and return fire only if faced with unusually strong and persistent resistance.[37] As far as is known, no such order regarding the Romanian units with the Wehrmacht was ever issued.

By the end of March, there was evidence of a considerable increase in the size of several partisan units and of a much closer tie-in of their operations with those of the Red Army. Four bands totaling some 8,000–9,000 men and united under a central command appeared in the rear of the *Fourth Panzer Army,* which was defending in the Tarnopol-Lwow area where the Soviet pressure was very heavy, carrying out tactical reconnaissance for the Red Army, attempting to prevent the destruction of important traffic installations by the retreating Germans, and striking at the supply lines. When the fighting moved in on Tarnopol, this force moved to the south, possibly to aid the Red Army in its attempt to destroy the *First Panzer Army* which had been surrounded and was attempting to fight its way out to the west.

In April the Naumov band, grown to some 1,500–2,000 men, reappeared, now operating against the rail line running east from Lwow. Due to the large number of German troops in the area, however, they had little success, and were continually badgered in their operations by UPA units, which had increased considerably in size and had grown very aggressive. A miscellany of a number of smaller bands was equally ineffective.

In May the Red Army pressure eased somewhat and the Germans were able to move more actively against these bands in a series of local actions. These combined with the growing strength of the UPA, which now fighting in its avowed homeland was successfully recruiting increasing numbers of native Galicians into its ranks, and the logistical difficulties the partisans were having because the number of Germans in the area precluded adequate supply by air drop, gradually scattered the remaining bands. Thus the partisan movement in the south, which had never been a factor in the fight there, faded out of the picture.

The Final Blow—The Central Sector

The Realignment of Partisan Strength

Before the end of January it had become obvious that the start the partisans in the central sector had made toward expanding and con-

---

[37] Rpt, *GFP 704,* quoted in memo, *Abt. Frd.H.Ost, 16.II.44., Frd.H.Ost, Vortraege und Notizen.* H 3/193.

solidating their areas of concentration during the last weeks of 1943 was part of a series of Moscow-directed steps to improve the operational efficiency of the movement and realign its mission more closely with that of the Red Army. Certainly the partisan support of the drive from Orel into White Russia had not been overly impressive. True, with their raids and sabotage the bands had hurt the Germans, but with a strength in excess of 60,000 men, with good support from the Soviet rear, and in terrain which heavily favored them, they had failed in their mission of cutting off the supply of the German units at the front and trapping them in the forward areas by blocking their axes of retreat. And this was against an enemy preoccupied with staving off literal disaster. Because they lacked experienced and aggressive leadership at the unit level and tight, centralized control from the top, they had dissipated much of their effort on areas and targets of lesser strategic significance where the opposition was light or nonexistent and had failed to follow up any advantages gained.

With the German rear now very shallow, the problem of correcting these deficiencies was simplified considerably. Especial emphasis was placed on tightening the regional and central command structures. Operations group commanders in key areas were replaced with Red Army officers of combat experience and proven aggressive leadership, and command channels between the partisan staffs and the Soviet rear were improved to the point where by the end of January almost every move and change in disposition of the bands was dictated by the Central Staff and subordinated to the future operational intentions of the Red Army.[38] At the same time the expansion and linking up of the concentration areas continued until the bands were spread in almost continuous blocks through the countryside just off the supply corridors. By 1 March this realignment of strength was virtually complete with hardly a portion of the army group rear area or the *Reichskommissariat Weissruthenien* outside the larger population centers where the partisans were not either dominant militarily or poised in considerable numbers along all the highways and railroads or which was not under a Communist Party administration. Although the Germans still maintained a few strong points in these regions, the garrisons were so heavily outnumbered

---

[38] *H. Gr. Mitte, Ic/AO (Abw.), Nr. 63/44 geh., 3.I.44.* in *KTB, H. Gr. Mitte Bandenmeldungen, Nov 43—Maerz 44.* 65002/69; *H. Gr. Mitte, Ia. Nr. 1620/44 g.Kdos., 8.II.44.* in *ibid.; H. Gr. Mitte, Ia, Nr. 14550/43 g.Kdos., 8.XII.43., Anl. z. KTB. H. Gr. Mitte, 1.X.–31.XII.43.* 65002/24; *H. Gr. Mitte, Ia. Nr. 279/44 g.Kdos., 8.I.44., KTB, H. Gr. Mitte, 1.I.–31.III.44.* 65002/48; 1st Lt. Larry Wolff, "The Partisan Situation in Army Group Center, 1 January to 31 December 1944," pp. 1–8. OCMH files.

and the posts themselves were so isolated that they were almost valueless tactically or in an administrative sense.[39]

The Soviet Plan

Once the bands were realigned and under tight control, the Central Staff turned its attention to their utilization in the months to come. As before, they were to operate in direct support of the Red Army when it resumed the offensive with the coming of summer, striking the German supply axes concurrently with the assault from the east. In this offensive, however, their operations were carefully planned not as a series of isolated blows but as an integrated whole fitted far more closely into the over-all battle picture than in previous campaigns.

This was the plan. They were to hold tightly to their newly aligned areas in the face of all attacks, all the while strengthening them, until the Red Army struck the Dnepr line in a general offensive. Then, after making the Germans' withdrawal on a broad front slow and difficult, they were to split the front and drive the Germans into the narrow corridors along the roads and railroads now dominated by the concentration areas where they might be blocked or successively checked until destroyed from the east. The bands disposed closest to the front, entrenched in extensive field fortifications, constituted the blocking-canalizing force (*Sperriegel*) which was to turn them into the east-west axes; the remainder comprised the interdiction group.[40]

As such, the plan was well adapted to the German situation. *Army Group Center* lay pressed back against the dense forests of White Russia and the Pripyat barrier with its divisions far below strength and with few reserves. The road and rail net available to it was sparse. There was only one heavy capacity, double-track line traversing the sector and five of medium capacity, plus three highways, only one of which might be classed as primary in the American sense. The secondary roads were so poor that they could be interdicted with little effort. Thus with the terrain precluding cross-country movement on other than a small scale, almost all ordered German movement and supply would have to go over the rail lines and the three highways. And these were the partisans' targets.

---

[39] 1st Lt. Larry Wolff, "The Partisan' Situation in Army Group Center, 1 January to 31 December 1944," pp. 1–8; *Bandenlage im Bereich der H. Gr. Mitte, Stand: 1.I.44., Anl. z. KTB H. Gr. Mitte, Ic/AO (Abw.)*. 65003./5; *H. Gr. Mitte, Ic/AO (Abw.), Nr. 63/44 geh., 3.I.44. in KTB, H. Gr. Mitte Bandenmeldungen, Nov. 43–Maerz 44.* 65002/69; *H. Gr. Mitte, Ia. Nr. 1620/44 g.Kdos., 8.II.44. in ibid.*

[40] This was the estimate of the situation made by *Army Group Center* in January and was borne out by subsequent intelligence reports and the situation maps for the period. See: *H. Gr. Mitte, Ic/AO (Abw.), Nr. 63/44 geh., 3.I.44. in KTB, H. Gr. Mitte Bandenmeldungen, Nov. 43–Maerz 44.* 65002/69; *Bandenlage im Bereich der H. Gr. Mitte, Stand: 1.I.44., Anl. z. KTB H. Gr. Mitte, Ic/AO (Abw.).* 65003/5. See also: Extract from Order of the Day 48, Lepel Partisan Brigade Stalin, 4 Mar 44, in *AOK 16, Ic/AO, Fnb., Bandenlage, 1.IV.–15.VII.44.* 54323/8.

Operations During the Winter and Spring Months [41]

Once the bands had become established in their concentration areas, there were few changes in their dispositions. The rear of the *Second Army* in the middle and lower Pripyat area was an exception, with the westward shift of emphasis that had started before the turn of the year to conform with the progress of the Red Army divisions driving into the western Ukraine continuing through the month of March. The heavy concentrations in the Ushachi-Lepel-Senno region west of Orsha-Vitebsk received a number of reinforcements, and several sizeable bands were fed into that area just north of Polotsk which the Germans had cleared in late December to increase the pressure in the Polotsk-Dvinsk line.

Throughout the remainder of the winter the partisans launched no sector-wide campaign of sabotage. Within their particular areas they continued their raiding and demolitions, but the attacks were sporadic and generally uncoordinated, as they had been in the fall, and bore no relation to their strength of some 130,000. They most frequently hit the roads and signal facilities away from the communication corridors and attacked German-occupied villages and strong points within their own areas. In some regions they burned all villages that they were forced to evacuate or that they thought might furnish shelter for their enemies. They continued to place pressure on the railroads; in March they set off 1,837 demolitions out of approximately 3,300 attempts, damaging 237 locomotives and 824 cars. The lines radiating out of Brest-Litovsk received the heaviest attention, especially during the latter half of the month when a number of German units were being shifted south to the Kovel sector to reinforce *Army Group South*. The total sabotage was roughly equivalent to that of the two preceding months. Their demolition techniques showed no improvement, however, for all during the winter the general supply of the German armies remained unaffected: Local supply, which often had to be funneled through areas controlled by the bands, was hindered somewhat by a lack of control of the secondary road net, portions of which were so endangered that maps were issued indicating the roads safe for single vehicle travel, safe only for convoy travel, or unsafe for all travel.[42]

For the most part the bands confined themselves to building up their own strength and combat readiness and to constructing fortifications both for local protection and to reinforce their strategic position for the coming campaign, while their staffs and intelligence sections concentrated on espionage. This latter had been given a high priority by the Central Staff, and intercepts by the Germans indicated that it had

---

[41] Unless otherwise noted, the material in this section is taken from Wolff, "The Partisan Situation in Army Group Center, 1 January to 31 December 1944." OCMH files.

[42] *Strassenverkehrslage, Stand: 1.III.44., Anl. 5 z. Pz AOK 3, Ia. Nr. 2327/44 g.Kdos., 2.III.44., KTB, H. Gr. Mitte, Nov. 43–Maerz 44.* 65002/69.

become very efficient and was passing an increasing volume of accurate and up-to-date information across the front to the east.

German Counteraction

Throughout most of the winter the security commands were haunted by their old nemesis, shortage of manpower, and in the face of the numerical superiority of the partisans they were able to offer little more than token resistance to their consolidation of the countryside. Lacking sufficient troops to perform even routine functions, any offensive moves they undertook always had to be at the expense of fundamentally necessary static security. Occasional operations of battalion or regimental scope accomplished little of permanent military value when they were launched. In most such instances the bands followed their old tactics of refusing battle and slipped away deeper into the forests and swamps where they merely waited for the enemy to retire before they returned, knowing from experience that their enemy had too few troops to garrison any region cleared. Only when a probing force penetrated too near one of their primary bases would they react positively; then they resisted fiercely from prepared positions. For the most part the security commands confined their active efforts to maintaining contact with the bands for reasons of intelligence and to attempting to curtail the partisans' espionage activities which were causing more and more concern at army group headquarters. As a result, the bands had things very much their own way.

With the coming of the spring thaws indicating the nearness of the operating season, the Germans became increasingly conscious of the bands concentrated along the army group's life lines to the west. They correctly deduced the plans of the Soviet high command for the use of the partisans and realized that, if they were to mount any sort of effective defense against the Red Army attacks which were sure to come or withdraw as an integrated force should the pressure prove too great, they would have to regain at least a modicum of control over their rear.

Since the partisans in the rear of the *Second Army* had shifted much of their strength and the majority of their operations well to the west, the most critical portion of the army group rear in terms of partisan strength and strategic importance for German defense was that behind the *Third Panzer Army* and the left wing of the *Fourth Army,* the region comprising the territory about the towns of Ushachi, Lepel, and Senno west of Vitebsk and Orsha. This area dominated the two major east-west corridors. In view of the large number of divisions the Soviets had massed opposite it, at least one arm of the Red Army main effort seemed sure to come through it. The Germans knew that the Soviets

had been strengthening the bands in this area for some months, probably to the exclusion of all others, and had kept them well supplied by
air. This, combined with frequent attacks on garrisons and the increasingly stubborn resistance offered patrols and probing actions on the
fringes of the region, convinced them that this was the most formidable
block in their rear and that it was manned by units whose training and
leadership had brought them almost to the level of regular Soviet troops,
with a high morale and an excellent will to fight. In view of all this,
the area had to be broken or at least neutralized. Consequently, late
in March the army group command projected a series of major antipartisan sweeps through the entire area in a final attempt at a solution.

This series of clearing actions began on 11 April and continued almost
uninterruptedly until the opening of the Soviet general offensive on
23 June. The Ushachi region, considered the strongest of the concentrations because of its tight-knit command structure, was attacked first.
As the opening move, elements of the *Third Panzer Army* attacked westward down the left bank of the Dvina River, where bands disposed as
the left wing of the blocking-canalizing force had built up a formidable
defense line, cleared it, and drove on into the lake region just south of
Polotsk. Contrary to expectations, the partisans there, caught by surprise and mistakenly believing that the Germans would withdraw after
the operation, pulled back across the lake line and into the depths of the
Ushachi area with hardly a fight, despite orders to the contrary. The
attacking force consolidated its gains and dug in. This was Operation
REGENSCHAUER.

In Operation *FRUEHLINGSFEST,* which followed almost immediately, the units which had executed *REGENSCHAUER* remained in
place along the lakes as a blocking force, joined on the north and west
by elements of the *Sixteenth Army.* Attacking in close order from the
south and southeast and supported by three *Stuka* squadrons, additional
elements of the *Third Panzer Army* and a large force of police and SS
units drove into the area as the hammer against the anvil of the blocking
line.

From the start of this second attack, the partisans resisted stubbornly
all along the line, fighting doggedly from positions prepared in depth
and protected by abatis and extensive mine fields. Aided by close-in
tactical support from the Red Air Force as well as reinforcements brought
in by glider, the bands forced the Germans to advance slowly from position to position, giving ground grudgingly and frequently counterattack-
ing. Attesting to the importance Moscow accorded the area, the Red
Army went so far as to launch a limited offensive against the right wing
of *Army Group North* in an attempt to pull some of the weight off the
beleaguered bands. When the attack groups were joined by elements

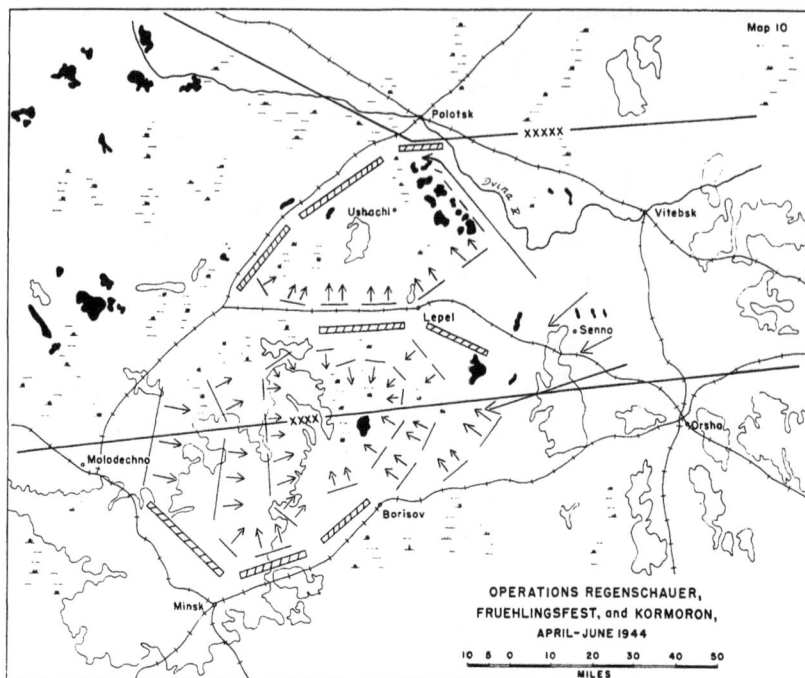

*Map 10.   Operations REGENSCHAUER, FRUEHLINGSFEST, and
KORMORON, April–June 1944.*

of the *95th Infantry Division,* however, the pressure became too heavy,
and the partisans began a series of attempts to break out to the south.
By the middle of May the operation was essentially complete with the
area cleared and the bands badly scattered. Partisan casualties were
listed at slightly in excess of 14,000, with an estimated 3,000–4,000
escaping to the south and southwest.

At the conclusion of the two operations the Ushachi area lay free of
the bands and the Orsha-Lepel rail line-extended, which the *Third
Panzer Army* felt so vital to the defense of the Orsha-Vitebsk sector of
the front, secured at least momentarily from partisan interdiction. The
threat of the partisans in the Senno area and south of Lepel remained,
however, and to consolidate the gains of the earlier sweeps and to prevent
reinfiltration, the army group first garrisoned the area just cleared and
then mounted a third drive designed to clear the entire region north of
Molodechno-Minsk-Borisov. This was Operation *KORMORON.*

The operation opened on 22 May with elements of the *Third Panzer
Army* striking westward through the Senno area, and police and SS units
attacking to the east and northeast from the vicinity of Molodechno. To
prevent a mass escape of bands to the north and south, additional elements of the *Third Panzer Army* had set up a blocking line on the north-

ern fringe of the region while police and SS units under the *Wehrmacht-befehlshaber Weissruthenien* and elements of the *Fourth Army* had established similar positions along the rail lines to the south and southwest. Unlike the partisan units in the Ushachi battles, which had fought as a unified command under the leadership of a single operations group, the bands resisting the *KORMORON* drive operated under at least two headquarters, one headed by a Red Army general officer, the other by a Communist Party functionary, and were unable to offer a coordinated defense. While they fought stubbornly at times, their resistance lacked cohesion, and they were slowly pressed into a small swampy area and cut to pieces. The fight was brought to a premature conclusion by the opening of the Red Army summer offensive and a number of small groups of partisans escaped. OKH considered the area cleared and listed partisan casualties as 7,697 dead, 5,286 taken prisoner, and 342 camps and 900 bunkers destroyed.

While these operations were in progress, there was a steady increase in all types of partisan activity throughout the rest of the army group rear. Not concerted enough to represent a "softening up" effort, it seemed rather to be a deliberate attempt to make life miserable for the Germans and whittle away at their strength while waiting for the Red Army to strike. The bands not only increased the number of their raids and the volume of their sabotage, but struck at larger and more critical targets. Often supported by heavy weapons, they hit, beside the lines of communication and signal facilities, at strong points, German-occupied villages, and troops billets, and burned all settlements which might be developed by the enemy into additional strong points. They ceased withdrawing except in the face of overwhelming odds and offered stubborn resistance to patrols, both of which were indicative of heightened morale. Their supply by air was stepped up appreciably, especially during the first three weeks of June,[44] and additional specialists and Red Army officers were air-landed or parachuted in to them. Late in May a number of the bands in the *Second Army* rear which had moved west in March to aid in the Red Army drive on Kovel were driven back by a German counterattack to their old concentration areas astride the supply corridors through the Pripyat. There they reorganized in their old positions under the original blocking-canalizing plan. Such was the picture when the storm broke.

The Final Blow

On the night of 19–20 June the partisans opened the preparation for the long-expected Soviet offensive with their greatest single blow of the war against the German lines of communication. That night,

---

[44] *Bericht, Mai, Juni 44, AOK 16, Ic/AO, Fnb. Bandenlage, 1.IV–15.VII.44.* 54323/8.

surpassing even the mass attacks of 2–3 August 1943, they successfully set off demolitions on the rail lines at 9,600 places in some 14,000 attempts and followed up with an additional 892 the next night. The demolitions were well planned and executed and carried out under the protection of strong covering parties to the accompaniment of heavy attacks on German security posts.[45] The lines Minsk-Orsha and Mogilev-Vitebsk were especially hard hit and almost completely paralyzed for several days. There were no demolitions reported for 21–22 June or for 22–23 June. Of other sabotage committed those first nights or of rail demolitions on succeeding nights nothing is known.

On 23 June, the Red Army struck, with masses of artillery fire and attack units of the Red Air Force adding to the havoc the bands had created. The main efforts were launched on both sides of Vitebsk and south and east of Bobruysk, generally in the direction of Minsk. As the fighting swept through their concentration areas, the partisans worked in close cooperation with the regular units. For the most part they held their formations and hit at their targets with a good degree of precision. In a number of instances they were identified fighting in the line as units under direct Red Army control.[46] As the advance neared the Polish-White Russian border, however, their units slowly fell apart. Many were absorbed into the line divisions, while others broke off in small groups in an effort to avoid induction into the Regular Army. Some few held their ranks and moved westward into the *Generalgouvernement* in the van of the fight.[47]

---

[45] *Lfl. Kdo, 6, Ic. Nr. 8000/44 geh., 20.VII.44., Anl. z. KTB, H. Gr. Mitte.* 65002/8. Actually, with the exception of the *Second Army* rear, few of the details of this partisan offensive are known. All the records of the *Fourth* and *Ninth Armies* were lost when those units were destroyed in July and only one *KTB* of the *Third Panzer Army* has survived. The number of attempts on the night of 19–20 Jun—14,000—is an approximation based on the known number of successful and "prevented" demolitions behind the *Second Army* on that date. See also: Genmaj Alexander Ratcliffe, "Lessons Learned from the Partisan War in Russia," pp. 5–6. MS # P–055a. Foreign Studies Br., OCMH.

[46] This was the experience behind the *Second Army.*

[47] *Ibid.*

CHAPTER 12

SUMMARY AND CONCLUSIONS

Summary

The Soviet Partisan Movement which was established in the wake of the German armies invading the USSR in 1941 was, in both conception and scope, the greatest irregular resistance movement in the history of warfare. It combined all the classic elements of resistance movements of the past with modern means of communication and transportation and modern weapons, and at its peak involved a far greater number of men than had ever before been drawn into an irregular force. The modern military planner should study both the Soviet experience in organizing and utilizing the partisan movement and the German experience in combating it if he is preparing an operational campaign and its logistical support or an occupation of conquered territory.

When the German military and political leaders drew up their plans for the invasion of Russia, they made a number of errors in relation to the control and administration of the rear areas of the armies. These mistakes had a very positive and direct effect on the rise and growth of the Soviet Partisan Movement.

The errors of the military planners were largely ones of omission. From the first they predicated all their preparations on a winning campaign of no more than four months' duration; they made no provision for unforeseen contingencies which might prolong the campaign; they made inadequate provision for control of their immediate rear areas and protection of their lines of communication. In fact the military never conceived of such a thing as a resistance movement. As a result, the partisans were able to gain an early foothold.

With the political planners, the errors were those of commission. The policy they set for the occupation, which was to take over in the wake of the Wehrmacht and continue on after the cessation of hostilities, was almost wholly one of repression and served to accentuate the deficiencies of the military planning. The Soviet Union was first to be dominated, then administered and exploited, and finally broken up and placed under tight Nazi control to the greater profit and glory of the German Reich. There was to be no real attempt to win the Russian natives over to collaboration. What they thought or felt was not to matter in the least. Force was to be used "in its most brutal form." Whether the people starved as a result of the exploitation was of no moment. In short,

German planning laid a very fertile basis for the birth and growth of a resistance movement. The deficiencies of the military planning gave the movement its initial impetus in the form of a chance to establish itself unhindered; the political planning, by antagonizing and driving away the anti-Soviet segment of the population, in effect guaranteed its continued growth and development.

The partisan movement was established behind the German lines after the invasion was launched, partly through the independent activity of NKVD personnel and Red Army officers and NCO's, and partly under a Moscow-directed national defense effort that attempted to utilize the vast reservoir of manpower that German advances in Russia had made unavailable for the Red Army. In the first months of the war the movement accomplished little of a positive nature as far as the German Army was concerned. The organization of the early bands was anything but good. Their morale was poor, and their leadership, too often political, left a great deal to be desired. There was little coordination of effort among them and there was no real centralized control. They seldom showed any aggressiveness; the paramount interest of the individual members seems to have been one of immediate personal survival. When they did operate, it was generally against the rail net, but they struck more often in areas where terrain and the absence of opposition gave them maximum protection than where elementary strategy indicated. Their only true value lay in their inherent potential, the military know-how of the Red Army personnel, and the fanaticism of the Communist Party and NKVD people. Taken *in toto,* their activity during 1941 did not materially hinder German offensive operations, although at times it hurt temporarily. In some areas they made the establishment of a smoothly functioning occupation difficult, especially in regard to the relationship between the occupation administration and the natives, and they caused the line armies some inconveniences. But they never exercised any positive influence on the course of events which led to the Wehrmacht's failure to achieve it 1941 objectives.

Still, considering that they started from scratch, these bands did make some progress. Being largely ignored by the German military, they were able in a small way to orient themselves strategically and tactically and to develop their organization and communications net relatively unhindered. Further, under a growing clandestine Communist Party control and abetted by the German occupation policies, they were successful in some areas in gaining at least the passive support of a portion of the Russian people and in throwing considerable doubt in the minds of others as to the wisdom of supporting or collaborating with the invader.

The 1941 pattern continued throughout 1942. Although the bands increased considerably in number and size and caused repeated disruptions to the German occupation and economic administrations, their activity had no immediate effect on the operations of the Wehrmacht during the year. The Soviet counteroffensive which followed the failure to take Moscow breached the German front in the central sector and the right flank of the northern sector in a number of places, and opened the rear areas to widespread infiltration. This gave the Russians an excellent opportunity to improve the command structure of the individual bands and at the same time organize them into a more effective military instrument. Still, when summer came there was no visible organized or even disorganized attempt by the bands to upset either the German concentrations for the offensive toward Stalingrad and the Caucasus or the logistical support after the attack got under way, and no attempt to support the Red Army counteroffensive launched in late November.

In August and September of 1943, following the failure of the German attempt to reduce the Kursk salient in the ill-starred Operation *ZITADELLE*, the Red Army launched a general assault in great force, and at the same time the partisans mounted their first large-scale offensive against the Wehrmacht rear in direct support. On the face of it, this offensive seemed highly successful: more than 20,000 demolitions set off on the rail lines behind *Army Group Center*, which was bearing the brunt of the Soviet attack; extensive sabotage to railway installations other than trackage, to highways, and to signal facilities; and a propaganda and terror campaign that resulted in widespread defection among the German native auxiliaries.

In analysis, however, the picture is not so bright. The plan had been for the partisans to paralyze the Germans' supply and troop movements by destroying the rail lines, cut them off from the west by blocking their axes of retreat, and help crush them in an east-west pincer. But the results fell far short of the original design. Throughout the period the German withdrawals proceeded smoothly and almost on schedule, with a low percentage-wise loss of troop and supply trains. The bands never paralyzed the rail lines; they never blocked the German axes of retreat; and the withdrawals never became a rout, remaining rather under German control throughout.

There are several reasons for the partisans' failure to accomplish their mission during these two months. First, they had been ordered to follow up "continuously" and "systematically." This they did not do. If their heaviest attacks had been made on successive nights, or even no more than several days apart, the blows might well have proven fatal. But instead the attacks were spaced far apart, and the German traffic continued to move. Second, the demolition techniques they used were generally poor. Many of the rail demolitions listed as successful must have done slight or no damage at all; otherwise the Germans simply could not have operated the volume of traffic they did following the attacks. As far as can be told from the record, the Germans listed as successful any demolition charge or mine which was actually set off, irrespective of damage, and as unsuccessful any charge removed or disarmed prior to detonation. Third, the strategic placement of demolitions left much to be desired. If the Central Staff worked out the specific sections of trackage to be hit, and there is reason to believe that they did, at least in the early phases of the offensive, the bands simply did not carry out the directives issued them. As before, they appear to have hit where the natural cover was the heaviest and the opposition the lightest, not where they might have done the Germans the most damage.

The German security units were weak throughout the occupied areas, and with one exception there were no regular units guarding communication facilities during this period. The bands had a superiority in numbers in their areas of concentration and ample time for thorough preparation. Yet in many cases they wasted demolitions and hit important lines only lightly. There were over 15,000 attempted rail breaks in the sector during August, yet the most vital artery in the whole area, the Brest-Litovsk-Minsk-Smolensk line, suffered but 903 demolitions of all sizes in more than 400 miles of double track and only 4 mass demolitions. The most heavily hit lines were the Minsk-Gomel in the Pripyat and the Polotsk-Molodechno deep in the broken forest country behind the *Third Panzer Army* in White Russia. Certainly the Minsk-Gomel was a most important line during the withdrawal to the Desna, and later in the retrograde movement to the Dneper. The bands hit it hard, but they never knocked it out for an appreciable length of time, even though it ran through terrain so difficult as to make it almost impossible to protect. Instead they wasted over two thousand demolitions on small feeder lines, demolitions which set on the tracks between Gomel and Minsk would have doubled the destruction where it would have hurt the Germans the most.

The operations of the partisans in the rear of the *Eighteenth Army* during January and February 1944 were something else again and exercised a very definite influence on the course of the battles along that portion of the front. From the opening of the Soviet offensive there on 14 January to the stabilizing of the German line south of Pskov early in March the bands set off demolitions on the rail lines at but 1,564 spots. Yet with these they "completely paralyzed" one of the two tactically most important rail connections in the sector during the highly critical period of the initial Red Army breakthrough, forcing a badly needed reinforcing division off the rails and so delaying it that it never arrived as a unit and had to be committed piecemeal. They so continually interdicted the major rail axis of the sector that another reinforcing division, an armored one, was too late to join the biggest battle of the campaign and finally had to be committed elsewhere because a third reinforcing division, similarly forced off the rails and continually harassed as it moved cross-country on foot, was days late. In addition, they interdicted highways and swamp tracks with demolitions and road blocks; cut wire communications; laid mine fields; scouted for the Red Army; and on, occasion engaged the Germans in showdown combat.

These were considerable contributions; still it cannot be said that they were in any wise decisive. The Soviet offensive could hardly have failed to succeed, with or without the efforts of the partisans, because of the overwhelming superiority of the Red Army units and the thinness of the German line and its lack of reserves. The partisans neither won the campaign nor prevented the Germans from winning it. The Red Army was simply too strong at the points of main effort and the Wehrmacht too weak. That the bands did much to speed up the expulsion of the Germans from the area between Lake Ilmen and Lake Peipus, however, is obvious. Certainly they did much to prevent the Germans from stabilizing the situation in the Luga area by paralyzing the Dno-Soltsy line when they did.

Why did the partisan effort in the northern sector in January and February of 1944 to a large degree realize its potential while that in the central sector the previous summer fail? There are several possible answers to this question. Admittedly the areas were not comparable except as to terrain, which was extremely difficult in both cases, thus adding to the partisans' advantage; the *Eighteenth Army* rear comprised but a fraction of that of *Army Group Center;* trackage in the central sector totaled thousands of miles, that in the northern but a few hundred; behind the *Eighteenth Army* there were some 13,000 partisans in something less than 20 units; in the central sector there were some 70,000 in a large number of organizations; and finally there were probably more security troops per square mile in the northern sector. In the northern sector the critical targets were more concentrated geographically and there were fewer of them. But there were fewer partisans there and the defenders also were more concentrated in the vicinity of the targets. Even more important, the targets lay close to the front lines and thus more subject to defense by line troops than they had been in the central sector. In other words, neither sector could be said to have had all the advantages.

In large part, however, the answer lies in the difference between the partisan units in organization, training, and leadership. It seems obvious that the Central Staff had seen the mistakes committed in the past and by 1944 had passed on to the bands in the north the fruit of experience in other sectors. This showed very definitely in the overall direction of the campaign, the selection and priority of the targets, and the like. But more important was the relative efficiency of the bands in the two areas. The partisans in the north had remained relatively undisturbed to organize and develop as they might, in their own home areas, almost since the beginning of the war. Their numbers had always remained small, so that the problem of control never became a really difficult one. And they had never expanded past the point where they could be adequately trained and provided with competent leaders. The results speak for themselves. Where this over-all leadership was furnished them, unit leadership and discipline were vastly improved, and an aggressiveness, heretofore absent, became evident throughout. The bands showed little hesitation in working close behind the front lines and even in facing the German regulars in show-down fights. The incidence of such clashes was high. The tactically and strategically important targets were picked and attacked. The attacks were well timed and were boldly followed up. The rail lines were hit until the Germans were forced into the swamps and forests where they were hit again. Percentage-wise, the number of bridges blown was higher than ever before. Demolition techniques showed vast improvement.

In attempting to evaluate the irregulars' part in the Soviet offensive of June–July 1944, there is far less evidence to go on. Just what they added to this, the greatest of the Red Army assaults, is a difficult question to answer. Obviously, the Soviets would have swept through the Wehrmacht defenses even without the partisans' blows at the rail lines. They were simply too strong at every point and the Germans too weak. The plan for the support of the offensive by the bands, on paper at least, was a sound one. But it was obviously far too complex for the command organs which were to execute it, demanding as it did a degree of precision and tightly centralized control which would have taxed the capacities of an experienced regular staff. It demanded a skill and doggedness in execution which the irregulars did not and could not have. And it appears to have been drawn up without reference to possible countermoves by the Germans. The dispositions of the bands under the plan were badly upset on the northern flank, where they were supposed to be the strongest and do the most damage, by the three German large-scale antipartisan operations there; and they were weakened in the lower Pripyat when the bands there were shifted westward to aid in the investment of the Kovel-Brest-Litovsk area in January and February and then driven back again by German pressure several months later. As a result, the German flank units, the *Third Panzer Army* on the north and the *Second Army* in the south, when forced to withdraw, were successful in brushing aside what opposition the bands offered and pulling back to the west in relatively good order and without undue losses.

In the center of the sector, as far as the *Ninth Army* was concerned, the plan was made superfluous by the rapid Soviet advance. In the case of the *Fourth Army* the plan simply did not work because the bands had neither the skill nor the strength to cope with the German line divisions, preoccupied as they were. The canalizing positions nowhere forced the Germans into the communications corridors, and the bands which were to block these corridors further to the west were left without a definite mission. Until it was cut off by the Russian armor, the army's withdrawal was orderly.

More important, the attack on the rail lines itself, obviously made on Moscow's signal, was either badly timed in relation to the general assault, or the bands' reserves of demolition material were grossly miscalculated by the logistics people responsible for their supply. Whatever the case, the error was one of command. The Red Army had such a superiority that there was no great need to depend on the element of surprise for the success of its first blow. The Germans were woefully weak, and at this stage of the war the Soviets could not have been ignorant of the fact. It seems too obvious that they could have afforded to indicate an imminent assault in exchange for a 72-hour period of concentrated attacks on the enemies' communications. The first blow, delivered four days before the general assault, which was launched on 23 June, totaled 9,600 successful demolitions; the second, delivered one day later, some 90 percent fewer. There was no blow delivered the next night, and none in the hours immediately preceding the general attack. The bands did not lose heart over night, and the Germans did not have the manpower to drive them off. Obviously, they ran out of explosives. As a result, the Germans were given a period of some forty-eight hours to recover somewhat. Either this recovery was phenomenally rapid or the demolitions were poorly executed, or both, for on 27 June the Dvinsk-Molodechno, Minsk-Orsha, and Minsk-Bobruysk lines, all primary trunks, were still open and reinforcements were moving over them from other sectors. Such a one-shot blow should have been delivered either simultaneously with the general assault or after it. In short, in this instance the movement did not accomplish what it might have, and had the strength of the German units been more nearly equal to that of the Red Army, this circumstance might well have been the deciding factor.

Conclusions

The Soviet Partisan Movement had a certain measure of success, perhaps as much as a resistance movement can have when opposed by a first-class military power. But this success was definitely limited. A war waged by a "regular" army has been defined as an attempt to take, hold, or deny terrain to an enemy; one waged by "irregular" forces as an attempt to prevent or avoid exploitation of terrain by an enemy. The partisans were never regulars, but rather irregulars, and as such were never able to stand up against the regulars of the German Army even in areas and in circumstances of their own choosing, and they were able to "deny" only that terrain which was tactically unimportant to the Germans at a particular time or which because of manpower limitations the Germans were unable to occupy or clear. Despite the fact that the bands as they were in 1943 and 1944 were often extremely difficult to combat, whenever the Germans saw the need to clean up a sector of their rear and were not too heavily committed at the front, they were always equal to the task. Certainly the bands hurt the Wehrmacht. Every rail break, every piece of rolling stock damaged or destroyed, every German soldier killed, wounded, or diverted from other duties to guard against the bands hurt. But the damage was never decisive. As far as preventing German exploitation of the terrain, as irregulars they were more successful, although more so in relation to the occupation and economic administrations than to the German Army itself. Since the occupation as planned was never put into operation, this again was never decisive.

In 1943 and 1944 the strength of the partisan movement lay in the following factors: The movement had a wealth of manpower available, manpower innately tough, frugal, and inured to hardship, and often intimately familiar with the area in which it operated; a majority of the Russian people were at least neutral, and these grew progressively more openly sympathetic as the war progressed; and the Wehrmacht, a seemingly irresistible force in 1941 and 1942, was, after Stalingrad, a losing army, sapped of much of its former strength, and attempting only to avoid defeat.

But the two great weaknesses of the movement, its basic "irregularity" and the problem of over-all control, far more than offset these positive qualities and clearly mirrored the limitations inherent in any partisan force. Irregularity is the great universal weakness of all resistance movements, and the Soviet movement was no exception. The partisans were irregular in almost every sense of the word. Because of the conditions under which they were formed they could never be integrated into the Red Army, and thus they could never be organized, equipped, trained, and controlled to the extent that they would ever approach the level of or be utilized as a "regular" force. Taken as a whole, the majority of their units, despite a hard core of Communist fanatics and Red Army personnel, were little better than third-rate militia. For the most part the rank and file were poor and unenthusiastic soldiers in ill-disciplined units. Most of the volunteers had joined to escape the German forced labor draft, while the forcibly enlisted generally had little heart for the whole business. Furthermore, unit leadership in the bands was almost universally poor, and it was probable that there were far fewer Red Army men in their ranks than the Germans thought.

The problem of control was perhaps an even greater weakness. A company or battalion of infantry is often extremely difficult to control from a distance of no more than several hundred yards. In comparison, the problem of effectively ordering 60,000 to 80,000 irregulars in a number of loose-knit units a hundred miles or more beyond the enemy's lines, even with dependable communications which more often than not were unavailable, was almost insurmountable. The difference in operational efficiency between the 60,000 to 80,000 deep in the central sector and the handful, by comparison, close in behind the rear of the *Eighteenth Army* was an excellent example. If a resistance movement is ever to become a decisive instrument in a regular war, these weaknesses must be eliminated or at least minimized to a large degree.

Considering what the partisans did accomplish, however, the effect they would likely have had on a permanent occupation is something else again. Had the Wehrmacht been able to force a military decision which left sizeable portions of the USSR in German hands to occupy and administer on something approaching a permanent basis, the 100,000-plus partisans, supported as they were by a large proportion of a population antagonized by German occupation policy and practice, would have made the establishment of a workable administration extremely difficult and perhaps prevented it entirely. Considering the extent to which the movement had grown as early as mid-1943 and the tremendous expanse and difficult terrain of European Russia, to make such an occupation successful the Germans would have had to devote a far larger number of line divisions to the task of policing and protecting the lines of communication and population centers and openly battling the partisans and garrisoning their concentration areas than state of their strategic position on other fronts would have made feasible. Anything less would have left at least a part of the bands intact and operational, and merely scattered or driven underground the remainder, with the result that the cancer would have remained.

Lessons Learned

There are many sound lessons to be learned from this Soviet experiment in rebellion and the German experience in combating it.

1. For a resistance movement to come into being and to grow to maturity, certain conditions must exist:

   a. The people must favor it;

   b. The terrain in which its units operate must be difficult enough to give security to its bases and cloak its operations and to discourage continued pursuit;

   c. The regular army at which it strikes must not be overly strong.

2. Individual irregular units operating independently can be destroyed by timely action of line troops, but an organized resistance move-

ment, once well started, is extremely difficult to combat. Therefore the surest way to combat a resistance movement is to strike at its roots, that is, never let it get started.

3. The best preventive measures are:

a. Proper detailed occupational planning executed prior to the occupation;

b. A clear understanding of the people themselves with whom the occupation must deal, psychological, ethnological, and ideological characteristics;

c. A unified and centrally controlled administration of the areas occupied; and

d. A firm but fair occupation administration combining, as Jomini saw it, courtesy, gentleness, severity, and just dealing. If the mass of the people can be won over, or at least induced not to aid the partisans, the movement will die on the vine.

4. If an army in the midst of an operational campaign should find itself confronted by a resistance movement in its zone of communications, it should:

a. Never allow the partisans to divert it from its primary mission of front-line combat to the extent of weakening that front.

b. Rather view the situation in its proper perspective, remembering that partisans as such have a very limited combat value, and react accordingly.

c. Strike hard with sufficient first-line troops or, if such should not be feasible at the time, pull itself in on its major communication axes and let the rest go for the time being, confident that it possesses the organization and strength to clear the rear if it later becomes necessary.

In the field of antipartisan tactics the following basic principles should be applied:

1. The objective of an antipartisan operation should always be complete annihilation of the enemy in the attacked area, not expulsion from the area.

2. Command should always be unified under an experienced frontline commander no matter how diverse the composite elements of the force.

3. Preparation for an antipartisan operation should be made by a General Staff operations section and as carefully as in the case of an operation at the front.

4. The most complete and up-to-date information possible should be obtained prior to the operation and should be kept current during the course of the operation.

5. The most complete security possible should be maintained during the planning and the assembly of troops in order to preserve the element of surprise.

6. In view of the difficult terrain generally encountered in this type of operation, the units comprising the attack force should be provided with ample signal equipment.

7. Encirclement of the entire area to be cleared should be closely followed by a surprise attack.

8. The area should be carefully combed during the course of the operation.

9. Following the completion of the operation, the area cleared should either be secured by strong garrisons or, if such should not be feasible, all buildings in the area should be completely destroyed and all persons evacuated from the area in order to dissuade the partisans from returning.

BIBLIOGRAPHICAL NOTE

The Soviet Partisan Movement, 1941–1944 is based almost entirely on documents now in the custody of the United States Government. These comprise the voluminous collection of German Army records, including the Rosenberg and Himmler files, now located in the Captured Records Section of The Adjutant General's Office and the records of the various trials of war criminals following World War II which are now in the National Archives.

Specifically the German Army records used were those portions pertaining to German planning and operations and to partisan organization and operations. These included army war diaries (KTB's) and their supporting papers, operations and intelligence reports, minutes of conferences, telegrams, and transcripts of telephone conversations, and the like, from division level through army group and army group rear area to include the High Command of the Army (OKH) and the Armed Forces High Command (OKW). They were supplemented by manuscript histories prepared after the war by more than two hundred German officers working under the direction of the Historical Division, EUCOM. Limited use was made of German naval and air force records, for the most part in relation to the political aspects of the decision to attack the Soviet Union. For the period to September 1942, the most valuable single source for over-all guidance and general information was "The Private War Journal of Generaloberst Franz Halder." For the political aspects of both the planning for the invasion of Russia and the political occupation as far as it was put into effect, the Rosenberg and Himmler files and the records of the war crimes trials were used extensively.

Secondary sources were used only for orientation and general background material. No Soviet secondary sources were used because of their general unreliability. A selected bibliography of secondary sources is appended.

Balzak, S. S., V. F. Vasyutin, and Ta. G. Feigin. *Economic Geography of the USSR.* New York, 1949.

Berchin, Michel, and Eliahu Ben-Horin. *The Red Army.* New York, 1942.

Beloff, Max. *The Foreign Policy of Soviet Russia, 1929–1941.* London, 1949. 2 vols.

Churchill, Winston Spencer. *The Gathering Storm.* Boston, 1948.

——————————. *The Grand Alliance.* Cambridge, 1950.

Ciano, Galeazzo. *The Ciano Diaries.* New York, 1946.

Cross, Samuel Hazzard. *Slavic Civilization Through the Ages.* Cambridge, 1948.

Dallin, David. *Soviet Russia's Foreign Policy.* New Haven, 1942.

Davies, Joseph E. *Mission to Moscow.* New York, 1941.

De Mendelssohn, Peter. *Design for Aggression.* New York, 1946.

Dwinger, Edwin Erich. *General Wlassow: Eine Tragoedie Unserer Zeit.* Berlin, 1951.

Garbutt, P. E. *The Russian Railroads.* London, 1949.

Gorer, Geoffrey and John Rickman. *The People of Great Russia.* London, 1949.

Guderian, Heinz. *Panzer Leader.* New York, 1952.

Hitler's Secret Conversations, 1941–1944. New York, 1953.

Kendrew, W. G. *The Climates of the Continents.* Oxford, 1937.

Liddel Hart, B. H. *The German Generals Talk.* New York, 1948.

Lochner, Louis P. (ed.). *The Goebbels Diaries.* New York, 1948.

Maynard, Sir John. *Russia in Flux.* New York, 1948.

Pares, Bernard. *A History of Russia.* 5th ed.; New York, 1947.

Picker, Henry (ed.). *Hitler's Tischgespraeche im Fuehrerhauptquartier 1941–42.* Bonn, 1951.

Rosinski, Herbert. *The German Army.* Washington, 1940.

Rothstein, Andrew (tr.). *Soviet Foreign Policy During the Patriotic War.* London, _____. 2 vols.

Sherwood, Robert E. *Roosevelt and Hopkins, An Intimate History.* New York, 1948.

Simmons, Ernest J. *USSR, A Concise Handbook.* Ithaca, 1947.

Strakhovsky, Leonid I. (ed.). *A Handbook of Slavic Studies.* Cambridge, 1949.

Tannehill, Ivan Ray. *Weather Around the World.* Princeton, 1943.

Teske, Hermann. *Die Silbernen Spiegel.* Heidelberg, 1952.

Thursfield, H. G. (ed.) *Brassey's Naval Annual, 1945.* New York, 1948.

Trewartha, Glenn T. *An Introduction to Weather and Climate.* New York, 1937.

Trial of the Major War Criminals Before the International Military Tribunal. Nuremberg, 1947. 42 vols.

Trials of War Criminals Before the Nuernberg Military Tribunals. Nuernberg, 1946–1949. 12 vols.

United States Army (or War Department):

   Biennial Report of the Chief of Staff of the United States Army to the Secretary of War, July 1, 1941 to June 30, 1943. Washington, 1943.

   Biennial Report of the Chief of Staff of the United States Army, to the Secretary of War, July 1, 1943 to June 30, 1945. Washington, 1945.

   Handbook on German Military Forces. Washington, 1945. [TM E 30–451.]

   Order of Battle of the German Army. Washington, 1945.

   The World at War. Washington, 1945.

UNITED STATES ARMY IN WORLD WAR II:

   Harrison, Gordon A. *Cross-Channel Attack.* Washington, 1951.

United States Army, Office, Chief of Military History:

   Russia, Planning and Operations (1940–1942). Washington, 1954. [DA Pam 20–261a.]

United States Government:
    Department of State. *Nazi-Soviet Relations, 1939–1941.* Washington, 1948.
    _____. *Peace and War: United States Foreign Policy 1931–1941.* Washington, 1943.
Vernadsky, George. *A History of Russia.* New Haven, 1929; rev. ed. 1945.
Virski, Fred. *My Life in the Red Army.* New York, 1949.
Voznesensky, Nikolai A. *The Economy of the USSR During World War II.* Washington, 1948.
Walsh, Warren B. and Roy A Price. *Russia, A. Handbook.* Syracuse, 1947.

U. S. GOVERNMENT PRINTING OFFICE: 1956

www.ingramcontent.com/pod-product-compliance
Lightning Source LLC
Chambersburg PA
CBHW060423100426
42812CB00030B/3280/J